What people are saying about ...

THE INFLUENCE COURSE

"Politics made possible, politics made positive, politics made pressing. If you're daunted by the prospect of getting involved in politics, or jaded by what you've seen of party politics, but want to help contribute to a kinder, more just, more Jesus-shaped, flourishing society, here's an upbeat, practical, biblically rich, creatively written and successfully tested guide to help you and your church get purposefully and productively engaged ... whoever you vote for."

Mark Greene, Mission Champion, LICC

"Christians aren't meant to get their ultimate meaning from politics, but the Bible is very clear that we should definitely care and enter into the struggles of the world around us, and to find joy in serving our communities. This course is the perfect entry for putting our Christian faith into practice in the public sphere."

Tim Farron, MP

"Doing the course really highlighted that the church trains people to do church-related stuff—preaching, leading, teaching children, leading worship—but doesn't train people to get involved in the outside world.... We can spread the gospel by working to improve people's lives and that means getting involved in political decision making."

Lizzie Jewkes, Liberal Democrat
Christian Forum

"I encourage everyone to step through the Influence Course, which serves as a very digestible, practical and motivational course to help you explore your place in political engagement to serve in the public square, to pray, to partake and to represent."

Rachael Maskell, MP

"The gospel is political. Standing for the lost, the last, the least and the lonely is political. Believing in a God who loved the world so much that He gave up His only Son to save it—that is political and it leads to a people that are … ready to be counted at every level of society.… The Influence Course is something that … creates space for a church community to engage with challenging teaching and gives practical advice on where we can action that teaching. I am excited to see what future material comes from Christians in Politics and we will be running the Influence Course again."

Rev Jonathan Phillips, St Peter's Chester

"Engaging with the political world and public life, either as a Christian or Church, is something for which many of us feel unprepared for or uncertain about. The Influence Course gave us the Biblical foundations, the tools and the confidence to begin that engagement."

Kevin Thomas, Christchurch Baptist Church

"People in churches did an amazing job in supporting their communities during the pandemic. I recommend this biblical course to those who want to move on to have real influence in the public square, and I hope there will be many."

Stephen Timms, MP

"Through my work with Tearfund, I see the justice-seeking passions of the church rising up around issues like the climate crisis, but often Christians feel ill-equipped to channel those passions in constructive ways. The Influence Course is a practical way to help people take those first baby steps to being influencers in the public square."

Ruth Valerio, Global Advocacy and
Influencing Director for Tearfund

"The direct link between Faith Policy and politics has been popping out all over the place since our gatherings—it really has altered my lens on the world."

David Yardley, Course Participant

Christians in Politics

THE

INFLUENCE
COURSE

YOUR JOURNEY INTO GOD'S HEART
FOR GOOD GOVERNANCE

DAVID C COOK

transforming lives together

THE INFLUENCE COURSE
Published by David C Cook
4050 Lee Vance Drive
Colorado Springs, CO 80918 U.S.A.

Integrity Music Limited, a Division of David C Cook
Brighton, East Sussex BN1 2RE, England

The graphic circle C logo is a registered trademark of David C Cook.

The website addresses recommended throughout this book are offered as a
resource to you. These websites are not intended in any way to be or imply an
endorsement on the part of David C Cook, nor do we vouch for their content.

Unless otherwise noted, all Scripture quotations are taken from Holy Bible,
New International Version® Anglicized, NIV® Copyright © 1979, 1984, 2011
by Biblica, Inc.® Used by permission. All rights reserved worldwide. Scripture
quotations marked KJV are taken from The Authorised (King James) Version.
Rights in the Authorised Version in the United Kingdom are vested in the Crown.
Reproduced by permission of the Crown's patentee, Cambridge University
Press. The author has added italics to Scripture quotations for emphasis.

ISBN 978-0-8307-8248-2
eISBN 978-0-8307-8249-9

The Team: Ian Matthews, Paul Owen, Jeff Gerke,
Jo Stockdale, Jennie Pollock, Susan Murdock
Cover Design: Pete Barnsley (CreativeHoot.com)

Printed in the United Kingdom
First Edition 2021

1 2 3 4 5 6 7 8 9 10

061721

CONTENTS

Introduction   9

Session 1   Busy Church   13
Session 2   What Belongs to God?   35
Session 3   Transformation   53
Session 4   Behind the Scenes   69
Session 5   We Can't Agree   85
Session 6   What's Next?   103

Conclusion   123
Acknowledgements   125
Notes   127

INTRODUCTION

All over the UK, the church is doing an incredible job serving communities. From foodbanks in Cornwall to debt counselling in the Highlands, the Word is becoming flesh in local neighbourhoods. The transformation in individuals and communities is tangible and exciting.

Is there a danger, however, that the church could become just the paramedic of the nation, giving first aid to the victims of a fallen system, rather than also speaking and installing truth, righteousness, and justice into the systems and structures of our land? Might we be so busy fulfilling our pastoral calling that we ignore our prophetic calling?

This course will take all the members of your church on a journey into God's heart for good governance—and into the truth that we all have a part to play, no matter how small. We'll look at the biblical call to public leadership, the huge need for people of integrity to be involved, and the simple baby steps we can take to get there.

It's important to note that this is a 'starter course' for *all* the small groups of a church to do for a season, not just a course for those who have some pre-existing political interest. The teaching and activities are broad-based and applicable to all believers, not only to those who feel a particular call towards politics.

Many of us in the church have become 'armchair activists.' We have political opinions and passions, but they often aren't connected relationally or having an impact on actual structures, aside from the often toxic world of social media. This course will lead us up out of those armchairs.

How to use this book

The sessions are a toolbox. Not everything may be applicable for your context. The different sections of each session are designed to complement one another, but don't feel bad if you need to curtail certain sections for the purposes of time. Please just make use of what works for you.

The sessions will obviously work best if the leader has spent a decent amount of time watching and reading the material. That way, you can make connections between sections and answer people's queries intelligently!

Each session is comprised of a short video introducing the overall theme, followed by feedback, a bit of teaching, an activity, a 'takeaway' (a challenge before the next meeting), and prayer.

From our experience, it is the times of discussion that are hugely beneficial in 'earthing' this material for people. The desire of this course is not just to bombard people with information but to create a context where we are able to hear and explore God's call for our lives. Therefore, having space to grapple with and respond to the ways in which we have been provoked will be key.

We've suggested activities that can be done with groups meeting in person, but there are ideas for alternatives or adjustments if your group is meeting online (found here: http://influencecourse.co.uk/). It obviously depends on the size of your group, but for the feedback sessions it is probably best to stay in the main group. And then for the discussion and prayer sections, please use your judgement as to whether smaller sub-groups would encourage more interaction and prayer, feeding back where appropriate.

The response to this course has already been exciting. Some kind churches trialled the material, and already two participants are likely to become local councillors, two have formed a campaigning organisation, some have joined various political parties, and one has begun working for an MP. Many groups wrote to their MPs, and one group had their question asked on the floor of Parliament. Another group managed to get some roadworks quickly sorted by their local council!

We couldn't be more thrilled that Christians are truly getting involved. Come join in!

Session 1

BUSY CHURCH

Summary

This first session will look at how loving our neighbour in the biblical sense leads to questions which may require political answers. We will celebrate the church's efforts that are having a huge impact all over the UK, and we will also ask if perhaps we need to be more strategic in order to see sustainable kingdom transformation. There will also be a chance to solve some of society's biggest problems using the power of clothes pegs!

Structure

Each week will involve Bible-based input from videos and talks, group discussion, prayer, and a practical activity. This week, we recommend you do them in this order:

- Welcome (8 minutes)
- Video (2 minutes)

- Feedback (8 minutes)
- Activity (12 minutes)
- Talk (10 minutes)
- Discussion (20 minutes)
- Prayer (10 minutes)
- Takeaway (2 minutes)

72 minutes total

To run this session, you will need:
- Access to the internet or the downloaded video (and if needed, a projector and laptop setup) to watch the 'Show Up 2.0' video.
- Pens.
- Three pieces of string or similar to act as temporary 'washing lines' stretching across the room.
- Twenty clothes pegs.
- About twenty small pieces of card or paper that you can peg to the washing lines.
- Two large sheets of paper.

Welcome (8 minutes)

Invite each person in your group to introduce themselves and answer the question, 'Would you consider yourself "political"?' Then open the session with a prayer asking God to speak to everyone present, deepening our understanding of what it means to love your neighbour.

Video: Show Up 2.0 (1:38 minutes)

Play the Christians in Politics video 'Show Up 2.0.'

Here is the video script to give you an idea of its content:

> All over the UK, the church is doing an incredible job. We're running foodbanks, mentoring at-risk teenagers, counselling those in debt, being friends to the elderly, sheltering the homeless, running parent-toddler groups, homework clubs, music/arts workshops, healing on the streets, and sports camps, working with prisoners and community choirs. This is wonderful. But there is a danger.
>
> Martin Luther King said that as Christians we enjoy being the Good Samaritan on life's roadside. It often feels good to help someone and see the change up close. But he went on to ask, 'Who is going back to the Jericho road?' In other words, who is making sure that no one else gets mugged? Do we need more street lighting? More CCTV cameras? More police on the beat? The thing is that those political decisions happen in fairly dull committees poring over statistics and reports. Not as exciting as seeing that change right in your face. But if we don't show up in those places, the church may spend the next fifty years as the nation's paramedic, treating the victims of a flawed system but failing to bring righteousness and justice to the system itself.

It's good to be the Good Samaritan, but it's also good to give him the odd day off. Some of us need to be in the system. Might that be you? Don't just vote. Show up.

> It's good to be the Good Samaritan, but it's also good to give him the odd day off.

Feedback (8 minutes)

The aim of the discussion time is to ease the group into reflecting and engaging with the session topic, not necessarily to have all the answers.

1. What jumped out at you from the video?
2. What needs are you aware of in your local neighbourhood/s?
3. How could your church try to meet some of those needs and how is it doing so already? Note that here we are including the church gathered (for example, through church projects) and the church dispersed (for example, through individuals in their work).
4. What insights have these efforts given you into those needs?

Activity (12 minutes)
The personal and the political—joining the dots

On the left-hand wall of your room, put up a sheet of paper that says PERSONAL, and on the right, one that says POLITICAL.

Ask the group to now choose just one problem that impacts the lives of people or an individual in their community—it may be a need or issue that has just been mentioned in the discussion. It doesn't have to be the most challenging problem in your area, but it will help if it is an issue of which at least some of the group have some understanding. Some examples could be debt, not being able to speak English, isolation/loneliness, alcohol dependency, home-lessness, or youth violence. Write the one you have chosen on a small piece of paper or card.

Stick or hang the 'problem' on the far left of the room (not implying the political far left!). From that point, stretch three 'washing lines' of string across the room to three separate points on the right-hand side. Now ask everyone, 'What is the "problem behind the problem"?—and what might the steps towards solving it be? What would it look like to "go back to the Jericho road" for this problem?' Scribble these steps down in short form and hang them in sequence to the right of the problem on the washing line.

There will of course be more than one 'problem behind the problem', but just choose three, and each gets its own washing line. It should look something like this … using the example of road traffic casualties.

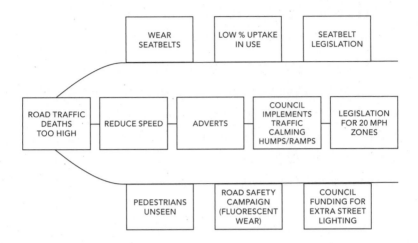

You might also jump straight across to the right-hand side, to a political reason for why this problem exists or to a political solution that might address it. Hang this on the far right of the 'washing line.' You can then also work backwards towards the left, perhaps meeting in the middle.

You may want to split into teams, taking a washing line each, to discuss what connects the left to the right. Your answers on these sheets will hopefully join the dots between the personal and the political.

For example, you might choose 'youth violence' as your problem. One person may suggest that the root causes are 'boredom' linked to 'lack of adequate youth resources in the area' linked to 'council cuts' linked to 'lack of funding from central government' linked to 'poor management of the economy.'

Someone else may say 'lack of good role models' linked to 'family breakdown' linked to 'lack of parenting support' linked to 'lack of national government priority around family.'

One person may say 'drugs' linked to 'lack of effective deterrent' linked to 'failing policing strategies' linked to 'home office policy.'

That gives you three 'lines' emanating from the same problem.

Think not only about how the problem could be alleviated but also about how it might be prevented in the first place. Think about the physical, psychological, and 'spiritual' reasons why these problems exist or why they may be difficult to ameliorate. Note that we are not claiming that the causes or solutions for these problems are purely political, but that they certainly have a political component!

If you have time, you can repeat the exercise with another problem.

It's not that the group will work out exactly how to 'solve' all these issues, but it is an exercise in strategically thinking about the wider context of our communities and the processes by which things can change in our society.

Talk (10 minutes)

From our experience, some people prefer to simply read the talk out to the group (it takes about 7 minutes, plus the Bible readings), or if you'd like to develop your own version, please do—we've put more ideas and resources in the notes at the end of the session. We've also put some suggestions in brackets for where you might like to add examples from your own church. Either way, the material will be much more powerful if the leader has 'lived in it' for some time, considering some of the applications of the material for themselves and the others who will be present.

We're going to look together at a couple of passages from the Gospels. *Read—or ask someone else to read—Mark 12:30–31 and Luke 10:25–37.*

> 'Love the Lord your God with all your heart and with all your soul and with all your mind and with all your strength,' [and] 'Love your neighbour as yourself.' There is no commandment greater than these. (Mark 12:30–31)

> On one occasion an expert in the law stood up to test Jesus. 'Teacher,' he asked, 'what must I do to inherit eternal life?'
>
> 'What is written in the Law?' he replied. 'How do you read it?'
>
> He answered, '"Love the Lord your God with all your heart and with all your soul and with all your strength and with all your mind"; and, "Love your neighbour as yourself."'
>
> 'You have answered correctly,' Jesus replied. 'Do this and you will live.'
>
> But he wanted to justify himself, so he asked Jesus, 'And who is my neighbour?'
>
> In reply Jesus said: 'A man was going down from Jerusalem to Jericho, when he was attacked by robbers. They stripped him of his clothes, beat him and went away, leaving him half-dead. A priest happened to be going down the same road, and

when he saw the man, he passed by on the other
side. So too, a Levite, when he came to the place
and saw him, passed by on the other side. But a
Samaritan, as he travelled, came where the man
was; and when he saw him, he took pity on him.
He went to him and bandaged his wounds, pouring on oil and wine. Then he put the man on his
own donkey, brought him to an inn and took care
of him. The next day he took out two denarii and
gave them to the innkeeper. "Look after him," he
said, "and when I return, I will reimburse you for
any extra expense you may have."

'Which of these three do you think was a
neighbour to the man who fell into the hands of
robbers?'

The expert in the law replied, 'The one who
had mercy on him.'

Jesus told him, 'Go and do likewise.' (Luke
10:25–37)

The Good Samaritan is one of the best-known stories that Jesus
told, and the church today has got a pretty good grasp of the idea
that we're called to be good neighbours to one another. As we saw
in the video, many churches across the UK are now having a sus-
tained impact on their communities, through working *with* people
rather than doing things *to* them—debt counselling, youth clubs,
pregnancy advice centres, and foodbanks, to name just a few. [*Do
mention the kinds of things your church is involved with.*]

However, as Archbishop Desmond Tutu once said, 'As Christians, we need to not just be pulling the drowning bodies out of the river. We need to be going upstream to find out who is pushing them in.'[1]

What does it mean to go upstream and find out how people are getting pushed into the river? What happens when we start to ask why people even *need* foodbanks or debt advice? Well, more often than not, it brings us into the realm of politics.

'I'm not interested in politics,' you've probably heard someone say. 'Those politicians—they're all the same. They haven't a clue about what's going on out here in the real world. Politics does nothing for me. Why should I give them my vote? They don't care about me.'

Given what we pick up about politics from the media, you can't blame us for being cynical. But when somebody says, 'I don't care about politics,' we have to ask the question in return, 'But do you care about your neighbourhood? Do you care about [*insert the name of your town*]?'

Jesus said, 'Love your neighbour as yourself.' So we need to love others in the way that we love ourselves. But how do we love ourselves? We love ourselves by a huge variety of mental, physical, and spiritual attitudes and practices that keep the show of life on the road.

We feed ourselves. We brush our teeth. We buy clothes for ourselves. We try to find meaningful work and somewhere to live. We get educated. We look after our health (sometimes!). We get a National Insurance number. We try to save money. We try to make friends and do things we enjoy. We look for purpose. We reach for God. We don't manage all of them, many of us, but these are some of the ways we love ourselves.

Loving our neighbour 'as ourselves' must mean caring about all these aspects of other people's lives too. It doesn't have to be more complicated than that. Our love must be holistic. For example, we would never cease feeding ourselves because we decided that all that mattered was our spiritual needs. If we love someone only enough to see their 'spiritual' life sorted out, then our love runs the risk of not addressing the needs of the whole person in the way that Jesus did.

Mick Duncan from Urban Neighbours of Hope lived for twelve years in a slum in Manila with his family. He speaks about one of his neighbours for whom being a friend meant simply being involved in her life on many levels. She was in extreme poverty, so there were times when, as her friend, he simply needed to share meals with her or give gifts of cash and items that would help her survive. He was fighting on a *practical front*.

She was also heavily involved in some of the occult practices that ensnare many in the Philippines, so Mick had to fight on a *spiritual front*. There was much prayer and deliverance.

The land on which they lived was not acknowledged as 'real' by the government, so she was not an official citizen with all the benefits, like healthcare and education, which that would bring. It also meant that the area did not receive proper sanitation or refuse systems. So Mick had to fight for her on a *political front* for the land and for all of her neighbours to be recognised.

The point must be made in the midst of all of this that she was also blessing him, and he was learning huge amounts from her. But you can see that to focus on any one of these areas to the neglect of the other would be to avoid being the neighbour she needed.

And of course we don't understand someone's context the moment we meet them. As we get to know them, and they get to know us, we come to understand more about each other's context and one another's needs, and we come to care about the bigger picture of one another's lives.

As we learn to really love people, we find that compassion draws us into questions of justice. We come to care that someone's wages are too low to allow them to feed their family, or that when they cannot get out of their house there is no healthcare provision that can go to them, or that they live in the midst of a culture of worklessness.

That is why it simply isn't an option for us to opt out of political activity, leaving it to someone else. If we choose to love others as Jesus taught us to, there will be a political dimension to our lives. We do not live abstract lives. We all live in a certain area of a certain town in a certain country. The life that is possible for us and for others is hugely influenced by the laws of that society at both the local and national levels. We cannot avoid their influence. You cannot love someone in a vacuum, removed from the rest of their life. You have to love them in context.

> If we choose to love others as Jesus taught us to, there will be a political dimension to our lives.

Let's think about someone specifically, someone in this neighbourhood. Perhaps you have an elderly neighbour? It might be someone you know and have spoken to or just someone you've seen nearby. Can you picture them? Now think about your answers to these questions.

- Do you care that their bins are collected?
- Do you care that their local hospital has a long waiting list for the surgery they need?
- Do you care that their bedroom is damp?
- Do you care about their noisy neighbours?
- Do you care about whether there is any decent public transport they can use to get around?

If we care about even one of these things, we care about politics. We care about politics because we care about people. Quite often, the wonderful projects that churches are involved in are what awaken us to the reality of other people's lives and needs. This can be the start of a journey.

Politics simply describes how we order society and people. God loves people, and he calls us to love one another; there's no limit to how far that will take us. In the coming weeks, we're going to explore where that might lead when it comes to politics.

Paramedics are important. We need first aid. We need to be the Good Samaritan. But does God have even more in store for some of us?

Discussion (20 minutes)

1. What kinds of actions do you picture when you think of the call to love our neighbour as ourselves?

2. What might 'engaging with politics as an expression of love' look like?

3. Do you think that the church is more concerned with 'pulling the drowning bodies out of the river' or 'going upstream to find out who is pushing them in'?

4. Why do you think the church is often hesitant to 'get political'?

5. Does anyone in this group know anything about our local MP or local councillors? If so, what?

Prayer (10 minutes)

Invite the group to pray (perhaps in smaller groups) and reflect on all the issues that have been discussed. Ask for God's direction in terms of what our responses should be. Jesus did only what he saw the Father doing (John 5:19). This course is not about adding yet another 'to-do' to an already lengthy to-do list, but widening our understanding of the sort of things God may call us to. Perhaps God may be calling us to stop doing some other things to make room for some political engagement?

This powerful prayer, written by Mother Teresa, is available as a PowerPoint presentation on the course website (http://influencecourse .co.uk/).

Closing prayer

> O God, we pray for all those in our world
> who are suffering from injustice:
> For those who are discriminated against
> because of their race, color or religion;
> For those imprisoned
> for working for the relief of oppression;

For those who are hounded

for speaking the inconvenient truth;

For those tempted to violence

as a cry against overwhelming hardship;

For those deprived of reasonable health and

education;

For those suffering from hunger and famine;

For those too weak to help themselves

and who have no one else to help them;

For the unemployed who cry out

for work but do not find it.

We pray for anyone of our acquaintance

who is personally affected by injustice.

Forgive us, Lord, if we unwittingly share in the

conditions

or in a system that perpetuates injustice.

Show us how we can serve your children

and make your love practical by washing their feet.

Amen.[2]

Takeaway (2 minutes)

Each week, we'll suggest something that the group could do in the coming week to explore things further. It's a great way of getting people to flesh out the journey of this course. Research shows that if we don't do something within a few days of a challenge, our behaviour is unlikely to change!

- Why don't you write to your local MP or your local councillors? Do you know who your local councillors are? If not, you can find out at www.gov.uk/find-your-local-councillors. First, thank them for the service they are giving and assure them of your support and prayers. Show that you understand what a challenging job it is, and perhaps find something specific that they have done to encourage them about. Then you could mention an issue that is of particular concern to you in the local area (perhaps one which your church is engaged in addressing). Share your experience, ask them how they see the issue, and explore how you could work together to address it. Let God lead your pen or typing fingers to kick-start a kingdom relationship.

Further talk resources
Loving your neighbour—testimony of Gavin White (Councillor in Old Moat Ward)

My background is as a church leader involved in finance and administration with a relatively large church in Manchester. I was also involved in the local community where I live, in Old Moat, helping to set up events in local parks and being on the board of governors where my kids went to school.

I started to realise, though, that there were certain things that weren't going to change until I got involved earlier in the decision- and budget-making process for things locally in my community. That's why I decided to transition from my church leadership role in administration and finance into one which involves more of the administration of our city here in Manchester.

I joined the Labour Party back in 2004 as I have always had a heart and passion for social justice and for true equality of opportunity for all, regardless of background.

I embarked on the journey of becoming a local councillor in the summer of 2015 and was duly elected as a local Labour Party councillor for the Old Moat ward in Manchester on 3 May 2018. It is such an incredible honour to serve my local community in this way and take the hallmarks and values of the kingdom into the community that I represent, and to be salt and light whenever I can in our city.

Charity versus justice?

Here is another framing that may be helpful for the discussions of this session. Sometimes it helps to differentiate between *charity* and *justice*.

- *Charity* is the sticking plaster that is required because injustice remains. Charity deals with the symptoms of a sick global system.
- Seeking *justice* pursues a cure for the disease with which the system is riddled. Here, we should point out that we mean justice in its broadest, truest sense, which is not the preserve of one political faction!

Our charitable efforts mostly come from a pure heart. However, we often prefer charity to justice because it can make us feel good or look good, but *challenging systems involves inevitable conflict with powerful vested interests for whom the present system probably works very well.* Those may be powerful voices on Twitter that attempt to silence any dissent on social issues, or powerful CEOs being paid one hundred times what their cleaners are paid. These conflicts rarely make us comfortable.

> Challenging systems involves inevitable conflict with powerful vested interests for whom the present system probably works very well.

One example of the church making a journey from *apathy* to *charity*, which then led to some justice-seeking, was 'Hope 08.'

It was a united social justice and evangelism campaign across the UK during 2008. Some 1,500 villages, towns, and cities took part in unified missional efforts and were exposed to huge needs in their communities. Many reported that it was the first time they had realised the depth of need in their communities. Many said they had been shaken from their *apathy*. This led many to start local projects and NGOs to address these needs.

Once you start asking why local needs exist, you inevitably come up with *answers that need political expression.*

It's important to note that this may also lead *Christians in different political directions from the same motivational starting point.* Christians often shy away from this part of the process because we want to avoid conflict with each other. Time spent living on a council estate may lead some Christians to campaign for a living wage and may lead others to campaign for more support and training for parents.

In this challenging part of the journey, as we move from charity to justice-seeking, it's not that we leave compassion and charity behind.

It's not like this:

Perhaps a better description of that journey would be a spiral where we revisit different areas of engagement as we journey outwards from our selfish self towards God's world.

It's like this:

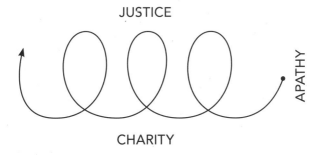

Speed

The reality is that churches often spend more time engaged in their own programmes because, if we're honest, they can be faster at making change happen.

Churches can help people pretty much straightaway, and they can do it without the constraints of people we may not agree with or who may ask us to fill out many forms.

Change in the political realm is often slow—it can take many years to get from the moment of inspiration to the moment of legislation, and then many more years until it has impact.

But:

- Change brought about in the political realm can influence a whole nation or the world, rather than just a few people.
- Political change may also be longer-lasting—not based on only immediate opportunities—and may reach parts of the nation that churches don't yet reach.
- For example, a few years ago, folks could have campaigned to stop people smoking in just their local pub, or just prayed for the habits of

individuals known to them to change to improve their health. But against huge opposition from vested interests, a broad coalition of people challenged the government, and legislation was enacted that has improved the health of millions of people across the UK for the long-term by outlawing smoking in workplaces.

- Here is an utterly unscientific graph to help explain:

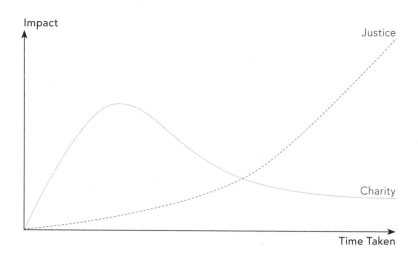

Of course, it's *both/and* rather than *either/or*, but again a bird's eye view of the UK today reveals that there are more Christians involved in transformative, hands-on, church-based mission projects than in efforts that seek to shape the structural make-up of a village, town, city, or nation.

Could we stop seeing the work as our mission and start trying to find our place in God's overall mission to see the redemption, reconciliation, and restoration of all things?

WHAT BELONGS TO GOD?

Summary

This second session will look at how God has authority over all things, including politics, and what that means for us as Christians. We'll look at the sacred-secular divide and play a game that will make us feel like we're in a youth group again!

Structure

- Welcome (5 minutes)
- Activity (10 minutes)
- Video (3 minutes)
- Feedback (10 minutes)
- Talk (10 minutes)
- Discussion (20 minutes)
- Prayer (10 minutes)
- Takeaway (2 minutes)

70 minutes total

To run this session, you will need:

- Access to the internet or the downloaded video (and if needed, a projector and laptop setup) to watch the 'Jesus and Politics' video.
- Perhaps a large piece of paper (at least A3) with GOD written at one end and CAESAR at the other end, and a counter for each group member. (If you are able to do the first activity on your feet instead, then you won't need these things—read through the instructions first so you can decide!)
- *Those Who Show Up*—the book by Andy Flannagan. Not essential but helpful!

Welcome (5 minutes)

If anyone carried out the 'takeaway' action from the last session, get them to tell the group. (It involved contacting the local MP or councillors, and it's quite likely that they won't have heard a response yet, but it's great to encourage anyone who has stepped out and begun a conversation.)

Open with prayer that brings these potential new connections before God.

Activity (10 minutes)

If you have a large enough room and your group are able to be mobile, then this is an activity to do on your feet. Otherwise, you will need a large, long piece of paper and enough counters for each group member to have one each.

Explain to the group that this time we are thinking about the story from Matthew 22 in which Jesus says: 'Give back to Caesar what is Caesar's, and to God what is God's.' Surely Jesus made that division clear, so we're going to do the same.

One end of the room (or the piece of paper) is labelled GOD (by means of a speedily made poster!), and the other, CAESAR (similarly made!). When you read out each word, each person responds with their honest gut reaction (not their lengthy consideration!) as to whether they associate it more with God or Caesar—i.e., is it physical or spiritual?

If you're doing the activity on your feet, each person will stand near the corresponding end of the room (or somewhere in the middle if they think it's unclear, or a bit of both); if you're using counters, each person will place the counter on the piece of paper nearest the word GOD or CAESAR.

These are the words to read out, one at a time: *broadband, gambling, a worship song, an industrial park, a foodbank, the rail network, the stock market, daily devotionals, council tax, prayer ministry, nuclear weapons, debt counselling, journalism, youth work, high-street shopping, gardening, playgrounds, social media, sermons, the Bible,* and *mortgages.*

Don't comment on where people have chosen to stand or put their counters, but you might occasionally ask someone why they have chosen to stand in a particular place for a certain word. There will be inevitable comedy, which is to be encouraged!

Video: Jesus and Politics (2:34 minutes)

Play the Christians in Politics video 'Jesus and Politics.'

Here is the video script to give you an idea of its content:

> A group of spies once tried to trap Jesus, asking, 'Is it right to pay taxes to Caesar?' In other words, 'Are you a revolutionary opposed to Roman rule, or are you a compromiser supporting Roman rule?' He refuses to be tricked into giving a simplistic answer and instead asks for a coin, asks his own question, and then famously declares, 'Render unto Caesar what is Caesar's, and render unto God what is God's.'
>
> Now, we hear those words with our Western mindsets and think, 'Ah, easy! Let Caesar look after all the practical, logistical, political stuff, and let God and his people get on with all the spiritual stuff. The Sunday morning stuff—prayers, hymns, invisible things—that's God's turf. Taxation, roads, healthcare—that's Caesar's turf. How convenient to have that separation. None of that awkward mixing of religion and politics.'
>
> But for those listening to Jesus in the first century, there's not a chance they would have heard Jesus' statement that way. For the Hebrews, body, soul, and spirit were not separate entities. Life was one. For example, the temple wasn't just a place where you worshipped; it was a civic centre looking after

many aspects of communal life. For the Hebrews, their religious leaders were also their political leaders.

So when we talk about what is God's and what is Caesar's, we're not talking about two separate realms where God has jurisdiction in the sacred, and Caesar has jurisdiction in the secular. It's not like this. It's more like this: Caesar has a small, delegated area of authority within the context of God's overall authority.

He is the supreme creator who is reconciling all things in heaven and earth to himself. Jesus reiterated this when he told Pilate that he would have no authority unless 'it had been given you from above.' Note that he doesn't dispute that Pilate has real authority, but he reminds him where it comes from.

So God has an opinion on everything—including taxes—because he is in authority over all of it. As the ex-Dutch prime minister and theologian Abraham Kuyper said, 'There is not one square inch of creation over which the Lord Christ does not cry, "It is mine."'

Feedback (10 minutes)

The aim of this discussion time is to ease the group into reflecting and engaging with the session topic, not necessarily to have all the answers.

1. Did anything in the video challenge or inspire you? What was it?

2. If we subconsciously adopt a view of life that separates everything into two areas of authority—one under God and the other under Caesar—what kinds of things will we spend our time doing as individuals or collectively as the church?

3. How might it change our priorities if we saw every dimension of life as coming under God's authority, and if we believed that God is concerned about all of it? What practical difference might it make in your life or your church's life?

Talk (10 minutes)

You can read this out to the group (it takes about 7 minutes, plus the Bible readings), or if you'd like to develop your own version, feel free—we've put more ideas and resources in the notes at the end of the session.

We're going to look together at that story from Matthew 22, alongside a short passage from the Old Testament.

Read—or ask someone else to read—Matthew 22:15–22 and Genesis 1:26–28.

> Then the Pharisees went out and laid plans to trap [Jesus] in his words. They sent their disciples to him along with the Herodians. 'Teacher,' they said, 'we know that you are a man of integrity and that you teach the way of God in accordance with the truth. You aren't swayed by others, because you pay no attention to who they are. Tell us then,

what is your opinion? Is it right to pay the poll-tax to Caesar or not?'

But Jesus, knowing their evil intent, said, 'You hypocrites, why are you trying to trap me? Show me the coin used for paying the tax.' They brought him a denarius, and he asked them, 'Whose image is this? And whose inscription?'

'Caesar's,' they replied.

Then he said to them, 'So give back to Caesar what is Caesar's, and to God what is God's.'

When they heard this, they were amazed. So they left him and went away. (Matt. 22:15–22)

Then God said, 'Let us make mankind in our image, in our likeness, so that they may rule over the fish in the sea and the birds in the sky, over the livestock and all the wild animals, and over all the creatures that move along the ground.' So God created mankind in his own image, in the image of God he created them; male and female he created them. God blessed them and said to them, 'Be fruitful and increase in number; fill the earth and subdue it. Rule over the fish in the sea and the birds in the sky and over every living creature that moves on the ground.' (Gen. 1:26–28)

Last time, we reflected on a challenge that Archbishop Desmond Tutu brought to the church about why we spend so much time pulling drowning people from the river when we need to go upstream and see who is pushing them in. This week, we begin with a different challenge from him. He says, 'When people tell me that the Bible has nothing to do with politics, I ask them, "Which Bible are you talking about?"'

So much of the Bible is interested in the questions at the heart of politics—such as how we order society and how we structure things so that people can flourish. And it's not just the abstract, big picture. In the story of God's people, the nation of Israel, we see so much of the nitty-gritty of how this works out, how God leads his people, what angers and frustrates him, what kinds of laws matter, and what good leadership looks like.

And this shouldn't surprise us. Bearing in mind he invented the world, people, and everything, we should imagine he has the best insights on how it can all hold together.

But before we get to any specifics, there are deep theological questions that underlie our confusion or discomfort with the idea of engaging with politics at all, and so let's look at some of them.

In those verses we read from Genesis, God clearly gives humans authority. It's the authority to steward and care for the creation, to ensure that it continues to flourish, and to be fruitful. What it means to be human is tied up with this notion that we are image-bearers of the Divine. We carry something of God. He has somehow imparted or shared the mandate of leadership and stewardship—governance, if you like—to humanity. And it is all tied to this idea of being created in the image of God.

So to understand what it means to bear authority in its true sense, we look to God. We look to his nature and character to learn how we should be. And Scripture paints a vivid picture for us. We find in the Bible depictions of his goodness, his mercy, his faithfulness, his anger at injustice, his sacrificial love, and his wisdom. These are the qualities we are to embody.

When we think about Adam and Eve's call to public leadership, we are so impressed by the *what* that we forget *when* it happens. In light of the fall, politics and government have often been seen as a 'necessary evil' to restrain sin, but this ignores the fact that responsibility for the earth was given to humans even *before* the fall. Organisation is needed even in the context of perfection. God has always been intending to share his reign with us, and we will reign with him even when evil is no more. So our engagement is not just pragmatically 'sorting out the problems of the world'—this is a divine vocation, a holy calling.

Humanity was created in God's image, so we should be a physical embodiment of his leadership, his governance, his priorities. And what began in creation then grew into the particular calling of the nation of Israel and then the church. The calling is to make God known, to make him visible. To be a blessing to the nations.

More than anything, God desires to be known—because he knows that this knowledge and relationship is what humans need to be fully human and thereby whole as individuals, communities, or societies.

And there are so many ways we work to make him known, to make his love real and tangible to the people around us. There are, in fact, no limits to the ways in which we continue to give ourselves to him and his work, to love the people around us, and to take on the authority he has given us.

There is no such thing as 'secular,' no part of life God is not in authority over. Franciscan writer Richard Rohr often reminds his readers of this. There is no 'secular,' he says, only sacred and 'de-sacralised' or desecrated, where humanity has sucked the holiness out of something that was meant for good.

> There is no such thing as 'secular,' no part of life God is not in authority over.

As the psalmist writes, 'The earth is the LORD's, and everything in it, the world, and all who live in it' (Ps. 24:1).

And of course we find in Jesus the perfect embodiment of this. He was fully God and fully human—and that in itself tells us that there's no room in his theology for dealing with the two states separately!

To bear authority in any sense is to step into what it means to be human. We have an innate authority in us because we are image-bearers of God, the ultimate authority. And so it is natural that we would step into opportunities to exercise that calling. It is not that we are all called to be one type of leader, but we are all called to contribute to the flourishing of God's creation. We are *his* stewards over *his* creation. And God is God over everything, not just the church. We are called to invest ourselves in the fruitfulness and flourishing of every corner of creation, not just our holy buildings.

In the story we've just read in Matthew 22, the Pharisees seemingly ask Jesus a legitimate question, one that relates to this issue of where God's authority reaches. What does it actually relate to? What practical and political matters should our religious life be concerned with? Does our faith affect what we think about tax?

Only, it's really a trap. They aren't actually looking to Jesus as a wise teacher who will guide them in matters of financial ethics. Despite the smooth flattery with which they begin, they actually want to corner Jesus into one of two dangerous answers. It looks like Jesus has two choices. It's basically a yes or no answer: Should we pay taxes to Rome?

Jesus, of course, will not be trapped. If he goes with a, 'Yes, they should pay taxes to Caesar,' they could depict him as a sell-out and unpatriotic. With another framing, he also won't allow a clear yes because that would imply that some things are out of God's jurisdiction and shouldn't be a matter of theological concern. Nor will he answer no, setting himself up as a political revolutionary out to overthrow Caesar. He gives them an answer which makes them do the thinking: 'So give back to Caesar what is Caesar's, and to God what is God's.'

He makes the Pharisees answer the question of how far they believe God's authority reaches. Do they think their money belongs to Caesar or to God? Where do they want to draw the lines?

What is God's? Everything. And what is Caesar's? Whatever God has temporarily delegated to Caesar. The two should never be confused. But this is also why we are called to respect and pray for our leaders. The authority they/we carry *is* real. But it is delegated!

(You might like to draw out the diagrams below as a way of explaining how God's authority and Caesar's authority aren't separate realms—one sacred, one secular or political—but that it all lies within God's ultimate authority.)

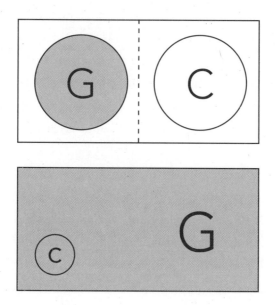

Let's finish with these inspiring words from author Jane Collier: 'There is no part of our existence, cultural, political, historical or communal, which is not called, through conversion, to become the stuff of which the Kingdom of God is fashioned.'[3]

Discussion (20 minutes)

1. Are there any areas of life that you tend to think of as being unrelated to God and to your faith? Your investments, perhaps? Your

woodwork? Your fashion or eating habits? Share these honestly with the group.

2. How do you feel about the idea that all humans are called to participate in the flourishing of the whole creation? Do you feel like you have the agency or authority to help make that happen?

3. Many of us do believe that there is no sacred-secular divide in life, but this doesn't always translate into how we organise ourselves as the church. Do you think your church spends more resources (staffing, training, relational efforts, maintenance) on what happens on a Sunday or from Monday to Friday?

Prayer (10 minutes)

Spend some time praying—as a group, in smaller groups, or individually—about what you have covered in this session. This may include a time of repentance for ignoring some aspects of God's whole creation and our responsibility. You might like to close with the prayer below, 'God of All Government.' The PowerPoint presentation is available from the course website (http://influencecourse.co.uk/).

Closing prayer

God of all Government,
Send workers into the harvest field of political life.
Call your people. Not simply those who pay you
        lip service,
But those who hear your voice and know your name.

Those who will not serve two masters,
Those who will choose kingdom over tribe,
Those who are not ashamed of the gospel,
Those who will speak up for those who cannot
        speak for themselves.

Those who will seek justice, encourage the
        oppressed, defend the cause of the fatherless,
        and plead the case of the widow,
Those who will seek to reconcile more than separate,
Those who will seek to co-operate more than
        compete,
Those who will seek peace more than power.

Those who will choose your glory over
        self-promotion,
Those who will choose truth over expediency,
Those who will listen to the still, small voice more
        than the megaphone of the media,
Those who will care for the least of these, rather
        than genuflect to the greatest.

Those who find their identity and security in divine
        election more than their election by man,
Those whose citizenship is in heaven, and whose
        primary allegiance is to another King,

Those who cannot help but speak of the reason for
    the hope that they have,
Those who know your grace for their failings.

Call out an army that will march on its knees in
    humility
To fight not with the weapons of this world
But with the invisible ammunition of your
    kingdom.

Amen.

Takeaway (2 minutes)

Each week, we'll suggest something that the group could do in the coming week to explore things further. It's entirely optional, but it's a great way of getting people to deepen the journey.

- This week, try to make a list of the things you spend your time doing that you have not really thought of before as 'spiritual' activities. They might relate to your work or your chores or what you do with your spare time. When you have your list, bring them all to God in prayer, asking him to help you see them as 'the stuff of which the kingdom of God is fashioned.'

Further talk resources
ROUTE 66

In Andy Flannagan's book *Those Who Show Up* (definitely recommended reading for anyone doing this course), there is a chapter called 'ROUTE 66,' which takes you on a whistle-stop tour of all sixty-six books of the Bible, illustrating how God's heart for good governance is not confined to a few specific texts, but screams out of all of Scripture. It underlines the key message that God cares passionately about *all* of life!

An effective way of communicating this, that some groups have used, is to read short excerpts aloud at high speed, with each person taking one book of the Bible in turn. You can source the book from all the usual places you buy books or download the chapter 'ROUTE 66' from the course website (http://influencecourse.co.uk/).

Journey into local politics—testimony of Israel Imarni

As a young single parent in the early 1990s, my only way out of a lifetime of poverty was to further my education. Without affordable rent, this was impossible. I was fortunate, after years on the waiting list, to be offered a council flat.

After moving in, I immediately signed up for a degree course in fashion, and I successfully graduated. Upon graduating, I was able to secure work as a fashion buyer and progress my career over a number of years. I eventually purchased a house of my own, and now live independent of state benefits, and can provide for my child. I know first-hand the difference good-quality housing can make.

We are all here to fulfil our God-given purpose, solving problems such as providing those in need with a truly affordable place to live. This enables them to make choices and realise their potential. It frees both individuals and communities.

Although I worked in the creative industries, I had a passion to enable others to make the same choices I had been afforded. Politics seemed far removed and boring compared to my day job. A chance meeting with the director of The Conservative Christian Fellowship showed me that I could champion the cause for social housing much sooner than I had imagined. I enrolled on their leadership development course and was trained and mentored, and I networked with people who showed me how to apply to be a borough councillor. It was much easier and much more accessible than I expected.

Against all odds, I won a seat in the 2015 election. After a year, I was promoted to Vice-Chairman of the Housing & Communities Scrutiny Committee, and before long I was promoted to Chairman, and also Chairman of the Tenants & Leaseholders Committee. Having been a council tenant myself, I am able to bring a customer viewpoint, and my contributions are more than just theory. There is a need for a conscious Christian voice at all levels of government and input from people with real-life experience to inform policy making.

Recommended reading

- Craig G. Bartholomew and Michael W. Goheen, *Living at the Crossroads: An Introduction to Christian Worldview* (Ada, MI: Baker, 2008).

- John Gray, *Black Mass: Apocalyptic Religion and the Death of Utopia* (New York: Penguin, 2007).
- Jonathan Haidt, *The Righteous Mind: Why Good People Are Divided by Politics and Religion* (New York: Penguin, 2012).
- Tim Keller, *Generous Justice: How God's Grace Makes Us Just* (London: Hodder & Stoughton, 2010).
- David T. Koysiz, *Political Visions and Illusions: A Survey and Christian Critique of Contemporary Ideologies* (Grand Rapids, MI: InterVarsity Press, 2003).
- Nick Spencer and Jonathan Chaplin, *God and Government* (London: SPCK, 2009).

Session 3

TRANSFORMATION

Summary

This session looks at why politics is a part of God's mission to transform all things. It looks at how we can play our part in that mission in the different spheres of life. Also, many planets will appear all over your walls!

Structure

- Welcome (5 minutes)
- Video (3 minutes)
- Feedback (10 minutes)
- Talk (12 minutes)
- Discussion (20 minutes)
- Activity (10 minutes)
- Prayer (10 minutes)
- Takeaway (2 minutes)

72 minutes total

To run this session, you will need:

- Access to the internet or the downloaded video (and, if needed, a projector and laptop setup) to watch the 'Show Up' video.
- Paper, pens, scissors, sticky-tak, wall space, lining paper, or large board.

Welcome (5 minutes)

Open with prayer. Again, include some feedback from the 'take-aways' from the last two weeks.

Video: Show Up (2:56 minutes)

Following the opening prayer, start the session off with the Christians in Politics video 'Show Up.'

Here is the video script to give you an idea of its content:

> 'For in him all things were created, things in heaven and on earth, visible and invisible, whether thrones or powers or rulers or authorities, all things have been created through him and for him. He is before all things, and in him all things hold together. And he is the head of the body, the church; he is the beginning and the firstborn from among the dead so that in everything he might have the supremacy.'

All things means all of creation. God's desire is for every sphere of culture to be transformed. Business, media, education, arts, religion, family, and even politics. But most of our energy, time, and resources as the church seem to be invested only in the religious sphere. We're training people to be better worship leaders, better preachers, better small group leaders. But not so much of our time is spent training people to be better teachers, better journalists, or better politicians. In fact, we may be impacting only one-seventh of culture.

These spheres are transformed by the presence of prayerful, trained-up believers within them. For too long as Christians, we have been shouting from the sidelines rather than getting on the pitch. It's easy to send an email or a postcard. It's harder to build relationships and work with those we may not necessarily agree with. In politics, decisions are made by those who show up.

We have a choice as believers in the UK: Are we going to spend the next few years just commentating on and complaining about the state of our country? Or are we going to follow the biblical precedent of people like Joseph, Esther, and Daniel, who served in the midst of regimes that make present-day politics look positively virtuous?

Surely, it's time for Christians to show up. We can just follow, or we can serve and lead. Your vote could just be the start of you making decisions, not the end. So why don't you join a political party or a campaign or connect with your local councillors or MP? And, above all, pray. Rather than shouting from a distance, you could be whispering from up close.

We will see God's will be done and his kingdom come on earth as it is in heaven. The question is, will we be part of making it happen?

Show up. Jesus did.

Feedback (10 minutes)

The aim of this discussion time is to ease the group into reflecting and engaging with the session topic, not necessarily to have all the answers.

1. What jumped out at you from the video?

2. What aspects of culture do you think most influence you or (if you have them) your children? How do you see the power of the spheres at play?

3. In terms of the political sphere, do you ever disagree with the decisions our politicians make, nationally or locally? What influence have those decisions had on you? Give some examples.

4. Do you ever complain about those decisions on social media? How does that usually go?

5. Can you think of some proactive, relational ways to engage with these issues?

Talk (12 minutes)

You can read this out to the group (it takes about 7 minutes, plus the Bible readings), or if you'd like to develop your own version, feel free—we've put more ideas and resources in the notes at the end of the session. We've also put some suggestions in brackets here of where you might like to add examples from your own church.

We're going to reflect today on the passage of Scripture that we heard in the video—Colossians 1:15–20—and we're also going to consider a couple of other short passages of Scripture.

Read—or ask someone else to read—Matthew 5:13–16 and 1 Corinthians 15:58. (Do read Colossians 1 again if you would like to.)

You are the salt of the earth. But if the salt loses its saltiness, how can it be made salty again? It is no longer good for anything, except to be thrown out and trampled underfoot.

You are the light of the world. A town built on a hill cannot be hidden. Neither do people light a lamp and put it under a bowl. Instead they put it on its stand, and it gives light to everyone in the house. In the same way, let your light shine before others, that they may see your good deeds and glorify your Father in heaven. (Matt. 5:13–16)

Therefore, my dear brothers and sisters, stand firm. Let nothing move you. Always give your-selves fully to the work of the Lord, because you

know that your labour in the Lord is not in vain.
(1 Cor. 15:58)

Jesus 'is before all things, and in him all things hold together,' wrote Paul in his letter to the Colossians. When we talk about seeking the kingdom of God above everything else, we are looking towards the renewal of everything, every part of life. God's desire has always been for every sphere of culture to be transformed, every corner of creation—not just our churches, and not just our hearts. The kingdom of God touches everything about how we live, how we flourish, how we order our society, how we spend our time, how we raise children, how we make money, how we care for the wider creation. It is expressed in business, media, education, arts, religion, family, and even politics.

So, if we are to be partners in the transformation of all life, what might that practically mean?

Social scientists talk of seven broad areas of life that influence culture: government, religion, business, education, family, media, and the arts. These are the areas that have been shown to have the most profound influence on how we think and live, forming our culture.

The word *culture* comes from the same Latin root as the word *cult*. Culture leads us, though it is an invisible leader. It is what is in the ether. It is the air we breathe, causing us to believe what is right and what is wrong, what is allowable and what is not.

Jesus famously describes his followers as the light of the world and as the salt of the earth, as we just read. Salt enhances the flavour of our food when small amounts of it are spread out within the rest of the ingredients, which is a compelling picture of influence. But where are we bringing our influence to bear?

The problem for us as the church is that, even though we have desired change in the various spheres, we have not always been meaningfully present *in* those spheres. We have often sought change via prayer and petitioning from the outside but have not always followed Christ's pattern of incarnation by being involved on the inside.

> The problem for us as the church is that, even though we have desired change in the various spheres, we have not always been meaningfully present *in* those spheres.

As the video mentioned, we spend so much time and energy in the church training people to be better worship leaders, better preachers, or better small group leaders. There's a place for that, but what about helping one another to influence the rest of culture?

The church has been waking up to this problem, but sometimes the framing for our endorsement of jobs in the spheres—people in business, healthcare, education, the arts—has been purely evangelistic. As if the work we are involved in has value only inasmuch as it gives us opportunities to explain the good news and save people's souls.

Another consequence of not understanding what drives culture is that because we haven't been proactively present in the spheres, our political exploits have often been a reflex reaction rather than a salt-and-light relational engagement.

In the past (and sometimes still in the present), the church often got 'political' only when we felt someone had come and trampled on 'our turf,' invading our religious sphere. For example, when there are issues of marriage, start of life/end of life issues, or Sunday trading. Not that these aren't important issues. But when we only react and try to 'defend our turf,' it has a profound impact on the tone of our communication. It allows us to become pigeon-holed to those issues because we haven't been engaging proactively across the breadth of the issues.

Here is another place where what we believe about the end of all things makes a huge difference. When you are confident in knowing how the story of our world will unfold, you can still fight for what you believe to be right, but you can do it in an open-handed, smiling, confident way because you know how things are going to turn out in the end.

In each sphere and part of culture, there are enormous challenges which we need to be wise about. The gospel grinds up against principalities and powers in every sphere, including the religious sphere. Different theological questions are thrown up by each context and kind of work. The temptations are different. The glories are different. Each subculture is different and tries to influence our thinking in different ways.

That's why it doesn't work to just do this kind of engagement on our own, in isolation. We need each other to stay accountable. We need to be the body of Christ and not lone wolves. So we seek not just the transformation of individuals to be more aligned with his ways, but also the transformation of systems and structures so they are more aligned to his ways. And the two obviously interact with one another.

Senator Roy Herron writes in his book *How Can a Christian Be in Politics?*, 'If people of faith refuse to participate in politics, then others will make the crucial decisions. In a democracy, the people get the government they choose—and work for. You could say we get the government we deserve. Government can be awful or it can be good; often it is some of both. It is our duty, both as citizens and as Christians, to make it better. The question, then, is not, how can a Christian be in politics? The question is, how can a Christian not be in politics?'[4]

Jesus compared the kingdom of God to a mustard seed— seemingly small, but when it's grown it spreads everywhere. This is an image of infiltration, not of domination, and it's a good one to apply to our thinking about the spheres. Andy Flannagan, in his book *Those Who Show Up*, says, 'The challenge for Christians in Politics who are meeting locally is that in the final analysis, you want them to be mostly dispersed rather than gathered.'

Comforting as it might be to always have strength in numbers, so we feel less vulnerable, God rarely seems to work like that. 'Not by might nor by power,' God says, 'but by my Spirit' (Zech. 4:6).

It's not a takeover we're orchestrating. That's not the model of the mustard seed. Or the seed that must fall into the ground and die in order to produce fruit—that's a picture of something that seems to disappear completely.

We choose to be *present*, even when we feel tiny and insignificant in the face of a giant institution or area of culture. We turn up to our local political party meeting even when it feels like it won't change anything in the grand scheme of things, and maybe even feels a bit dull. We show up. We build relationships. We pray for wisdom. We look for ways to work for good.

> We choose to be *present*, even when we feel tiny and insignificant in the face of a giant institution or area of culture.

We look to the model of a figure like Daniel, who was an embodiment of salt and light within the pagan empire. We keep our hearts focused on God above all. We hold to our ethics. We try to communicate God's nature and his priorities through the kind of people we are—loving, gracious, faithful, holy. And we get stuck in. We don't remove ourselves from the fray.

We look for ways to support one another. In any single congregation, there may not be enough Christians who are passionate about politics to form a sustainable support group. But in *all* the churches of a town or borough, there will be enough people who could come together to form a critical mass. Across the UK, the same churches that have partnered for mission across a town to collaborate on foodbanks or youth work are now gathering Christians from across a town who are engaged with politics, or the media, or the NHS to pray for these spheres and support one another. It is inspiring to see. You may want to start one in your town—if so, Christians in Politics have resources to help!

Although we're talking a lot about politics specifically in this course, it's not the whole deal! Yes, it is strategic, but we engage with politics not because it controls all of life, but because—along with the arts, media, education, family, religion, and business—it creates the culture in which we live and breathe. Like it or not, that culture directs what our children grow up believing is right and wrong.

And of course one of the things we as Christians bring to politics is some perspective on the limitations of politics—there is only so much transformation that can be wrought from the 'external' work of politics. The externalities of life which politics influence tell only a portion of the story of our lives.

In summary, we gather to be dispersed because there is no sphere of life that God is not working to transform.

We are the salt of the earth. We are the light of the world. But to be those things, we have to get out of the church building and show up in the rest of our culture.

> There is no sphere of life that God is not working to transform. We are the salt of the earth. We are the light of the world. But to be those things, we have to get out of the church building and show up in the rest of our culture.

Discussion (20 minutes)

1. The seven spheres of culture we mentioned are government, religion, business, education, family, media, and the arts. Does anyone identify particularly with one of those spheres in terms of their work or interest? (Note this is not designed to be an exhaustive list. For example, there is no specific mention of sport or healthcare. These seven spheres are simply the areas that have been shown to have the most influence on culture.)

2. Reflect on your involvement or work and how you feel it connects with your faith—where are the opportunities?

3. Do you feel like you have any influence over the culture of the place you live or work? What are the different ways people could 'infiltrate' and influence this particular area for the sake of the kingdom?

Activity (10 minutes)

Some participants may be able to clearly identify a sphere of culture they operate within or have most interest in. Others may benefit from a conversation and helpful questions from fellow participants about where they feel they may be called to influence.

It is also worth noting that these spheres have huge areas of intersection and cross-over. It is not an exact science, just a helpful conceptual tool. For example, the realm of politics obviously influences the realm of business, and vice versa.

Give everyone two pieces of paper that have been cut into circles, to represent a 'sphere.'

Ask each person to spend a couple of minutes writing down on the pieces of paper the glories and darknesses of the particular sphere they have chosen. The positives go on one circle and the negatives go on the other. Then go around and ask each person to share one positive and one negative aspect from their spheres as they stick them on a wall or board. When people have chosen the same sphere of influence, encourage them to stick those circles near one another. This display will provide a potent kick-start to our prayers in the next section. For example, for politics, someone may list the glories as 'keeps society from chaos,' 'leaders give a sense of national identity,' and 'prevents dictatorships,' and the darknesses as 'tribalism,' 'self-promotion,' 'economy with the truth.'

Ask people to think up one way in which their sphere could be transformed in a positive way. For example, 'Our local council could become known as a place where all kinds of people are listened to,' or 'Our local businesses could be role models in sustainability.' This will lead us into our time of prayer.

Some participants may not feel as comfortable sharing as others do, so you may need to facilitate their participation sensitively.

Prayer (10 minutes)

Spend some time praying about the specific spheres of influence you have been discussing. Pray for each sphere to operate as it has been designed by God to operate. After some time of free prayer, you may want to use the following song as well. Listen to it at http://bit.ly/wsyk-video, or just sing it, as it is written to the tune of 'Abide with Me.'

We Seek Your Kingdom

We seek your kingdom throughout every sphere
We long for heaven's demonstration here
Jesus, your light shines bright for all to see
Transform, revive and heal society

Before all things, in him all things were made
Inspiring culture, media and trade
May all our work serve your economy
Transform, revive and heal society

Peace, truth and justice reigning everywhere
With us be present in our public square
Fill all who lead with your integrity
Transform, revive and heal society

Forgive us Lord, when we have not engaged
Failing to scribe your heart on history's page
Make us again what we were made to be
Transform, revive and heal society

Faithful to govern ever may we be
Selfless in service, loving constantly
In everything may your authority
Transform, revive and heal society[5]

Takeaway (2 minutes)

Each week, we'll suggest something that the group could do in the coming week to explore things further. It's entirely optional, but it's a great way of getting people to deepen the journey of this course.

- Visit the Christians in Politics website (www .christiansinpolitics.org.uk) and look over the resources and articles. Take some notes on what most jumps out at you as homework to share with the group next week.
- If you are involved in some of the other spheres, you may also like to look at www.transform workuk.org or www.licc.org.uk, who support believers engaged in the various spheres. For further reading on the theology of God's holistic mission of transformation, see the resources listed below.

Recommended reading

- Dr Richard Bauckham and Trevor Hart, *Hope against Hope: Christian Eschatology at the Turn of the Millennium* (Grand Rapids, MI: Eerdmans, 2009).
- Christopher Wright, *The Mission of God: Unlocking the Bible's Grand Narrative* (London: IVP, 2006).

- Tom Wright, *Surprised by Hope: Rethinking Heaven, the Resurrection, and the Mission of the Church* (New York: Harper Paperbacks, 2008).
- When it comes to the theology of Christian engagement in politics, some amazing work has been done by thinkers like Oliver O'Donovan, Jonathan Chaplin, Anna Rowlands, and David Landrum. Browse their online writing!

Session 4

BEHIND THE SCENES

Summary

This session looks at the often ignored but vital role that Christians can play behind the scenes within politics and government, both locally and nationally, and more broadly considers how patient, godly relationship-building is key. We'll also experience the rough and tumble of politics with blindfolds on!

Structure

- Welcome (5 minutes)
- Activity (10 minutes)
- Video (3 minutes)
- Feedback (10 minutes)
- Talk (10 minutes)
- Discussion (20 minutes)
- Prayer (10 minutes)
- Takeaway (4 minutes)

72 minutes total

To run this session, you will need:

- Access to the internet or a downloaded video (and if needed, a projector and laptop setup) to watch the 'Influence' video.
- For the activity: a couple of blindfolds and a stopwatch!

Welcome (5 minutes)

We recommend opening with prayer. If anyone carried out a 'take-away' action from any of the last few weeks and hasn't yet told the group, encourage them to share their experience.

Activity (10 minutes)
Blindfold obstacle course

Before the group arrives at the location, arrange a simple obstacle course. It could be around the church hall or throughout someone's house. It could just be around one large room or through a few rooms. You could use boxes, chairs, sticks, piles of books, or just use your own fiendish creativity to make life difficult for the travellers.

Divide the participants into two teams. Each team must nominate three players, who will then be timed traversing the course blindfolded. Add a ten-second penalty for every obstacle that is touched. The lowest combined time wins. Each traveller is allowed a companion from their team who can walk alongside them and whisper instructions. They may have quite a job, however, as the role of the other team is to make as much noise as possible and give unhelpful instructions. Obviously, this game may not be suitable for some participants, but hopefully they can still cheer encouragement … or seed confusion!

After playing, ask the group to reflect on what the experience of being out of their comfort zone felt like. Might that environment feel suspiciously like our noisy, present-day public square? Most importantly, ask who had more influence on them: the 'whisperer' or the cheering/baying crowd.

Video: The Influence Video (3:32 minutes)

Watch the Christians in Politics video 'The Influence Video.'

Here is the video script to give you an idea of its content:

How much do you know about Obadiah? If you're anything like me, not very much. That's because he worked behind the scenes—you could say he was the sound guy to Elijah's worship leader.

King Ahab has been leading Israel astray, and Elijah is told to challenge his dabbling with other gods. But Elijah doesn't just rant about this dysfunctional political leadership from the desert, screaming into the ether on social media and drumming up signatures for his 'Down with Baal' petition. He seeks a connection with an actual human being.

Obadiah managed Ahab's palace and affairs, and it couldn't have been easy for this God-fearing civil servant to be present at the heart of a regime that was doing such damage to God's honour.

But he stayed. He was faithful. Then, at the right moment, he meets Elijah and is perfectly placed to broker a very unlikely meeting. The distant is brought close.

So the rap battle to end all rap battles takes place on Mount Carmel. The prophets of Baal suffer total humiliation, and an impossible bonfire that even Bear Grylls couldn't have managed leaves a lasting impact on the consciousness of the people of Israel. But it wouldn't have happened without the event management skills of Obadiah.

It's as important to be holding the clipboard as it is to be holding the microphone.

Elijah constantly confronted King Ahab from outside the court. We need brave people like him. But fewer of us are working on the inside, like Obadiah. We need more brave people like *him*. Let's face it—it's much more exciting to see dry altars burst into flames than to be forwarding emails around a government department. Elijah gets to be the hero of Sunday school stories. Obadiah—not so much.

We can refine our message until it's perfect, then pump it out with every piece of technology we can find, but if we don't connect with any real people who are willing to listen, it may not bear the fruit it could.

The difference between noise and influence is *relationship*.

If the very nature of God is a set of relationships—*perichoresis*—could it be true that the kingdom of God never moves faster than the speed of relationships?

We live in a noisy world. So much information, but not much wisdom. How do we filter it? How do we work out which words to believe? We believe what's said by people we know and trust. So wouldn't it be better if people were hearing our message from people they know and trust?

Making noise helps us feel better but may not be so great for the rest of the world. Noise may make you move away from something. Relationship draws you closer to someone.

Do we want to feel like we've done our duty, or do we want to have real influence? If the latter, we need to do the hard yards of relationship-building. It may not be fast, and it may not be pretty, but we will learn and be transformed in the process. And it may just lead to moments when impossible and beautiful things cause everyone to stop and stare and say, 'The LORD—he is God.'

Feedback (10 minutes)

The aim of this discussion time is to ease the group into reflecting and engaging with the session topic, not necessarily to have all the answers.

1. Did anything in the video challenge or inspire you?

2. Which approach do you think comes more easily to you—getting involved with an issue more vocally from a distance or building longer-term relationships on the inside? There is no right or wrong answer!

3. In our modern world, what information sources do you trust? Have you encountered any of the perils of un-relational arguments on social media?

Talk (10 minutes)

You can read this out to the group (it takes about 7 minutes, plus the Bible reading), or if you'd like to develop your own version, feel free—we've put more resources in the notes at the end of the session.

Today, we're going to study a passage from the Old Testament that looks at the influence God's people can have when they are in administrative roles in government. It will be more interesting than it sounds!

Read—or ask someone else to read—1 Kings 18:1–6.

> After a long time, in the third year, the word of the LORD came to Elijah: 'Go and present yourself to Ahab, and I will send rain on the land.' So Elijah went to present himself to Ahab.
>
> Now the famine was severe in Samaria, and Ahab had summoned Obadiah, his palace administrator. (Obadiah was a devout believer in the LORD. While Jezebel was killing off the LORD's prophets, Obadiah had taken a hundred prophets and hidden them in two caves, fifty in each, and had supplied them with food and water.) Ahab had said to Obadiah, 'Go through the land to all the springs and valleys. Maybe we can find some grass to keep the horses and mules alive so we will not have to kill any of our animals.' So they divided the land they were to cover, Ahab going in one direction and Obadiah in another. (1 Kings 18:1–6)

To begin to understand this story, we need to have some sense of who Obadiah was. He isn't a character we tend to hear much about in church. Of course, there is an Old Testament book called Obadiah, named after Obadiah the prophet. But this is not the same guy. Prophet Obadiah came later.

Verse 3 tells us that this Obadiah was a senior civil servant, the 'palace administrator.' Only by being a faithful worker in the palace would he have risen to this position. Verses 3 and 12 also tell us that he was a devout believer in God. Fittingly, his name means: 'Servant of the Lord.'

To best understand Obadiah's influence, we need to appreciate his context. At this point in Israel's history, King Ahab rules over Israel, and 1 Kings tell us that he 'did more evil in the eyes of the Lord than any of those before him.' That's some government to choose to work inside. The prophet Elijah had announced a drought from God on the land as a direct consequence of Ahab's wickedness. Ahab tried hard to find and kill Elijah (v. 10), while Jezebel 'was killing off the Lord's prophets' (v. 4).

So what did Obadiah do in the context of so much corruption, abuse of power, and immorality? How did he see his calling? What did it mean to him to live a life devoted to God whilst working for that regime?

He did his work well. Verses 5–6 show how Obadiah was trusted by Ahab. Think about how this trust would have been earned, despite the fact that Ahab and Obadiah had vastly different morals and attitudes towards God. Try to imagine how Obadiah would have had to restrain himself for the greater good. I would imagine he showed great respect, conscientiousness, loyalty, and integrity.

But he went further than just being 'a good guy' or 'a safe pair of hands.' When Ahab's wife, Jezebel, was killing off all the prophets, Obadiah stepped in and secretly put them into hiding. He was bold in doing what he could to *mitigate the effects of wickedness*. And he not only hid the prophets, he also kept them alive with provisions. He put his life at risk by doing this.

Maybe that recalls to you more recent stories of how so many people living under the Nazi regime hid Jews, risking their lives in the process. Being faithful to God usually demands more than just being a conscientious employee.

You could also say that Obadiah showed *wisdom in his caution*. When he was hiding one hundred prophets from Jezebel, he split them into two locations for safety, in case either was discovered. However, despite his initial caution, he was willing to *keep in step with God's Spirit*, which ensured he was in the right place at the right time.

In the story we started to read, Elijah tells Obadiah to take him to Ahab, which strikes Obadiah as an act of insanity that might prove fatal for him. If he shows up with Elijah after Ahab has been searching for him across the known world, it would be hard for Ahab not to jump to the conclusion that Obadiah had known where he was all along. But Elijah insists that God wants the meeting to go ahead, so Obadiah goes to Ahab with the news. Consider how this willingness, given the context, showcases his godliness and true allegiance.

This willingness was pivotal to what happened next. You probably know the story of Elijah and Mount Carmel. When Elijah and Ahab meet, Elijah tells Ahab to summon all of Israel for a face-off between the prophets of Baal and Elijah, as the only remaining prophet of Israel's God.

Each team gets a bull to sacrifice and an altar and they have to pray for their God to send the fire. Team Baal pray all day and go to all kinds of extreme lengths to make their God send fire, but to no avail. Elijah pours water all over his altar, and then God sends an enormous fire that consumes everything. The showdown leads to the people of Israel acknowledging the Lord as God.

That incredible outcome was made possible, in human terms, because Obadiah did as Elijah asked of him and arranged the meeting with Ahab. He was the only one who could make that meeting happen. The insider.

We read nothing more of this Obadiah in Scripture. Just this one story of how a guy on the inside made possible this extraordinary demonstration of God's power in front of the nation of Israel. His faithfulness to God is a permanent record in Scripture.

Despite the events of Mount Carmel, King Ahab continued to disregard God. He committed injustice towards an upright citizen, which you can read about in 1 Kings 18 if you keep going after the Mount Carmel story.

The verdict on Ahab's life and rule is brutally honest: he was unprecedented in his wickedness, and his actions set the Northern Kingdom of Israel firmly on a course of idolatry, leading to eventual captivity and assimilation, as prophesied. But over the centuries, the showdown on Mount Carmel became a foundational faith-building episode for the people of Israel. They became more convinced that their God was not just *a* god but *the* God.

The story of Obadiah is not about how one man changed every-thing. What we get is an evolving, complicated story of faithfulness and regression, of devotion and rebellion—and at the heart of it all, God's faithfulness in spite of everything.

Obadiah's story is fascinating because he was present in the heart of a notoriously corrupt regime. He worked for it. He isn't the only figure in Scripture like that—Daniel is another obvious example—and it's hard to say how much say they had in the roles they were assigned. But that was his calling. At the same time that Elijah was called to his prophetic critique and challenge of the regime, God called someone else to work inside the system.

At any time of rampant godlessness and religious persecution, the need for a godly presence at the heart of government is height-ened. It can be easy to think that this is when Christians should get out, keep themselves pure, and run for the hills. But if the story of Obadiah shows us anything, it is that something else is also possible—that God calls us to take on different roles.

> At any time of rampant godlessness and religious persecution, the need for a godly presence at the heart of government is heightened.

Obadiah's devotion to God showed his commitment to *righteousness,* and his actions towards the prophets showed his desire for *justice.* In that regard, he was for Israel what King Ahab was supposed to be. Although his actions didn't lead to permanent revival, he did what he could to be a positive influence within his role. He operated within the space between the prophet and the king, a servant of God and of Ahab.

Discussion (20 minutes)

1. How important do you feel it is to work inside a political party, at a local council, or in the civil service? Why is that the case?

2. Where do you already have influence? Where may God be calling you to have influence?

3. Obadiah had to 'put up' with many things that were wrong in the regime for which he was working. We're often uncomfortable with this kind of compromise. Can you think of contemporary parallels in our current political system? How can we know, as Daniel seemed to, when it is the right time to comply and the right time to deny?

4. If it's all about relationships, then with whom is the next relationship that God may be calling you to? Who may represent your next step deeper into political waters?

Prayer (10 minutes)

Spend some time praying—as a group, in smaller groups, or individually—about what you have covered in this session. In line with our focus on the things that go on behind the scenes, this week we will try to be silent and still, rather than enjoying the sound of our own voices! This prayer may help as an introduction. It is to be read by a leader, and everyone should join in the bold type. The PowerPoint file is available in the resources section online (http://influencecourse.co.uk/). Then spend five minutes in silence waiting on God, in the hope of keeping in step with God's Spirit as Obadiah and Elijah did.

> In this world of conflicting opinions, **we choose
>   to listen.**
> In this world where those who speak loudest are
>   heard, **we choose to listen.**
> In this world where we speak without being spoken
>   to, **we choose to listen.**
> In this world where we're running to stand still, **we
>   choose to listen.**

> In this world where we want our voice to be heard,
>   **we choose to listen.**
> In this world where we long to be noticed, **we
>   choose to listen.**
> In this world where we often listen only to those
>   who agree with us, **we choose to listen.**
> In this world where we have to fight to find silence,
>   **we choose to listen.**

> **May we be like the One who says he will hear
>   our cry—the great Listener.
> The One who is all ears to hear the complaints
>   of a people whose only language is often
>   complaint.**

The One who cannot look, as he hears the
    screams of the trafficked, the bullied, and
    the insane.
The One who tenses his fists as he overhears the
    arrogance of men who would play God as
    they trample on the poor.

We choose to listen because you have listened
    to us.

Psalm 10:17
    You, LORD, hear the desire of the afflicted;
    you encourage them, and you listen to
    their cry,

Amen.

Takeaway (4 minutes)

Each week, we'll suggest something that the group could do in the coming week to explore things further. It's entirely optional, but it's a great way of getting people to deepen the journey of this course.

- In response to the call to relationships and meaningful influence, take some time to pray and reflect about just one relationship God may be leading you into. If appropriate, make contact with that person. It may be someone you already know or someone you need to reach out to. Who knows what influence you may have? We have many stories of 'normal' people getting remarkable responses from politicians. Another way to think about this is to consider who is just a few steps further along the political journey than you are and who might be able to help you. If you are struggling to find someone like that, do get in touch with us at info@christiansinpolitics.org.uk, and we can match you up with a mentor, or maybe you would like to be a mentor!

• In the next session, we will be thinking about how we can disagree well as believers. So, in preparation, encourage the group to browse the websites of the main political parties in the UK to appraise themselves of their policies and style. Suggest they take note of what they agree with and what they don't.

Extra prayer

Heavenly Father, we thank you for your loving care for the world you created and for your concern for society.

We praise you for the abilities you give us to order society and to promote peace and welfare. We pray for those in office within our government.

We ask that you would give them wisdom, humility, and a desire to govern with righteousness and justice.

We pray especially for believers within Parliament, both in elected public office and in behind-the-scenes, supportive, administrative roles.

May your Spirit of wisdom come upon them, granting them discernment; and may your peace be within them in all that they do—especially in times of tension and disagreement.

We pray that you would raise up your people to be Christ's ambassadors in the places of power in our nation, towns, and cities.

We pray this for the sake of your kingdom.

In Jesus' name we pray.

Amen.

Recommended reading

- Chapters 8, 14, and 15 of Andy Flannagan, *Those Who Show Up* (Edinburgh: Muddy Pearl, 2015).

Session 5

WE CAN'T AGREE

Summary

This session looks at the challenges and the importance of Christians disagreeing well in politics. We'll look at what true unity is, and we'll get a chance to interrogate our fellow participants in a mock radio studio!

Structure

- Welcome (5 minutes)
- Video: Order from Chaos (3 minutes)
- Prayer (3 minutes)
- Feedback (10 minutes)
- Talk (10 minutes)
- Video: Disagree with Tea (5 minutes)
- Discussion (20 minutes)
- Activity (10 minutes)
- Prayer (10 minutes)
- Takeaway (2 minutes)

78 minutes

To run this session, you will need:

- Access to the internet or the downloaded files (and if needed, a projector and laptop setup) to watch the 'Order from Chaos' and 'Disagree with Tea' videos.
- Enough pens and paper for everyone taking part.

Welcome (5 minutes)

Video: Order from Chaos (2:40 minutes)

We recommend opening with prayer for unity and reconciliation in response to this video. Feel free to follow naturally wherever it leads. Some may even want to confess their part in our divisions. As ever, if anyone carried out a 'takeaway' action from any of the last few weeks and hasn't yet told the group, encourage them to share their experience.

Prayer (3 minutes)

Feedback (10 minutes)

The aim of this discussion time is to ease the group into reflecting and engaging with the session topic, not necessarily to have all the answers.

1. How can Christians hold different views on political issues and maintain relationships (rather than just avoiding each other)?

2. Why may it be a good thing for congregations to have people who have different political views and loyalties?

3. Can you identify something positive in the approach or policies of each of the main political parties in this country, even if you would not normally vote for them? (If you are struggling to think of any policies, even after the research homework, then it is very easy to do some quick Googling!)

Talk (10 minutes)

You can read this out to the group (it takes about 8 minutes, plus the Bible readings), or if you'd like to develop your own version, feel free—we've put more ideas and resources in the notes at the end of the session.

We're going to think today about unity and what that means as we approach politics.

Read—or ask someone else to read—Psalm 133 and 2 Chronicles 30:12.

> How good and pleasant it is
> when God's people live together in unity!
>
> It is like precious oil poured on the head,
> running down on the beard,
> running down on Aaron's beard,
> down on the collar of his robe.

It is as if the dew of Hermon
    were falling on Mount Zion.
For there the LORD bestows his blessing,
    even life for evermore. (Ps. 133)

Also in Judah the hand of God was on the people
to give them unity of mind to carry out what the
king and his officials had ordered, following the
word of the LORD. (2 Chron. 30:12)

What is it that we understand from the word *unity*? What is unity? It's not the same as uniformity, being the same, so what does it mean?

Well, let's go back a step. What is a unit? We use the term in all kinds of different ways. We use it in maths—you might remember learning to add up *units,* tens, and hundreds in the classroom, depending on how long ago you went to school.

The military talk about units. A group of soldiers on the same team and living in the same place get referred to as a unit. Ikea will sell you all kinds of units and give you instructions on how to assemble them at home. You can rent a unit, meaning a flat or apartment in a bigger building. (*You could ask the group if they can think of other ways in which the word is used.*)

Couples or families sometimes get described as a unit. They are individuals, but somehow they have this togetherness that also makes them some kind of joint entity or team.

Describing disparate parts as making up a unit conveys a sense of togetherness, oneness. It implies that they are not just independent parts but also form something bigger. It's not that they lose the sense of being something distinct, but they also function in this added way as a part of something else. Something bigger. And *unity* is the term given to describe that state of harmony.

So let's think back over some of those meanings of *unit* and think about how unity is displayed amongst the different parts—and how it makes a difference.

- Maths?
- Military?
- Furniture?
- Buildings?
- Couples/families?
- Any others you came up with.

At the heart of our faith is a unit of three persons: the Trinity. In the Bible, God is revealed as Father, Son, and Spirit. The Trinity is the model of a perfect unit, and the relationship that the three of them share was even depicted by the early Church Fathers as a dance—known as *perichoresis*. It's a powerful picture of being in step with one another, sharing a rhythm and a sense of movement.

But what does unity mean when it comes to the church, to God's people? We get a sense of its importance from the Old Testament in the verses which we just read. Psalm 133 talks about unity as something beautiful to which God's people should aspire. The whole psalm is dedicated to this one idea that when God's people live together in unity, it is a profound joy and blessing to everyone. The psalmist uses images of oil and dew pouring out over everyone, these beautiful, life-giving liquids that cannot be contained.

In the New Testament, the theme of unity is presented in both theological and practical terms. Paul famously wrote to the church in Philippi, in the second chapter of his letter:

> Therefore if you have any encouragement from being united with Christ, if any comfort from his love, if any common sharing in the Spirit, if any tenderness and compassion, then make my joy complete by being like-minded, having the same love, being one in spirit and of one mind. (Phil. 2:1–2)

It is assumed that through our faith in Jesus, we have been united to him in a profound way. Paul urged us that if this is really true, if we have experienced his love, then it must lead to a practical unity with other believers, which is described in terms of having one mind and one spirit.

Does this mean that Paul is urging us to have all the same opinions as every other Christian, to embrace a uniformity of perspective on everything? Is that what any of us have experienced in the church? Christians have always had things they disagree about—you can see that in the New Testament as well as in today's church, and even in the video we just watched. Christians join different political parties!

So what else might it mean to share the same love, being one in spirit and mind? It means that we are filled with the same Spirit, God's Holy Spirit, and perhaps this means that we affirm and recognise that in one another even when we disagree. It means that we are held together by our love for Jesus and our complete trust in him as the source of our salvation. It might mean that these things that unite us are more important than the things we disagree about, and that we hold in mind this unity, this togetherness in the face of anything else. We choose to put kingdom before tribe.

> These things that unite us are more important than the things we disagree about.

We all have our own experiences of church life, and perhaps we have stories about when we have witnessed unity and when we really haven't. All kinds of issues threaten church unity. Leadership styles. Ways of leading meetings. Who is welcome in church. Ethical questions around lifestyle and sexuality. Often what tears churches apart are the attitudes and relationship breakdowns involved more than the different opinions people hold. It is especially tragic when these attitudes override the love which we are called to extend to one another in every circumstance.

The early church faced a huge number of challenges as it learnt how to be a united community. It was comprised of people from social classes at opposite ends of the spectrum. In one congregation, a slave would worship alongside their owner—united as equals in Christ Jesus (see Gal. 3:28), and Scripture instructs both in how to act wisely and rightly towards the other.

We are not required to have the same opinions on issues which the Bible does not address directly, including political matters. It is worth remembering that all rulers, whether democratically elected or otherwise, are ruling on behalf of God and are accountable to him. We do not live in a theocratic society, so we are expected to learn how to live as a Christian community within a pluralistic environment.

Individual Christians will each have different political ideas and will vote accordingly. They will join different parties. Some will stand for election for opposing parties. They all need our prayers, whether we agree with their political ideas or not.

The ability to disagree on secondary matters within a context of unity around primary matters is priceless. The media are constantly looking for spats and points of contention between different camps within political parties, as they make for good headlines. Christians are called to be humble towards each other, realising we are all sinners prone to pride. Sometimes the *way* in which we discuss and debate political matters may be more important than the outcome.

> Sometimes the *way* in which we discuss and debate political matters may be more important than the outcome.

This is a distinctive that we can hopefully bring to society. As Archbishop Justin Welby says in the foreword to *Those Who Show Up*, 'Politics would be extremely dull if we all agreed on everything. There is joy in diversity, and we should not be afraid to disagree with one another, but in a way that models the reconciling love of Jesus. Good disagreement is a gift that the church can offer the world around it—and our political system could certainly do with a healthy dose of it.'

Good disagreement is rarely fostered outside the context of good relationships. When we don't know each other, we judge each other. We need to intentionally build relationships with those with whom we may disagree. And that takes time and effort. And humility.

Ephesians 1:10 says that 'when the times reach their fulfilment, [God will] bring unity to all things in heaven and on earth under Christ.' The new creation (Rev. 21–22) will usher in an eternal age of perfect cosmic, and societal, unity. What a beautiful hope that we have. We cannot force unity, but God is bringing it about as he works to restore and redeem the whole creation.

Debate is part of democracy, and disagreements over ideas and policy are inherent, but they all must be understood in the context of the great, perfectly united, eternal future that God has for his people in glory.

Video: Disagree with Tea (4:20 minutes)

Show the Christians in Politics video 'Disagree with Tea.'

Here is the video script to give you an idea of the content:

As you can imagine, there are many issues on which we fundamentally disagree.

'Well, I always say to my Labour friends I admire your political principles but I just think that Labour Party policy can sometimes lead to dependence on the State.'

'Well, I get angry when Conservative policies treat people as economic units. An economy should serve the people rather than people being slaves to the economy.'

'Well, I don't think the Liberal Democrats got the credit they deserved in the last Parliament for things like increasing the income tax threshold.'

As Christians in politics, we are team players in our individual political tribes, but as Christians, we do owe our primary allegiance to our King.

For us, it has to be kingdom before tribe every time—not that that's always easy to work out.

That's why we compassionately disagree on different issues but do it over a cup of tea.

And as the Archbishop of Canterbury himself says, Christians should debate politics and debate passionately, but as Christians, we should model disagreeing well.

It's what we can offer to society—one of the major things as an alternative to the Punch and Judy we see in things like Prime Minister's Questions.

But I do think if we're not careful we can be easily lured into believing that any difference of opinion is automatically a split or a rift. I think our media and our political campaigning, and probably our own laziness of thought as well, don't really help that. We start to think that acceptance and agreement are the same thing. I mean, it just takes reading one news story and you can be totally forgiven for thinking that any two people—or two groups of people—who disagree on the same issue can't also accept one another. But that's just not the case. We can disagree and extend the arms of embrace at the same time. That's just not the story that newspapers want to write.

Absolutely, we live in this tabloid culture where we play the man or the woman but not the ball. You know, when we're discussing policy—whether it's the EU or Trident, whether it's education or law and order—we need to disagree gracefully and humbly. You know, it says in the Bible that we see only in part, and Christians need to model that. Perhaps this is a bit like a beautiful conservatory with hundreds of different coloured panes of glass. There are over 400 denominations, but maybe the church needs to learn a bit about community from political parties. There aren't 400 political parties. There are just a handful. And let's face it, those in stained-glass houses probably shouldn't throw stones.

One of the main reasons I hear from people telling me they don't engage in party politics—from Christians, especially—is that they couldn't agree with everything that a party stands for. And I understand that. I mean, that's where I was for a long time, as well. But if you wait around for the perfect party, you'll be waiting a long time.

The reality is, every day in our workplaces we work alongside people who we fundamentally disagree with on certain issues. You know, we probably don't agree with everything that our husband or wife believes. We certainly don't agree with everything that our church believes. And yet we find common cause and we work together.

You know, at this point, I should probably confess that there is one party and I agree with 100 percent of their policies, but it's called the Andy Flannagan Party, and it has only one member, and sadly, it's me. That is the philosophical thick end of the wedge we get to. You know, we just paint ourselves isolationist into a corner until there's nowhere left to go and there's nobody left to go with.

So, I guess, why don't you think of joining a political party? You know, it's important to not lose your identity to the tribe, but it's important to be in one. That surely is where the missional, faith-stretching adventure is. You know, working with people that we don't necessarily agree with on everything. For me, that's being salt and light.

So disagree. But disagree well. And don't just talk. Get involved. And not just in our parties.

'Politics would be extremely dull if we all agreed on everything. There is joy in diversity, and we should not be afraid to disagree with one another, but in a way that models the reconciling love of Jesus. Good disagreement is a gift that the church can offer the world around it—and our political system could certainly do with a healthy dose of it.'—Archbishop Justin Welby[6]

Discussion (20 minutes)

1. Do you think you are someone who is 'quick to listen, slow to speak and slow to become angry' (James 1:19)? What's an example of that in your life? What might happen if we applied this to our interactions on social media?

2. As Jesus showed us, there are of course times for 'turning over the tables' as well as times for 'turning the other cheek.' How do we discern the right response in the right moment? How did Jesus?

3. Do people talk about politics in your church? Did people talk about Brexit in your church? What are some of the genuine fears of 'doing politics'?

4. Are any of the group members of political parties? Ask them to share their experiences, both positive and negative.

5. What might stop you from joining a political party?

Activity (10 minutes)

Choose one of the following issues and ask for three volunteers to help with a 'media interview roleplay.' No specialist knowledge required!

- The best flavour of crisps
- Whether or not shops should open on a Sunday
- A contemporary political issue of your choice

Ask the three volunteers to perform a radio or TV interview. One person will be the interviewer, and the other two people will take intentionally opposing positions on the chosen issue. It will be most effective if you create a 'stage' to help people get into their parts. You may want to invent a fictitious local radio station! Make sure the interviewer keeps things moving and cuts off answers with challenges, as a normal interviewer would.

The participants should be encouraged to be as caustic as they like to make sure they 'win' the argument. It is no-holds barred! You may already know which members of your group would revel in this experience! Someone should have a stopwatch, ready to sing a radio jingle when the clock hits zero. Four minutes is about right. You rarely have that long in these situations!

Next, reveal that you will repeat the experience with three new volunteers, whom you will brief to find a way to still disagree but disagree well. How can they stay respectful while disagreeing strongly?

You may have so much fun that you want to do it all again with a new topic. Controlling the timing can be up to you. At the end, allow the group to reflect on what they learned through the experience. Pray for any relationships that may need mending!

Prayer (10 minutes)

Spend some time praying—as a group, in smaller groups, or individually—about what you have covered in this session. It may be appropriate to have a time of confession, and you could use this prayer.

Confession

Father, Son, and Holy Spirit,
We come before you, unworthy of your grace,
Unworthy of your love, unworthy of you.
We are sinners. Have mercy on us, O Lord.
Too often have we chosen the fruit over the garden.
Too often have we bowed down to the golden calf.
Too often have we begged for a sign.
Too often have we declared Caesar to be Lord.
Too often have we demanded to see the wounds in
    your hands.

Too often have we substituted our image of you,
   for you.
Too often have we neglected your call to be salt
   and light.
Too often have we mutilated the body of Christ to
   individual parts.
Too often have we reduced Christianity to a list of
   our particular passions.
Too often have we chosen our tribe over your
   kingdom.
Too often have we been content in our comfortable
   silos.
Too often have we rushed to judgement of the
   other.
But too often have we cowered in fear when you
   may call us to turn over tables.
Too often have we forgotten Jesus' life, death, and
   resurrection.
Too often have we acted on sight and not on faith.

Lord, have mercy.
Christ, have mercy.
Lord, have mercy.

(Silent prayers of confession)

Heal us now of our sinfulness and of the hatred
   that divides us.

Take away our hardness of heart.

Open our eyes which are often blind to the needs
of others.

Remove our selfishness and our greed.

We pray for the reconciliation of our land and our
world, whose division condemns us.

We pray for the courage to admit our fault,

The strength to amend our actions,

And the hope that your grace awaits us.

Give us self-control at all times, and fill our hearts
with your eternal love.

O Jesus, we ask you now to heal and bless us, and
fill us with your peace.

Amen.

Takeaway (2 minutes)

Each week, we'll suggest something that the group could do in the
coming week to explore things further. It's entirely optional, but it's
a great way of getting people to deepen the journey of this course.

- Do you have a friend, colleague, or family member who has different political opinions to you
  and maybe supports a different party? It might
  just be someone who holds very strong views
  compared to your own. This week, make a point

of doing some intentional relationship-building. You may even want to talk to them about politics—or rather, listen. Ask them to help you understand why they hold these views and why they support one particular party. If they ask your opinion in return, great. If they don't, then leave it there. Just see it as an opportunity to listen, build relationship, and understand a different viewpoint better.

Extra prayer

We thank you that we can pray to you, our heavenly Father, in the name of your Son, Jesus Christ, through your Holy Spirit.

We thank you for your unity and the diversity within the Trinity.

We praise you for the love you have for your people, your bride.

We are excited by the eternal joys that await in the new creation where we will experience perfect, unhindered unity in a perfect heavenly world.

We pray for our witness as your people until then.

We pray that you will keep us faithful as citizens, engaged and interested in your world.

We ask that you would give us the Spirit of peace which enables us to discuss, debate, and disagree on political issues without compromising our love for each other.

Forgive us for our pride and our inability to listen well to each other.

We pray for politicians who are believers—may you help them to model gracious disagreement and point to you. Reveal to us whether we might be those politicians in the future. In Jesus' name we pray. Amen.

Recommended reading

- Luke Bretherton, *Christianity and Contemporary Politics: The Conditions and Possibilities of Faithful Witness* (Hoboken, NJ: Wiley-Blackwell, 2010).
- Michael Wear, *Reclaiming Hope* (Nashville: Thomas Nelson, 2017).
- Nick Spencer and Jonathan Chaplin, ed., *God and Government* (London: SPCK, 2009).
- John Micklethwait and Adrian Wooldridge, *God Is Back: How the Global Rise of Faith Is Changing the World* (New York: Penguin, 2009).

Session 6

WHAT'S NEXT?

Summary

This final session will look at what it means to see God's will be done and his kingdom come on earth as it is in heaven—and what part politics may have to play in that. We'll have a chance to get poetic and prophetic! We'll also have time to reflect on what participants might do next in their political engagement after the course finishes.

Structure

- Welcome (2 minutes)
- Video (4 minutes)
- Feedback (15 minutes)
- Talk (12 minutes)
- Discussion (20 minutes)
- Activity (15 minutes)
- Prayer (10 minutes)
- Takeaway (2 minutes)

80 minutes total

To run this session, you will need:

- Access to the internet or the downloaded video (and if needed, a projector and laptop setup) to watch the 'Heaven and Earth' video.
- Enough pens and paper for everyone taking part.

Welcome (2 minutes)

We recommend opening with prayer. If anyone carried out the 'takeaway' action from last week, (or even if they did a previous week's takeaway a little late), ask them to share with the group.

Video: Heaven and Earth (3:57 minutes)

Following the opening prayer, start the session off with the Christians in Politics video 'Heaven and Earth.'

Here is the video script to give you an idea of its content:

When Jesus famously encouraged his disciples to pray 'your kingdom come, your will be done,' he was giving us a clue to what he actually meant every time he spoke of the 'kingdom of heaven.' When you look at what he said, he could not have just been talking about a distant place, a 'pie in the sky when you die.'

Jesus was giving the people of the first century images and metaphors to understand what was taking place in front of their eyes, and what continues to happen in front of our rather more sceptical twenty-first-century eyes. Yeast, mustard seeds, and fields were telling the story of this incredible kingdom that was being inaugurated through healings, deliverance, and words of knowledge. He was demonstrating the future perfection of heaven in the present.

The problem is that our idea of heaven is often based more on what we have subconsciously imbibed from culture than from the Bible. We imagine long, fluffy beards sitting on clouds playing harps in *The Simpsons*, medieval art in the National Gallery, or certain popular, apocalyptic, rapture-based novels.

There is still a hangover in church culture from a time when we believed that Christianity was solely an escape ticket to a disembodied heaven that was just a geographical place beyond the stratosphere (but this side of Mars).

It's not so much like this.

So when Jesus speaks of heaven, he is not speaking of a disembodied place which our 'souls' float off to, but the sphere of reality where God's will is always perfectly done. There is also the sphere of earth where, sadly, his will is not exclusively adhered to yet, as we know all too well.

So perhaps we could more accurately draw it like this.

Which creates this fascinating little intersection. This is where Jesus' life and actions sit. His very person was heaven and earth fused. His was the life fully surrendered to God's perfect will. He was heaven on earth, the fulfilment of the ancient stories of tabernacles and temples. And every healing, act of mercy, and speaking of truth to power sits in here.

Similarly for us in the twenty-first century, every moment that tells of his righteous rule and reign is in there—every moment of compassion, every cry for justice, every piece of good legislation, and every thread of pure thinking demonstrate that future perfection in the here and now. We pray for and we demonstrate heaven on earth. It makes sense of 'your will be done, your kingdom come—on earth as it is in heaven.'

But the glorious thing is that we know where this picture is going. Nobody can claim to know exactly how it all happens, but we are promised in Scripture that the end of the story is an incredible, total fusion of the new heaven and the new earth, as described in Revelation 21 and 2 Peter.

Ridiculously, we are called to be partners with God in his mission to see the restoration, redemption, and reconciliation of all things. If that is the ultimate goal, then suddenly our involvement in all the structures of this world starts to make sense.

Can you see how motivating that is? Our efforts are not wasted. Every effort to choose kindness over cynicism, to choose truth over expediency, to choose cooperation rather than competition, to choose love over apathy, makes a mark on the map of forever.

Where are you going to make your mark?

> Ridiculously, we are called to be partners with God in his mission to see the restoration, redemption, and reconciliation of all things. If that is the ultimate goal, then suddenly our involvement in all the structures of this world starts to make sense.

Feedback (15 minutes)

The aim of this discussion time is to ease the group into reflecting and engaging with the session topic, not necessarily to have all the answers. (Note that paper and pens are required.)

1. As a child, how were you taught to think about heaven, and how do you think about it now?

2. Can you think of things you have experienced or seen which would sit in the overlap of heaven and earth—moments when God's will was done, moments that show us what God's rule looks like? Suggest that participants draw two large circles with a large intersection, and write a list of things in it. (Leave some space for question #3!) Here are some to get you started (only if you need a nudge): compassionate actions, pure thoughts, warm hospitality, a miraculous healing, a prophetic dream, a well-crafted spreadsheet, or a well-tended garden.

3. What kind of *political changes* in this area might sit in the 'intersection' to demonstrate the kingdom of God? Add these to your picture. Here are some to get you started (only if you need a nudge): truth-telling, accountability, just taxation, family support, or available healthcare.

Talk (12 minutes)

You can read this out to the group (it takes about 8 minutes, plus the Bible reading), or if you'd like to develop your own version, feel free—we've put more ideas and resources in the notes at the end of the session.

We're going to think today about unity and what that means as we approach politics.

*Read—or ask someone else to read—*Revelation 21:1–5.

> And I saw a new heaven and a new earth: for the first heaven and the first earth were passed away; and there was no more sea.
>
> And I John saw the holy city, new Jerusalem, coming down from God out of heaven, prepared as a bride adorned for her husband.
>
> And I heard a great voice out of heaven saying, Behold, the tabernacle of God is with men, and he will dwell with them, and they shall be his people, and God himself shall be with them, and be their God.
>
> And God shall wipe away all tears from their eyes; and there shall be no more death, neither sorrow, nor crying, neither shall there be any more pain: for the former things are passed away.
>
> And he that sat upon the throne said, Behold, I make all things new. (Rev. 21:1–5 KJV)

There is a story told about a family of American tourists arriving at Heathrow, who hired a car with SatNav and excitedly headed for Windsor Castle. They were confused when, three hours later, they pulled up outside the Windsor Castle pub in Weston-super-Mare.

When we get our destination even just slightly wrong, it can make a huge difference.

As Christians, is it possible that we have done that with heaven?

We explored that idea when we watched the video a little earlier, and we challenged the idea that many people still hold, that heaven is a place we will one day escape to, leaving earth far behind.

This passage in Revelation is a beautiful picture of what we are talking about—the promise of the end of the story. That Jesus will return, and there will be a new heaven and a new earth. Note that he descends here to us; we don't have to go up to find him. God's dwelling will be here with us. And there is no more pain and no more death. What a beautiful passage that is, and what a beautiful promise it contains. What a vision we have for the future. The moment when God restores all things, makes all things new, makes it all right.

The world of modern politics seems murky by comparison, and so far away from this grand and glorious hope we have. How are the two possibly connected? How do we focus our sights on the dream of what God is doing and also get involved with today's imperfect systems? It's a struggle that is real and difficult and perhaps one of the reasons we pull back from trying.

Sometimes, Christians will nod with a smile and say that it's great that some believers are politically 'involved' but that it's not a priority for them. Church leaders sometimes say they can't divert any time or resources in that direction. However, more often than not, it is actually a theological issue.

Which takes us back to the spheres …

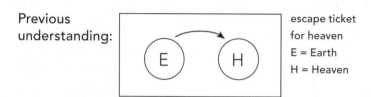

Previous understanding:
escape ticket for heaven
E = Earth
H = Heaven

If that picture is true, then of course we won't invest as much time in how we are governed, in caring for the environment, or in addressing structural injustice.

Why would we? Any time spent doing that would inevitably mean less time telling people about their need of Jesus. The argument goes like this: 'Helping the poor is great. In fact, bless you—you are a great example of compassion. But actually, what is eternal is more important.' And who could disagree? But if we draw it like this …

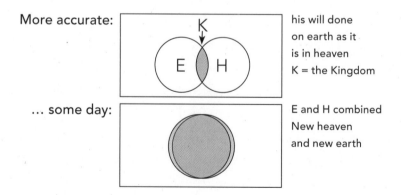

More accurate:
his will done on earth as it is in heaven
K = the Kingdom

… some day:
E and H combined
New heaven and new earth

Things may start to fall into place, because we believe that a better explanation of heaven is 'the realm where God's will is perfectly done,' and there are beautiful moments where his will *is* done on earth as it is in heaven. Every action and thought surrendered to his will sits in this intersection.

> Jesus's resurrection is the beginning of God's new project not to snatch people away from earth to heaven but to colonize earth with the life of heaven. That, after all, is what the Lord's Prayer is about.[7]

He did not say, 'I make some things new.' *All* things will be made new. This passage in Revelation simply echoes the reality of this restoration that has been promised in many other places in Scripture, such as Isaiah and Paul's letters.

The word used here in Revelation 21 implies re-creation, rather than creation from scratch *(see 'Further Talk Resources' later in this session)*. This is the return to how things were always meant to be.

> New creation is precisely that future of the present world, of all created reality, which does not emerge from the history of this world but will be given to it by God. It requires an originating act of God, just as creation in the beginning did, but in this case it will be an act which preserves the identity of the first creation while creatively transforming it.[8]

Jesus' life, death, and resurrection announced this new creation. None of this is possible without the cross. We are all called to follow in his footsteps, demonstrating the now-and-not-yet of his kingdom, as he did. Jesus' resurrection gives us a huge clue here. On Easter

Sunday morning, the tomb was *empty*. Jesus' new body was not a brand-new body, but a transformed version of his old body. It was the same molecules but transformed. There weren't any bits of him left in that tomb.

> *But our citizenship is in heaven.* And we eagerly await a Saviour from there, the Lord Jesus Christ, who, by the power that enables him to bring everything under his control, *will transform our lowly bodies so that they will be like his glorious body.* (Phil. 3:20–21)

In Scripture, it is promised that we and all of creation will similarly be transformed. So as with Jesus, the stuff of now will not be swept away and discarded. It will be gloriously transformed:

> I consider that our present sufferings are not worth comparing with the glory that will be revealed in us. For the creation waits in eager expectation for the children of God to be revealed. For the creation was subjected to frustration, not by its own choice, but by the will of the one who subjected it, in hope that *the creation itself will be liberated from its bondage to decay and brought into the freedom and glory of the children of God.*
>
> We know that the whole creation has been groaning as in the pains of childbirth right up to the present time. Not only so, but we ourselves,

who have the firstfruits of the Spirit, *groan inwardly*
as we wait eagerly for our adoption to sonship, the
redemption of our bodies. (Rom. 8:18–23)

Do you see what innate dignity that confers on to the stuff of
now? It is not just 'secular matter' waiting to be thrown away; it is
all under God's authority awaiting transformation. Honouring this
truth leads us to grieve about our world, to care about our world, to
pray for our world, and to attempt to demonstrate truth, justice, and
righteousness in the systems, structures, and stuff of our world. This
matter matters.

> This matter matters.

It's important to explain here that we are not engaged in trying
to 'improve the earth to make it fit for Christ's return.' We are not
'building the kingdom' or the New Jerusalem. We are *demonstrating*
the kingdom. We are living lives of integrity that reflect the future
reality of a world transformed in every way. To demonstrate the
kingdom now is to erect signposts to that future perfection.

Jesus' miracles operated in the same way. They were real flesh-
and-blood examples of 'heaven on earth,' but they were also a
foretaste of what was to come for the whole world. Demonstrating
the kingdom is Jesus' way. Building the kingdom is the human,
workaholic way, in which we falsely think we are called to meet

every need around us and exhaust ourselves in the process. Jesus did not meet every need. He did only what he heard the Father calling him to do. It feels like it is time for more Venn diagrams!

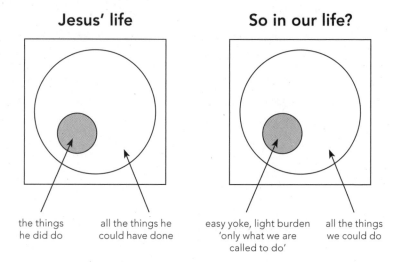

Jesus' life

the things he did do

all the things he could have done

So in our life?

easy yoke, light burden 'only what we are called to do'

all the things we could do

Now, none of us can claim to know the exact methodology of how the spheres of heaven and earth become fully and finally fused. At some point, God will perform an extraordinary act of power that will dwarf any feeble attempts that we have been involved in. But we do know that this is our direction of travel. This is our trajectory. Our actions can be woven into the eternal fabric. They can be of eternal worth.

Back in the day, in a place called Eden, governance was perfect. And one day, it will be so again. We will be involved as kings and priests ruling and reigning with him forever, so in this in-between phase we may as well begin our apprenticeship!

Discussion (20 minutes)

1. Do these thoughts about the future reality of the new creation inspire you with any thoughts about your own future? Which ideas impact you most?

2. What might God be calling you to, as individuals or as a group, to be a part of his kingdom coming into politics?

3. Are there any obstacles (practical, theological, or philosophical) to that calling that have been removed during this course? Are there any that still remain? If so, what are they?

4. Do you already have a Christians in Politics group in your town? If not, would you be interested in launching one? How could you find out if there are folks from other churches who may be interested?

Activity (15 minutes)

The concept of a new creation and a restored earth can seem remote, so this activity is about making it local. If there is a new heaven and a new earth, then might there not be a new Milton Keynes, a new Edinburgh, or a new Chipping Norton? What might they look like?

Spend 10 minutes writing some sentences that describe what a new [*enter your town or village name*] would look like if it were fully restored, healed, redeemed. What would be present? What would be gone? It could become a poem.

You might like to read aloud some of 'New Camberwell' to give everyone the idea:

New Camberwell

It was 8 o'clock on Monday morning.

I was standing by Camberwell Green.

And I saw a new London coming down from the
heavens.

I saw a teenager leap out of bed with joy, laughing
with the freshness of the morning.

I saw elderly ladies skipping down Denmark Hill.

I saw children paddling in the river Thames.

I saw a football match in Peckham Rye Park and
the teams were mixed people from every
people group—asylum seekers and taxi
drivers, policemen and prisoners, pensioners
and politicians. People from every race and
class playing and laughing in the sun.

I saw a street party where the people were eating
amazing home-made food, and dancing
because there was hope again.

And I looked across the community of South
London; a community of hope; a community
of grace; a community of warmth.

I saw gardens scattered everywhere—some small,
tucked into small corners, some sprawling
and shared by many, with people of every age
tending to them. Some were full of beautiful
flowers, others had every kind of fruit and
vegetable and herb.

And in the clearness of the morning I looked
down to Peckham and there was no more
asthma, no more unwanted pregnancies,
no more debt, no more violence, no more
overcrowding, and nobody was too busy.

And there was music across the city—music of
every kind. People from every background
were collaborating and creating.
New and beautiful murals were being painted
on empty billboards—all the ads had
gone and were replaced by breathtaking
art and messages of hope. Teams of artists
would search out new corners of the city
to make beautiful again.

The dividing walls were gone. Everyone
belonged.
Poverty was unthinkable because everyone took
care of each other.
Everyone had a job and a purpose—mind-
numbing jobs were gone.
Families and neighbourhoods were restored.
Nobody was lonely, or could even remember
what that felt like. There was no more
hopelessness, no more depression.
There was no more litter, no dealers, no guns,
no knives, no dangerous dogs.

There were no more racial tensions, just one
    harmonious mix in technicolour.

And I looked and I saw kids playing cricket on the
    streets, and neighbours cheering them on.
I saw homes without locks on the doors, where a
    welcome was always guaranteed.
I saw a playground with climbing frames that
    weren't rusty, where children threw
    themselves into the air without fear of
    harm, where the teenagers helped the little
    ones up to the highest frames.

I saw a London where everyone had a family.
Where no-one had a broken heart.
I saw a London where tears were wiped away.[9]

Prayer (10 minutes)

Spend some time praying—as a group, in smaller groups, or individually—about what you have covered in this session. Encourage people to pray prayers for their towns, expressing their longings that have been expressed in their 'New X' writing. Pray his will be done and his kingdom come.

    You may want to use the song 'We are Blessed (Bring Heaven to Earth Lord)' to help with the reflection.[10] A link can be found here: https://andyflan.com/songs/organic-worship.

Takeaway (2 minutes)

Each week, we'll suggest something that the group could do in the coming week to explore things further. It's entirely optional, but it's a great way of getting people to deepen the journey.

- Encourage everyone to share at least one tangible action they want to take as a result of doing this course. What's the next step? Joining a party? Getting to know the local council better? (For further ideas, please see the Conclusion.)
- Find a way to stay in touch so you can check in on each other's plans and progress.

Further talk resources
Transformation and re-creation

Kainos: the Greek word for 'new' used in Revelation 21 implies *re-creation* rather than creation from scratch.

William D. Mounce suggests *kainos* should be understood as 'fresh life rising from the decay and wreck of the old world'[11] The word speaks of the earth being renewed rather than re-created *ex nihilo*. This sits in congruence with the manner in which Jesus was raised from the dead. His new body was *different but in continuity* with his old one.

John Blanchard says, 'The new body is not identical but will be identifiable with it.'[12]

Aperchomai: the verb which we read as 'passed away' in Revelation 21:1 means 'to depart, go away.'

The sense here in the context of John's vision is that the old earth has not been incinerated but simply disappeared from his sight. Theologian Gale Heide feels the most important point is that, 'John is not saying that God has simply wiped everything away to begin again with nothing.'[13] Blanchard backs this up: 'If God were to annihilate the first cosmos and start again, it would at least suggest that Satan had ruined the first beyond remedy.'

This is the return to *how things were always meant to be*: from minute individual decisions to huge ecosystems, they will *all be transformed to operate in the way that God first intended*. In perfection with him for eternity.

Marriage

The biblical analogy of marriage is powerful in helping us think about demonstrating the kingdom. Sometimes, married couples struggle because we believe the hype (increased by the Spice Girls!) that some sort of mystical, magic dust transformation happens on the wedding day. 'Two become one.' Job done. Just like a rom-com. We don't have to 'tend to the garden' of our marriage beyond that. Yes, of course we know that two become one flesh in a real sense, but have we co-opted that thinking to naively believe these two distinct individuals will now operate flawlessly as one entity?

Anyone who is married knows that a more accurate description might be 'two *becoming* one'—an ongoing, beautiful process of increasing understanding, compromise, and sacrificial love.

This is an excellent metaphor for the fusion of heaven and earth. We have bought into a myth that as with a wedding, all that matters is the one-off, climactic, end-of-time event. This means we do not fully realise our role in demonstrating the kingdom in the here and now, hoping to see those spheres ever closer together. Just like a marriage, there may be moments when that overlap seems huge, and moments where it seems barely discernible.

Useful quotes

- 'Living as a demonstration of what God plans to do in and for all creation in Jesus Christ.'[14]
- 'The congregation comprises the people of God, called to be formed into a unique social community whose life together is the sign, witness and foretaste of what God is doing in and for all of creation.'[15]
- 'This means that those who live by this story live within it. It gives us our identity, our place in the story, and a part to play in the still-to-be-completed purposes of God for his world.'[16]
- 'God after all is the creator. He has no interest in leaving earth to rot and making do for all eternity with only one half of the original creation.'[17]
- 'To be a Christian, a person of faith … is precisely to live as a person for whom God's future shapes the present.'[18]

CONCLUSION

So we've reached the end, but it's really only the beginning. Our journey into the world of politics and public leadership won't end here. But if we've learnt anything from this course, it's hopefully that we need the support of each other to continue the journey. As the African proverb says, 'If you want to go fast, go alone. If you want to go far, go together.'

Our prayer is that you will stay connected to each other, and also to the wider family of Christians in Politics. We'd love to hear how the course has gone, so please let us know. There are also many ways to get involved and volunteer with us, so please get in touch. These are just some of the things that you could join in with:

- Local Christians in Politics groups are springing up across the country, learning to put kingdom before tribe and disagree well.
- Many folks are being trained further in public speaking and in media interview skills.
- Christians from across the political spectrum are coming together to pray, often online.
- People are seeing politics as a mission field, joining parties and the Christian agencies that

operate to influence and serve those parties like the Conservative Christian Fellowship, Christians on the Left, the Liberal Democrat Christian Forum, and others.

- It's not everyone's job to be a candidate, but everyone can be praying, and some are giving financially.
- Hundreds have joined the UK councillors' prayer network who are local, borough, or county councillors.
- Many young people are embodying this message as Young Christians in Politics. They are being mentored by more mature folks. Could that be you?
- Join in any of these by getting in touch via info@ christiansinpolitics.org.uk

ACKNOWLEDGEMENTS

Material: Sarah Hickey, Simon Hutton, and Andy Flannagan
Logistics: Benita Hussain
Editing: Jenny Flannagan

www.christiansinpolitics.org.uk

NOTES

1. Seminar on Faith and Politics, Johannesburg, January 1989.

2. Mother Teresa in Heidi Schlumpf, *The Notre Dame Book of Prayer* (Notre Dame, IN: Ave Maria Press, 2010).

3. Jane Collier, *From Complicity to Encounter: The Church and the Culture of Economism* (Harrisburg, PA: Trinity Press International, 1998).

4. Roy Herron, *How Can a Christian Be in Politics?* (Carol Stream, IL: Tyndale, 2005).

5. Music: 'Abide with Me,' by Henry Francis Lyte (Public Domain). Lyrics: Noel Robinson, Andy Flannagan, Rev Graham Hunter.

6. Justin Welby in Andy Flannagan, *Those Who Show Up* (Edinburgh: Muddy Pearl, 2015), 4.

7. N. T. Wright, *Surprised by Hope: Rethinking Heaven, the Resurrection, and the Mission of the Church* (London: HarperPaperbacks, 2008).

8. Richard Bauckham and Trevor Hart, *Hope against Hope: Christian Eschatology at the Turn of the Millennium* (Grand Rapids, MI: Eerdmans, 1999), 128.

9. Adapted by Jenny Flannagan from an original piece of writing by Dave Steell called 'New London.'

10. 'We Are Blessed—Andy Flannagan feat Tearfund Friends and Partners,' YouTube, 20 November 2013, www.youtube.com/watch?v=Cd72zi3i2XY.

11. William D. Mounce, *Mounce's Complete Expository Dictionary of Old and New Testament Words* (Grand Rapids, MI: Zondervan, 2006).

12. John Blanchard, 'Whatever Happened to Heaven?' *Reformation and Revival: A Quarterly Journal for Church Leadership* 6, no. 2 (Spring 1997).

13. Gale Z. Heide, 'What Is New about the New Heaven and the New Earth? A Theology of Creation from Revelation 21 and 2 Peter 3.' *Journal of the Evangelical Theological Society* (March 1997).

14. Alan J. Roxburgh and Fred Romanuk, *The Missional Leader: Equipping Your Church to Reach a Changing World* (Minneapolis, MN: Fortress Press, 2020), xi.

15. Roxburgh and Romanuk, *Missional Leader*, 14.

16. Bauckham and Hart, *Hope against Hope*, 36.

17. Tom Wright, *How God Became King: Getting to the Heart of the Gospels* (London: SPCK, 2012).

18. Bauckham and Hart, *Hope against Hope*, 83.

EMPEROR AND ARISTOCRACY
IN HEIAN JAPAN

BY THE SAME AUTHOR

Yodo no tsukai ou le système des quatre envoyés, Paris: Presses Universitaires de France, 1966.

Fonctions et fonctionnaires japonais au début du XIe siècle, 2 vols. Paris: Publications Orientalistes de France, 1977.

Bibliographie japonaise, Paris: Publications Orientalistes de France, 1986.

Histoire du Japon des origines à la fin de l'époque Meiji: Matériaux pour l'étude de la langue et de la civilisation japonaises, Paris: Publications Orientalistes de France, 1986.

Notes journalières de Fujiwara no Michinaga, ministre à la cour de Hei.an (995-1018). Traduction du Midō kanpakuki, 3 vols. Genève-Paris: Droz, 1987, 1988, 1991.

Ed., *L'Histoire du Japon des origines à nos jours*, Le Coteau: Horvath, 1990. [Reprinted with additions, Paris: Hermann, 2009]

Poèmes de Fujiwara no Michinaga, ministre à la cour de Hei.an (995-1018), Genève-Paris: Droz, 1993.

La cour du Japon à l'époque de Heian aux Xe et XIe siècles, Paris: Hachette, 1995.

Notes journalières de Fujiwara no Sukefusa. Traduction du Shunki, 2 vols. Genève-Paris: Droz, 2001, 2004.

Gouverneurs de province et guerriers dans les Histoires qui sont maintenant du passé: Konjaku monogatarishū, Paris: Collège de France, Institut des Hautes Études Japonaises, 2004.

La cour et l'administration du Japon à l'époque de Heian, Genève: Droz, 2006. [Revised edition of *Fonctions et fonctionnaires japonais au début du XIe siècle*, 2 vols. 1977]

Recueil de décrets de trois ères méthodiquement classés, Ruijū sandai kyaku, 2 vols. Genève-Paris: Droz, 2008, 2011.

Notes sur de nouveaux divertissements comiques, Shinsarugakuki, Paris: Les Belles Lettres, 2013.

Un fonctionnaire lettré Miyoshi no Kiyoyuki 847-918, sa vie, ses oeuvres. [In preparation]

FRANCINE HÉRAIL

EMPEROR AND ARISTOCRACY
IN HEIAN JAPAN
~10th and 11th centuries~

Translated by WENDY COBCROFT

Emperor and Aristocracy in Heian Japan
Copyright © 2013 Francine Hérail & Wendy Cobcroft
All Rights Reserved

First Published 2013

The original French edition, *La cour du Japon à l'époque de Heian aux Xᵉ et XIᵉ siècles*, was published by Hachette (Paris) in 1995. Copyright © reverted to Francine Hérail in 2011.

ISBN-10: 1-492-26282-X
ISBN-13: 978-1-492-26282-4

Printed in the United States of America

ILLUSTRATIONS

Map 1:   The imperial palace (*daidairi*).

Map 2:   The inner (residential) palace (*dairi*).

Source: *Atlas historique de Kyōto* (Unesco/Les Éditions de l'Amateur, 2008) ed. Nicolas Fiévé. By kind permission of N. Fiévé.

Note: These two maps replace the eight scroll illustrations in the 1995 French edition. *L'Atlas historique de Kyōto*, together with *L'architecture et la ville du Japon ancien* (Maisonneuve et Larose, 1996) by Nicolas Fiévé and *Nihonshi jiten* (Iwanami, 1999), may be consulted for other maps and illustrations of certain palace buildings, the layout of Heiankyō and the location of its major residences.

CONTENTS

Translator's Preface   viii

Acknowledgements   ix

Preliminary Notes   x

Introduction   1

1   *Style of Government: Bureaucracy and Aristocracy*   5

The "codal system", 5
The Fujiwara family, 14
The aristocracy in power, 20

2   *Rituals and Celebrations*   37

Choice of rituals as a method of government, 37
The annual cycle of celebrations, 46
The court as patron of the arts, 58

3   *Living Environment of the Aristocracy*   75

Formalism and spatial organization in the capital, 75
Inner palace and aristocratic residences, 87
Interior spaces: harmony and refinement, 96

4   *Private Life*   109

Marriages and successions, 109
The stages of life, 122
Women in society, 134

5   *Failure and its Remedies*   151

Socially acceptable ways of arresting the decline, 152
Taking religious vows, 162
Socially unacceptable ways: the descent into
criminality, 170

6   *Prescriptions for Success and Salvation*   181

Shintō, 183
Buddhism, 190
The way of Yin and Yang, 197

Conclusion   205

Appendix 1   *Writing in Heian Japan*   209

Appendix 2   *Learning and Artistic Pursuits*   215

Appendix 3   *Status and Role of Provincial Governors
                 at the Apogee of the Heian Period*   233

Bibliography   265

Index   273

Map 1:   **The imperial palace** (*daidairi*)   314

Map 2:   **The inner (residential) palace** (*dairi*)   315

TRANSLATOR'S PREFACE

La cour du Japon à l'époque de Heian, published in 1995, remains the most succinct account of a period of Japanese history that is now receiving more attention by scholars than ever before. In this slim volume, Francine Hérail was able to distil an impressive amount of material, culled from her unsurpassed knowledge of the primary sources.

The author, who was present when Charlotte von Verschuer asked me to prepare an English translation, warmly endorsed the proposal. My task was greatly facilitated by Francine Hérail's supportive involvement throughout: answering queries, providing additional information and readily agreeing to my suggested changes. She very kindly took the time to carefully re-read both texts, and has assured me that the final result meets with her approval.

It has been a pleasure and privilege to translate this book, which is offered as a modest tribute to an inspirational scholar whom I am honoured to be able to call my teacher, mentor and friend. I sincerely hope that *Emperor and Aristocracy in Heian Japan* will make the work of Francine Hérail more widely known and stimulate further interest in the history of the period to which she has devoted the best part of her long and distinguished career.

Wendy Cobcroft
Sydney, Australia
July 2013

ACKNOWLEDGEMENTS

The author and translator especially wish to thank Charlotte von Verschuer (Francine Hérail's successor at the École Pratique des Hautes Études, Paris), who provided the initial impetus for this project and closely followed its progress. We welcome this opportunity to place on record her tireless activity and infectious enthusiasm in promoting Heian studies wherever the occasion presents itself, both in France and abroad.

The translator is indebted to Royall Tyler (Emeritus Professor, Australian National University) for his unwavering support and his invaluable advice on a number of matters, including the choice of cover image. As a long-time admirer of Francine Hérail's work, he was most anxious to see this book in print.

Warmest thanks go to Lawrence Marceau (University of Auckland), always willing to assist and generous with his time, who provided the translator with some very useful, practical information at the final stage; and to Anna Beerens (an experienced academic publishing editor in Leiden), likewise generous with her time and knowledge, who read the completed text and whose comments were very much appreciated.

Lastly, we express our gratitude to Ariane de Pree-Kajfez of Stanford University Press, who solved a long-standing "mystery" for us; and to Hachette, Paris, who returned the copyright of the French edition to the author, thereby facilitating this publication.

PRELIMINARY NOTES

Author's note (modified):

Appendix 1 (*Writing in Heian Japan*) gives brief details of the administrative and literary texts used as source materials. Appendix 2 (*Learning and Artistic Pursuits*) and Appendix 3 (*Status and Role of Provincial Governors at the Apogee of the Heian Period*) have been added to provide a broader picture of the occupations of the lesser nobility.

Dates are given in the notes according to the system of era names (sometimes changed more than once during a reign). Each is followed by three figures: the year, month and day; then by the corresponding year of our era. Kankō 1.3.3. is the 3rd day of the 3rd month of the 1st year of Kankō. However this cannot be translated as 3rd March, because Japan used a luni-solar calendar, the months of which do not correspond to those of the Gregorian calendar. The difference is approximately from three to six weeks. Kankō 1.3.3. is 26th March 1004. Kannin 2.8.19. is 30th September 1018.

The transcription of Japanese words follows the Hepburn system. Vowels written with a macron are long. The *e* corresponds to *é* [Eng. *ace*], and *u* to *ou* [Eng. *boot*]. The *g* is hard, *s* is unvoiced and *h* is aspirated; *ch* is pronounced *tch*.

Translator's note:

In close collaboration with the author, quite a few minor changes and/or corrections have been made to the text and notes, the latter being placed for convenience at the end of each chapter. The inclusion of many additional names (and dates) will enable the reader to easily identify the people mentioned, and the index (now with Chinese characters) has been expanded in order to provide some information on all but the most obscure personages. (This was considered preferable to a series of genealogical tables, which may be found in other works by the author.) The revised and updated bibliography takes account of new publications in French and English since 1995.

Unlike French, where the comprehensive terminology drawn up by Francine Hérail for *Fonctions et fonctionnaires japonais au début du XIe siècle* (POF, 1977; revised edition *La cour et l'administration du Japon à l'époque de Heian*, Droz, 2006) is the norm, there is unfortunately no such standard in English-language scholarship. Thus, while gratefully acknowledging many helpful suggestions from the various sources consulted, we have necessarily been guided first and foremost by the author's own work, most notably regarding the classification of the Heian administrative levels: Ministry (*kan*), Department (*shō*), Office (*ryō*), Bureau (*shi* or *tsukasa*) and Service (*shiki*). The use of initial lower-case for functions (e.g. prime minister) reflects the preference of the author and translator.

In line with Japanese usage, the family name precedes the given name (commonly used on its own), and the traditional 'no' has been retained, e.g. Fujiwara no Michinaga. Ages are according to the Japanese way of reckoning: the birth year is counted as "one" and a person is a year older each New Year's Day of the lunisolar calendar (i.e. January or early February).

INTRODUCTION

The apogee of the Heian period, the 10th and 11th centuries, is nowadays often called the "age of the court" (*ōchō jidai*), contrasting with the expression "code-governed State" (*ritsuryō kokka*) that characterizes the 8th and 9th centuries. This contrast is also expressed, in a somewhat simplified way, as the transition from a bureaucratic-type system to an aristocratic regime. However the term translated as "court" has two meanings in early Japan: "the place from where the emperor (or the imperial dynasty) governs the country", and "State" or "country". When discussing the "age of the court", contemporary historians therefore add to the original meaning, which is also perfectly applicable to the 8th and 9th centuries, a new shade, that of a brilliant worldly existence dominated by an aristocracy.

The Heian court experienced a magnificent flowering of arts and letters, and the comparison with the court of Louis XIV (1638-1715) comes quite naturally to mind.[1] In Japan, as in France, ceremonial, the beauty of the setting and the bringing together of high-born personages were intended to show off the glory of the reign and thus had a political dimension. But Louis XIV made a distinction between courtiers and administrative organs, whose respective roles were more or less separate, whereas it must not be forgotten that the members of the Heian court remained officials, even if the central administration devoted at least as much, if not more time to the organization of celebrations as to the actual business of government. This was because, for the senior nobles and officials of the time, ceremonies were not simply a means of acting upon the minds of the lesser officials and the common people by arousing admiration and respect; they were also considered to be an effective way of influencing supernatural powers and obtaining their protection. Thanks to these ceremonies, the court believed itself capable of fulfilling its mission: assuring the peace and prosperity of the country. The privileged interlocutor of these powers remained the emperor. He was thus the focal point of everything. Yet his person mattered little, because his maternal family, the Fujiwara, had placed him firmly under its control. Nothing was done without his being informed and he felt responsible for everything, but he could take no decision without the advice of the regent or, if he were an adult, of the chancellor.

The emperor and his court ended up living and acting to fulfil what they deemed to be the essence of their mission: to maintain, in accordance with the precedents, the annual cycle of ceremonies. No-one in the Japan of the time could contest this prerogative. Celebrations were therefore government matters, prepared and carried out in a bureaucratic way, with a great many consultations, deliberations, investigations into precedents, reports, and promulgations of decrees and orders. In fact, the bureaucratic formalities survived in what is often described as the shipwreck of the codal institutions, when the court gave up its fastidious control of the work of the provincial administrators and allowed them considerable freedom of action, counterbalanced, however, by the requirement to submit accounts at the end of four years and to wait a long time in some cases for a new appointment.

The extraordinary brilliance of Japanese civilization in the early 11th century owes nothing to the emperors; it is a collective phenomenon produced by the whole of aristocratic society. However aristocrats and officials, together with their families, their servants and the monks who moved in their orbit made up only a very small part of the population of Japan in the 10th and 11th centuries, at most several tens of thousands of people out of the seven or eight million in the archipelago at that time, virtually all of them living in the capital Heiankyō, the City of Peace and Tranquillity. But they have left a considerable mark on the history of the country, though this is unknown to many present-day Japanese. Some scholars, even in Japan, have in fact maintained that modern society, institutions and customs have been shaped by those of the Edo period and that what had existed at the dawn of history – aristocratic society – could only be an object of curiosity and of no use for an understanding of our own time. Yet, besides the fact that it is perfectly justifiable to take an interest in a society that has left a brilliant literature, it is also to forget that the Edo regime (1603-1867) had inherited from early Japan the principles of order and of minute and stringent control formulated by the administration of the early period (which in Japan broadly encompasses the 7th to the 12th century), the partiality for census-taking, land registers, reports, and all the weight of the bureaucracy. It also knew and admired the sense of ceremonial and the regard for hierarchies: everything that had given the early court part of its prestige. In the Edo period, as in those that preceded it, people read, wrote commentaries on, imitated, and even parodied the masterpieces of the early literature, some of which are among the greatest in world literature and remain a source of inspiration for contemporary writers.

Notes

1. The only possible comparison with French history, albeit an imperfect one in most respects. While it is true that the rules governing protocol were very strict in both cases, the most obvious difference is the highly public nature of the life of Louis XIV and the highly private nature of the life of the Japanese emperor, notwithstanding that he too was fundamentally a public personage.

CHAPTER 1

STYLE OF GOVERNMENT:
BUREAUCRACY AND ARISTOCRACY

The "codal system"

In the course of the 7th century, Japan gradually came to know and imitate the institutions of Tang China. In 701, full penal and administrative codes were put into effect, then revised in 718. These texts, called *Yōrō ritsuryō* after the name of the era during which they were given their definitive form, henceforth remained sacrosanct. But certain points were modified or completed by means of decrees, issued in large numbers up to the early 10th century, and several collections are extant. In addition, detailed regulations meticulously set down the procedures and tasks of the various administrative organs. Those of the Engi era (901-923) survive: they were probably no more than a reworking of the regulations issued at the beginning and end of the 9th century. This large volume of texts provides the most complete information about the organs of government and the role of each one.

However this legislation is almost silent on the emperor. It has become customary to translate by "emperor" the various names given over the centuries to the personage who ruled in Japan. Yet none of these terms suggests that the emperor is the one who holds power and who commands. What concerns him has nothing whatever to do with decrees or regulations or articles of the administrative code, but with a mandate from the founding deities of the country, his ancestors. This is apparent from the way history was written in the early 8th century under the direction of the imperial family. To describe the emperor as being all-powerful or a law-maker or above the law would be to distort reality. He belongs to an order different from that of power. In Japanese he is called *akitsu kami*, "visible deity", and his presence somehow makes manifest the protection that the deities grant to the country: this protection establishes and maintains it. The emperor's influence extends far and wide and, provided his conduct is ethical and he serves the deities in the appropriate manner, it ensures peace and prosperity for his subjects. In the official texts written in *kanbun*, that is, Chinese, even if heavily "Japanized", he is called *tennō*, "celestial ruler", a term influenced by Taoism. *Tennō* denotes the Pole Star, the one that enables bearings to be taken, the fixed star around which the heavens revolve. Another expression used, also borrowed from China, is *tenshi*, "son of Heaven", which may recall the celestial ancestor, the goddess Amaterasu. The imperial ideology therefore tended to remove the emperors from the business of government. This had not been entirely the case in the late 7th century, when the regime referred to by historians as the "code-governed State" became established. In a sense, it would seem that the formulation of this ideology, as evidenced by the Chinese-style titles bestowed on the ruler, played a role in removing him from the direct conduct of affairs. The Japanese also found in the political ideas imported from China the one requiring the emperor to surround himself with wise counsellors and to heed their advice. His beneficent influence was thus transmitted through the officials and the large volume of legislative texts deals above all with them.

The organization of the administrative code and its formulation show how skilfully the Japanese were able to adapt the Chinese texts to the needs of a country far smaller and far less populated than the great continental empire. One can also read into this the obvious wish to set themselves apart from China, even if only by giving pride of place to the organ in charge of the worship of the national deities, the Ministry of Religious Affairs (Jingikan), which kept the lists of shrines for the entire country, as well as of their clergy, prepared and presented the court offerings to the most important shrines and celebrated the rituals. But the officials of this ministry held only relatively low ranks and performed only very specialized functions: purifications, prayers, offerings and divination.

The principal organ was the Ministry of State Affairs (Dajōkan), which grouped together the functions of three Chinese organs – the departments of Affairs of State, Imperial Chancellery and Grand Imperial Secretariat – that respectively controlled the administration, received reports and requests and drafted imperial edicts. This ministry had at its head a college of ministers, counsellors and auditors: the council of senior nobles. The head of the college was the prime minister (*dajōdaijin*), designated a "living norm", but his function was more honorary than real and seldom filled. From the late 10th century, it served to honour the most senior member of the Fujiwara family, a minister but not a close relative of the emperor and as such without any authority. Or else the head of the council took this title in order to perform an emperor's coming-of-age ceremony. The two principal ministers were those of the left and the right (*sadaijin*; *udaijin*), as the important functions were duplicated in this way. The left, identified with the east, took precedence over the right and the west, but the prerogatives of these two ministers were the same. Leaving aside the prime minister, whose post was more often vacant than occupied, a third ministerial post was created after the codes were compiled. Since the literal translation of his name *naidaijin* – "minister of the centre or interior" – could be misleading, as he was not seated at the centre, was not entrusted with confidential matters and came lower down in the hierarchy than the ministers of the left and the right, we have called him "third minister". The council also included major and second counsellors (*dainagon*; *chūnagon*), as well as auditors (*sangi*), this latter function created after the code was formulated. These last-mentioned of the group of senior nobles did not have the right to put forward proposals, but they gave their opinions and often took notes during deliberations. At different times in its history, this college had six to fifteen, or even twenty members. It proposed decisions regarding appointments and promotions of civil and military personnel, local administration, finances and more generally the management of property, as well as severe sentences of death or exile.

The council had at its disposal two organs with secretariat functions. One was the Control Board (Benkan) divided into two sections, left and right, each responsible for four departments: Court Affairs (Nakatsukasashō, primarily the issuing of imperial edicts), Regulations Relating to Civil Officials (Shiki-bushō, the management of careers), Noble Affairs (Jibushō, matters concerning the organization of the families holding titles and ranks, selection of the family head, successions) and Population (Minbushō, principally the tax system) for the left section; and Military Affairs (Hyōbushō), Justice (Gyōbushō), Treasury (Ōkurashō) and Palace Affairs (Kunaishō) for the right section. The two major controllers were sometimes members of the council and nearly always destined to join its ranks. They were assisted by two second and third controllers, as well as by Control Board secretaries. These officials were responsible for reading the correspondence – requests and reports – from the departments within their jurisdiction and from the provinces, ensuring that it conformed to the rules and in this way preparing the work of the council. They also supervised the documents issued in reply. On the other hand, a bureau of ministerial secretaries consisting of four to five officials was consulted whenever the council needed lists of precedents. The heads of the principal departments were sometimes members of the council. But it had become customary to appoint imperial princes to head Court Affairs, Regulations Relating to Civil Officials and on occasion Military Affairs: in this case the function was carried out by the assistant directors.

The eight departments originally had within their jurisdiction two services (*shiki*) with eight officials, eighteen offices (*ryō*) with six or seven officials, and thirty bureaux (*shi* or *tsukasa*) with two or three officials. Except for the offices of Accounts (Shukeiryō) and Public Resources (Shuzeiryō) responsible for overseeing the collection of taxes and the management of the public rice reserves, thus with the provincial administration, the activities of these organs were really only concerned with the life of the court, whether it be the Library Office (Zushoryō), the offices of Palace Storehouses (Kuraryō), Imperial Tombs

(Shoryōryō), Medicine (Tenyakuryō) and Grains (Ōiryō), or the large number of technical bureaux, such as Saké (Zōshushi), Blacksmiths (Kaji no tsukasa), Gardens and Lakes (Enchishi) and Utensils (Kyotōshi), many of them being quite short-lived. However, after modifications, closures, mergers and changes of classification, at the end of the 10th century there remained only two services, those of the Empress (Chūgūshiki) and the Table (Daizenshiki) – because the officials in service were fed and the emperor sometimes offered banquets to his faithful servants –, nineteen offices and seven bureaux. The most active were the offices of Divination (Onmyōryō), responsible for drawing up the calendar, divination and the formation of specialists in these sciences, Palace Storehouses, which managed some of the products needed both for daily life and for the offerings made to shrines, Higher Learning (Daigakuryō), which controlled the formation of officials in the fields of classics, law and mathematics, Public Resources and Accounts, which verified the tax registers and all matters relating to finances, Constructions (Mokuryō), responsible for repairs and rebuilding of the palace, and Medicine, which, besides the preparation and supply of medicines, trained physicians. Water (Shusuishi), Saké and Weaving (Oribe no tsukasa) remained indispensable bureaux.

Each organ had a director, an assistant director, a maximum of two or three officials of the third class and the same number of the fourth class. According to their grade, these men were invested with one of the thirty levels of the nine ranks: two levels for the first three ranks and four for those below, down to the ninth or starting rank. They worked full time, which enabled them, in theory, to be promoted at the end of four years. Had the provisions of the administrative code been followed to the letter, their total number would have been less than a thousand: around five hundred for the central administration, three hundred for the provincial administration, fifty or so guards officers and about a hundred technicians of equal ranking with officials, teachers and specialists in the various branches of learning: the classics, reading, writing, law, mathematics, medicine, music, the calendar and divination. And of these thousand functions, only a hundred and fifty were held, in principle, by men of the first five ranks. It was only officials of the fifth rank and above who benefited from being granted rice fields commensurate with their rank, and for whom the special ranks given to their sons when they began their careers could provide a significant advantage. In a word, only men of the first five ranks were considered part of the aristocracy.

The central organs also made use of around ten thousand minor officials, who were not denied access to the lowest ranks but who had hardly any opportunities for advancement, as they were required to wait ten years to have their merits examined. Of these ten thousand, there were around two hundred clerks (the provinces employed roughly the same number), some eight hundred students of the various branches of learning, artisans, soldiers of the guards and servants in the crown prince's household. The households of princes and senior nobles, as well as the provincial administrations, also had the possibility of recruiting temporary staff who, while in service, benefited from tax advantages. Regulations, never very strictly enforced, attempted to limit their number.

For the administration of the sixty-eight provinces and islands, the capital dispatched for a four-year term just two to six officials, depending on the size of the province (there were four categories – very large, large, medium and small –, the second being by far the best represented), and three clerks. But much of the work was done by local recruits belonging to prominent families.

When one reads the large volume of codes, regulations and decrees issued up to the beginning of the 10th century, it is clear that, on the one hand, the emperor and his officials supported, at least in words, the ideal of a benevolent government, whose every action must contribute to the good of the people and that, on the other hand, in order to achieve this ideal they adopted a bureaucratic-type system. Hierarchy, clearly defined sharing of powers, annual assessment of officials and promotion on merit every four years, stipends paid from the government store-houses on fixed dates and according to the grade and rank of each official, strict control exercised over the totality of the country's products, need for a written order for the most insignificant acts: all these characteristics give the system established by the codes its bureaucratic form. Over time, the articles in the regulation relating to the rendering of accounts when the hand-over of provincial administrators took place increased to the point where the regulation of the early 10th century was twice as long as that of the early 9th century.

However this apparent determination to preserve and increase the number of regulations and controls in order to maintain the regularity of the system went against another aspect of the regime, also present since its inception: the importance of the aristocracy. When the "code-governed State" was established, it replaced institutions founded on the pre-eminence of large clans allied with and subordinate to the family who ruled over Yamato (the only name for Japan up to the end of the 7th century). They were not abolished but became part of the new organization. As in China, but with an even more distinct advantage, the code authorized men invested with the highest ranks to enable their sons to benefit from special ranks. In the first century of application of the codes, promotions were very slow, as the legally requisite times were respected. The advantage given to the sons of senior nobles was thus significant. Furthermore, since the emoluments allocated to the important personages were far higher than those of the middle-ranking officials and they benefited from the revenues of households that had been granted to them, they had huge incomes, which allowed them to keep many more servants than stipulated by the regulations.

Our knowledge of the first two centuries of the early period is based largely on the official histories,[1] and these make it very difficult to get a detailed picture of the mutual relationships between individuals and families. But there is plenty of evidence to suggest that the impersonal regulations were often circumvented and that factions and clienteles already played an important role among the officials and in their dealings with the population, especially the local notables. Do we not find in a biography written to extol the merits of a good provincial governor[2] that he accepts the gifts of those under his jurisdiction when he leaves his post?

Promotion decided solely on the criterion of merit always remained a stated ideal, but was seldom applied. The most conscientious officials even risked being penalized. One can read some examples in the official histories, especially in the last of them. According to the obituary of an auditor named Masami (799-863) in the *Nihon sandai jitsuroku* (*Veritable Record of Three Reigns of Japan*), this man, who left behind the reputation of being a "good official", was demoted in 846 as a disciplinary measure because he had wanted to prosecute a person guilty of maladministration.[3] The most celebrated doctor of law in the 9th century, Sanuki no Naganao (783-862), was once exiled because he had given an opinion that had displeased a man in favour, but that was later proven to be correct.[4] The few judicial incidents related in the *rikkokushi* (the general term for the six official, national histories) clearly show that the result of prosecutions often depended on the personal situation of the accused. It is true that the known cases are often linked to factional rivalries at the court.

Recruitment by competitive examination, in theory the fairest way of determining merit, did exist, but only allowed access to relatively minor posts. Significantly, in the early 9th century, Saga Tennō (r. 809-823), steeped in Chinese culture, tried to compel the sons of men of the first three ranks to compete for entry into a new branch of learning, that of letters, the pinnacle of the way of the classics, since it consisted of a study of the *Three Histories* of China – *Records of the Historian* (J. *Shiki*; Ch. *Shiji*), *History of the Former Han Dynasty* (J. *Zenkanjo*; Ch. *Qian Hanshu*) and *History of the Later Han Dynasty* (J. *Gokanjo*; Ch. *Hou Hanshu*) –, as well as of the great 6th-century poetic anthology, *Monzen* (Ch. *Wenxuan*), the most suitable curriculum, it was thought, for the training of future members of the ruling class. Saga Tennō had therefore taken care to reserve this competitive examination for the sons of the most senior nobles. But these young men had no wish to be judged by teachers whom they considered as their inferiors. On the other hand, students who were deserving and poor felt frustrated at not being able to reach the highest level of learning. After six years, Saga's successor Junna Tennō (r. 823-833) abandoned this project and, in 827, the way of letters was opened up to everyone.[5] It benefited both newcomers and off-spring of struggling branches of the most prominent families. Those versed in letters certainly claimed to be teaching political morality and affirmed that all careers should be based on merit. However birth and alliances were always the key factor, even if a place was reserved for merit, notably in middle-level posts. Two families, the Sugawara and Ōe, were able to gain entry into the group of senior nobles thanks to their success in literary studies, yet they themselves later relied on heredity, ensuring a virtual monopoly of the functions of doctor of letters.

Less cumbersome than those of China, the codal institutions were still too unwieldy for what turned out to be their main task: the administration of the court. The normal procedures were so complicated – for the issuing of an imperial edict, several shuttles between the emperor, the secretary drafting it and the senior nobles – and the hierarchy between agencies caused so many delays and errors, deliberate or not, because requests and decisions had to move along the chain and many officials of different grades had to be apprised of them, that, from the early 9th century, it became necessary to close down some bureaux and above all to create new organs, called "extracodal", which could act more promptly. The holders of these positions always combined them with a function in a regular agency; therefore, in theory, the number of posts was not increased. The two most important new organs were the Chancellery (Kurōdodokoro) and Police Bureau (Kebiishichō).[6]

The Chancellery was headed by two men, usually a major controller and a second general of the palace guard (Konoefu). They had at their disposal about ten Chancellery members: two or three of the fifth rank, with the others being young officials who had not yet attained this rank, and subordinates. Their role was to serve the emperor in his daily life and to coordinate the work of the offices and bureaux involved. The two heads and, on occasion, for minor matters, other members were tasked with liaising between the emperor and the council of senior nobles. This organ was thus entrusted with a confidential mission and the officials belonging to it were those who had most occasion to see the emperor and to hope for honourable careers.

It was also from the 9th century that some officers in the gate guard (Emonfu) were chosen especially for police duties. Under the direction of an intendant, either a second counsellor or an auditor, the inspectors of the Police Bureau, originally responsible for making inquiries and arrests, ended up encroaching on the prerogatives of the Department of Justice and almost completely taking them over. They not only arrested criminals, but also interrogated and sentenced them – at least those who were not officials of the first five ranks. They ordered beatings to be carried out and kept prisoners locked up: those accused of crimes as well as those sentenced to hard labour.

The bureaucratic methods – too complex given that the work of the administration was centred almost exclusively on the court –, the customs dating back to before the 8th century, the regulations relating to promotion that blocked the path to success for newcomers, and the trend towards heredity: all these factors attest to the shift of the institutions towards an aristocratic regime based on personal relationships and the pre-eminence of a few important families. The family whose influence was the most effective and that experienced the most brilliant success was the Fujiwara.

The Fujiwara family

The Fujiwara had an ambivalent attitude towards the codal system. They in fact contributed significantly to its decline and, at the same time, considered it one of their crowning glories. The founder was Nakatomi no Kamatari (614-669), who was the chief advisor of Tenji Tennō (626-671) when, in 645, this emperor set the country on the path of the reforms that led to the establishment of the "code-governed State". In 669, the emperor visited Kamatari on his death-bed and gave him the name of Fujiwara. This name then passed to Fuhito, Kamatari's son, but not to the other branches of the Nakatomi, which for the most part remained attached to the service of the national religion and whose members only occasionally held general administrative functions. Fuhito (659-720) played a key role at the court in the early 8th century. He is credited with the transfer of the capital from Fujiwarakyō to Nara in 710 and, during the Yōrō era, in 718, the revision of the codes. He was also able to very cleverly play the game of matrimonial alliances. Whereas in the 7th century the imperial family had favoured endogamy, no doubt to protect itself from the excessive influence of the major clans, Fuhito married one of his daughters (Kyūshi, ?-754) to Monmu Tennō (683-707). Her son, in 724, became the emperor known as Shōmu (701-756); he already had among his consorts a younger daughter of Fuhito, Kōmyōshi (701-760), the half-sister of his mother. In 729, following the birth of a son who was immediately named crown prince, but who died when only a few months old, the influence of Fuhito's four sons, especially the two eldest, Muchimaro (680-737) and Fusasaki (681-737), was so great at the court that they succeeded in bringing about the suicide of the last prince of the imperial family holding the highest offices in the council, Prince Nagaya (684-729), on the pretext that he had been responsible for the death of the infant crown prince by means of magical practices, and declaring their sister empress (consort of an emperor),[7] a title previously granted only to princesses. The empress Kōmyō added to the merits acquired by her father and grandfather that of founding charitable institutions, the Hospital of Compassion (Hiden-in) and Hospice (Yakuin), and in this way contributing to realizing the ideal of a benevolent government. Thus, in the early 8th century, two important precedents were established: an emperor who was the son of a Fujiwara daughter and a Fujiwara daughter elevated to the rank of empress.

All the Fujiwara were descended from Fuhito's four sons, who were the founders of the four branches of this family,

designated respectively Hokke, Nanke, Shikike and Kyōke –
after the part of the capital in which their residences were
located for the first two, and the functions held by their founder
in the Department of Regulations Relating to Civil Officials and
in the prefectural office of the capital for the other two. The
fourth branch did not expand very much. The generation of
Fuhito's grandsons already produced eighteen senior nobles and
many officials. Three centuries later, the number of non-
Fujiwara senior nobles was negligible and more than half of the
middle-ranking officials belonged to one or other of the Fujiwara branches and their countless lines of descendants.

During the 8th century, the family suffered a number of
setbacks: in 737, following a smallpox epidemic that took the
lives of Fuhito's four sons, and because of court intrigues or the
unbridled ambition of one of its members in 740 and in 764.[8] In
the early 9th century, when the court's move to Heiankyō had
become permanent, the Northern branch gained the ascendancy
over the others, in the person of Fuyutsugu (775-826). Even
from this time on, however, the rise of the Fujiwara was not
direct and straightforward. The emperors attempted to slow it
down by reducing the majority of their many sons to the rank of
subjects. These sons therefore founded various families with the
name of Taira and others, even more numerous, with that of
Minamoto. Having thus become members of the aristocracy,
princes could take up a career, usually fast-tracked as they
started at the fourth rank, and several were made ministers. But
in the 9th century, it was only in very rare cases that their
descendants could maintain their place in the group of senior
nobles beyond the first generation.

Under the reigns of Kanmu (781-806), Saga (809-823) and
Ninmyō (833-850), the recruitment of senior nobles was quite
varied: new men came into the council because they had been
good administrators or had distinguished themselves by their
talents and learning. And in the late 9th and early 10th century,
Uda Tennō (r. 887-897) and his son Daigo Tennō (r. 897-930)
raised the most brilliant scholar-official of the time, Sugawara
no Michizane (845-903), to the post of minister of the right. But

despite the reservations of certain emperors and the jealousy of families in decline like the Tachibana and Tomo, the Fujiwara were able to gain the ascendancy because of their superior numbers, the precedents they could draw on, the marriages of their daughters with emperors, and the prestige they derived from the work of their founders Kamatari and Fuhito. They took particular care to ensure that all the empresses were Fujiwara by birth, or in exceptional circumstances imperial princesses, and made certain that the mothers of the crown princes were always Fujiwara daughters, not hesitating to stir up trouble, like the incident in 842 that resulted in the death in exile of the renowned literatus and calligrapher Tachibana no Hayanari, no doubt falsely accused of involvement in a plot, thereby enabling them to rid themselves of a crown prince born of an imperial princess in order to replace him with a grandson of Fuyutsugu. It was also because they had accused him of having elevated his daughter to the rank of imperial consort that they caused the exile, then in 903 the death of the illustrious Michizane.

It was from 842, when Fuyutsugu's grandson Montoku (b. 827) was designated crown prince, that the Fujiwara of the Northern branch began their ascendancy and extracted every possible advantage from their position as the grandfather or maternal uncle of the emperors. In spite of the codal rules, which had been modelled on those of China and privileged the paternal line, Japan had preserved a tradition of uxorial marriage, thus giving the maternal grandfather an influence over the education of his daughter's children. This distinctively Japanese custom was exploited by the Fujiwara. Fuyutsugu's successor, Yoshifusa (804-872), was the grandfather of Seiwa Tennō (r. 858-876), whose father, Montoku Tennō, died prematurely in 858. Seiwa, though only nine years old, was placed on the throne. This situation of an under-age emperor was new and until then had been avoided. At the beginning of the 8th century, when Shōmu, the grandson of Fuhito and designated crown prince, had at the age of six lost his father Monmu Tennō, he had not immediately ascended the throne and two female reigns – those of his grandmother Genmei (r. 707-715) and his aunt Genshō (r. 715-724) – had allowed him to attain his majority. A century and a half later, it would also have been possible to organize a transitional reign, as there was no shortage of imperial princes. However Yoshifusa preferred to impose a minor and appoint himself as the protector of his grandson, which he remained after Seiwa had celebrated his coming-of-age: he thus laid the foundation for the function of regent (*sesshō*) and even for that of chancellor (*kanpaku*). His nephew and adopted son and heir, Mototsune (836-891), was named regent when, in 876, Seiwa Tennō abdicated in favour of one of his sons, a nephew of Mototsune, Yōzei Tennō (r. 876-884). This time a regency was officially declared: the imperial edict promulgated on this occasion entrusted Mototsune with the task of protecting and assisting the young emperor, as well as dealing with government business. This concerned promotions and appointments. The regent thus had the opportunity of establishing a clientele among the officials.

Mototsune forced the abdication of his nephew Yōzei Tennō, because he was showing signs of mental illness. He was not closely related to the following three emperors – Kōkō, Uda and Daigo –, which was a disadvantage. But Kōkō Tennō (r. 884-887), an elderly imperial prince who owed his accession to the throne to Mototsune, allowed him to keep the prerogatives and privileges he had had during Yōzei's reign. After Kōkō's death, Mototsune, who had emerged victorious from a dispute over the definition of the prerogatives of the chancellor and which put him at odds with certain scholar-officials backed by Uda Tennō,[9] took the step of having an edict issued in his favour that set down, more or less definitively, the role of the chancellor: in essence to see beforehand all documents submitted to the emperor and all replies issued in the emperor's name. This was the privilege of "unofficial document examination" (*nairan*), which gave its recipient the same prerogatives as those of the chancellor, even if he did not formally hold the title.

At this point in time, the Fujiwara did not have everything entirely their own way. When he abdicated in 897, Uda Tennō decided that, while he was alive, his under-age son Daigo

Tennō had no need of a regent. He nonetheless maintained the document examination function, but he divided it between Tokihira (871-909), the eldest son of Mototsune, and Sugawara no Michizane, who was disadvantaged by the fact that none of his forebears had been a minister and that no literatus had ever been appointed to this office. Tokihira, with the help of his father's faction at the court, was able to rid himself of Michizane, but he died in 909 and the examination function was not conferred again during Daigo Tennō's lifetime. However, of the fourteen sons of this emperor, it was a grandson of Mototsune who was named crown prince. When Suzaku Tennō (923-952) became emperor, he was eight years old and Tadahira (880-949), the younger brother of Tokihira, took on the function of regent. After Suzaku came of age, Tadahira retained the document examination function right up until his death, that is to say, into the early years of Murakami Tennō (r. 946-967), also his nephew. But with his death there was another break, because this emperor followed the example of his father, Daigo Tennō, and avoided conferring the function of chancellor or that of document examiner.

It was only from 967 that the functions of regent (for an under-age emperor) and chancellor (for an adult emperor) were continuously held by a descendant of Tadahira. Early on, there was rivalry between two of Tadahira's sons, Saneyori (900-970) and Morosuke (908-960), and their descendants. But the factor that gave victory to Morosuke's sons and among them to the third-born, Kaneie (929-990) was that, on the one hand, a daughter of Morosuke (Anshi) was the mother of the two emperors who succeeded Murakami Tennō – Reizei (r. 967-969) and Enyū (r. 969 984) – and, on the other hand, Kaneie's two daughters (Chōshi, ?-982 and Senshi, 961-1001) also gave birth to princes who were the sons of these emperors, whereas Saneyori's son Yoritada (924-989) may indeed have made his daughter an empress, but she failed to produce a prince. The randomness of princely births therefore contributed to Kaneie's success. After little more than a century, the principal line of the Northern branch, which had taken care not to allow the precedents at its disposal to become obsolete and to ensure that others did not attempt to imitate it, embarked on its most illustrious period. This coincides with the golden age of early Japan and the development of an aristocratic-type regime.

The aristocracy in power

According to the code, the aristocracy began at the fifth rank. However, when the Fujiwara were at the height of their power, ranks were bestowed more liberally and more rapidly and thus in a sense devalued. One may therefore consider the only true aristocrats to be men of the first three ranks, and those of the fourth and fifth ranks who were destined to attain this status, either by birth, or because of superior talent or special services.

The individual who brought the glory of the Fujiwara to its peak, and whose conduct and methods of government best reflect the aristocratic system is Michinaga (966-1027). He is the main hero of the long historical narrative *Eiga monogatari* (*A Tale of Flowering Fortunes*), probably written a short time after his death by the lady Akazome Emon (960?-1041?), who had been in the service of his principal wife Rinshi. In the early 12th century, the *Ōkagami* (*Great Mirror*), a series of biographies of the most important Fujiwara ministers, ends with that of Michinaga, which is far more detailed than the others. The people, it says, worshipped him like a bodhisattva, so awed were they by his majesty. But these accounts suggest that his successes owed more to his having been chosen and protected by the deities and buddhas than to his personal qualities. At an early age, a physiognomist had apparently predicted his destiny. Yet his qualities as a statesman, at least as this term was understood at the time, must have been evident, for the minister of the left, Minamoto no Masanobu (920-993), who, in the face of competition from the Fujiwara daughters, despaired of his daughter Rinshi entering the palace as an imperial consort, gave her in marriage to Michinaga, even though he was only a younger son and just beginning his official career. He proved to be very skilful at managing his vast clientele and was able to protect himself from his enemies by a combination of strictness and generosity.

Michinaga was the fourth son of Kaneie and the third of his principal wife Tokihime (?-980). His full sister (Senshi) gave birth to the only son of Enyū Tennō and another of his sisters (Chōshi) to several sons of Reizei Tennō. Kaneie's career had been held back on occasion by the enmity of his older brothers, but in 984 he had the good fortune to be the only living grandfather of imperial princes who were entitled to become emperor, as the sons of a Fujiwara daughter descended from Tadahira. When Enyū Tennō abdicated in 984, his successor was the son of his brother Reizei Tennō, a retired emperor who had no possible way of protecting his son because his own mental state was not quite normal. The young Kazan Tennō (968-1008), aged sixteen, could count neither on the protection of his maternal grandfather Fujiwara no Koremasa (924-972), the eldest brother of Kaneie, nor on that of his maternal uncle Fujiwara no Yoshichika (957-1008), who was not yet at a stage in his career where he could aspire to being invested with the document examination function. Kaneie cleverly managed to persuade him to abdicate, achieved in dramatic circumstances, as Kazan secretly left the palace with the complicity of Kaneie's second son Michikane (961-995), in order to retire to a temple and perform the first act needed to become a monk. He was later to lead a rather worldly life. In 986, Kaneie therefore had his young grandson, a seven-year old crown prince and son of Enyū Tennō, placed on the throne, and another grandson, then aged eleven and a son of Reizei Tennō, named crown prince. Ichijō Tennō (b. 980) ruled until 1011, then his successor Sanjō Tennō (b. 976) until 1016. Kaneie naturally took on the function of regent and began to vigorously promote his sons' careers. The eldest, Michitaka (953-995), succeeded him as regent in 990, then as chancellor in 993. The third son, Michinaga, at age twenty, as would be expected, was only a member of the Chancellery and an adjutant of the (largely ceremonial) military guard (Hyōefu): entry-level posts. In 988, his father made him a second counsellor, bypassing the intermediate grade of auditor, and three years later he was promoted to major counsellor.

If his two older brothers had lived and had time to arrange posts for their sons, it is probable that Michinaga would not have progressed much further. However, in 995, the chancellor Michitaka died. He was succeeded by his younger brother Michikane, who died seven days after his appointment. The way was open for Michinaga. Michitaka had hoped that his eldest son Korechika (974-1010), aged twenty-two and already third minister, would succeed him, all the more so as his daughter Teishi (976-1001), who had been elevated to the rank of empress, was much loved by the young emperor (Ichijō) and could soon give him sons, whose protector would be their maternal uncle. But the emperor's mother (Senshi) had apparently advised him to confer the function of chancellor on Michitaka's last surviving brother, Michinaga. Alarmed at the early deaths of his two older brothers, Michinaga refused this honour, but accepted the document examination function. Paradoxically, the most powerful of the Fujiwara never became chancellor, a title that posterity nonetheless gave him, since he is known by the name of Midō kanpaku, the chancellor of the chapel – an allusion to his very strong Buddhist faith.

Michinaga's position nevertheless remained precarious, as his eldest daughter Shōshi (988-1074) was only nine years old in 996. His niece the empress (Teishi) gave birth to a son (Atsuyasu) in 999, which raised the hopes of the two uncles of the young prince. In 996, Michinaga had had them exiled in the wake of a rather obscure incident involving an attack by their men on the escort of Kazan Tennō, who had taken religious vows. It was said that Kazan was visiting the same residence as the third minister Korechika. Michinaga magnanimously permitted them to return to the capital after a short time, but the third minister lost his post and had only his rank reinstated, while his younger brother Takaie (979-1044), a second counsellor, did not rise any further in the hierarchy.

Michinaga had two wives of almost identical status by birth and both Minamoto: Rinshi (964-1053), daughter of a minister of the left (Masanobu) and grandson of Uda Tennō; and Meishi (965?-1049), daughter of a son of Daigo Tennō, Takaakira (914-982), a minister who had been disgraced in 969, following a plot no doubt hatched by Fujiwara no Moromasa (920-969), a brother of Morosuke. Rinshi gave birth to two sons and four daughters and Meishi to four sons and two daughters: these twelve children were counted among the number of Michinaga's successes. Thanks to Rinshi's daughters, born between 988 and 1007, he was the grandfather of the three emperors who reigned from 1016 to 1068. His eldest daughter, Shōshi, took the place of her cousin Teishi, who died prematurely, and was elevated to the rank of empress in 1000. She gave birth in 1008 and 1009 to two princes who reigned in succession: Goichijō, from 1016 to 1036, and Gosuzaku, from 1036 to 1045. Michinaga's second daughter Kenshi (994-1027) was the empress during the time of Sanjō Tennō, but she had only one daughter. The third daughter Ishi (999-1036) was married to her nephew, Goichijō Tennō, and in her turn became empress, but she too only had daughters. The fourth daughter Kishi (1007-1025) died prematurely, but as the consort of the crown prince, her nephew the future Gosuzaku Tennō, she gave birth to a son, who from 1045 to 1068 was Goreizei Tennō. When Michinaga retired in 1017, he left the regency to his son and heir, the eldest of Rinshi's sons, then aged twenty-five. Until his resignation in 1068, Yorimichi (992-1074) was to exercise the function of chancellor for his three nephews.

Michinaga's success as a statesman is measured by the relative peace enjoyed by the country during his lifetime. This contrasts with the difficulties experienced by his son with the Ise Shrine and the monks of Hieizan, as well as with the quite violent disturbances that shook the eastern provinces between 1029 and 1032 and those of the North from 1056. Yet it is not easy to find a positive quality for him. Leaving aside the military capabilities that a senior noble could not but despise, as only fit for inferiors and dangerous, because killing could expose a person to the vengeance of angry spirits, one cannot credit him with the talent of a legislator, or that of a reformer.

The number of documents issued in his time is quite small and they mainly relate to religion and ceremonial. He did not seek to improve or modify the system he had to run, but he cleverly used the precedents inherited from his forebears and he did not waste his opportunities. His main talent lay in his ability to manage the court personnel, make wise choices, exploit rivalries and balance firmness with generosity.

Up against the regent, the chancellor or the holder of the document examination function, the position of the emperor was very uncomfortable, as it was almost impossible for him to reject a decision proposed by the man who was his protector and advisor, even if it displeased him. If the result was not satisfactory, it was the emperor who felt responsible. Certainly Michinaga did not push the emperor too far and did not refuse to accept a suggestion from him, especially on minor matters. But he was strict and even brutal with Sanjō Tennō, whose prompt abdication he wanted in order to replace him with his own grandson (Atsunari). When Sanjō was ill and suffering from problems affecting his vision, Michinaga refused on various pretexts to attend to the business of government, notably to hold an appointments session expected by the officials, which distressed the emperor who felt responsible for a delay that was prejudicial to his servants; he deferred various decisions and refused to accept the post of chancellor, which would have enabled him to sign documents in place of the emperor who could not do so.[10] For his part, Sanjō wished to name as crown prince to succeed Michinaga's grandson his eldest son Atsuakira (994-1051), who was not related to the powerful minister, and his refusal to abdicate was designed to obtain this concession. Michinaga gave him what he wanted, but he made sure there was a vacuum around the new crown prince, who, humiliated at seeing the best officials decline to enter his household, waited only for his father's death to resign.

In Yorimichi's time, Gosuzaku Tennō suffered greatly from the heavy tutelage of his uncle. When the latter's choices of candidates to lead the Tendai sect or oversee the administration of the Ise Shrine caused unrest within the clergy, the emperor

was so tormented by his sense of responsibility and helpless-
ness that he increased the number of his prayers, sometimes
spending several hours of the night praying in the cold turned
towards Ise, to the point where he became ill.[11] Generally
speaking, Michinaga always managed to maintain some restraint in his dealings with the emperor and he kept up
appearances. Yorimichi was less respectful and allowed officials to come in droves and curry favour with him, while the
emperor's service was not properly attended to and it was very
often necessary to hastily convene the staff in charge of the
imperial meals. The chancellor was openly hostile towards men
like Fujiwara no Sukefusa (1007-1057) who were liked by the
emperor. Gosuzaku Tennō was deeply hurt and considered that
the insults directed at his close retainers were directed at him, as
he remarked one day to his Chancellery head Sukefusa. When
the latter had a dispute over precedence with a colleague of the
palace guard, Fujiwara no Yukitsune (1012-1050), and the
chancellor was refusing to decide in favour of Sukefusa as head
of the Chancellery and thus a special servant of the emperor,
Gosuzaku told him in confidence:

> The conduct of Yukitsune on the question of seating is most
> impertinent. This insult was not directed at you, but at me. All
> this is due to the chancellor's negligence regarding the service
> of the court.[12]

Yet Sukefusa, whose journal often mentions the displeasure
and confusion of the emperor, also does not hesitate to criticize
his faint-heartedness when facing his uncle the chancellor.

In the aristocratic system, birth, personal relations, appearances and weight of precedents were more important than
regulations, controls and even force. Ambitions were partly
kept in check because each person knew what his birth allowed
him to aspire to. Anyone whose forebear had not been a
minister or a senior noble could not become one, and the same
applied if the precedent was too far removed in time. This was
the case for all posts. Since the central administration had not
persisted in its aim of controlling everything in the country, it

did not expand. A few extra posts were created – a second controller, some guards officers and secretaries –, but these creations were offset by the large number of cumulative functions, so that in the late 10th century the candidates always exceeded the available posts and many officials spent much of their career waiting for a vacancy: a source of frustration, because having a post enabled one to live better and even profit from it. Whoever held the key to appointments thus had considerable prestige and, by this very fact, had a strong grip on power. Since there were many candidates, it was always possible to select the best ones. Requests accompanied by gifts, intrigues and rivalries were commonplace. However, as the precedents could not be flouted too openly, personal preference could not be carried to extremes. Men of equal birth and promoted together naturally wished to progress together, and it was perfectly acceptable for an official unhappy with what he believed to be an unfair promotion to refuse to turn up for duty. In 1005, Fujiwara no Kintō (966-1041), who had begun his career shortly before Fujiwara no Narinobu (967-1035), was overtaken by him. Both were the sons of ministers and distinguished by their poetic talents: a highly prized attribute. Kintō no longer appeared at the court or at Michinaga's residence. Michinaga took no offence at this and even sent him a poem reproaching him for having absented himself from a session of poetic composition:

> Are you shut away in your valley dwelling? I was awaiting its last song, but the nightingale keeps silent and spring has passed.

Kintō replied:

> He did not know that spring had passed. Voice of the nightingale hidden in the mountains, where no flowers bloom.[13]

Promotions took place at the beginning of the year, in spring. Kintō compares himself to the nightingale concealed deep in the woods, far from the court and its benefits. His wish was immediately granted and he received his promotion.

Michinaga succeeded admirably in obtaining the ideal mix for the council of senior nobles. He was minister of the left and head of the council and was careful to select "insignificant men" as minister of the right and as third minister. The first was one of his cousins, Akimitsu (944-1021), eldest son of Kane-michi the seven-day chancellor; he was awkward, had little education and was even slightly foolish, or at least portrayed as such. The second was Michinaga's only surviving uncle, Kinsue (957-1029), who had the reputation of being fairly easy-going and was satisfied with an honorary post. On the other hand, Michinaga was able to surround himself with capable major and second counsellors, that is to say, literate enough to compose poetry and write a draft proposal, very familiar with procedures and ceremonial minutiae, and endowed with a good memory that enabled them to find useful precedents. He also demanded their loyalty and, if need be, information on the mood at the court and any potential enemies. Fujiwara no Kintō was both a poet and versed in matters of protocol. Fujiwara no Narinobu excelled in poetry composed in Chinese. Fujiwara no Yukinari (972-1027), who held the post of major controller for many years, had a practical knowledge of administrative details and was also the greatest calligrapher of the age. Minamoto no Toshikata (960-1027) was very devoted and hence a good informant. Minamoto no Michikata (969-1044), whose entire career was spent at the Control Board from 995 to 1019, was an able administrator. Fujiwara no Sanesuke (957-1046), heir to the branch of Saneyori, was a long-time enemy of Michinaga, as is evident from the many criticisms in his journal (*Shōyūki*). However, when he retired in 1017, Michinaga had him appointed minister of the right. He did not wish to deprive his son Yorimichi of the long experience of Sanesuke, an acknow-ledged expert in procedures and ceremonial, notably in matters pertaining to relations with the shrines. Moreover, Sanesuke's only heir was an adopted nephew, Sukehira (986-1067), who could not pose any threat to Michinaga's sons. In making his choices, Michinaga seems to have preferred men who were flexible and adaptable.

Since the work of the administration had come to be largely concentrated on managing the court, the number of officials actually required had decreased. It was essential to have available men who were very familiar with the precedents and could quickly provide the advice requested of them, notably on matters of celebrations and appointments: one or two of the ministerial secretaries filled this role, sometimes for ten years and more. The Control Board was indispensable, as all reports, especially those relating to the supplies needed for the daily life of the palace and the central administration, passed through it. Most of its members were competent and remained in their posts for many years; some, like Minamoto no Michikata, rose in it through all the grades. The officers of the palace guard had a largely ceremonial role, but some good administrators among them were also useful when it came to preparing celebrations. It was necessary to have a capable intendant of the Repair Service (Shurishiki) or a good director of the Constructions Office, for rebuilding or repairs to the palace, as well as for setting up the décor for ceremonies. The Chancellery also required discerning choices, as its members had the privilege of seeing the emperor and could be the bearers of important messages and reports. The same applied to the Police Bureau.

These functions do not seem to have been affected by venality, or only to a very limited extent. The most influential man at the court, or the chancellor when he held this title, seldom tolerated men about whom he had the slightest doubt. Sanesuke negotiated for a long time with Michinaga the appointment of his nephew and adopted son Sukehira to the post of head of the Chancellery. However, given the lineage and abilities of the candidate, this appointment was fully justified. But Michinaga feared the advice that Sanesuke might secretly pass on to the emperor through his son. The same problems were repeated when Sukefusa, Sukehira's son, was in his turn appointed head of the Chancellery: Gosuzaku Tennō desired his appointment, but Yorimichi disliked him and had reason to distrust him, for Sukefusa's journal clearly shows that he secretly provided information to the emperor. He naively writes at the beginning of 1040, when the emperor expresses his surprise that the chancellor has not ordered any action to be taken against the household of the major counsellor Fujiwara no Yorimune (993-1065) whose members had been found guilty of attacking an inspector of the Police Bureau:

> This affair had been known for some time and I had secretly reported it to the emperor. But it is most annoying that he is suddenly talking about it. What's to be done? It's fate. If the chancellor and this major counsellor hear of it, they will certainly bear me ill will. An order to take action could have serious consequences. Loyalty would be of no use at all.[14]

The chancellor had nonetheless taken care to have Fujiwara no Tsunesuke (1006-1081), one of his loyal followers and a rival of Sukefusa, as the joint head of the Chancellery.

The choice of some sixty provincial governors (*zuryō*) was extremely important, as the material life of the court was dependent on them. Their role had been gradually reduced to being no more than that of tax farmer and keeper of the peace. But the court did not look too closely at their activities: it restricted itself to asking them at more or less fixed dates for what it needed and not tolerating disturbances and complaints from those under their jurisdiction. Any governor who was so inept as to be unable to prevent protests from reaching the capital was dismissed. The most celebrated case is the petition in thirty-one articles (*Owari no kuni gebumi*) presented in 988 by the district administrators (*gunji*) and (well-to-do) peasants of Owari province against the governor, Fujiwara no Motonaga (?-?).[15] The text is somewhat ambiguous, as certain grievances concern taxes raised in accordance with the regulations, albeit subject to the customary reductions. However, the text as a whole does not give the impression that this governor was a conscientious official. Rather it appears that he kept the additional taxes raised, and the inhabitants of Owari are aggrieved that he has grown rich. Another source of income for governors was trade. Taxes were levied in rice, but the court required a variety of products: cloth, oil, paper, and so on.

Governors often arbitrarily set at a very low level the price of the goods they obtained by means of the tax rice, not observing what were regarded as normal prices. There are some ten known cases of complaints brought to the court by provincial inhabitants over fifty years, which is quite a small number. As a tax farmer, the governor made no distinction between his personal goods and the taxes he levied. He stocked together in his warehouses the products required by the court and what he kept as profit. It frequently happened that he also made advance payments to the court agencies he was responsible for supplying. As the upholder of public order, he himself recruited and paid a band of men (*rōdō* or *rōtō*) whose duty it was to assist and protect him and, by force if need be, collect the taxes. He also made use of notables of the province, with whom it was in his interest to be on good terms. The court only looked into the governors' management in a general way when they left office, and even then based on partly fabricated documents, as it was necessary to keep up the appearance of supervision, whereas the protection of an important personage in exchange for services, such as having ensured that he was paid on time and in the prescribed amount the allowance granted by reason of his rank, or to have protected his property from an excessive tax burden, were often the main qualifications for obtaining a discharge. These posts as governors, by which the court maintained its control over the country and its own means of subsistence, were thus highly sought after by the middle-ranking officials, and by all those who had no possibility of being promoted to the council. To have served as a ministerial secretary, as a member of the Control Board or an official of the Department of Regulations Relating to Civil Officials, and less often of Court Affairs or Military Affairs, was a qualification for an appointment as governor. But, for the others, these appointments were secured through the patronage of an important personage to whom they had rendered services or by their undertaking to provide building works for the court. Fires were a common occurrence, so it was often necessary to reconstruct pavilions, corridors, doors or surrounding walls.

This amounted to a kind of unofficial venality. There was no clearly prescribed fee.

On the other hand, certain minor posts, notably in the offices of Horses (Meryō), could be bought. They sometimes cost a great deal. Fujiwara no Sanesuke, in 1031, undertook to obtain the appointment of a son of one of his housemen, a minor official in the Accounts Office whom he protected, to the post of fourth-class official in the Accounts Office or the Office of Public Resources. The father was prepared to offer eight hundred bushels of rice, but Sanesuke thought he should pay a thousand bushels.[16] Moreover, a right of presentation to minor functions, or even to ranks, was officially granted to the senior nobles, which enabled them to receive payment for their patronage. Many holders of minor posts in the central administration were in fact merely the servants of high- or middle-ranking officials. One sees in the journal of Fujiwara no Sukefusa that his confidential agent, the man who managed the property of Sukefusa's father-in-law Minamoto no Norisuke (979-1039), the governor of Mikawa province, was a third-class official in the Library Office. It is very likely that he too was rewarded for his trouble with a share of the profits made in the province.

Stipends were no longer paid regularly, as the public storehouses were empty. However the senior nobles and officials of the capital received rights over products from the provinces. Some men were invested with more than one provincial function that they did not take up, but which allowed them to draw the stipend attaching to such posts. If the resident governor felt that he was dealing with a man out of favour, he made very little effort to ensure that the beneficiary was sent the rice and textiles to which he was entitled. In the late 10th and early 11th century, the members of the most important families usually took the daughters of provincial governors as their wives. In this way, they could be kept by their wife's family, without having to wait for a stipend that might not be paid. On the death of his father-in-law, who had housed and fed him for eighteen years, Sukefusa was very distressed, saying that he had lost his arms and legs.[17] Personal relationships had thus also encroached on this important aspect of the bureaucratic system, namely the rules governing stipends. Through patronage, one obtained a position, sometimes by paying the patron, and, in return, he presented gifts when he received a service. Goods circulated in the world of the court by means of gifts and return gifts, but the vocabulary made a clear distinction between what the inferior was obligated to offer in order to express his gratitude and loyalty, and what the superior gave out of generosity. Moreover, the gifts given by the superior had often been received and sometimes demanded from the inferior.

Client relationships thus played a vital role in the court administration. It was thanks to them that the chancellor maintained his hold over the officials and obtained their loyalty and services. It was also thanks to them that each man found a way of making a living. But certain people still paid lip service to the idea that service was owed to the emperor and the country. Fujiwara no Sanesuke, an enemy of Michinaga, it is true, did not deny himself the pleasure in his journal of mocking those of his colleagues whom he considered too deferential towards the powerful minister. When Michinaga was forced to agree to the first consort of Sanjō Tennō, Seishi (971-1025) – daughter of Fujiwara no Naritoki (941-995) –, who had borne him several sons, being named second empress, alongside his own daughter Kenshi, a more recent consort not yet a mother but still declared first empress, it was very difficult to go ahead with the solemn proclamation of the imperial edict and the setting up of Seishi's household, because no-one wished to displease the highest personage of the court. Sanesuke, who had wisely declined the position as head of that household, wrote:

> Everyone is very fearful because of the minister of the left. The messengers sent to summon the senior nobles to the palace and called before these same senior nobles were mocked and insulted and could say nothing. This conduct shows precious little loyalty towards the emperor.[18]

In such circumstances, Sanesuke and later his grandson Sukefusa did not fail to display righteous indignation. Yet, in everyday life, they considered it normal to be the patrons of low-ranking officials and to expect personal services from them.

It must also be noted that these relationships did not involve very onerous obligations. Nothing like what was expected – at least in theory – in the world of the warriors. Middle-ranking officials were concerned above all with survival. Their loyalty did not exclude a degree of calculation. They did not hesitate to abandon a protector whose influence was on the wane in order to attach themselves to a more powerful one. Many kept several irons in the fire and considered themselves bound to a number of important men.

Despite the shift of the institutions in favour of the aristocracy and the personal relationships that permeated the world of the court and allowed it to operate and survive, its members of all ranks – covering the central administration and its agents in the provinces, the governors – still regarded themselves as officials. One piece of evidence for this, perhaps so obvious as to hardly need mentioning, is that the writers of journals always identify those about whom they are speaking by the name of their function: major counsellor, second controller of the left, assistant director of the Department of Regulations Relating to Civil Officials, ministerial secretary, head of the Office of Higher Learning, and so on. Only for ministers do they sometimes add the name of his residence.

One of the main characteristics of this system is the very great importance attached to ceremonial, and to maintaining procedures and celebrations, so much so that one of the major productions of this society consists of protocol manuals or collections of models and that at least two-thirds of the work of the central administration was concerned with ceremonies.

Notes

1. Compilation of the *Kojiki* (*Record of Ancient Matters*) in 712, and the *Nihon shoki* (*Chronicle of Japan*) in 720, the first of the six official histories (*rikkokushi*), continued by other works covering the years up to 887, the last, *Nihon sandai jitsuroku* (*Veritable Record of Three Reigns of Japan*), having been compiled at the beginning of the 10th century.
2. Biography of the model official Fujiwara no Yasunori (825-895), *Fujiwara no Yasunori den*, written by the scholar-official Miyoshi no Kiyoyuki in 907.
3. *Shoku Nihon kōki* (*Later Annals of Japan, Continued*), the fourth of the official histories; account of the incident in 846, Jōwa 13.11.14., and *Nihon sandai jitsuroku*, obituary of Prince Masami, in 863, Jōgan 5.5.1.
4. Sanuki no Naganao was the foremost jurist of his day; see his obituary in *Nihon sandai jitsuroku* in Jōgan 4.8.17., 862.
5. Decree by the Ministry of State Affairs in 827, in the anthology *Honchō monzui* (*Literary Essence of Our Country*), chap. 2, text 21. The curriculum for the classics included, besides *The Analects of Confucius* (J. *Rongo*; Ch. *Lunyu*) and *The Classic of Filial Piety* (J. *Kōkyō*; Ch. *Xiaojing*), *The Book of Changes* (J. *Ekikyō*; Ch. *Yijing*), *The Book of Documents* (J. *Shokyō*; Ch. *Shujing*), *The Zhou Rituals* (J. *Shūrai*; Ch. *Zhouli*), *The Book of Etiquette and Ceremonial* (J. *Girai*; Ch. *Yili*), *The Book of Rites* (J. *Raiki*; Ch. *Liji*), *The Book of Odes* (J. *Shikyō*; Ch. *Shijing*) and the *Commentary of Tso on the Annals of the Duchy of Lu* (J. *Shunjū sashiden*; Ch. *Chunqiu Zuoshizhuan*). The curriculum for letters was enriched by the *Records of the Historian* (J. *Shiki*; Ch. *Shiji*), *History of the Former Han Dynasty* (J. *Zenkanjo*; Ch. *Qian Hanshu*), *History of the Later Han Dynasty* (J. *Gokanjo*; Ch. *Hou Hanshu*), the *Anthology* (J. *Monzen*; Ch. *Wenxuan*) and dictionary (J. *Jiga*; Ch. *Erya*).
6. The Chancellery and Police Bureau date from the reign of Saga Tennō, but the precise date on which these two organs were established is not known.
7. A clear distinction is made in Japan between a female ruler, called *tennō* like a male ruler, and an empress, consort of an emperor, *kōgō* or *chūgū*.

8. In 740, the insurrection of Fujiwara no Hirotsugu (?-740) in Kyūshū and, in 764, the downfall of Fujiwara no Nakamaro (706-764) who had dominated the court since 757.

9. A famous incident called "*akō*", from the term chosen to designate the function of the minister invested with the office of document examiner; the literatus taking notes used the word *akō*, which displeased Mototsune, as it had been used in China as a title, admittedly honorary, but not guaranteeing the possession of any real power. This incident gives an idea of the weapons in the hands of the literati. This term could later give rise to a challenge to the authority of the person invested with it.

10. See in the *Shōyūki*, the journal of Fujiwara no Sanesuke, in 1015, Chōwa 4. from the 5th to the 10th month, the successive refusals of Michinaga to give the emperor any comfort by holding religious celebrations and by replacing him in some of his functions.

11. *Shunki*, the journal of Fujiwara no Sukefusa, Chōryaku 4., 1040, end of the 8th month. For about ten days, the emperor went down each evening from nine until midnight to pray in the garden. *Shōyūki*, Chōgen 4.8.12., 1031, during disturbances at Ise, his brother Goichijō Tennō had gone at night to pray in the palace pavilion housing the sacred mirror.

12. *Shunki*, Chōryaku 2.10.7., 1038. This affair lasted several months and gave rise to some comical scenes, Sukefusa placing himself above Yukitsune, even though there was insufficient room for him to be seated.

13. *Shōyūki*, Kankō 2.4.2., 1005, and the collection of poems by Fujiwara no Kintō, *Kintō shū*, Nos 527 and 528. Similar cases, of an official displeased at not having obtained the promotion to which he believed he was entitled and afterwards failing to present for duty, are quite common.

14. *Shunki*, Chōryaku 3.12.15., beginning of 1040. Sukefusa very often writes that the emperor asks him to consult the minister of the right Fujiwara no Sanesuke secretly or unofficially, meaning without informing the chancellor.

15. *Heian ibun* (archives of the 8th to 12th centuries compiled by Takeuchi Rizō), text 339. The governor named in the petition was dismissed, but incurred no other punishment.

16. *Shōyūki*, Chōgen 4.2.23., 1031. The amount paid, quite large for what was after all a minor post, suggests that the holders of these

functions had opportunities to be offered bribes by provincial governors.

17. *Shunki*, Chōryaku 3.10.7. and 3.11.24., 1039.
18. *Shōyūki*, Chōwa 1.4.27., 1012. Michinaga had seen to it that the procedure for the appointment of the second empress coincided with the entry of his daughter into the palace as first empress, so that most of the senior nobles and officials had gone to escort her. The two ministers had found excuses for staying at home.

CHAPTER 2

RITUALS AND CELEBRATIONS

Choice of rituals as a method of government

"Ritual is reason, music is measure": this old play on the words *rei*, 'ritual', and *ri*, 'reason', was fully accepted by the Japanese of the early period and explains their interest in ceremonial, which was elevated to the rank of an essential task of government. So it was that at the end of the 9th century, in the south-east corner of the Pavilion of Purity and Freshness (Seiryōden), where the emperor conducted his daily life, a large screen was erected, on which month by month and day by day the activities prescribed for the court were set out. These consisted of procedures, but treated as rituals, as well as court, Shintō and Buddhist rituals. In the early 9th century, the court had had compiled, on the one hand, very detailed regulations pertaining to each administrative organ, including the Ministry of Religious Affairs, and, on the other hand, *Inner Palace Regulations* (*Dairishiki*). The first concern the daily work and finances of each service, while the second deal mainly with ceremonial. At that time, the two categories, one devoted essentially to procedures and the other to ceremonial, were fairly well differentiated. In the late 10th century, the administrative regulations seem to have been consulted far less often than the protocol manuals, new works that made significant progress during the 10th century and include the administrative procedures. Whereas the compilation of regulations in the 9th century had been done at imperial command by committees of officials, whose work was officially presented to the throne, the protocol manuals were individual works, often written by the highest personages. Several are attributed to emperors, such as the *Shingishiki* (*New Ritual Procedures*), ascribed to Murakami Tennō. Also preserved, more or less complete, are those by

Fujiwara no Sanesuke and Fujiwara no Morosuke,[1] showing slight differences that would have been almost imperceptible to outsiders, but to which their respective descendants were very attached.

The most important and most often consulted work is undoubtedly the collection titled *Saikyūki* (*Notes of the Western Residence*). The owner of this residence was a son of Daigo Tennō, Takaakira, who was removed from the registers of the imperial family and given the name of Minamoto. He attained the rank of minister of the left, but was disgraced following a plot hatched by Moromasa, a son of Fujiwara no Tadahira.[2] The *Saikyūki* provided the definitive model for this kind of work: it contains, on the one hand, a calendar of the annual activities, whether celebrations, rituals or procedures, each accompanied by a description of the location, with a list of the requisite objects, such as curtains, mats, screens and tables, details of the participants, with their ranks and grades, the series of actions performed and the words pronounced; and, on the other hand, detailed information concerning special celebrations such as enthronement, abdication, the celebration of the Great Thanks-giving (Daijōsai) at the start of a reign, the proclamation of an empress, and the ceremony marking the coming-of-age of a prince. It also includes the method of drafting certain imperial orders or other official texts, the circumstances occasioning the drafting of such texts, notes relating to dress and a host of other details. A reading of the *Saikyūki* makes it possible to perfectly reconstruct the décor of each celebration, as it always takes place in a location divided into equal sections by pillars: the place of each object and each participant is precisely defined; for example, at the third bay from the west, or at the second bay from the north. When an official is to come forward with a document or a cup or any other object, the route he must follow is shown down to the last detail. The phrases used to call participants and the orders issued are noted as well. This work also contains lists of precedents, sometimes irregular, with an explanation of the circumstances that made it necessary to disregard the rules. It was completed over time and includes examples dating from after the death of its author Takaakira. A reading of the journals of the senior nobles shows that all of them were familiar with and assiduously put into practice *Notes of the Western Residence*, since they quote from these as a matter of course.

In the early 11th century, the major counsellor Fujiwara no Kintō compiled *Hokuzanshō* (*Notes of the Northern Hills*), which owes its name to his place of retirement, north of Kyōto. Although a descendant of Fujiwara no Saneyori, known as the Lord of Ononomiya, for the most part he did not keep the rituals specific to his branch of the family, but in general adopted those of Morosuke's branch, as he appears to have worked for his son-in-law, Fujiwara no Norimichi (996-1075), a son of Michinaga: he gives, in particular, a very detailed description of the appointment of the general of the palace guard and the congratulatory banquet that followed. Norimichi was appointed to this post in 1017 at the age of twenty.

In the early 12th century, Ōe no Masafusa (1041-1111), a descendant of renowned literati and himself a doctor of letters, as well as a senior noble, produced *Gōke shidai* (*Order of Procedures and Celebrations According to the Ōe Family*), which shows some differences with the notes of Takaakira that pre-date them by about a century. In spite of the scrupulous respect for the precedents, a few changes, such as in the order of courses for a banquet, had been introduced. Yet, for the most part, there is a remarkable continuity.

These manuals present another noteworthy feature, one still found in modern works that refer to them or provide commentaries on them, as the tradition of studies of this type has never been interrupted over the centuries. The writers give almost no explanation as to the reasons for the arrangements adopted and the significance of the gestures performed. Nonetheless, the various influences that shaped the annual cycle of celebrations can be discerned. That of the Chinese classics is clearly visible in the court rituals, notably solemn greetings, banquets and poetry sessions. The important point is that, on each occasion, everything was arranged in order to display hierarchies. As is written in *The Book of Rites* (J. *Raiki*; Ch. *Liji*):

> The great ceremonies imitate the different degrees that exist in heaven and on earth.

The rules were virtually the same: the superior was turned towards the south; the officials lined up in a row from east to west or from north to south; the solemn bow consisted of three movements, two deep bows punctuated by a dance-like gesture; whoever was honoured by the emperor with a cup of saké did not take the cup proffered by the emperor but exchanged the cup and went down into the courtyard to make his bow of thanks. Needless to say, the Japanese adapted and often simplified the prescriptions found in the Chinese classics, *The Book of Rites* or *The Book of Etiquette and Ceremonial* (J. *Girai*; Ch. *Yili*).

The national religion, Shintō, also provided a number of important annual rituals associated with the request for good harvests for the year and with thanksgiving at the end of the agricultural work cycle. Specifically, on three occasions during the year, the emperor offered a meal to the deities. Other rituals recalled the national myths, notably that of the sun goddess Amaterasu who, exasperated at the violent conduct of her brother Susanoo no mikoto, went into the cave, and emerged only when the deity Amanouzume no mikoto began to dance and made the other deities laugh. A woman belonging to a clan said to be descended from the goddess Amanouzume no mikoto performed this dance each year towards the time of the winter solstice. This ritual was intended to keep the emperor in good health by pacifying his spirit (or rather his spirits), in the same way as the dance in front of the cave had placated the sun goddess. The emperor did not personally attend most of the Shintō celebrations, just as he did not go in person to the great shrines that received his regular gifts on the occasion of their two annual festivals. However he was required to undergo purifications and abstain from certain foods, and do obeisance to the deities in his apartments when the officials of the Ministry of Religious Affairs were performing their functions.

Buddhism was also present. One of the most widely used *sūtras*, the *Benevolent Kings Sūtra* (*Ninnōkyō*), contained a passage stating that kings who ordered it to be read would keep their countries safe from wars and calamities. It was therefore decided that such readings were beneficial. But the annual cycle of celebrations was not as rich in Buddhist elements: there were celebrations at the beginning and end of the year (Gosaie and Obutsumyōe), as well as the commemoration of the Buddha's birth in the 4th month (Kanbutsue). Yet it should be noted that if, by an accident of the calendar, this latter festival happened to coincide with that of a shrine, it was cancelled at the court. In fact, the presence of Buddhist monks was considered defiling and prohibited if a celebration of the national religion was being held. It is interesting to note that this rule, which seems to give absolute priority to the national religion, permitted no exception, whereas individuals exhibited more devotion to the buddhas than to the deities and had far more numerous and far closer relations with the Buddhist temples and their monks than with the shrine priests. At the court, too, Buddhist celebrations were very frequent and the emperor often attended them, but apart from the three mentioned earlier, they were not held on a regular basis.

In summary, the court rituals, of Chinese origin or inspired by China, were designed to show in concrete terms the order of the country, those of Shintō to remind people of the close ties of the emperor with the national deities and his role as intercessor between them and his subjects, and those of Buddhism to obtain aid at the beginning of the year and above all in cases of need: illness of the emperor, epidemics, drought or excessive rains.

In their everyday work, the senior nobles and officials of the 11th century attached more importance to protocol manuals than to legislative texts, regulations and decrees, and appear to have known and applied them better. How did this come about? It seems that the development of the study of letters played a part. This discipline trained the best exponents of Chinese thought and literature. In the 9th century, its members, while not holding the most prestigious posts, nonetheless succeeded in making significant inroads into the upper level of the administration. Some entered the council of senior nobles, and many were employed at the Control Board and in the secretariat of the Ministry of State Affairs. They were lecturers to the emperors and tutors to the aristocrats. They authored the official histories regarded as collections of precedents and models to be followed, and compiled the administrative regulations. They were thus in a position to exert an influence. Masters of political morality, they praised the kind found in the Chinese classics, namely that the government must be benevolent, take measures to ensure that the people lived in peace and prosperity, and favour example over punishment. However, in order to achieve this ideal, there were in fact two methods: one involved acting in a direct way, as it were rationally; the other took an indirect approach, based on magic. The literati did not really make a choice and by turns or at the same time advised both. The first prescription was the one put into practice by the good official – honest, fair and moderate – who acts by example, kindness, persuasion, raising the moral standards of the people and not using punishments. To achieve the ideal of benevolent government, it was essential to have officials who were assessed, promoted and inspected at regular intervals, devoted to the common good, constituting a well-ordered administration, capable of taking the precautionary measures required to avoid food shortages.

The second method derives from other aspects of Chinese thought, which greatly interested the literary specialists. The titles of the compositions set for graduates attest to this: Taoism, the cosmic rhythms, the calendar, the art of divination and geomancy aroused their curiosity. They tended on occasion to neglect questions of practical administration in favour of problems they deemed to be of a higher order. There was an Office of Divination, responsible for formulating the calendar, explaining omens and teaching a body of doctrine, *onmyōdō*, "the way of Yin and Yang", namely the two principles whose alternation regulates the entire universe, maintains it and causes it to evolve. This discipline therefore studied everything taught by natural phenomena, as well as the interactions between the physical and human universes. While not the recognized specialists of this branch of learning and while not fulfilling the normal tasks – providing consultations for interpreting abnormal phenomena and fixing auspicious dates – of those called "masters of the way of Yin and Yang", the literati were themselves very familiar with it and appear to have contributed to its success in the 9th century, a success that only increased with time. According to this mode of thought, acting on the microcosm makes it possible to influence the macrocosm, because rituals, gestures and signs are effective mediums. This can be seen in different fields, such as those of names, colours and directions. One task of the literati, at each change of the era name used for dating, was to propose words with an auspicious meaning: for example, Chōwa, "Enduring Harmony" (1012-1016); Kannin, "Generosity and Humanity" (1017-1020); Jian, "Peaceful Government" (1021-1023), and so on. The characters signifying harmony, duration, generosity, protection and virtue were especially favoured. These changes were generally proposed in the 10th and 11th centuries when an epidemic, a lack of rain or any other ill-starred event occurred, making it advisable to begin a new era. The literati also intervened at the Heian palace, far more than at the palace in Nara, to assign to the palace buildings and gates auspicious names in keeping with their orientation. They no doubt had confidence in this method of protection, as there exist written opinions signed by literati explaining the burning of a pavilion by the failure to assign a suitable name.[3] Similarly, the ill-considered use of the colour red was believed to cause fires.

The literati found in China the idea that there is no distinction or conflict between the natural and human worlds, but rather unity and continuity. It was thus necessary to first of all establish harmony in the country, the kind that results when each element is in its proper place. The way of Yin and Yang led to an emphasis on processes that were in a sense magical.

The religions too, Shintō and Buddhism alike, proclaimed that their rituals were efficacious. The monks knew rituals against diseases and natural disasters. The shrine priests promised misfortunes if the prescribed form of worship was not followed.

The authors of the classics, for their part, considered ritual rather from a moral and social point of view: ritual made it possible to discipline bodies and minds, to which music and dance also contributed, and it allowed each person to examine in concrete terms his place in the world. Their approach was often rational, free from any superstitious posturing, and in accord with what is stated in a commentary on the *Annals of the Duchy of Lu* (J. *Shunjū Sashiden*; Ch. *Chunqiu Zuoshizhuan*):

> When the country is becoming prosperous, the prince heeds advice for governing that takes account of the needs of the people. When the country is in decline, the prince heeds advice for governing that takes account only of the protection of the gods.

The scholar-officials, for their part, had no fear of contradicting themselves and refused none of the ritual functions. Ōe no Masahira (952-1012), a doctor of letters, considered the greatest literatus of his time, quotes the *Annals of the Duchy of Lu* to criticize his colleagues who, when candidates for a post, performed ceremonies for the deities. Yet when he wished to obtain a post in the Chancellery for his son Takachika (978?-1046), he went on a pilgrimage to the Atsuta Shrine and made a request to the goddess.[4]

When Sugawara no Kiyotomo (770-842), a doctor of letters who was responsible for the subsequent prosperity of his family, accompanied an embassy to China at the beginning of the 9th century, what he brought back from his voyage, at least officially, was a plan for the reorganization of the court ceremonies. The monk Kūkai (774-835), some of whose relatives taught at the Office of Higher Learning and who was himself highly educated in all branches of knowledge, and especially well versed in the classics, brought back from the same voyage the doctrines of the esoteric Shingon sect of Buddhism and the rituals relating to it. The monk of the Tendai sect, Ennin (794-864), who left for China with the last embassy, that of 838, brought back with him the doctrines of Tendai esoterism. In the early 10th century, Miyoshi no Kiyoyuki (847-918), the last doctor of letters to enter the council without having had a senior noble among his forebears, wrote a reform project. One article concerns the misappropriation of offerings to the shrines, the cause, according to him, of misfortunes for the country.[5] These facts are sufficient to show that the men most conversant with the Chinese texts, although aware of the rational bent of the principal classics, by no means excluded the use of rituals in order to obtain a material result.

As time passed, the celebrations became as it were sacrosanct, the most important duty of the court, to which the officials devoted more time than to any other purpose. When misfortune or danger struck, the council's deliberations did not deal with the specific measures to be taken but with the choice of the most effective rituals. The special ceremonies, in particular, were a heavy burden. In his journal, Fujiwara no Sanesuke, at the time a major counsellor, sets out in detail everything that needed to be done for almost a year to prepare for a pilgrimage of a few hours by the emperor to the Kamo Shrine.[6]

At least two-thirds of the deliberations of the council of senior nobles concerned decisions relating to celebrations. The other third involved discussions centring on the examination of the accounts of the provincial governors and the subsequent appointments.

Respect for the precedents had as a consequence that the annual cycle of court celebrations did not change; it became the main preoccupation of the administration. Only the emperor and his entourage were able to perform it. As no-one could contest their role, this may have helped to ensure the survival of the imperial court during the centuries of government of the country by the warrior class, who respected rituals and customs inherited from the past.

The annual cycle of celebrations

In a sense, this cycle places on the same level what we call administrative procedures, court rituals and religious celebrations. This distinction is somewhat anachronistic, since the celebrations had a political dimension: they were considered to be efficacious and necessary for the good governance of the country. A quick count gives around a hundred celebrations, sixteen of them Buddhist, and eighty procedures that are listed in chronological order, but these last-mentioned, for the most part, were not elaborated on in the protocol manuals. The twelve months (lunar, as the calendar was lunisolar and seven times in nineteen years an extra month was added) had a variable number of events: the busiest were the first and last months. The hot summer season, the 5th and 6th months and the beginning of the 7th, which mostly correspond to July and August, had far fewer events.

The 1st month was exceptionally rich in celebrations, as it was necessary to enter the new year under auspicious circumstances. Court rituals, rituals drawn from Buddhism, Taoism and the way of Yin and Yang, and administrative procedures, but not Shintō rituals, followed one another. In this 1st month, the 1st day was especially full. The first act of the emperor on the morning of this day, which, in the lunisolar calendar, coincided with the beginning of spring, was to bathe in order to purify himself, then go down into the garden and there, facing north, invoke seven times the star for the year, one of the seven of the Lesser Bear (the constellation known as the Little Dipper), this being intended to ward off disasters. The emperor next bowed to Heaven, Earth and the four cardinal points and, finally, he bowed in the direction of the graves of his father and mother. The various elements of this ritual, which combined Taoist beliefs with those of the way of Yin and Yang, as well as filial piety, came from China, but it was in Japan that they were organized into a coherent whole.

Having returned to his apartments, the emperor then drank three cups of saké in which prophylactic substances had been dissolved. The potion in the first cup had a name signifying that it destroyed harmful influences and promoted good ones. These remedies were prepared with great care and kept facing a suitable direction. On three successive days, they were offered to the emperor. This was also a Chinese custom, adopted in the 9th century.

Next, from the top of the Pavilion of Purity and Freshness, where he lived, the emperor received the homage of his servants – senior nobles and officials – lined up in the garden. In the 10th century, this "Minor Reverence" (*kojōhai*) replaced a far more elaborate ritual that took place at the Court of the Eight Departments (Hasshōin or Chōdōin), in the Great Hall of State (Daigokuden). It seems that they wished to avoid the complications associated with readying the Court of the Eight Departments, as well as the transfer of the emperor to another palace courtyard, which would have required the use of the palanquin and the provision of an escort. But, in so doing, some of the official and majestic character of the ritual was lost, as the garden in front of the Pavilion of Purity and Freshness could not accommodate all the officials.

Finally, in the Southern Pavilion (Naden or Nanden), facing south and at right angles to the southern end of the Pavilion of Purity and Freshness, the emperor offered his servants a banquet. On this occasion, he was presented with the calendar for the year – as the master of time, it was he who promulgated it – together with a report on the ice-houses – well filled they signified a saintly reign – and a red fish, red being an auspicious colour. The emperor was seated on his throne, in the centre of the pavilion, some distance away from the senior nobles seated to the south, in the gallery that encircled the building. The ladies were seated behind the northern partition. The officials of the Control Board and the ministerial secretariat, as well as the members of the Chancellery and the men who had the privilege of going up to the Courtiers' Hall (Tenjō no ma), were at the foot of the pavilion on either side of the central staircase. The guards officers were stationed around the courtyard in front of the east pavilion for those of the left sections, and the west pavilion for those of the right sections, lined up from north to south. First the emperor took his place, showing as it were that the country, of which the court was a miniature version, would not exist without his presence. Then the minister in charge of the ceremony had the formal invitation read out and all the participants entered the courtyard in hierarchical order, stood still and bowed. After the ritual of thanks for the saké about to be offered, the senior nobles went up to take their places and the others made their way to their seats. The emperor was served first, being brought in two servings no less than eighteen small cups or bowls, not counting the condiments and rice. The senior nobles received only about ten kinds of food. The other officials seated in the courtyard were served even fewer dishes. As for the minor officials, they were given shared dishes of rice mixed with fish and vegetables. Next came three rounds of saké, each with three cups. During the first and third rounds, there was a musical interlude: the first of songs said to be from a place called Kuzu, whose inhabitants had reputedly offered entertainments to an emperor of a very distant time in the past; the second presented by the Office of Music (Gagakuryō). Thus after a piece considered to be of Japanese origin came a performance of music from the continent. The participants then reassembled in the courtyard, standing in hierarchical order, to hear the reading of an imperial edict and make their ritual bows, before receiving gifts: garments and fabrics of greater or lesser value according to the rank of each recipient.

Almost all palace banquets followed the same programme. Some work was often involved, if only for the sake of appearances: on the 7th day of the 1st month, the proclamation of the lists of promotions; at the beginning of the 4th month, the days inaugurating the summer work; and in winter, at the beginning of the 10th month, the presentation to the emperor of the ministerial reports and the affixing of the imperial seal to documents. These banquets of the 1st and 7th days of the 1st month and the 4th and 10th months always took place, except in cases of the death of a very close relative. But they were often shortened, as the emperor did not attend even half of them, on various pretexts: inauspicious day, tiredness, move to a temporary palace, or another excuse.

Three banquets were devoted more especially to artistic activities. According to the annual cycle of celebrations, in the 1st month of the year, on one occasion, the emperor assembled the senior nobles and scholar-officials to compose Chinese poetry, in a semi-private session, as it did not take place in the Southern Pavilion. In the 3rd month, a banquet was sometimes organized by the side of a winding canal, during which poems had to be composed while the current brought cups in the shape of birds. This was no doubt a very ancient Chinese ritual with a purificatory value. But in Japan it seems rather to have been considered an exotic curiosity. On the 9th day of the 9th month, the annual cycle prescribed the holding of a banquet, called Triple Yang (Chōyō no sechie), with the composition of poems. These three banquets, while included in the annual cycle, were in fact very often cancelled and officials only took the trouble to organize them once or twice during a reign. Nonetheless, gatherings for the composition of poems in the 9th month were still frequently held in the early 11th century, but without the inconvenience of a formal session.

Two banquets were closely associated with the very ancient practices of an agrarian society. On the 16th day of the 1st month, while a meal was being served to the court in the Southern Pavilion, a group of women beat the earth with their feet in order to awaken its energies and danced in circles around the buildings of the inner palace. The banquet held the day after the First Fruits Festival (Shinjōsai or Niiname no matsuri), in the 11th month, was very seldom cancelled. It was enhanced by a programme of dance, greatly appreciated, at which young female dancers and their retinues performed.

Banquets could also be ordered in exceptional circumstances. When the emperor moved into a temporary palace during the rebuilding of the palace and when he returned to his usual residence, the new period had to be ushered in by an auspicious act: imbibing the drink that gladdened and warmed the heart. The same applied to the coming-of-age celebration of an imperial prince. Whether the year was good or bad, each one had at least five or six great banquets. These celebrations, held regularly or only on special occasions, were an opportunity to listen to music and often to watch dances, which were performed on a platform in the courtyard in front of the Southern Pavilion. As these gatherings often took place towards evening, torches were lit in the later stages. But when the moon was shining, they were extinguished. If, in addition, a gentle breeze could be heard, it was a delight for the participants to contemplate the scene in the moonlight and listen to the sounds of the instruments mingling with the murmur of the breeze. Banquets always began in a very orderly and formal manner, and this is what the protocol manuals and the journals of the senior nobles describe in great detail. Very often, though, they ended in drinking bouts; the participants sang in unison or improvised a concert, ranks were broken for the exchange of cups, and quite a few of the senior nobles were no longer capable of returning unaided to their carriage. It seems that as long as only music-making was involved, the emperor could participate: Ichijō Tennō was an accomplished flute player. However he did not attend disorderly drinking sessions.

In the 1st month, the main procedures were the deliberations concerning promotions and appointments, these last-mentioned over three days. But additional sessions could be scheduled throughout the year, whether it be to alter postings at the request of the men appointed, or to rectify errors, or because a vacancy had occurred. These deliberations took place in the inner palace, in the council chamber where the senior nobles spent most of their time issuing the final discharges required by the provincial governors in order to obtain a new post. Decisions were taken in the emperor's presence: the senior nobles proceeded to the Courtiers' Hall in front of the sovereign's apartments in the Pavilion of Purity and Freshness. These were procedures that could never be cancelled under any circumstances; at most they could be postponed if the emperor was ill or a death had occurred. Two other sessions were nearly always retained. They did not take place in the inner palace but in the buildings of the Ministry of State Affairs. In the 8th month was the examination of the merits of officials, and in the 2nd month the review of the minor officials nominated for promotion. In fact, these procedures had become very formal: examining merits consisted of reading out a record of the number of days' attendance by each person. It seems that for the officials who participated in this exercise, the main interest was that they were served refreshments and several rounds of saké. At different times throughout the year, the court distributed various allowances – garments and the costs associated with the use of a horse to certain officials – and alms, especially at the beginning of the year, to the poor of the capital. This meant drawing up lists of recipients, designating those in charge and requisitioning provinces for the products such as cloth, rice and salt to be divided up.

The Japanese court borrowed from China a bi-annual ceremony in honour of Confucius and other sages (Sekiten), at the beginning of the 2nd and 8th months. This took place in the buildings of the Office of Higher Learning, where there was a kind of chapel. Officials who specialized in the classics and letters, as well as one or two senior nobles in charge of proceedings, first made an offering of food to the spirits of the sages. Then the assembled company made its way to one of the Office pavilions for the reading of a classic, a banquet and a session of composition of Chinese poems, followed by a more informal drinking session. In the 8th month, on the day after the celebration at the Office, doctors of both disciplines, followed by their students, came to the Southern Pavilion of the inner palace for a public session of disputation over the meaning of one of the classics. In principle, the emperor was present. But this session was far from being held every year and the emperor seldom attended it. There was always a good reason for cancelling it; in such cases, the customary gifts were still frequently distributed. It also happened that the scholar-officials went on strike, claiming that they were not treated with sufficient respect. In 1013, as the bureaux had not issued the permits needed to organize the final examinations for the graduates, they and the examiners did not turn up at the session, which had to be cancelled.[7]

The Shintō celebrations mentioned in the annual cycle and of interest to the court were very numerous, but for the most part they were held outside the palace, in the shrines themselves. The palace, nonetheless, prepared offerings that the emperor reverenced, after having purified himself. Twenty-one shrines were thus given regular offerings at the time of their two annual festivals, in addition to those sent on special occasions. However, for the festivals at Kasuga in the 2nd and 11th months, Iwashimizu in the 3rd month, and Kamo in the 4th and 11th months, the emperor watched the procession leave. Kasuga, in Nara, was the shrine of the Fujiwara, the maternal family of the emperors. Iwashimizu, south of Kyōto, housed deities including Ōjin Tennō and Jingū Kōgō, believed to be the ancestors of the emperor. The two Kamo shrines, north of the capital, were dedicated to the deities of the area, but when the court moved to Heian it worshipped them in a very special way and an imperial princess was dedicated to their service. For each festival of these three shrines, the son of a senior noble was designated as imperial messenger and a programme of music and dance was prepared. The day of the festival (or the previous day for Kasuga), the messenger and his retinue went to the palace, where the emperor reverenced the offerings and watched the dances that were to be presented to the deities, as well as the procession's departure. The processions for the festivals at Iwashimizu and Kamo attracted large crowds along the entire route. The senior nobles and ladies watched from inside their carriages. There were also platforms of a kind along the First Avenue, from where one could view the Kamo procession without being seen. On arrival at the shrine, the messenger presented the offerings and a prayer was read. To please the deities, a line of caparisoned horses paraded around the buildings, the dances were performed, and sometimes a horse race was organized. Then, at night, the procession returned to the palace. For the Kamo festival, a fire was lit in the courtyard east of the Pavilion of Purity and Freshness. By its light, members of the palace guard performed a dance evoking an episode relating to the deities and designed to have them come and enjoy the spectacle, which was also greatly appreciated by the members of the court. Refreshments with saké were served to the participants.

In the 2nd month, at the start of the agricultural year, there took place the ceremony called Prayers for the Year (Kinensai or Toshigoi no matsuri), intended to obtain the protection of the deities of the entire country for an abundant harvest. The regulations stipulated that on this occasion the emperor was to have offerings sent to the deities of all the provinces, either directly for seven hundred and thirty-seven shrines, or indirectly through the governors for three thousand one hundred and thirty-two. However, in the 11th century, this was no longer faithfully observed, and only the most important shrines continued to be presented with offerings by the court. The sovereign did not attend the prayers recited at the Ministry of Religious Affairs, or the departure of the messengers entrusted with the offerings, which consisted mainly of cloth. But he himself and all the senior nobles and officials who, in one way or another, were involved in the preparations and took part in the ritual, had to be ritually pure in the three days leading up to it and observe various interdictions. This celebration was postponed only on very rare occasions, for example when the palace had been touched by a defilement and some time was needed to remove it.

The 6th and 12th months began with a series of purificatory practices that the emperor observed up to the 11th day – the date of a ceremony with the misleading name of Monthly Celebration (Tsukinamisai). The senior nobles and officials involved, all ritually pure, made their way to the Ministry of Religious Affairs for a prayer of thanksgiving and a distribution of offerings destined in principle for three hundred and four shrines. The following night, the emperor in person offered up a meal to the goddess Amaterasu in the building set aside for that purpose in the inner palace: the Pavilion of Divine Happiness (Shinkaden) within the Court of Central Harmony (Chūka-in or

Chūwa-in). He bathed and put on a pure garment in order to enter the hall where serving women came and laid out the trays. He offered up a first service towards ten in the evening and a second towards three in the morning. Then he changed his costume and returned to his apartments. Officials, both men and women, from the Ministry of Religious Affairs then came and sprinkled rice and saké and called down upon him happiness and safety. At daybreak, he drank a bowl of rice gruel, which signified the end of the period of interdictions, food and others, begun on the first day. Everything concerning these interdictions, as well as the purifications, was rigorously observed, but the emperor very seldom went in person to offer up the sacred meal. Officials from the Ministry of Religious Affairs conducted the ritual in their buildings.

The 6th and 12th months ended with a great purification, which took place at the south gate of the palace. The emperor remained in his apartments, where a ritual was celebrated for him. On the last night of the year, an exorcism ritual was conducted. Men from the guards played the role of demons and were driven out. Purifications, which were the preserve of specialists, were always performed, as was the exorcism. This caused great animation in the palace: torches, races around the pavilions and shooting of arrows. The guards chosen to become demons reluctantly obeyed.

The 11th month began, like the 6th and 12th, with a period of interdiction for the emperor and the officials selected to participate in the preparations for the First Fruits Festival, which involved offering up to the deity a meal consisting of new rice, saké made with new rice and several fish dishes. When the emperor officiated in person, the ritual was held at night in the Shinkaden, the special pavilion used for the sacred meals of the 6th and 12th months. The meal took place at two different times: nine in the evening and one in the morning. The emperor, seated facing the place of the deity, served her and ate a little of the rice himself. Meanwhile, outside the pavilion, by the light of torches and braziers, officials danced and sang short pieces in honour of the deities. This part of the celebration – the emperor going to where the meal was served – was in fact very often omitted and Religious Affairs officials made the offerings of food within the Ministry buildings.

On the other hand, only the death of a close relative could cause the court to abandon the festivities marking the end of the agricultural year that took place on the days preceding and the day after the First Fruits Festival. A month beforehand, two senior nobles and two officials were chosen to prepare a young dancer and her attendants: a very onerous task, as several costumes were required for each dancer. On the 2nd day of the Rat (which came around every twelve days, so there were two or three each month), a first rehearsal took place in the presence of the emperor in the Pavilion of Constant Tranquillity, Jōneiden, the pavilion of the inner palace reserved for the dancers. Two days later, there was celebrated in the buildings of the Department of Palace Affairs the ritual of the Pacification of Souls (Chinkonsai), to ensure the continuation of the emperor's vital forces, symbolized by one of the garments worn by him. On the evening of this same day, a second dance rehearsal was held in the Pavilion of Purity and Freshness, in front of the emperor and a small gathering. The next day, the First Fruits Festival was celebrated, and the following day the emperor offered his servants a banquet called "Redness", namely "Intoxication" (Toyo no akari no sechie), during which the young dancers performed. From the time they entered the palace and for five days, the courtiers indulged in all kinds of demonstrations of gaiety. Informally dressed, they went through the palace singing.

An anecdote in the *Konjaku monogatarishū* (*Tales of Times Now Past*) relates the sad story of a provincial governor chosen to present a young dancer. He has never had the privilege of entering the inner palace and is not familiar with its ways and customs. He accompanies his daughter to the place set aside for the dancers, where a space enclosed by curtains is reserved for each one. The sight of the young courtiers letting their hair down fills him with astonishment and they make fun of him and hold him up to ridicule.[8] Things sometimes ended in an orgy. In

1039, Fujiwara no Sukefusa writes that four young courtiers, including his younger brother Sukenaka (1021-1087), sought out a young novice, their favourite, took him into the rehearsal room, where the leader of the group slept with him and, for two days, forced this boy to have relations with the musicians and the dancers' attendants. The emperor, having been informed somewhat belatedly, demanded that they be punished, for, he said, the shame of such conduct reflected badly on the imperial family.[9]

The Ise Shrine enjoyed a very special position, because here was worshipped the great solar deity Amaterasu, ancestor of the imperial family and from whom it held the mandate to rule over the country. The emperor sent a messenger to Ise at least four times a year: on the occasions of the Prayers for the Year, the two Monthly Celebrations, and the First Fruits Festival at the shrine (Kannamesai), which took place in the 9th month. He also sent a messenger when the "sacred objects" were moved into a new shrine, every twenty years, and each time an unusual event occurred at the court or in the country.

The two main Buddhist ceremonies took place at the beginning and end of the year. From the 8th to the 14th day of the 1st month, the court summoned thirty-two monks and their acolytes who were invited to read the *Golden Light Sūtra* (*Konkōmyōkyō*) for two sessions a day in the Great Hall of State. On the first and last day, the senior nobles attended and a musical programme was performed. On the evening of the last day, the participants made their way to the inner palace, where two monks, who had been chosen beforehand, faced each other in a doctrinal disputation. At the end of the year there was celebrated over three successive nights, in the emperor's apartments in the Pavilion of Purity and Freshness, the Litanies of the August Names of the Buddhas (Obutsumyōe), to wipe out the year's misdeeds.

In spring and autumn, on a movable date, one hundred monks were invited to the Southern Pavilion to recite over three days the *Large Sūtra on Perfect Wisdom* (*Daihannyakyō*), for the protection of the country. On the 8th day of the 4th month, the Aspersions of the Buddha (Kanbutsue) commemorated the birth and first bath of the Buddha. However, since the 4th month had an abundance of Shintō celebrations, this ritual was often cancelled.

Some of the most popular rituals were competitions. In the 1st month, over two successive days, there were archery contests, which had been adapted in Japan from ancient Chinese customs designed to ward off evil spirits and misfortunes. From the 10th century, the emperor attended only the second session. A left side competed against a right side and the archers faced off in pairs. The wins for each side were then added up. The senior nobles, who entered the men of their escorts, all members of the palace guard, took a very keen interest in the results of their champions. The mounted archery contest, included in the annual cycle for the 5th month, was no longer held from the late 10th century. In the last two months of the year, there was organized in the inner palace an archery session called "Inauguration of the Archery Ground" (Iba hajime), because the target removed during the summer was put back for the occasion. Senior nobles were not too proud to take part. Prizes were awarded to the winners.

The wrestling matches (the origin of present-day sumo competitions) at the end of the 7th month undoubtedly went far back into the past. They pitted very strong men against each other: a left side recruited in the east of the country and a right side recruited in the west by the palace guard. The sessions took place in the inner palace and lasted for several days. They originally had a religious meaning: to stir up the energies of the earth through the use of human forces at a critical moment, namely the ripening of the rice. The spectators – emperor and senior nobles – often looked for omens concerning their future and that of the country in the results: victory of the left or right side, first victory of the competition awarded to a man of the left or the right, number of successive victories of one side. The sessions ended with the performance of pieces of music. The wrestling matches were cancelled in the event of a death or natural disasters. They were very much appreciated by the court. Disputes over which side had won were common and spectators sometimes came to blows in front of the emperor, who nonetheless had the final decision in doubtful cases. The officials lost all sense of decorum and, in the affray, caps went flying.[10]

This cycle included a considerable number of celebrations, to which must be added the many supplementary religious ceremonies, mainly Buddhist, but also offerings to shrines, ordered when required. Nevertheless, the court certainly did not bother to celebrate all of them and often cancelled or shortened them on various pretexts, the most usual being rain. Gosuzaku Tennō was extremely devoted to the deities and would have liked to officiate more often for the sacred meal, but the chancellor Fujiwara no Yorimichi, who did not wish to give the senior nobles and officials the inconvenience of a night-time escort or perhaps simply to show the sovereign who was in charge, often refused him that solace.

This annual cycle thus combined diverse elements: procedures and celebrations of indigenous and Chinese origin, Shintō, Buddhism, Taoism and the way of Yin and Yang, as well as popular rituals from China or native to Japan. They usually took place in the inner palace, and even those that began in other palace buildings (at the centre of which was the inner palace) often concluded in the Southern Pavilion. What unified them was that the emperor was always at the centre, as the intercessor between the country and the deities and buddhas, as the benefactor of his people and primarily of his close servants whom he appointed, promoted and rewarded, and as the upholder of civilized society and patron of the arts.

The court as patron of the arts

Early Japan took from China the notion that poetry is the pinnacle of all literature, that ritual is, above all else, a means of governing, and that dance and music contribute to the success of a reign. It says in the chapter "On Music" in *The Book of Rites*:.

When rituals and music are practised, there is virtue, for virtue is to possess rituals and music. If the rulers of old regulated rituals and music, it was not to gratify the senses, but to teach the people to discipline their feelings and to return to the correct way.

Echoing this, the Japanese literatus of the early 11th century, Ōe no Masahira, writes:

Ours is the country of poetry, letters shine here and therefore the ruler is happy; rituals and music flourish here and therefore the country is well governed. Thus, thanks to a saintly ruler, peace reigns in all things.[11]

For another of these literati, Fujiwara no Arikuni (943-1011), drawing heavily on Chinese texts, the ability to compose poetry is the mark of the perfect man. Poetry is a source of knowledge about people, and makes it possible to suitably praise the virtue of a good ruler or a good minister.[12] It is the best way of presenting good examples, which is important for those advocating government by example. In all of Chinese literature, what the Japanese literati considered to be the noblest form was poetry. A doctor of letters of the early 10th century, Ki no Haseo (845-912), author of a collection of poems and in competition with a colleague, Miyoshi no Kiyoyuki – more a prose-writer and author of biographies of worthy officials or eminent monks, as well as a project for the reform of the administration –, states that among the best Chinese writers, one should imitate those who devote themselves to poetry and place beauty above all else, and not those who cogitate on the classics.[13] For another doctor of the 10th century, Sugawara no Fumitoki (899-981):

"The *Anthology* is the foundation of the great work of the government of a country and the moralization of the people."[14]

In other words, a knowledge of this anthology containing poems and prose composed in China before the 6th century is deemed essential for those who govern.

Poetry and music are the tools of a good government and their prosperity attests to this. Which is why the literati never stopped repeating that the ruler must treat them honourably. Ōe no Masahira, in a preface to a collection of poems, writes:

> When the country is well governed, letters naturally flourish; as for music, it is the diversion of an enlightened reign. When the government is regulated, songs of praise resound on all sides. Ever since our ruler has watched over his people, scholar-officials have been in favour, and musician-officials have been well received.[15]

This is also why the great minister and master of the country, Fujiwara no Michinaga, was superior to his son and successor Yorimichi, not only because Japan was more peaceful in his time, but also because he encouraged a revival of poetic composition and participated in this himself through his Chinese and Japanese poems. For it was also said of these last-mentioned that they express what is hidden in a person's heart: joy, sadness, regret, and emotion in the presence of beauty. A further indication of the high status of music and poetry is that the only gifts suitable for a minister to offer the emperor were either a musical instrument – flute, lute or mouth organ – or scrolls or books of poems, preferably with fine calligraphy.

Imbued with these ideas and not wishing to be inferior to China, its model, the court reserved an important place in each ceremony for music and dance; at least from time to time, it endeavoured to have an entire formal banquet devoted to poetic composition in Chinese and, quite frequently, informal invitations to composition sessions, which were often accompanied by a prepared or improvised concert. One cannot deny, however, that justifications of high political morality were not always paramount and that, especially with music and dance, aesthetic pleasure came first.

With the establishment of the codal system, an Office of Music was set up to oversee the training and recruitment of musicians, singers and dancers, as well as to ensure the correct interpretation of the pieces and the organization of programmes suitable for each occasion. This Office had on its staff four singing teachers, four dance teachers, two flute teachers, a choir of thirty men and one of a hundred women, about a hundred dancers, eight flute players, and teachers and students for the performance of Chinese and Korean music, as well as for music classified as national. However, over time, various reorganizations took place. The staff of the Office was greatly reduced and extracodal agencies developed, like the Choir, whose role it was to perform the musical programme for the celebration of the First Fruits Festival and those for the shrine festivals, mainly so-called national music: pieces in honour of the deities or pieces of popular music from various provinces adopted and adapted by the court, called "stable-boy songs" (*saibara*).

The female dancers were attached to the Naikyōbō: under the overall direction of a senior noble, the officials in charge dealt with recruitments, rehearsals and the management of the costumes and accessories.

The Office of Music, for its part, was responsible for the performance of Chinese or "left" pieces and Korean or "right" pieces. An intendant, who was a senior noble, had his assistants recruit the musicians – instrumentalists and singers – as well as the dancers, conduct the rehearsals and see to the accessories for each celebration. They could thus call on every kind of talent. In fact, the sons of senior nobles learned music and dance at an early age and many officials were known for their mastery of one or other instrument. Officers – lower-ranking officers and men of the palace guard in particular – cultivated these arts and served as teachers to the young aristocrats. This more flexible organization, which no longer called on specialists whose sole function was to play an instrument, sing or dance, but on all those who had distinguished themselves by their talent, clearly reflects the taste and growing interest of the members of the court for music and dance. An important minister like Fujiwara no Michinaga could order performances too and he had the necessary costumes at his disposal. There were also costumes in some religious establishments, to which musicians were doubtless attached.

At each banquet, each shrine festival and each visit of an emperor to the residence of the chief minister, generally to see there a newborn child of his own, a programme of music and dance was performed, as in Buddhist temples on the occasion of major celebrations. For example, when Sanjō Tennō went to Michinaga's residence after the birth of his daughter Princess Teishi (1013-1094), he was able to enjoy the spectacle of horse races, boats filled with musicians moving around on the lake, and then, towards evening, writes this minister:

> The emperor took his seat. The senior nobles were called into his presence and received their meal trays. The musicians were summoned. While the great noblemen and courtiers performed several pieces, the musicians arrived in boats, playing their flutes. The sounds coming from the lake and those coming from the pavilion harmonized. After having thus played many pieces, the musicians approached the step. The emperor was served the second course of his meal. My household had prepared it: two small lacquer tables inlaid with mother-of-pearl and silver utensils. The clouds disappeared and the sky cleared. The moon was so pure and bright that members of the Palace Office removed the torches. The surface of the water glistened, very clear; the sound of the water cascading onto the sandy shore harmonized with the sound of the instruments.[16]

When dancers were especially skilful or touching, the senior nobles who were present at the entertainment removed one of their garments and gave it to them as a reward. The author of the *Eiga monogatari*, relating the banquet organized for the sixtieth birthday of Michinaga's wife Rinshi, describes a lower-ranking officer of the palace guard who was an excellent dancer and the teacher of one of the minister's grandsons, Kaneyori (1014-1063):

> Michinaga removed a cloak of light brocade and gave it to this young lord. Then his dance teacher, the captain of the palace guard Masakata, placed the garment on his shoulders and had the child continue dancing while increasing the tempo, to the point where the chancellor Lord Yorimichi got up and came to

the foot of the southern gallery of the eastern pavilion to remove his cloak, [...] he gave him a jacket that the dancer placed on his head, continuing to dance without letting fall the garments he had received. [...] The great noblemen, delighted at the spectacle, removed their garments, so that the dancer could no longer carry them on his shoulders: they then placed one upon the other at the spot where the young lord was dancing, so that beneath the trees there seemed to be piles of leaves of every colour; it was a charming sight. Masakata had received so many garments that he was quite overwhelmed.[17]

The costume, consisting of several layers of jackets under the cloak, made possible this generosity.

The ability to compose Chinese poetry was perhaps less widespread than that of playing an instrument or even dancing. In fact, Chinese poems by only a few senior nobles have been preserved. This exercise tended to be the specialty of doctors of letters and a certain number of former students. A famous literatus like the renowned Sugawara no Michizane sometimes composed in an individual way, more for himself, choosing his subject according to his inspiration at the time or the events that were occurring, and his poetry often has a very personal tone. He was thus able to compile an anthology of his poems, which he presented to the emperor. But the collected works of Ōe no Masahira consist almost exclusively of pieces composed on demand and no other individual anthology of this time has survived. So, for the majority of those who devoted themselves to Chinese poetry, it was a collective exercise and a kind of competition, organized either at the palace or at the residence of an important minister. We have few accounts of an exchange of Chinese poems between two individuals, whereas sending a Japanese poem as a letter and in order to elicit a response was commonplace. One of the rare examples known is perhaps not without political connotations, given the names of those involved. In 1004, at the end of autumn, Fujiwara no Kore-chika, the nephew whom Michinaga had removed from political affairs, sent him a poem about the deserted cell of a monk who had left for China. Michinaga replied and the emperor, having been informed of this exchange, in his turn sent a poem to his minister.[18] Korechika, for his part, had answered with a second poem. This time, Michinaga, touched by the emperor's interest, replied to him. Korechika was determined to show off a superior talent that everyone acknowledged: that of composing good Chinese verse. It could also happen that someone who had not been invited to a session of poetic composition or who had been unable to attend later sent a poem to the organizer. But generally speaking, people only composed on a set topic and in a group.

From 995 until 1011, when Michinaga was the most important personage at the court of Ichijō Tennō, around thirty-five sessions of poetic composition were held at the palace and nearly forty at Michinaga's residence. It is likely that the record kept for this period was more or less complete. From 1011 to 1016, during the brief reign of Sanjō Tennō, who, unlike his cousin Ichijō, does not appear to have composed poetry himself, there was no invitation to a session at the palace. But Michinaga made up for this deficiency and organized eighteen at his residence, a subtle way of showing everyone that he, at least, knew how to keep up the good traditions. Later, during the first years of the reign of Goichijō, when he was a child, the invitations became fewer: Yorimichi seems to have had neither the gift nor the taste for Chinese verse and the court no longer had a large number of good poets, as had been the case at the beginning of the century. Nevertheless, Goichijō Tennō and Gosuzaku Tennō seem to have wished to follow in the footsteps of their father Ichijō. In the time of Goichijō, around twelve gatherings were recorded at the palace, two at the residence of the crown prince, the future Gosuzaku. Yorimichi, for his part, did not completely ignore his father's example and invited literati on eight occasions.

There were two types of gathering: the formal ones requiring lengthy preparations and the others, more numerous, usually convened in the 3rd, 7th or 9th months, namely when the cherry trees come into bloom, at the start of the cooler weather, when people watch the sky, the Milky Way is shining and the union of the Weaver and Cowherd stars is anticipated, and at the time when the chrysanthemums bloom and the maple leaves turn red. Thus Michinaga and Yorimichi sometimes issued invitations to compose verse on the occasion of an excursion into the country-side, especially in autumn. When guests travelled to the Uji villa, they began composing during the boat trip on the Uji River.[19] Another excursion was for maple viewing, on the Ōi River to the west of Kyōto: boats moved along the river and participants were reminded of an invitation from the retired Enyū Tennō in the autumn of 986. The guests, according to their particular talents, were grouped in three boats: one for the musicians, one for those composing Chinese poems and one for those composing Japanese poetry; everyone composed on the topic "Reflection of red leaves on limpid water". An anecdote praising Fujiwara no Kintō relates that he managed to climb into each boat, one after the other.[20] On the nights called *Kōshin*, that is, of the day determined by the signs "Senior of Metal and Monkey", it was advisable not to fall asleep, for, according to Chinese beliefs adopted by the Heian nobility, on this night the worms that live in the body go and divulge the secrets of each man to the celestial ruler. To prevent their departure and the risk of seeing one's life cut short, a vigil was organized at which verse was composed and music was played. No doubt in order to show even more clearly the interest taken by the court in the formation of capable literati, the competitive recruitment examination for students of letters was sometimes held in conjunction with a formal court session. But the candidates composed on a different topic and were not seated in the same place as the emperor, important personages and accredited literati. The most usual form, and the one used in the composition sessions, was the poem in two quatrains with lines of seven characters.

Once the time allowed for composition had elapsed, the poems were collected and a literatus was asked to read them aloud, often at dawn, by torchlight. Each poem had to strictly conform to the rules of Chinese prosody, based on the tones and their arrangement in each line and each quatrain, as well as on the rhyme. There were many prosody manuals and collections of examples. However the Japanese read the poems in the Japanese manner, by transposing from one language into the other, which nullified all the effort made to adhere to the rules.

Whether the session was formal or less formal, one of the literati present was asked to write a preface to the collection resulting from the poems of the participants. Here he set out the circumstances, described the setting and time of year, and used the opportunity to praise either the emperor or the minister who had issued the invitation. For him it was a chance to show off his ability to construct elegant sentences and to display his knowledge of Chinese literature. The praise, therefore, was never direct, but expressed through an allusion to an event or a personage of Chinese antiquity, to which the emperor or the minister was implicitly compared. Thus Ōe no Masahira, invited in the 5th month of 999 to Michinaga's residence, writes:

> Our host has cast a hook into the Iyo River, he has cultivated the paulownia where the phoenix comes to nest and is now a great minister.[21]

Casting a hook into the Iyo River calls to mind a Chinese emperor who, meeting an old man fishing and being at once impressed by his worth, took him into his service. The paulownia is the image of the great minister and the phoenix that of the emperor.

The topics proposed in the sessions at the court mostly called for the description of a landscape in keeping with the season, which at the same time praised the sovereign or the minister. In fact, it was believed that if the government was benevolent, the seasons would quite naturally follow one another as normal, and snow, rain, fine weather, blooming of flowers or reddening of leaves would occur in their season. As the literatus who composed a preface on the occasion of an excursion to Uji organized by Michinaga in 1004 says:

> Poetry expresses what is in the heart, it shows the way to those who govern. From the wonders offered by nature – fish,

insects, grasses, trees – poetry makes a choice and makes visible the beauties of the universe.[22]

The topics proposed were thus seldom original: for example, in spring, "Pond, when the spring flowers come into bloom", or "Dance of fallen flowers on the water"; in autumn, "Chrysanthemum, flower of the 9th day", or "The wind rises and the leaves that have died under the frost fall", or again "Autumn flies like a swift torrent". Often, they were drawn from a line of a Chinese poet. In order to compose on the topic, it was necessary to have the appropriate quotations in one's memory. But the participants were not caught out; as the dates of the sessions were announced in advance, they could guess the topic and be ready to compose on it. It even seems that it was often known beforehand, notwithstanding the protocol that gave the emperor the final choice at the beginning of the session. Michinaga, on a topic proposed early in April 1006, "Boat laden with fallen flowers",[23] in eight lines alludes to the celebrated *Peach Blossom Spring*,[24] a way of evoking a marvellous country where happiness reigns, to a line of the poet Bo Juyi (772-846) calling to mind a famous landscape in China, to a Chinese minister who, having had a very successful career, preferred to leave his post rather than risk the displeasure of his prince, and to a literatus without office intoxicated by the beauties of nature. All of which goes to show that the description of the beauties of the natural world expected of the participants at a poetry session did not need to be inspired by what was before their eyes. What was expected of them was to have in their memories the most amusing, touching and ingenious allusions and quotations and be able to skilfully interweave them. It was therefore an exercise reserved for the few people who were capable of recognizing behind each expression the many and varied shades of meaning that it drew from the different contexts in which it had been used by the Chinese poets. This learned poetry sometimes spilled over into excessive artifice. Hence candidates presenting as students of letters were often required to include in each line of their composition either a character from the name of a Chinese literatus mentioned in the *History of the Former Han Dynasty*, or a character from the title of a section of *The Book of Rites*.[25]

This poetry, which was so artificial, and even pedantic, nonetheless made it possible to express feelings – these also being very conventional for the most part – such as modesty, gratitude and the joy of living under an enlightened reign. The two allusions to prominent figures in Chinese antiquity from the brush of Michinaga in the poem referred to earlier can be nothing more than affectation, a way of showing a kind of detachment with regard to his successes. On rare occasions, a more personal note was evident. One day, when Michinaga was receiving Korechika, the nephew he had ousted, the topic "The flowers are falling and spring is departing" was proposed to the guests. Korechika's poem drew tears from those who heard it. It reads:

> Spring is slipping quickly away, short-lived; regrets cannot be stifled. The flowers fall and scatter.

The Chinese character used for 'scatter' has another meaning, 'slander', of which Korechika could count himself a victim. Further on he writes:

> Exhausted branch, oppressive peaks, the fog dulls the colours. Brittle glory, in the peaceful valley, the bird hides its song.[26]

The branch is Korechika, crushed by Michinaga's glory. The bird is the infant imperial prince Atsuyasu, nephew of Korechika, and his last hope at a time when the imperial princes Atsunari and Atsuyoshi, grandsons of Michinaga, are still unborn. In the quatrain composed on the occasion of the first reading lesson of Prince Atsuyasu, Michinaga uses a Chinese term in referring to him – one of the many synonyms permitted in poetry for the word 'prince', son of an emperor. In fact, this term was used in China for a prince who had been moved aside from the throne, even though he had hoped to rule. When this poem was read, the emperor and those taking part in the ceremony were left in no doubt that Michinaga would not allow

Atsuyasu to be named crown prince.[27] But cases of poems having real meaning are few and far between and, in this output, it is skill and memory that are admired above all.

Composition in Chinese was in a way a matter of State. It was practised by male officials. On the other hand, men and women composed in Japanese poems of five lines of five, seven, five, seven and seven syllables. This was the usual way of corresponding, when giving a gift or asking after someone, when a person had left the capital, to keep in touch with a friend, when offering a compliment or presenting condolences. At various times of the year, a poem was written to comment on the weather and seasonal symbols. Men and women expressed in them their loves, their regrets and their grievances. In Michinaga's time, at the end of the banquets organized to celebrate a birth, an appointment, a promotion or a birthday, the participants composed poems and often the guests sang the best of them in chorus. At the banquet organized to celebrate the elevation of his third daughter Ishi to the rank of empress, Michinaga wrote:

> Yes, this time is indeed my time, when I can think that nothing will cause the waning of the full moon.

He then asked Fujiwara no Sanesuke to compose a reply. However Sanesuke declined, saying the poem was of such excellence that it discouraged any response.[28] This excessive praise was perhaps an indirect criticism. Be that as it may, the gathering sang Michinaga's poem in chorus several more times.

Excursions in each season were also an opportunity to sing poems, as were Buddhist celebrations: Michinaga, in his fervent devotion for the *Lotus Sūtra* (*Hokekyō*), inaugurated a celebration of this *sūtra* that lasted a whole month. Some sessions included a banquet during which the participants were invited to compose poems on different parts of the *sūtra*.

Composing a poem always meant submitting oneself to the judgement of the person to whom it was addressed or a group. But certain gatherings also took the form of competitions. From the early 10th century, it had become the custom to organize contests of Japanese poems. Two sides made up of men and women were formed, one of the left and one of the right, a topic was given to each pair, or a general topic, each person having to compose their poem on the spot. The poems were read and an umpire decided which was the best and gave the reasons for his decision. In the time of Kazan Tennō (r. 984-986), some of these contests, *uta-awase*, took place at the palace. However, when they were in charge of the government, neither Fujiwara no Kaneie, nor his sons Michitaka and Michinaga held any at the court. They came back into favour in the mid-11th century and Yorimichi organized several very well known ones.

Japanese verse was far more closely associated with the everyday life of the aristocracy than Chinese verse and was used in many circumstances, more often private than public. Nevertheless, the court believed that it had a duty to patronize it and supported the compilation of anthologies considered as official works; the fourth, *Goshūi wakashū* (*Later Collection of Gleanings*), was presented to the emperor in 1086 and many others were to follow.

The custom of organizing competitions extended to objects other than poems. Often, on the occasion of a poetry contest, there was a request either for chrysanthemums, as far as possible in superbly decorated pots, or for trays containing miniature landscapes, embellished with plants and animals, such as the pine tree (symbol of endurance), the crane (symbol of good fortune) and the tortoise (symbol of longevity). There were other types of competition, such as fragrances or paintings or unusual objects. The collection of anecdotes *Tales of Times Now Past*[29] relates an amusing story in which the two sections of the palace guard were to present in this way something they had come across by chance. While a large crowd waited at the guard's racecourse in the presence of the chancellor Yorimichi, the champion of the left side arrived, superbly attired, mounted on a magnificent horse. The right side then brought out its champion, a wretched-looking old man dressed in rags, riding on a cow: a spectacle that provoked general hilarity.

Respect for ceremonial and a sense of hierarchies were required of officials in order for them to diligently perform the annual cycle of celebrations. Fear of making mistakes and fear of the judgement of others caused them stress and anxiety. Yet the members of the court sometimes gave themselves a little relaxation, spent sleepless nights in conversation and appreciated witty remarks, many of which are preserved in collections of anecdotes, not counting more unbridled diversions. They also took notice of and appreciated the beauty of the setting in which they lived and worked.

Notes

1. *Ononomiya nenjūgyōji*, the annual cycle drawn up by Sanesuke, who frequently mentions his grandfather Saneyori, known as the Lord of Ononomiya. *Kujō nenjūgyōji*, the annual cycle established by Morosuke, called the Lord of Kujō, from the name of his residence.
2. Disturbances of the Anna era, 969, caused not only by the wish to eliminate a Minamoto, Takaakira, who had married his daughter to a potential crown prince, but also no doubt by internal Fujiwara rivalries.
3. Opinions requested from the literati regarding the efficacy of the names of the palace gates: *Nihon sandai jitsuroku*, Jōgan 13.10.21., 871, and *Gonki*, the journal of Fujiwara no Yukinari, Chōhō 4.3.19., 1002.
4. *Honchō monzui*, chap. 7, letter to Yukinari of Chōhō 3.3.3., 1001, and *Chōya gunsai* (*Writings of the Court and Provinces*), chap. 3, text dated Chōtoku 4.12.9., 998.
5. *Honchō monzui*, chap. 2, text 24, *Iken jūnikajō* (*Opinions on Twelve Matters*), the response of Miyoshi no Kiyoyuki to the court, which had requested that it be presented with plans for reform.
6. *Shōyūki*, Kannin 1st year, *passim*. It was, in fact, essential to determine the most auspicious date and order preliminary celebrations to ensure the success of the pilgrimage; hence consultation to decide what kind of celebration, by whom and on which date to prepare the palanquin, have the shrines repaired,

name the men for the escort, the dancers and musicians and have them rehearse, sew their costumes, have the roads cleaned up, find the necessary funds, and decide how to reward the deities and their priests. All this work was completed with a great many consultations and investigations into precedents.

7. *Midō kanpakuki*, the journal of Fujiwara no Michinaga, Chōwa 2.8.7., 1013. Strike by graduates of the classics, who should have taken part in the disputation, in protest at the negligence of the senior nobles who did not issue the orders needed to enable them to obtain their graduation diploma.

8. *Konjaku monogatarishū*, chap. 28, anec. 4, "What happened to the governor of Owari in the rehearsal room for the dances of the First Fruits Festival". An elderly and deserving official, unfamiliar with palace customs and unaware that a kind of carnival takes place at the time of the festival, is astonished and panic-stricken when some young, facetious courtiers make him believe that all this uproar is intended to make him look foolish.

9. *Shunki*, Chōryaku 3.11.25., 1039. On several occasions, Sukefusa mentions this inclination of certain young courtiers for young men brought up in temples.

10. *Shōyūki*, Chōwa 2.7.29., 1013. Brawl in the emperor's presence, jostling, blows with sticks, shouting. Sanesuke, general of the right section of the palace guard, thinks the emperor's decision to award victory to the left side in an indecisive bout is unfair.

11. *Gōrihōshū* (*Anthology of the Ministry of Ceremonial's Official Ōe*), for the collection of Chinese poems composed at the palace in 999, Chōhō 1.9.30., with a preface by Masahira.

12. *Honchō monzui*, chap. 11, preface to the poems on the twenty-eight sections of the *Lotus Sūtra*. Arikuni in fact paraphrases the preface of *The Book of Odes*.

13. *Honchō monzui*, chap. 8, by Ki no Haseo, "Preface to the collection of poems I have composed since the Engi era".

14. *Honchō monzui*, chap. 9, text 6, preface composed by Fumitoki on the occasion of a banquet and a session of poetic composition organized to celebrate the end of a series of lectures on the *Anthology* at the court.

15. *Honchō monzui*, chap. 8, preface to the collection of poems composed in Chōhō 1.6.9., 999, on the topic "Refreshing oneself by turning towards a landscape of water and rocks", on the occasion of an all-night vigil at the palace for the day of *Kōshin*.

16. *Midō kanpakuki*, Chōwa 2.9.16., 1013, and *Eiga monogatari*, chap. 11.

17. *Eiga monogatari*, chap. 20. This celebration took place in 1023. Ō no Masakata (?-1045) was one of the most skilful dancers of the palace guard, in which he spent all his working life. His reputation as a dancer was so great that in 1040 he was given a minor provincial governorship. Already, *Midō kanpakuki*, Kankō 2.1.2., 1005, at a banquet at Michinaga's residence, the ministers and important personages had divested themselves of a garment to reward him.

18. *Midō kanpakuki*, Kankō 1.9. intercalary days 23. and 26., 1004. Korechika had a maternal grandfather reputed to be a good scholar.

19. *Midō kanpakuki*, Kankō 1.9. intercalary day 21., 1004. Michinaga's guests, in boats, composed "linked" poems, each one contributing a line. In the evening, at the villa, they composed on the topic "The landscape around the Uji villa".

20. Collection of anecdotes, *Kojidan* (*Remarks on Past Matters*), chap. 1, anec. 16; the event took place in Kanna 2.10.14., 986.

21. *Honchō monzui*, chap. 8, preface to the collection composed in Chōhō 1.5.7., 999. Invitation by Michinaga to his Higashi Sanjō residence. The best literati of the day were present. The topic proposed was "The thousand delights of a landscape of trees and water". The participants then played the game of "hidden rhymes".

22. *Honchō monzui*, chap. 9, text 37. On the occasion of the country outing at Uji in 1004, Ōe no Mochitoki (955-1010), a rival literatus of Ōe no Masahira was asked to write the preface for the evening's compositions.

23. *Honchō reisō* (*Outstanding Poems from Our Country*), an anthology of verse from the late 10th and early 11th century, chap. 1, No. 5. After a fire at the palace, the emperor had just spent several months at Michinaga's Higashi Sanjō residence. When he left in April 1006, Kankō 3.3.4., Michinaga organized a banquet with poetic composition.

24. *Tōkagenki* (Ch. *Taohua yuanji*), a short prose text by Tō Enmei (Ch. Tao Yuanming, 365-427), the epitome of the poor scholar who has retired to the countryside. In it he writes of a marvellous country inhabited by wise and welcoming people. Bo Juyi (J.

Haku Kyoi) was the Tang poet most admired in Japan during the Heian period.

25. *Gōrihōshū*, an examination poem by Ōe no Masahira, and *Hyakurenshō* (*Notes One Hundred Times Polished*), annals in *kanbun*, Chōkyū 4.9.9., 1043.

26. *Midō kanpakuki*, Kankō 2.3.29., 1005, and *Honchō reisō*. The session had begun with an archery contest.

27. *Honchō reisō*, No. 107; *Shōyūki*, Kankō 2.11.13. and 14., 1005. The emperor secretly attended the gathering, which took place in the pavilion of the palace where the empress Shōshi, stepmother of the young prince, resided. The topic proposed was "The first-born prince, on a winter's day, reads for the first time *The Classic of Filial Piety*".

28. *Shōyūki*, Kannin 2.10.16., 1018. When his third daughter, like the two older ones, was elevated to the rank of empress, Michinaga had the impression of having reached the pinnacle of all honours and he celebrated the event with a banquet organized at the Tsuchimikado residence.

29. *Konjaku monogatarishū*, chap. 28, anec. 35, "Object-guessing contest organized by the courtiers at the racecourse of the palace guard, section of the right".

CHAPTER 3

LIVING ENVIRONMENT OF
THE ARISTOCRACY

Formalism and spatial organization in the capital

The capital, Heiankyō, was established in 794 to house the palace and central administration buildings, as well as the residences of the nobility. Everything here was organized so as to make visible the social order, which was a reflection of the world order.

The first Japanese cities, the successive capitals Fujiwara-kyō, at the end of the 7th century, Heijōkyō or Nara, in the 8th century, and Heiankyō, the City of Peace and Tranquillity, also called Kyōto, the Capital or the City, were all created on the model of the Chinese capitals. They grew out of a political imperative, that of establishing a centre for the country that could house the palace, bureaux and officials in a spacious and stately manner, arousing the respect and admiration of the inhabitants of the country and foreign visitors. For, in the first two centuries of the "codal system", delegations from China or the Korean peninsula still came as far as the capital. However, from the 10th century, there were no longer official relations with neighbouring countries and Chinese, more rarely Korean, merchants were not given permission to leave the coastal areas. They were normally confined to the Government Headquarters in Kyūshū, the Dazaifu, near present-day Fukuoka, to which the court sent a trade mission or else instructed the governor-general to obtain for it the Chinese products it desired.

The choice of location was determined by various requirements, some purely geographical, and the others concerning the possibilities of the site indicated by geomancy. Heiankyō extended over a plain surrounded to the east, north and west by hills well suited to the building of temples, and bounded by rivers – the Kamo to the east and the Katsura to the west – that could provide water and places for purifications. Access to the sea was better than at Nara. By means of the Yodo River, Kyōto could access the port of Naniwa (in the western part of present-day Ōsaka), which received the products from the provinces bordering on the Inland Sea: rice, salt and fish. One river port was established south of the capital, at the junction of the Yodo and Uji rivers, and a second, a little farther north, at the junction of the Katsura and Kamo rivers. Here were stored, on the one hand, the products from the taxes of the western and southern regions and, on the other, the construction wood transported along the Uji River from the densely forested areas located to the south-east of Lake Biwa.

Heiankyō, a city planned as a coherent whole, was laid out in the form of a chessboard. It extended just over five kilometres from north to south and over four and a half kilometres from east to west. It was divided into two equal sections, left or east and right or west, by an imposing central avenue, called Red Bird (symbol of the south), Suzaku, about ninety-five metres wide. Unlike the Chinese capitals, Heiankyō does not seem to have been surrounded by a mud-brick wall. Yet Red Bird Avenue opened to the south with a massive gate, called Rashōmon, from a Chinese term meaning Enclosure Gate. This gate, built on a platform, had one storey and extended over seven bays. The pillars were painted red, contrasting with the white of the mud-brick walls. From the early 11th century, it was no longer maintained and the collection of anecdotes from the early 12th century, *Tales of Times Now Past*,[1] mentions the corpses that were piled up here. Each section was divided into districts about five hundred and twenty-two and a half metres along one side, each of them subdivided into sixteen blocks nearly one hundred and nineteen metres along one side. Districts and blocks were bounded by a network of avenues, thirty-five and a half metres or just under twenty-four metres wide delimiting the districts, and by streets nearly twelve metres wide between the blocks. Parallel to Red Bird Avenue, in the north-south direction, were six avenues and ten streets for each section, as the two districts closest to the central avenue were bisected by an avenue and not by a street. In the east-west direction, there were thirteen avenues and twenty-six streets. From the Ninth Avenue, at the southernmost end of the city, to the Second Avenue, these avenues ran alongside the district boundaries, but, between the Second and First Avenues, which formed the northern boundary of the city, were four avenues starting at the palace gates and named after these gates, *mikado*: Tsuchimikado ōji (Mud-brick Gate), Konoemikado ōji (Palace Guard Gate), Nakamikado ōji (Middle Gate) and Ōimikado ōji (gate near the Grains Office).

The extensive group of buildings formed by the palace – administrative complex and inner palace – was situated at the far end of Red Bird Avenue and occupied two districts in the east-west direction and two and a half in the north-south direction: a little over a thousand metres in one direction by thirteen hundred in the other. The city had nine and a half districts from north to south and eight from east to west: a total of thirty-four districts and five hundred and forty-four blocks for each section. It was bounded to the south by the Ninth Avenue, to the north by the First Avenue, to the east by Higashi Kyōgoku ōji and to the west by Nishi Kyōgoku ōji.

Each section had a separate administration controlled by a prefect, who was often a senior noble or a son of a high official. However, in the 11th century, it was an almost meaningless function. According to the regulations promulgated in the early 10th century, the role of the City administration was to keep the civil registers, maintain order and keep the public roads in good repair. But, in reality, the Police Bureau and its auxiliaries had a far more important role in these areas (except for the civil registers). Each district and each block was administered by heads appointed by the central administration. In the 11th century, however, this was no longer the case and one finds reference only to municipal officers called *tone*, often appointed by the Police Bureau and whose duty it was to oversee their block. They mostly appear in connection with the certification of land transactions. In fact, the presence of a sizeable number of large aristocratic residences, some occupying one or more blocks, made the work of the municipal officers, and even that of the Police Bureau, extremely difficult, because the important personages were very reluctant to accept the intrusion of low-ranking officials from the City administration or Police Bureau onto their property.

To the east and west of the central avenue, straddling the first and second districts in the east-west direction and the second and third districts in the north-south direction, were the east and west markets where, originally, fifty-one stalls in the east and thirty-three in the west had been set up. But the western market did not survive. These markets were dependent on the City administration. Officials and guards were attached to them; their task was to check the quality of the products offered for sale as well as cloth measurements, and to regulate prices.

The large and medium-sized residences had gardens and the entire city area was by no means covered with buildings: vegetable gardens and even rice fields continued to exist in the capital. Yet, in this city built for the administration and the court, there was no square or other area where the populace could gather. The market seems to have been the only place where people met. It was here that criminals arrested and sentenced by the Police Bureau were chained and flogged, a spectacle that each year in winter drew many commoners, but that some aristocrats were not too proud to watch, carefully concealed in their carriages. It is said that even Kazan Tennō was curious enough to want to see it.[2] It was also at the market that popular preachers were active. But during the 11th century, other stalls appeared elsewhere in the city.

On either side of the central avenue, in the south, not far from the Rashō Gate, two hostels had originally been built for foreign embassies, where the envoys from Parhae (a country located in the northern part of the Korean peninsula) often stayed in the 9th century. However, once foreigners were no longer admitted to the capital, these buildings had fallen into disrepair, and the land belonging to the eastern hostel had been given to the Office of Medicine, which had planted a herb garden there.

The religious establishments, Buddhist temples or Shintō shrines, very spacious enclosures dotted with chapels, could serve as meeting places and the inhabitants of the capital went there in droves during celebrations. The monthly festival of the Kiyomizudera drew large crowds and thieves were everywhere. But with the exception of the Tōji, "Eastern temple", and the Saiji, "Western temple", situated east and west of the Rashō Gate, at the southernmost end of the city, no religious establishment was permitted inside the city perimeter. They were scattered all around it in the hills or on the plain to the south. Some, like (to the east) the Hōjōji, the splendid temple founded by Fujiwara no Michinaga, or the Hōkōin, founded by Fujiwara no Kaneie, were built between the eastern boundary and the Kamo River. Others were farther away, such as (to the northeast) the holy mountain of Hieizan, called the Mountain, very auspiciously situated in a direction considered to be ill-omened, which enabled it to block evil influences. Rising to a height of eight hundred and forty-eight metres, the Mountain was dotted with smaller and larger temples organized into three groups. It was the headquarters of the Tendai sect, which had its ordination platform here. To the west, the Takaodera was associated with the memory of the founder of the Shingon sect, Kūkai. To the south-east, the Kiyomizudera had been founded in the early 9th century. In the 11th century, there existed around the capital a very large number of Buddhist temples, including (to the west) the Ninnaji founded by Uda Tennō, who had lived in retirement here. In the capital itself, there were private chapels in the great aristocratic residences. Moreover, many monks flouted the rule that forbad them to live in the capital. It seems that some moved into what they euphemistically referred to as carriage houses.[3] These dwellings could thus be used to set up unauthorized places of worship.

A number of large Shintō shrines were also located at various points around the city, some having existed before its foundation: to the north, the two Kamo shrines, upper and

lower, which the court so venerated that it assigned to their
service an imperial princess, just as at Ise; to the south-east was
the shrine of Inari, and to the west that of Matsunoo. Others
were established after the foundation of Heiankyō: to the north-
west Hirano, to the west Umenomiya, to the south-west
Ōharano, where the Fujiwara empresses worshipped their
family deities of Kasuga, to the south Iwashimizu, both a shrine
and a temple, where the emperors had installed the deities of
Usa in Kyūshū, and in the hills to the east the mixed establishment known by the name of Kanjin-in, where already in the
Heian period the very popular celebration later known as the
Gion festival took place. In the 10th century, directly north of
the palace, the Kitano Shrine was dedicated to the spirit of
Sugawara no Michizane, the minister who had died in exile in
903, because a fire at the palace had been attributed to his angry
spirit. All these shrines and temples protected the capital. They
drew a large crowd, both aristocrats and commoners, on the
occasion of their festivals. They also provided places for
excursions to admire nature in the different seasons, as well as
places at which to spend a few days, like the Kiyomizudera,
where Fujiwara no Michinaga received a poem from Kazan
Tennō, sent one to the lady Sei Shōnagon (966?-1017?) who
was staying there, and composed a Chinese poem in the autumn
of 1004:

> Kiyomizudera high up in the heart of the eastern hills; here for
> a time, far from this base world, I am hidden in this rustic
> temple ...[4]

The population of the capital is estimated at around one
hundred thousand people: senior nobles, the most powerful of
whom could have about a hundred servants; middle-ranking
officials, who, while they were between appointments, could
retain only a skeleton staff, three or four people at most; and
also domestic servants and members of the court workshops.
But the floating population seems to have been quite large. The
provincial governors left behind in their province, sometimes
for one or two years, part of the ancillary staff they had

recruited in the capital, and brought to Heiankyō men of the province to do work on their residences and transport products to them. In either case, the length of stay varied and could be quite protracted. Several lists of convicted people, from the late 10th century, preserved by chance because they were written on the back of another document, show that many of them were from the provinces, and had no doubt come in the hope of being able to make easy pickings and to join the gangs in the capital.

All types of houses existed side by side. However laws had been enacted in the 8th century regarding the area of land permitted for the residences of officials of different ranks. Men of the first three ranks, namely the senior nobles and those of equivalent status, could own a block, or a little over one hectare. Middle-ranking officials, of the fourth and fifth ranks, namely men considered part of the aristocracy, were entitled to half a block. Minor officials, from the sixth rank down, had to be satisfied, at most, with a quarter of a block, and common people with even less. In the 11th century, these rules were flouted, but they were not forgotten, as is shown by a document dating from 1030,[5] which prohibits provincial governors from owning a residence occupying a block, something that appears to have become quite usual at the time, given the opportunities for them to grow rich through their role as tax farmers. They were reminded that they were entitled to only a quarter of a block, if they belonged to the sixth rank, and furthermore that anyone below this rank was not permitted to enclose his house with a mud-brick fence (quickset hedges were allowed) and to roof it with cypress bark. Even in the early 12th century, one can read in the journal (*Chūyūki*) of Fujiwara no Munetada (1062-1141) announcing the installation of a major counsellor of the second rank in a new residence that this is in conformity with the law and occupies one block.[6]

Had the rules been followed to the letter, in the early 11th century there would have been about twenty-five residences the size of one block, but not so well-off senior nobles of the third rank had to be satisfied with more modest houses and some provincial governors had organized splendid residences in which to receive a young senior noble as a son-in-law. There were usually only around a hundred individuals of the fourth and fifth ranks, and thus about a hundred residences occupying half a block. However, many men holding these ranks no doubt made do with less land.

Over time, the capital had developed in an uneven way. From the late 10th century, the western section gradually fell into decay and the city tended to spread eastwards, a trend that continued in the medieval period. As the scholar-official Yoshishige no Yasutane (?-1002) writes at the end of the 10th century in his celebrated *Chiteiki* (*Notes from the Pavilion by the Pond*):

> For more than twenty years I have been observing everything in both sections of the capital. In the west, there are fewer and fewer houses; it has almost become a field of ruins. People are fleeing these areas [...]. Those who accumulate wealth and those who wish to play a part in affairs cannot live there even for a single day.[7]

The last grand mansion built there, Nishinomiya, was that of the minister Minamoto no Takaakira. He had the misfortune to be disgraced and exiled, and this fine residence disappeared.

The most sought after area was situated east of the palace between the First and Third Avenues and between Higashi Kyōgoku ōji and Ōmiya ōji that ran alongside the palace. It was here that Fujiwara no Michinaga owned the residences of Tsuchimikado, set on two blocks at the edge of the city, with its annexe Takatsukasa covering one block, Takakura and Biwa, each occupying one block, and Higashi Sanjō, covering two blocks, rebuilt by Kaneie and henceforth the official residence of the head of the Fujiwara family. His son Yorimichi added to these properties the Kaya residence, much larger still, since it extended over four blocks. In Michinaga's time, the minister of the right Fujiwara no Akimitsu lived at Horikawa and the third minister Fujiwara no Kinsue at the Kan-in, each therefore owning two blocks. This concentration of grand residences led to an increase in the price of land, driving the minor and middle-ranking officials from the area, either because they were unable to purchase sufficient land there on which to build, or because they were forced to sell. "How many small houses have been taken over, how many people of slender means are discontented", says Yasutane. He himself had only been able to build his house in the vicinity of the Sixth Avenue.

In 998, the Ichijō residence, occupying one block near the palace north of the capital, had been sold by the daughter of the former prime minister Fujiwara no Tamemitsu (942-992) for eight thousand bushels of rice to a provincial governor, Saeki no Kinyuki (?-?),[8] who immediately transferred it to the mother of Ichijō Tennō. (It is not known whether he received something in return: an appointment, or a valuable object?) In the capital, a block of land of about five hundred square metres with a house on it cost around six hundred bushels of rice. This may be compared with a price of one hundred and eighty bushels for about one hectare – an area twenty times larger – of rice fields in the countryside.[9] In fact, the construction and upkeep of these very spacious residences, built of wood and often destroyed by fire (not always accidental but sometimes expressions of opposition), was a heavier burden than the price of the land.

The palace was encircled by high mud-brick walls pierced by fourteen gates: three each in the north and south and four each in the east and west. At the Nara palace, it seems that the gates often had the names of those responsible for guard duties, but at the Heian palace the gates were given names believed to be efficacious, since what they signified had to be realized in concrete terms, whether it be Ankamon, Gate of Peace and Happiness, or Taikenmon, Gate of the Reception of Wisdom. The characters and their meanings were drawn from the Chinese classics, but care was taken not to exactly copy the names of the Chinese palaces from the Tang era. Nonetheless, the gates on the eastern side were mostly referred to by simpler terms: Grains Office Gate (Ōimikado) because it was near this bureau; Middle Gate (Nakamikado); Palace Guard Gate (Konoemikado) because its guard post was located nearby; and

Extra Mud-brick Gate (Tsuchimikado), which never had a more exalted name. The belief in the influence of names is expressed in a decision by the senior nobles in 1002, taken after a series of fires. They asked themselves whether the fact that on the north side of the palace in Japan there was no gate or building called "Black Warrior", as was the case in China, was not the cause of the fires. For the use of this name made it possible to obtain "the help of the Black Warrior's virtue so that he could support the Red Bird's grandeur".

In Japan as in China, Suzakumon was the name of the gate situated at the centre of the south side of the palace, but the corresponding gate on the north side was called Ikanmon, Gate of Excellent Vigilance. When asked for their opinion, the members of the way of Yin and Yang were unable to give a clear response to the question put by the senior nobles.[10]

These gates were quite imposing structures: Red Bird Gate was erected on a stone base, surmounted by one storey, and had seven bays. Most other gates had only five. Only three gates had no steps, enabling free access: two in the east, the Grains Office Gate and Middle Gate, as well as one in the west, Dantenmon, Gate of Heavenly Will. They allowed ox-drawn carriages or heavy materials to pass through. For no-one was permitted to enter the palace in a carriage. Those who were granted the privilege of riding – the regent, ministers or very eminent monks – changed their carriage at the entrance to the palace, at the Middle Gate, and entered in a lighter conveyance pulled by men and not by oxen. The crown prince and imperial consorts could proceed as far as the outer wall of the inner palace. Above these gates was a panel bearing their name, commissioned from the best calligraphers.

Within this outer wall, besides the inner palace and south-west of it, were two courtyards. The first, called Hasshōin, Court of the Eight Departments, formed a very elongated rectangle in the north-south direction. It was surrounded by mud-brick walls pierced by gates, four of them very imposing structures and twelve others less ornate. The south gate, Ōten-mon, Gate of Heavenly Obedience, was directly opposite Red

Bird Gate. The first courtyard had two large buildings, which in the Nara period were used to convene officials, in particular those from the provinces who were called to the capital at regular intervals to give an account of their stewardship and receive instructions: activities that are no longer mentioned in the 10th century. A second courtyard north of the first had twelve large halls, leaving in the centre a very large open space. To the north stood the Great Hall of State, Daigokuden (where the imperial virtue was displayed), flanked at the rear by a small pavilion (Koadono), where the emperor could rest before going to the Court of the Eight Departments. Behind it was the gate aligned with the Gate of Heavenly Obedience, namely the Gate of Light and Good Fortune, Shōkeimon, through which the emperor's palanquin passed when he went to the Hasshōin. Names of pavilions and gates were copied in part from those of the Tang palaces. Terms expressing the notions of sun, spring and Yang were always attributed to the buildings facing east, while the buildings with names relating to autumn, duration and Yin always faced west. Three main categories of ideas were used: brightness and light, happiness and good fortune, duration and persistence, namely everything that the imperial virtue, which was displayed in the Great Hall of State, for a long time the scene of the emperor's public life, was supposed to spread throughout the country. But in the 11th century, the emperor seldom came here, except for the departure of the Vestal-princess of Ise, his enthronement and, the following autumn, the celebration of the First Fruits Festival, which, for the start of a reign, took on an especially solemn character. The courtyard was mainly used for Buddhist celebrations that brought together a large number of monks. Nevertheless, large buildings were always kept in good repair, as if, in spite of the narrowing down of the activities of the court to the inner palace, long the scene of the private life, so to speak, of the emperor (if indeed the term "private" can be applied to the emperor, since at that time he was often designated by the term *kokka*, which in the modern period took on the meaning of "State"), there was a strong desire to preserve this place from where the emperor, whose throne was precisely on the axis of Red Bird Avenue, looked out over the capital and the country and from where his beneficent influence shone out upon them.

Parallel to this courtyard was the one called Burakuin, Court of Abundance and Pleasures. An enclosure pierced by ten gates was occupied by four long pavilions extending from north to south, facing each other in pairs. Whenever he went there, the emperor seated himself in the Burakuden, Pavilion of Abundance and Pleasures, situated to the north and facing south. This place had been set up for the court banquets. But in the early 11th century, the only time it is known to have been used was for the banquets that followed the celebration of the Great Thanksgiving at the start of a reign.

To the west of the inner palace, a wide open space had been provided, overlooked from the west by the small Butokuden, Pavilion of Military Virtue, where in the 9th century the emperor attended the mounted archery contests on the 5th day of the 5th month, a celebration that was no longer held from the late 10th century. To the south-east of this space was a Buddhist chapel (Shingon-in), which could not possibly be situated in the inner palace where the sacred objects of the dynasty were housed. The space extending along the north wall of the palace was occupied by the agencies responsible for storing government property: the Department of the Treasury, the Office of Palace Storehouses and their annexes, or by the agencies staffed by female officials, such as the Sewing Office (Nuidonoryō). On the east and west façades around the palace guard gates, the space was reserved for the palace guards and military guards who had bureaux and exercise yards there. East of the Court of the Eight Departments, and west and south of the Court of Abundance and Pleasures, a series of closed courtyards housed the bureaux of the two ministries and the various departments and offices. Only the Office of Higher Learning was located outside the palace precincts, directly south-east of Red Bird Gate, because some of the students could be recruited among men holding no rank and it would have been impossible to allow them to enter the palace. South of the palace and east of the Office of Higher Learning, the Garden of the Sacred Spring, Shinsen-en, occupied half a district. It was used in the 9th century as a recreational area for the emperors, who organized poetic composition sessions here at various times of the year. However, in the 10th century, this place dedicated to a female dragon deity took on a religious purpose and celebrations were held here in order to bring about rain and also to placate the angry spirits of the dead, to whom were attributed the illnesses of summer. Far removed as it was from the hard toil of the peasants, the court was in fact most alarmed when there was too little or too much rain.

Inner palace and aristocratic residences

The Great Hall of State, in the Court of the Eight Departments, occupied the central part of the palace, but the place where the emperor lived was the inner palace. He very seldom left it, except to make a pilgrimage to a shrine (at most twice in a reign), or to visit a minister, the father of the empress, when she had given birth. In fact, fires were so common that the emperor was often forced to move into a temporary palace, a residence of his grandfather or maternal uncle, the most powerful man of the court, the one who held the post of document examiner or that of regent. This residence was then for a time no longer referred to by its name and was simply called the palace. An attempt was made to reorganize the space there just as at the palace, giving the same names to the places where the life of the court was conducted. From the late 10th century, with the near total domination of the court by the Fujiwara regents, the number of palace fires increased: there were three under the reign of Enyū Tennō, three during that of Ichijō Tennō and two during that of Sanjō Tennō. Under the reigns of Michinaga's three grandsons, Goichijō, Gosuzaku and Goreizei, the palace was destroyed just as often.

The inner palace was enclosed by a double wall, the outer one pierced by four gates in the south, two in the north and one each in the east and west. Between the first and second walls, to the west, were the bureaux of the Imperial Table (Naizenshi) and Palace Women (Uneme no tsukasa), as well as the Pavilion of Divine Happiness (Shinkaden) in the Court of Central Harmony (Chūka-in), used when the emperor himself offered up the sacred meals to the deities in the 6th and 12th months, and for the First Fruits Festival. To the north, some buildings could be used as temporary lodgings for monks invited to celebrations at the palace, while another housed a library. To the south and east, the two walls were parallel, with no pavilions between them.

The inner wall was pierced by three gates on each side and enclosed a quadrilateral measuring two hundred and eighteen metres from north to south by one hundred and seventy-six metres from east to west. The most important part, that used for the public life of the emperor, was at the southern end. A large pavilion measuring nine bays along its façade overlooked to the south the very spacious courtyard where the senior nobles and officials lined up for the solemn greetings. It bore the very significant name Shishinden, Pavilion of the Pole Star, recalling the identification of the emperor's role with that of the Pole Star, sometimes called *tennō*, the celestial ruler. In everyday life, however, the officials usually referred to it as the Southern Pavilion, Naden. This courtyard was closed off in the south by the surrounding wall, pierced at its centre by the gate known as Received Light, Shōmeimon, and closed off in the east and west by four pavilions extending from north to south and connected in pairs by covered galleries pierced at their mid points by the Gate of the Sun's Radiance (Nikkamon) to the east and by the Gate of the Moon's Radiance (Gekkamon) to the west. The room where the senior nobles normally assembled was situated in the broad gallery that connected the Southern Pavilion to the north of the Pavilion of the Beneficent Yang Principle (Giyō-den), where the important personages had another meeting room and where might be found the apartment of the regent or the chancellor when he was at the palace.

To the north-west of the Southern Pavilion and connected to it by covered galleries was the Pavilion of Purity and Freshness,

Seiryōden, where the emperor lived. This building faced east and had eleven bays from north to south and five from east to west; it looked onto a small garden adorned with clumps of bamboo. The daytime apartment of the emperor was located to the east. There were also service rooms to the west and, to the south, the Courtiers' Hall (Tenjō no ma), where the men who had been granted the privilege had the right to enter. To the north, several rooms were set aside for relaxation and the imperial consorts could join the emperor there. The north of the inner palace was occupied by around eighteen pavilions, either aligned from east to west, behind the Southern Pavilion and on the wings, or aligned from north to south, all connected by fairly broad covered galleries, closed off in some cases by walls, depending on whether or not they contained small rooms. The pavilion just north of the Southern Pavilion, the Pavilion of Benevolence and Good Fortune, Jijūden, was used for those banquets at which literati were invited to compose poems. To the east of this pavilion, the one called Unmeiden, Warmth and Brightness, facing north-south, housed the sacred mirror of the palace (supporting the spirit of Amaterasu, divine ancestor of the dynasty) and the women's services. In the northern part, pavilions with plant names such as Paulownia Arbour (Kiritsubo), Pear Arbour (Nashitsubo) and Wisteria Arbour (Fujitsubo) were used to accommodate the imperial consorts, who took their name from them: Lady of the Wisteria Arbour or Lady of the Paulownia Arbour. In the famous novel *Genji monogatari*, the mother of Prince Genji, the lower-ranking imperial consort, the lady of the bedchamber, is installed in the Paulownia Arbour, situated in the north-east corner of the palace; she must therefore go past numerous galleries, either between two pavilions or alongside a pavilion, in order to reach the emperor's apartments and, on the way, she is exposed to all sorts of humiliations by her rivals and especially by their attendants.[11] The *Eiga monogatari* relates the unpleasant experience of Fujiwara no Genshi (?-?), an imperial consort of Ichijō Tennō, who, having announced that she was pregnant, left the palace to the jeers of her rivals' attendants concealed behind the blinds: an experience all the more painful as it later turned out that she had been mistaken and there was no pregnancy.[12]

Each pavilion was raised on a platform and right around it ran a paved pathway, sheltered under the eaves. The greater part of the structure was made of wood, with large round pillars supporting a heavy timber frame. Each bay was about three metres. The central part of the pavilion formed a space with no pillars: in the Shishinden, for example, it was five bays long in the east-west direction and two in the north-south direction. One or two galleries, the width of a bay, often slightly lower, surrounded the central part. Further out came the narrower external gallery, completed by a railing. Between this and the surrounding gallery, wooden shutters could be lowered, these generally being replaced during the day by blinds. In the Shishinden, the northern gallery could be separated from the central part by a movable wooden partition, enabling a space to be provided for the ladies and for the table service, when the building was used for a banquet. Access to each pavilion was by steps – eighteen in the Shishinden – or by connecting galleries, which were sometimes on a slightly lower level. These galleries could be wide, and in this case living quarters were arranged on a side closed off by a mud-brick wall, or they could be narrow. The surrounding galleries, like the central part of the pavilions, were covered with floorboards. The timber frame was normally concealed by a decorated roof. While the palace buildings and the Courts of the Eight Departments and Abundance and Pleasures were covered with glazed tiles, of a greenish or bluish hue, the inner palace buildings had preserved a roofing method native to Japan, using Japanese cypress bark. The buildings as a whole therefore retained a brown colour scheme: that of the wood, blinds and roofing.

Generally speaking, there were few partitions and they were movable. The appearance was thus one of large rooms that could only be tightly closed, hence very dark, when the wooden shutters were lowered, or wide open, as the blinds, which during the day concealed the interior, allowed the cold and wind to enter and yet made the interior quite dark. This arrangement was well suited to the summer heat, but hardly to the winter cold. However, when it snowed, the senior nobles in their journals, like the ladies in their diaries, far from complaining of the cold, seem to have enjoyed the sight. It was customary for the writers of journals always to include a reference to the weather, but they never comment on it from a personal point of view. As for the cold, it is probable that their garments with their multiple layers and sometimes lined with silk floss gave them sufficient protection.

Moreover, there were no strong locks: screens, sliding shutters and blinds did not allow people to isolate themselves. For some ladies in service at the palace, one of the unpleasant aspects of their lives was that they could not always prevent an undesirable intrusion. Furthermore, nothing stopped thieves; they operated freely even in the palace, especially at night. However, the palace guard was expected to make its rounds and to announce the hours. Braziers were kept burning in the courtyards. But nothing made any difference and this type of incident was quite common. In November 1038, Fujiwara no Sukefusa relates how, one night, towards two in the morning, garments belonging to some ladies had been stolen from one of the service quarters in the Pavilion of Purity and Freshness, and how the emperor, immediately informed, had ordered inquiries to be made by the guards attached to the Chancellery and a list drawn up of the names of the men present at the time in the guard posts.[13] All in vain.

What made possible a reasonable level of protection was that access to the inner palace and, within the palace, access to the various pavilions was strictly limited. The guard posts at the gates had lists of the people allowed to enter. The privilege of going up to the Courtiers' Hall and entering the Pavilion of Purity and Freshness was granted to only a small number of officials, in particular to the members of the Chancellery. Only the senior nobles were seated in the Shishinden gallery during court banquets; men of the fourth and fifth ranks remained at the foot of the pavilion. The sense of hierarchies and of the

almost sacred character of the place where the emperor lived
was especially well developed among the senior nobles. The
following two examples are taken from the journal of Fujiwara
no Sukefusa. When Gosuzaku Tennō took a new imperial
consort, Fujiwara no Seishi (1014-1068), he conferred on her,
according to custom, the right to move around the palace in a
litter. However, as the inner palace had recently been destroyed
by a fire, he was then staying at the home of his chancellor
Yorimichi, the Kyōgoku residence. There was only one wall
here and so it was at the northern gate of this wall that the new
consort left her carriage to get into the litter. Sukefusa
suggested that it would perhaps have been better to have had
her dismount further north, in order to respect the distance
existing at the real palace between the two walls of the inner
palace.[14] The other example relates the fury of Gosuzaku
Tennō, when he saw that the member of the Chancellery tasked
with preparing the décor for a dance rehearsal in the Pavilion of
Purity and Freshness was walking on the floorboards of the
external gallery in his shoes. He at once had him dismissed.[15]

The arrangement of the residences of the senior nobles was
similar to that of the inner palace; it was imposing and often
obeyed the rules of symmetry. When they occupied two blocks,
their area was roughly equal to that of the inner palace, as they
extended over a quadrilateral two hundred and forty metres long
(compared with the two hundred and eighteen metres of the
inner palace) by nearly one hundred and nineteen metres wide
(compared with one hundred and seventy-six metres at the
palace). But the part not built on and turned into garden was far
larger than at the inner palace. A mud-brick wall pierced by a
gate on each side completely enclosed a group of pavilions
connected by narrow, covered corridors or by larger connecting
galleries that could be turned into small servants' rooms. The
main pavilion stood in the centre, with the façade facing south,
towards the garden. It was connected to other pavilions, Eastern
and Western, quadrilaterals whose long side extended from
north to south. Behind the main pavilion was a Northern
pavilion; there could also be pavilions behind the Eastern and

Western pavilions. Towards the south, these latter two were continued by galleries pierced by gates to the east and west leading into various other small pavilions. Service buildings, the kitchen and baths were located towards the north; stables and carriage houses were usually situated towards the east and west gates, as was the guard post reserved for the men on escort duty.

This basic layout could be interpreted in different ways. Thus the residence of Tsuchimikado (also called Kyōgoku and Jōtōmon), thought to have belonged to his wife Minamoto no Rinshi but that Fujiwara no Michinaga had rebuilt after the fire of 1016, had a Northern pavilion behind the main one and another behind the Western pavilion. The gallery that ran south from this latter pavilion led in turn to a service building, a chapel and a dance pavilion. To the east, a shorter, symmetrical gallery led into a carriage house. A stable was located near the gate of the eastern wall. South-east of the garden was a residential annexe, from where Michinaga could send offerings to the deities without fear of the uncleanness that could have offended them when he was uncertain as to the state of purity of his home or when monks were conducting their offices in his chapel. To the south-west, a racecourse had been set up, together with a pavilion: Michinaga used it mainly when the emperor honoured him with a visit. In the south-east corner, well away from all the other buildings, no doubt to avoid the risk of fires, had been built the pavilion where archives, books and documents were stored. At the Ichijō residence, where the mother of Ichijō Tennō lived and where he himself resided on several occasions after a fire at the palace, the main pavilion, designated the Southern Pavilion when this place served as the palace, was flanked by the Eastern and Western pavilions. Directly behind the main pavilion and parallel to it was the one normally called the Middle Pavilion, but called the Pavilion of Purity and Freshness when the emperor was using it. It was followed by a third pavilion to the north and flanked to the east by one situated behind the Eastern pavilion. Their construction was similar to that of the palace pavilions, with the central part and the galleries surrounding it able to be doubled in width on one side.

The middle-ranking officials, for their part, made do with more modest dwellings, but mostly including two or three pavilions, even if only small ones, connected by corridors. It has been possible to reconstruct the plan of the house of Yoshi-shige no Yasutane described in the work already mentioned, *Notes from the Pavilion by the Pond.* Yasutane owned a block of land measuring seventy metres by fifty-five, enclosed by a hedge. To the north, he erected the main building, eighteen metres by fifteen, facing south towards the garden and con-nected on the east side to another building measuring thirteen metres from north to south and six metres from east to west. From this pavilion ran a corridor that led towards the south and ended in a small building measuring six metres by six, which served as a study. Between the two main pavilions, a water-course fed a pond located to the south of the main pavilion and to the west of the study. This pond was dotted with islands that were accessed by small bridges. Yasutane, a scholar-official, was also very devout (he finally became a monk), and had therefore built an oratory to the west of the pond. To the south, he cultivated a small vegetable garden and a small orchard.

The garden was one of the attractive features of the aristocratic residences, and their owners devoted as much care to them as to the buildings. It was necessary to construct a hill that represented a mountain, excavate a pond that suggested the sea and dot it with islands, and bring running water by means of a small canal that was equivalent to a river. Thus all the elements that made up the universe had to be present in these gardens, which were a kind of microcosm. In the late 9th century, a minister, Minamoto no Tōru (822-895), attempted to reconstruct in miniature some celebrated landscapes.[16] In the preface to a collection of poems composed at one of Michi-naga's residences, Higashi Sanjō, Ōe no Masahira writes:

> Our present minister, moved by the harmoniousness of this place, has added to its charm. Rapids blocked by stones, rocky

bays, where the wind reverberates like the one that makes the strings of the koto sing in the mountain gorges. Spring flowers, autumnal leaves, here the rain paints the colours of the valleys [...]. For whoever devotes himself to the service of the ruler, it is difficult to seek other means of making a living. For whoever appreciates nature alone, it is easy not to follow the vocation of those who serve in the palace. But here, how admirable![17]

Masahira is suggesting that Michinaga, thanks to his garden, can practise at the same time the Confucian virtues of good ministers and the wisdom of the Taoist hermit who lives according to the rhythm of nature. The Heian aristocracy, who knew nature above all through excursions to time-honoured places at times determined by convention, as well as through poetry, had a taste not so much for nature as for the representation of nature.

The most important personages were not too proud to personally oversee the arrangement of their garden. Michinaga supervised the positioning of the stones at Tsuchimikado.[18] Kazan Tennō, having abdicated and taken religious vows, was noted for his innovations:

He occupied himself with the plantings in his garden; he declared that the cherry blossom is wonderfully beautiful but that the branches are somewhat stiff, that the trunk too is not pleasing to the eye and that it was better to see only the ends of the branches: he therefore had the trees planted outside the median wall of his residence and everyone thought his idea excellent. He also had daisies planted on the mud-brick walls: on all sides, the effect was surprising, a real Chinese brocade, a vision of dreams.[19]

These gardens were not merely objects of contemplation. People strolled around the lake and sailed small craft on it. When Michinaga invited monks to celebrate the *Lotus Sūtra*, a procession made its way through the garden. When he invited the emperor, a dance platform could be set up on an island and boats with bird and dragon heads moved about filled with musicians.

The beauty of the gardens, the grandeur of the pavilions, the harmonious curve of the heavy brown roofs, the spaciousness of the layouts, the restraint and weight of the various elements – round pillars of natural wood, timber frames made using simple jointing, and the whiteness of the few mud-brick walls –, all this was accompanied by what may appear to be disadvantages: darkened interiors of the buildings, inadequate protection from the cold, and the impossibility of isolating oneself. But the austerity of the whole was compensated for by the refinement of the details.

Interior spaces: harmony and refinement

The brown and uniform colour of the pavilions, where the aristocracy lived and showed themselves to advantage in the ceremonies, was balanced by the elements of colour provided by the paintings on partitions and screens and by the fabrics used for curtains and garments.

A few wooden partitions and screens made it possible to divide up the internal space; many of these were decorated with paintings. The court had a Painting Workshop (Edokoro) and those in charge were responsible for placing orders. The artists were usually quite minor officials attached to other bureaux. The court had them work on decorating certain partition-walls, which always needed redecorating after a fire. It also requested from them series of screens for various occasions: when a minister introduced his daughter into the palace as an imperial consort, he had the screens prepared for her apartment. Again, when an important personage celebrated his or her fiftieth or sixtieth birthday, screens were commissioned for the banquet, just as they were for the banquet held on the appointment of a regent.

Some early texts give the names of the main artists, as well as information about their works. Kose no Kanaoka (?-?) was active in the late 9th century and began a line of court painters. He painted in a manner still very close to the Chinese style, which differed from the Yamato style, developed from the 10th century. The difference was not in the manner or execution but in the subjects. In the 10th century, Kose no Kintada (?-?) began the practice of signing the back of works. Azukabe Tsunenori (?-?), active in the second half of the 10th century, from 954 to 972, was an under-officer in the gate guard. Tradition attributes to him the painting of a kind of divine animal with the form of a lion on a partition-wall of the Pavilion of Purity and Freshness. After his death, Michinaga used some of his screen paintings when his eldest daughter Shōshi entered the palace, which proves that his works were preserved and in demand. The painter Kose no Hirotaka (?-?), active in the early 11th century, was director of the Palace Women's Bureau and a descendant of Kanaoka.

The partitions, which were put out on ceremonial days to separate the central part of the Southern Pavilion from the northern gallery, were decorated in the late 9th century with the portraits of thirty-two Chinese sages, in imitation of what a Han ruler had done to encourage himself to be more virtuous. In the Pavilion of Purity and Freshness, the Chinese and Yamato styles were found side by side. In the space called the Demon Room (Oni no ma), a mythical Chinese animal, a slayer of demons, was portrayed. According to legend, this animal appeared when the reign was benevolent. Also in this pavilion were paintings of horses, as well as partitions showing a Chinese subject on one side and a Japanese subject on the other: next to the Konmei lake, which a Han emperor had had excavated near his capital, was a hunting scene on the Saga plain to the west of Heiankyō; behind a Chinese-style panel depicting a landscape peopled by mythical figures with large hands and feet was a fishing scene on the Uji River.

The screen paintings done for the imperial consorts appear to have had as their subject the seasons and the corresponding labours or diversions. For the banquet held to mark the appointment as regent of his son Yorimichi, Michinaga used the same subject but associated with the annual cycle of court celebrations. These works were therefore done in the Yamato style. Once the paintings had been completed or selected, the minister instructed members of the court to provide him with poems in keeping with the images. He chose the best ones and had them brushed on the screens. He would have wished to compose some himself for the banquet in his son's honour.

Chinese-style paintings – landscapes, figures of sages or mythological creatures – like Japanese-style landscapes and genre scenes were always in delicate and sober shades. Bright colours and quite bold colour combinations were rather to be found in textiles. Sensibility in this area was highly developed. The description of garments and curtains occupies an important place, not only in the diaries of court ladies and the historical narratives, but also in the journals of the senior nobles. Veritable treatises were written on the décor of buildings: from the mid-12th century we have the *Ruijū zatsuyōshō* (*Classified Notes on Various Important Customs*). Certain officials specialized in this kind of knowledge, like Minamoto no Masasuke (?-?) in the late 12th century, who left the *Masasuke shōzokushō* (*Masasuke's Treatise on Costume and Décor*).[20] This person had gained a reputation as an expert in the arrangement of ladies' trains, which, showing beneath the blinds, contributed to the adornment of the ceremonies, proving that dress certainly had its place in the interior décor. It also had its place in the appearance of the carriages, which were crates pulled by oxen, quite light, made of wood, plaited stalks and bamboo blinds edged with strips of fabric ornamented with pompoms, for the ladies made sure they allowed their sleeves to hang down under the blinds.

Closed interior spaces were created by curtains. Screens were used: a stand of black lacquered wood one to one and a half metres high had at the top a perpendicular rod about two metres long from which hung a curtain. Since textiles were made in narrow widths, hardly more than thirty centimetres, the panels were sewn, and cords often red in colour were set at intervals along them. Curtains were decorated on a white background with plant designs in keeping with the season, using reddish tones in winter and greenish tones in summer. For a birth, the curtains were left white; for a Buddhist celebration, dark grey curtains were put up. These screens could be quite low, as the ladies lived at floor level and often moved around on their knees inside. Curtains could also be hung between two pillars. The bamboo blinds were adorned with ribbons and pompoms, often red. In the palace, for the emperor, and in the aristocratic residences, for the head of a household, there was a dais in the central part of the main pavilion. This was a kind of platform of lacquered wood, some ten to twelve centimetres high, and four pillars about two metres high supported a frame. A white silk cloth was stretched over it by way of a ceiling, and fixed curtains, decorated like those of the screens, were placed at the four corners and on the north side. On the other three sides, the curtains could be raised. Two mats were laid out on the platform; the important personage could sleep, rest or isolate himself in this enclosed space. On a visit to Michinaga, Sanjō Tennō lingered there while the court waited for him to appear. He had made himself comfortable and had had his newborn daughter Teishi brought to him. He replied to Michinaga who invited him to come out that he knew by heart the music and dances prepared for him.[21] During long ceremonies, this dais made it possible to rest for a short time.

The most vivid and unexpected registers of colours were provided by the costumes, in particular those of the ladies. For male dress was subject to stricter sumptuary laws: the code has a chapter regulating the appearance and colours of garments, according to rank. To visit the palace, or the residence of a retired emperor, an empress or the chancellor, the officials were required to wear formal attire, of a colour and composition in keeping with their rank and function. The obligation to wear formal court dress was such that, even on a day when a fire had occurred in the inner palace and the senior nobles and officials, in the middle of the night and in haste, had just brought out the emperor and installed him temporarily in the Weaving Bureau, they returned home to don formal attire in order to come back at four in the morning to discuss and decide where the emperor was going to reside.[22] Even in less formal gatherings and on excursions to view the flowers or red leaves, they seldom had any real freedom in their use of materials, colours and patterns. There was a limit that one could not exceed without being criticized. The greatest efforts were made for the festivals of the Kamo and Iwashimizu shrines; at these times, even subordinates were dressed in precious silk and bright colours, but their master was censured. The journals of the early 11th century mention that before the festival, the Police Bureau was ordered to uphold the law, but they often add that the inspectors did not dare to arrest anyone who infringed it. Fujiwara no Sukefusa notes the aggressive behaviour of an inspector who, having a grievance against a sergeant attached to the Chancellery and finding him dressed in a red tunic not in conformity with the regulation, tore it and struck him.[23] The custom, it seems, was to have the garment removed and tear it, but to do so discreetly and not violently. The same Sukefusa writes, in 1039, that for those attending the dance rehearsals for the First Fruits Festival, the prohibition on wearing fabrics with woven patterns, as well as pale red and violet, reserved for the first four ranks, has been renewed.[24]

A distinction was made between court attire and more comfortable dress, especially that including more varied colour combinations. The general rule of male dress (and female dress was no different) was to superpose fairly long jackets or gowns under a full tunic with very wide sleeves, under which passed the train attached to one of the under-jackets. The lower half of the body was covered by loose-fitting trousers, a kind of trouser-skirt of stiff silk that protruded slightly from under the tunic. A belt adorned with precious stones, of greater or lesser value depending on rank, a cross-belt holding a sword in a richly ornamented sheath, and a cap (a kind of flat cap of lacquered black silk ending in a flap at the back) completed this costume. The ivory or wooden insignia of rank and the folding fan (said to be a Japanese invention) were indispensable accessories. The fan sometimes served as a stalling device for officials who were not quite sure what they were supposed to do. The less formal costume had a closer fitting tunic, trousers drawn tight at the ankles and more freedom in the blending of colours. The number of layers, quality of the fabrics and patterns on the under-jackets differed according to the season. Regardless of the weather, the court began wearing winter dress at the beginning of the 10th month and summer dress at the beginning of the 4th month. Certain patterns were reserved for the emperor's costume. In 1000, a design combining phoenix, tortoise, dragon, tiger and unicorn – symbols of the four cardinal points (south, north, east, west) and the centre – was commissioned from the painter Kose no Hirotaka and the material was woven by the Weaving Bureau for a garment intended for the emperor.[25] The colour of the tunic differed. In fact, according to the code, men of the first rank were entitled to wear deep purple, those of the second and third ranks lighter purple, those of the fourth rank deep red, those of the fifth rank lighter red and those of the sixth rank green. However, from the late 10th century, the first four ranks wore a dark-coloured tunic with blackish tints, the fifth rank fairly light red and the sixth rank green. The members of the Chancellery, whatever their rank, as well as those who had been granted the privilege of going up to the Courtiers' Hall, were entitled to wear colours not permitted by their rank. But maroon, reserved for the emperor, and fairly pale orange, reserved for the crown prince, remained off limits, as did dark red, which, it was believed at that time, could cause fires. The under-jackets, like the train, were of various colours and patterns. Men who were dancing, practising archery or playing an instrument freed one arm from the sleeve of the tunic, thereby revealing a parti-coloured sleeve. Everyday attire, even for men, was less austere. The important personages liked to dress the men of their escort magnificently on the occasion of the processions organized for the festivals at the Kamo and Iwashimizu shrines. In 1010, Michinaga had made lavish preparations for the Kamo festival, as his younger son Norimichi was the imperial messenger. He relates with evident satisfaction in his journal:

Everything needed for the messenger's retinue was of outstanding quality; everything was new. The men leading the horses were in mottled brown and green garments, red trousers and, on their feet, socks and sandals. The pages were in garments fastened with laces, in double fine blue fabric, with reddish under-jackets over-woven with patterns, trousers with green patterns and red cloaks [...]. Sixty followers, of whom the four leaders were in white garments, six men in red hunting dress, with red trousers and mauve under-jackets, six in green trousers with yellow under-jackets, six in plum-coloured trousers with green under-jackets, six in pale green trousers with red under-jackets, six in yellow trousers with reddish under-jackets, six in blue trousers with red under-jackets. For the others, I omit the details: everything was magnificent ....[26]

The author of the *Ōkagami*, praising the refined taste and grace of a young aristocrat, describes him in a group of junior courtiers:

He arrived, modestly dressed in a tight-fitting yellow tunic and mauve trousers. Yet compared with those who had taken great trouble over their outfits, he was superb.[27]

Among many other elegant figures may be mentioned that of the young Fujiwara no Michimasa (991-1054) in deep purple trousers drawn tight at the ankles and a pale beige tunic with green lining, the red of the under-jackets showing at the neck and sleeves.[28]

Ladies wore over a loose-fitting red trouser-skirt a series of robes in the form of gowns of decreasing length, which allowed skilfully blended colours to show at the neck, sleeves and hem. A sumptuous mantle completed the formal costume. A train, of very ornate fabric, was tied at the waist. Colour combinations had names such as pine, wisteria and chrysanthemum. Murasaki Shikibu (973?-1014?), author of the *Genji monogatari*, has described in her diary several of the costumes worn by the court ladies:

Those ladies who have permission to wear these colours have put on a green or red mantle, a printed train and a purple-red outer robe. Only the lady Muma wears a reddish-purple outer robe. Underneath they have a robe of light or dark red, the colour of reddening autumn leaves; and under this, according to their taste, as usual, three layers of robes of dark or light yellow, or the colour of a mauve aster or chrysanthemum, with a green lining. Those who cannot wear damask of different colours and, as always, the older women, have put on ensembles of robes with five layers of the same colour, either purple-red or green. The trains with wave patterns give an impression of freshness contrasting with the tightly woven ties.

And:

The lady Sakyō wears a mantle all of willow-green over an ensemble of five green layers, and the lady Chikuzen a mantle over a chrysanthemum-coloured ensemble, with a printed train, as usual.[29]

Ladies mostly allowed their long hair to hang down. But in certain cases, notably when they had to serve the emperor's meal, they put it up, at least on the sides, and placed a metal ornament with three points on top of their head.

The interior décor included very few objects. Padded mats (*tatami*) were still unknown and mats were simply spread where people slept or sat. In the aristocratic residences, these mats were edged with rich fabrics in floral designs. Cushions were also used, as well as round sedge seats about six or seven centimetres high. The emperor and important personages (naturally away from the emperor's presence) were sometimes seated on a large bench about thirty centimetres high or on a chair – of red lacquered wood in the Southern Pavilion and black lacquered wood in the Pavilion of Purity and Freshness. There they assumed the same posture as on the floor, seated cross-legged or on their heels.

Furniture consisted of relatively small-sized objects that could always be easily moved. It included chests – the so-called Chinese chests had four feet – small chests, low or high tables for setting down the bowls and plates during meals, the saké service, the casket containing the sacred jewel or the sacred sword (the two objects that always had to be near the emperor), shelves, and chests with doors opening towards the front and often topped by a shelf. Everything was in red or black lacquered wood, with an incrusted decoration, often floral, gilded or silvered: a technique in which the Japanese had become so highly skilled that they are sometimes credited with its invention, although this took place in China, but did not develop there. Mother-of-pearl inlays and ribbons with pom-poms embellished this furniture.

Special care was taken of the small chests. Some contained writing materials, others were intended to hold documents and books, others were filled with toiletry items and combs, and still others with an assortment of jars (often of a substance called lapis lazuli, but which was no doubt coloured glass imported from the continent), filled with sweet-smelling substances. For the aristocracy made great use of perfumes in solid form, mostly derived from plants. The ladies were experts in the blending of fragrances. The empress Shōshi, Michinaga's eldest daughter, after returning to her father's residence for the birth of her first child Atsunari, took pleasure in having her attendants create perfumes. Garments were scented, either by the vapours from perfume-pans, or by sachets. Oil lamps and mirrors of polished metal, both on lacquered wooden stands, completed the furnishings.

On introducing a daughter into the palace as an imperial consort, a minister made every effort to provide her with objects that could hold the emperor's attention. When Michinaga married his twelve-year old daughter Shōshi to Ichijō Tennō, who was nineteen, it was necessary to ensure that he took some pleasure in visiting her. The author of the *Eiga monogatari*, Akazome Emon, a woman in the service of the mother of the young empress, describes in the following words the visits of the sovereign to his wife, who was still a child:

> As soon as the emperor stepped onto the bridge leading to her apartments, he could smell the perfume coming from them, the exquisite fragrance of unidentified origin, the fragrance of an exotic and unknown perfume, a fragrance that transferred itself to him when he visited her, a fragrance quite unlike that of the

other ladies. He admired everything that was charming and exotic in her apartments, beginning with the contents of her comb boxes and writing cases, which were of exquisite beauty. As soon as it was daybreak, he visited her and admired her jewel caskets… He delighted in looking at the books of poems illustrated by Hirotaka and brushed by Yukinari.[30]

Whether it was the actual palace, an aristocratic residence that had become a temporary palace, or the home of a senior noble, the overall appearance was much the same. It was in this setting not without grandeur, of a slightly austere elegance and a great lack of comfort, which exposed the occupants to the cold and wind and gave them little protection from indiscreet people and thieves, that the senior nobles and their client officials performed their duties and carried on their intrigues. The service of the emperor did not take up all their energies, and each man, whatever his rank, endeavoured to secure as best he could the interests of his family, through the education of his children, marriages and alliances, and making arrangements for his succession.

Notes

1. *Konjaku monogatarishū*, chap. 29, anec. 18: "Tale of the thief who saw corpses in the Rashōmon gallery". A subject used again in the 20th century by Akutagawa Ryūnosuke; see the English translation, *Rashōmon and Seventeen Other Stories*, by Jay Rubin, Penguin, 2006, and the French translation, *Rashōmon et autres contes*, by Arimasa Mori, Gallimard, 1968.
2. *Saikyūki*, chap. 21; this took place in Kanna 2.5.17., 986, just before the abdication of Kazan Tennō. That day there were reportedly more than forty carriages of onlookers.
3. *Shinshō kyakuchoku fushō* (*New Selection of Decrees and Edicts*); a new regulation (*shinsei*) of Chōhō 1.7.25., 999, prohibiting monks from living in the capital in so-called "carriage houses".
4. *Sei Shōnagon shū*, the collected poems of Sei Shōnagon, I, 7. Michinaga, from the capital, wrote: "Did I imagine, leaving you

in yonder hills, that I would contemplate the moon alone in the Capital?"; *Gyokuyō wakashū* (*Collection of Jewelled Leaves*), an official anthology, No. 2230. Michinaga replied to a poem by Kazan Tennō: "Falling leaves, sadness of the autumnal landscape, felt even more keenly at the sound of the waterfall"; *Honchō reisō*, No. 65: "At the end of autumn, above Kiyomizudera".

5. *Nihon kiryaku* (*Abridged Annals of Japan*), Chōgen 3.4.23., 1030.

6. *Chūyūki*, Gen'ei 1.11.26., 1118.

7. *Honchō monzui*, chap. 12; *Chiteiki*: a prose text probably written in 982. Yasutane seems to have been inspired by various Chinese authors, including Bo Juyi.

8. *Gonki*, Chōtoku 4.10.29., 998. A transaction showing how difficult it was for women without a protector to hold onto their property, and the affluence of provincial governors.

9. *Heian ibun*, text 621, Kantoku 4.10.29., 1045 says that for one *chō* (1.13 hectares) the price is 60 pieces of silk. In the *Engishiki*, article 101 of the *Shuzeishiki* (*Regulations of the Office of Public Resources*) deals with the price of a piece of silk according to the province: it varies from 30 to 60 sheaves. If 60 sheaves is taken as the average value, one piece is equal to 3 bushels, 60 pieces being equal to 180 bushels. In the case of 30 sheaves, 60 pieces of silk are equal to 90 bushels.

10. *Gonki*, Chōhō 4.3.19., 1002. (Same date as the Black Warrior quotation.) Discussion by the senior nobles concerning the rebuilding of the inner palace, which had burned the previous year, Chōhō 3.11.18.

11. *Genji monogatari*, chap. 1: *Kiritsubo*. When the unfortunate favourite makes her way to the emperor's apartments, her rivals have soiled objects placed at intervals along her path.

12. *Eiga monogatari*, chap. 5. When Genshi left the palace, the attendants of another imperial consort watched the procession hidden behind a curtain, which caused Genshi's attendants to say that the curtain was also pregnant. But when it turned out that there had been no pregnancy, the young pages, making fun of Genshi, sang about the pregnancy of the curtain.

13. *Shunki*, Chōryaku 2.10.29., 1038. Thefts at the palace generally involved valuable silk garments. The menial servants were probably complicit in them.

14. *Shunki*, Chōryaku 3.12.21., beginning of 1040.
15. *Shunki*, Chōryaku 3.11.15., 1039.
16. On the son of Saga Tennō, the minister Minamoto no Tōru and his magnificent garden (Kawara no in), see B. Frank, Extraits des rapports sur les conférences, Histoire et philologie japonaises, Annuaires de l'École pratique des hautes études, IVe section, 1977, 1978 and 1979.
17. *Honchō monzui*, chap. 8. A session of poetic composition organized by Michinaga in Chōhō 1.7.6., 999.
18. *Midō kanpakuki*, Chōhō 2.1.30., 1000.
19. *Ōkagami*, section relating to Fujiwara no Koremasa, the maternal grandfather of Kazan Tennō. Kazan had also contrived to have a sloping floor built in his carriage house to facilitate the exit of conveyances.
20. *Ruijū zatsuyōshō*, a work from the mid-12th century, dealing with banquets, furniture and the décor of pavilions, as well as the material elements of celebrations. *Masasuke shōzokushō*; a study and analysis of this text may be found in F. Joüon des Longrais, *Tashi, le roman de celle qui épousa deux empereurs (1140-1202)*, Maison Franco-Japonaise, 1969.
21. *Midō kanpakuki*, Chōwa 2.9.16., 1013. The emperor preferred to relax inside the dais chatting with the young empress Kenshi, his consort, rather than appearing before his court in formal attire. Sometimes, when preparations were slightly delayed and the emperor was already in the Southern Pavilion for a celebration, he waited inside his dais where he could assume a relaxed attitude.
22. *Midō kanpakuki*, Kankō 6.10.5., 1009.
23. *Shunki*, Chōryaku 2.12.9., 1038. In fact, the over-reaction of the Police Bureau inspector was due to a private dispute.
24. *Shunki*, Chōryaku 3.11.14., 1039. It was also customary before the festival of the Kamo Shrine, which was an occasion for the participants in the procession to try to outdo each other in ostentation, to remind the Police Bureau of its obligation to enforce the sumptuary laws. However those who issued these orders infringed them, seriously embarrassing the Police Bureau.
25. *Gonki*, Chōhō 2.7.4. and 2.8.19., 1000.
26. *Midō kanpakuki*, Kankō 7.4.24., 1010.
27. *Ōkagami*, section relating to Koremasa; description of his son Yoshitaka, the father of Yukinari.

28. *Eiga monogatari*, chap. 8. The elegance and grace of Michimasa, son of the disgraced third minister Korechika, are all the more poignant as his future can only be undistinguished.

29. *Murasaki Shikibu nikki*; passage concerning the emperor's visit to Tsuchimikado, after the birth of the first son of the empress Shōshi, the future Goichijō Tennō.

30. *Eiga monogatari*, chap. 6.

CHAPTER 4

PRIVATE LIFE

Marriages and successions

In the chapter "On Households", the code has several articles relating to marriages and successions. It states that men from the age of fifteen and women from the age of thirteen can contract a marriage. Women were completely dependent on their family; in the first instance on parents, and, for orphans, on grandparents, uncles, aunts and cousins who took the place of the deceased parents. A woman could choose her husband only if she had no family. The Japanese code makes no mention of the role of the man's family, unlike the Chinese code. As in China, there were seven grounds for repudiating a wife: barrenness, adultery, lack of filial piety towards her parents-in-law, thoughtless chatter, jealousy and illness. A man could have only one principal wife and was punished if he took a second or degraded the first without cause. On the other hand, secondary wives were permitted. Men or women guilty of adultery were severely punished, in accordance with the penal code.

On the father's death, immovable and movable property was apportioned. The principal wife and the heir were each entitled to two shares, the other sons to one share and daughters living at home as well as secondary wives to half of one share. The property brought by wives was excluded from the apportionment. Moreover, the father had the right, during his lifetime, to dispose in any way he wished of personal property owned and acquired by him. In fact, the apportionments concerned only the inherited family property. If there was no son, adoption was permitted, preferably from among the relatives, and the adopted son had the same rights as a son born into the family.

In the Heian period, much of this legislation was no longer applied. However the *Hossō shiyōshō* (*Compendium of Laws*)[1] has preserved the greater part of it, with important corrections. Thus the clause "for the daughters living at home" has been deleted and it is all the daughters who inherit. The article relating to successions returns to the clause on apportionments, but adds that if the property owner, during his lifetime, disposes of it by a duly certified deed, there is no need to apply the code. Hence the freedom to make a will was considered normal, even for the inherited family property.

The application of the code during the Fujiwara period shows that the crime of adultery hardly retained any legal force. Moreover, the vocabulary used blurs the distinctions between principal and secondary wives. Many cases show that adoption worked well only if the person adopting was in favour of it and that there were many kinds of adoption, some being merely formal and temporary: for example, to enable a young man to benefit at the start of his career from the protection of a man better placed than his father.

It was usual for a man to visit the house of one or more wives or even to live with his parents-in-law. This has led some historians to argue that a woman retained the management of her property and passed it on to her daughter, succession through the female line apparently being preferred. However this argument takes no account of the fact that, very often, the husband who lived at his wife's home was of a higher social standing than her family, which frequently allowed him to take control of his wife's property. For the sons of senior nobles readily accepted to marry daughters of provincial governors, officials who had good opportunities to acquire personal wealth. Until they reached the highest levels of the hierarchy, young aristocrats could thus be supported, together with the children born from these unions. Very often too, after the death of their father-in-law, they took charge of the landed property he had left and that their wife would have had difficulty keeping up on her own. Quite a few cases may be mentioned. One of the clearest is that of Fujiwara no Sukefusa, elder son of the second counsellor Sukehira and grandson (or great-nephew as his father had been adopted by his uncle) of the minister of the right Sanesuke. He was married at the age of sixteen to the daughter of a middle-ranking official, Minamoto no Norisuke – for all that of very good lineage since he was the son of a major counsellor, Tokinaka (941-1001) –, who was often appointed to provincial posts. When his father-in-law died in 1039, Sukefusa wrote in his journal that he had been supported by him for eighteen years.[2] He inherited the residence where he had lived with his wife's family. He undertook restoration work on the house and was able to complete it thanks to some income derived from an estate in the province of Mikawa, of which his father-in-law was governor at the time of his death. Even if she was kept informed, it seems unlikely that his wife took any part in its management. And if he was able to use workers from Mikawa for the repairs, this was certainly because he held the important post of head of the Chancellery.

The case of Fujiwara no Sanesuke may also be mentioned. The first woman he married was the daughter of a rather insignificant auditor, Minamoto no Koremasa (929-980). He inherited a residence belonging to his father-in-law, where he had lived with his wife. In fact, after the death of this woman and the child he had had by her, he sold this house.[3] His father-in-law had a large number of sons, all of whom had undistinguished careers. Even at the very highest level of the aristocracy, it was the same. The Tsuchimikado residence apparently belonged to Minamoto no Rinshi, the wife of Michinaga. However he was the one who managed it and, when it was destroyed by a fire in 1016, it was thanks to the prestige of this minister that it was magnificently rebuilt and refurnished by some provincial governors who were his clients.[4]

Other examples may be put forward to counter the argument that women would have been able to freely dispose of their property. These concern women who lacked a highly placed protector. The prime minister Fujiwara no Tamemitsu enjoyed the use of the Ichijō residence, as he had married, among others, one of his nieces, the daughter of his half-brother Koremasa and heiress to this residence. He had a number of children by her: at least two sons and several daughters. He left the Ichijō property to these daughters, but they were unable to keep it. The provincial governor Saeki no Kinyuki purchased it and it quickly became the residence of the mother of Ichijō Tennō, the empress Senshi who had taken religious vows and was known as the Lady of Higashi Sanjō.[5] A second counsellor, Taira no Korenaka (944-1005), disposed of his property when he was appointed to the Government Headquarters in Kyūshū in 1001 and had to leave for that distant region. Ten properties, of unknown size, located in the capital and in the central provinces as well as in Ōmi – houses, rice fields, dry fields and pastures – were bequeathed to a temple. Five other properties were given to the same temple, but the life interest was left to Korenaka's wife and daughter. Four other estates were transferred to the temple, but with a right of inspection by the wife and daughter. Korenaka further stipulated that, if his daughter had a son who became a monk, he would be the intendant of this temple.[6] This testament clearly shows that Korenaka did not think his wife and daughter would be capable of protecting their property as effectively as a religious establishment.

What may give the impression that women had full control over the property inherited from their father is that, in the families of senior nobles, an arrangement was often made to give daughters the enjoyment of property handed down through the maternal line. Two or three cases are fairly well documented. The Biwa (Loquat) residence belonged to Fujiwara no Mototsune who, it was said, had inherited it from his real father Nagara (802-956), the brother of his adoptive father Yoshifusa.[7] He bequeathed it to his second son Nakahira (875-945). According to the genealogy of the Fujiwara family, Nakahira had only one son, probably born to a mother of low extraction as he became a monk, and two daughters, Gyōshi (?-?) and Meishi (?-?). The younger one who married Fujiwara no Atsutada (906-943) inherited the Biwa residence. Still according to the genealogy, she apparently had at least one son and one daughter. It was this last-mentioned who owned the Biwa property. To it she welcomed three successive husbands, two of whom (the first and the last) died there, while the second was only a temporary spouse. She had no children by any of them. After these two successions through the female line, the first perhaps due to the lack of a male heir, the Biwa residence passed into the hands of Michinaga, although it is not known by what route. From 1002, he had work done on it. The Horikawa residence had a similar destiny.[8] Nakahira bequeathed it to his elder daughter Gyōshi, who married an imperial prince, Ari-akira (910-961), a son of Daigo Tennō. The couple had at least one son, but it was the daughter who inherited the Horikawa-in. She married Fujiwara no Kanemichi. However, in the next generation, this residence passed not to the son she had produced but to another of Kanemichi's sons, Akimitsu. A further noteworthy case is that of Sanesuke's daughter. She inherited her father's property, which included the splendid Ononomiya residence. Married to a son of Fujiwara no Yori-mune (son of Michinaga), she died before her father, leaving only a daughter who married a son of Nagaie (1005-1064) (brother of Yorimune). Succession through the female line ended with this couple's daughter. She had married a major counsellor, Minamoto no Moroyori (1068-1139), but none of his children is listed in the Minamoto genealogy as having been born to this woman and the Ononomiya residence passed to one of Moroyori's sons.

The code, which took over an article from the Chinese code, made a clear distinction between the principal wife and subsequent concubines or secondary wives, who, according to Chinese custom, all lived in their husband's house. However Japanese customs were different. Without it being possible to assert that it was long-standing and uniform throughout the country and in all classes of the population, there was a tradition of the husband visiting the home of the woman's parents, at least in the early stages of the marriage. Later, it seems that the man and woman, once things had become reasonably settled, especially after the birth of children, often went to live elsewhere. In the world of the aristocracy in the Fujiwara period, depending on the status of the father and the hopes of the young man, there were quite a few opportunities for nocturnal visits to several women. Not all of these ended in a marriage: even if not publicly announced, at least one where the children were acknowledged by the father and as such recorded in his civil register. For, until her death, a woman remained in the civil register of her own family, but the acknowledged children, even if raised by the maternal grandfather, belonged to their father's family.

As one would expect, women of very high birth could not be treated with the same casualness as the daughters of low- or middle-ranking officials. But while giving the name of wife, *tsuma*, to several women, it was still necessary to decide which of the children would be declared the principal heir and, for the very important personages able to support several sons, which of them would benefit from the father's assistance for their career. A time also came when the man finally settled down in a particular place, whether acquired by him, or inherited from his wife's family, or inherited from his own family, in order to live there with her. The wife of the principal residence was called the "lady of the north", *kita no kata*, because she often lived in the pavilion situated behind the main pavilion.

The conduct of each man differed according to his character, tastes or ambitions. Aristocratic society, generally speaking, had no problem at all with multiple relationships. From Fujiwara no Morosuke to Michinaga, with Kaneie and Michikane coming in between, one finds several types of marital conduct.

Morosuke had twelve sons listed in the genealogical tables and seven daughters, by at least four wives. While still very young, at the age of seventeen, when he had only just received his first promotion to the fifth rank and his father Tadahira was minister of the right and head of the council of senior nobles, he visited the daughter of a provincial governor, Fujiwara no Tsunekuni (?-?), who was nonetheless the grandson of a minister. While still occupying the very junior post of chamberlain, his first son Koremasa was born in 924. In the years that followed, he had by this woman, Moriko (?-?), the governor of Musashi's daughter, three other sons and three daughters. The three eldest – Koremasa, Kanemichi (b. 925) and Kaneie (b.

929) – each became regent in their turn. The youngest, Tada-kimi (?-968), died before his brothers achieved their successes. The eldest daughter, Anshi (b. 927), was the consort of Mura-kami Tennō and mother of the emperors Reizei and Enyū. Her younger sister, Tōshi (?-975), was also a lady in the palace of Murakami Tennō. Morosuke must have maintained around the same time a relationship with another daughter of a provincial governor, of a similar social standing to Koremasa's mother. This woman, the governor of Hitachi's daughter, gave him three sons and at least one daughter. Their dates of birth are un-known. However the date of death of one of them and his career are known, for at the end of his life he was appointed a non-participating auditor (*hisangi*) on the council. Such a title was conferred either on a very young man destined for a great career, or, out of courtesy, on an official already well advanced in his career and who it was clear would not progress any further: certainly the case for this half-brother of Koremasa, called Tōnori. He died in 989, most probably aged around sixty. The children of the governor of Hitachi's daughter were there-fore in all likelihood born around the same time as the youngest children of the governor of Musashi's daughter, namely when Morosuke had just been appointed an auditor. It is not known whether Morosuke lived with one of these two women, but that seems rather unlikely. Morosuke later contracted two other marriages, which, given the noble birth of both women, could only have been official. The women in question were two imperial princesses, daughters of Daigo Tennō. The first was Gashi (909-954), who had been corresponding, no doubt as a prelude to a marriage, with Fujiwara no Atsutada, a cousin of Morosuke. But this did not eventuate, as she was named Vestal-princess, required to serve the deities of the imperial family at the Ise Shrine, from 931 until 936. On her return, Morosuke visited her. By him she had three sons, two of whom became monks and one, Tamemitsu (b. 942), who later became prime minister, as well as a daughter. When Gashi died in 954, Morosuke set his sights on a second imperial princess, Kōshi, a full sister of Murakami Tennō and the daughter of his aunt

Onshi (885-954). This princess, born in 920, was not destined for marriage, as in theory no man was of sufficiently high birth to make her his wife. She was elevated to the first rank in 946, treated like the empresses and housed at the palace. Morosuke dared to visit her there in secret, no doubt around 955. It required all the good will that the emperor had always shown towards Morosuke for him to accept this marriage. Kōshi bore him two sons: one became a monk, and the second, who cost her her life, was born in 957. Kinsue, too, later became prime minister. Morosuke had taken the princess to his Kujō residence at the time of this second birth, which could not under any circumstances take place at the palace, for reasons of defile-ment. The sons of imperial princesses, Tamemitsu and Kinsue, had posts that were prestigious but lacked political influence. On the other hand, it was the sons of the governor of Musashi's daughter who were the true heirs of Morosuke, notwithstanding the more modest extraction of their mother. Certainly having a sister who was an imperial consort and the mother of emperors contributed greatly to their success. Perhaps the sons of the governor of Hitachi's daughter would have had more illustrious careers if their sister had had the good fortune of Anshi, who was probably born before her.

Morosuke's third son, Kaneie, is well known for having visited at least six or seven women and for his stormy relation-ship with the mother of one of his sons and the author of a work called *Kagerō nikki* (*The Kagerō Diary*), in which she describes the various stages over more than ten years. He visited at the same time at least three women whom he considered as wives. One, known by the name of Tokihime, was the daughter of a governor of Settsu, Fujiwara no Nakamasa (?-?), the son of a second counsellor; the second, author of the *Kagerō nikki*, was the daughter of Fujiwara no Tomoyasu (?-977), a governor of Mutsu: she speaks of a third woman, but gives no information other than the place where this person lived. By Tokihime, from 954 to 966, Kaneie had three sons (Michitaka, Michikane and Michinaga) and two daughters (Chōshi and Senshi), who were the consorts of the emperors Reizei and Enyū and gave birth to the emperors Ichijō and Sanjō. It seems that he installed her in his Higashi Sanjō residence after 970; in any case, her daughters lived there. By Tomoyasu's daughter (936?-995?), he had a son, Michitsuna, born in 955. The third wife apparently had a son by Kaneie in 956, but the relationship with the mother ended very quickly and in all likelihood the child did not survive. Kaneie had two other daughters, one of whom he did not officially recognize and who was adopted by the governor of Mutsu's daughter. Yet the mother was the daughter of an auditor. The second, Suishi, was born around 974. The mother was the daughter of an assistant at the Government Head-quarters in Kyūshū and a rather flighty person, but to whom Kaneie took such a fancy that he installed her at his residence, no doubt after the death of Tokihime. The historical narrative *Eiga monogatari* amusingly calls her vice-principal wife.[9] Kaneie attempted to provide for his youngest daughter and gave her in marriage to the crown prince, his grandson, the future Sanjō Tennō. However, being just as flirtatious as her mother, she had an affair with a young nobleman, Minamoto no Yorisada (977-1020), and was obliged to leave the palace. At the end of his life, Kaneie wished, like his father, to take as his wife an imperial princess, Hoshi (949-987), a daughter of Murakami Tennō, but his visits to her ceased very quickly. Like his father, Kaneie chose as his heirs the first-born sons and the brothers of the daughter (Senshi) he had introduced into the palace of Enyū Tennō, but his wives or pseudo-wives all belonged to the middle level of officials.

His son Michikane had a very different idea of marital relationships. He took only one wife, the daughter of Fujiwara no Tōkazu (?-?), a half-brother of his father. She gave him three sons and a daughter. Michikane, it is said, was unattractive, grumpy and not very courteous. Nevertheless, Michinaga notes in 1012 the death of a natural daughter of his older brother.

Michinaga provides another model. He had two wives, Minamoto no Rinshi and Minamoto no Meishi, but the children of the first were treated better than those of the second. Rinshi was a descendant of Uda Tennō and the daughter of the minister of the left Masanobu. The *Eiga monogatari* relates that Masanobu was most reluctant to give his daughter to the third son of Kaneie, and so to a man who, *a priori*, had no hope of attaining the highest rank. He apparently said that it was "foolish to take this callow youth as a son-in-law". But Rinshi's mother, Fujiwara no Bokushi (?-1016), "an exceptionally far-sighted and wise woman", persuaded her husband to accept this marriage.[10] According to all contemporary accounts, it was a very happy one. As the *Eiga monogatari* says, Michinaga was not a man to divide himself between several wives. However his sister Senshi, the mother of Ichijō Tennō, was looking after a daughter of the disgraced minister Minamoto no Takaakira, a son of Daigo Tennō. Wishing to assure the future of Meishi, she hoped to make her Michinaga's wife. So it was that he had two wives. But he normally lived with Rinshi at the Tsuchimikado residence that belonged to her family. She gave him two sons, of whom the eldest Yorimichi inherited the headship of the Fujiwara family and the post of regent, and four daughters: three empresses, the consorts of emperors Ichijō, Sanjō and Goichijō; the fourth, at her death, was the consort of the crown prince Atsuyoshi, younger brother of Goichijō Tennō. The marriage of the third daughter Ishi with her nephew Goichijō, the son of her eldest sister Shōshi, was totally disproportionate, as she was nineteen years old when it was announced and the young emperor was barely ten. Meishi also had six children: four sons, one of whom, Akinobu (994-1027), gave up his career early on to become a monk, and two daughters, Kanshi (998?-1025) and Sonshi (?-?), whose marriages were less spectacular than those of their half-sisters, since the elder was given as a consolation prize and a pledge of Michinaga's protection to Atsuakira, the son of Sanjō Tennō, when the minister forced him to renounce his position as crown prince. The Fujiwara genealogy and the lists of ecclesiastical dignitaries give Michinaga a seventh son, Chōshin, born in 1014, therefore after the other children, to a daughter of a second counsellor. She was quite young when her father died and no doubt had to accept a post on the female staff of the palace. Two other daughters appear in the genealogy, with no mention of the mother's name. Michinaga granted the status of wives to only two women, but his position at the court was such that few could refuse his attentions. He notes in his journal that one evening someone brought to his residence a little girl who, he says, appeared to be of good birth.[11] It is quite likely that this child was his. Yet he did not acknowledge her and simply entrusted her to a woman in the service of the court. The great personages, whether emperors or ministers, were thus in the habit of not acknowledging certain children born to women of very low extraction, but of having them adopted by their servants.

Marital customs therefore show considerable diversity. Polygamy was the norm for aristocrats, as the genealogical tables show. However some men, by inclination or a lack of prestige, could form only one union at a time. The marriage of daughters was an important element in family strategies. The daughters of wealthy provincial governors had no difficulty marrying above their father's status, which benefited their family, as can be seen for that of Tokihime.[12] But those of senior nobles, and also of emperors and imperial princes, were more difficult to marry off and many had to accept to move down the social scale. As for women born into families of impecunious middle-ranking officials, they had to be satisfied either with mediocre marriages, or being secondary wives of an important personage, or going to serve in the palace or even in the household of a princess or the wife of an important personage.

As regards succession, the intention of the property owner was the only rule, though it was necessary for him to leave it to a person capable of having this intention respected. Immovable property was of little or no value if it could not be maintained in the case of houses, easily damaged by inclement weather or destroyed by fire, or if it could not be cultivated and protected in the case of rice fields and dry fields. The position occupied in the court hierarchy and the influence that could be exerted made it possible to keep this property when one was obliged to live in the capital like the aristocrats and many officials. In fact, the local notables employed in the provincial administrations and the provincial governors who had come from the capital did not fail to attack the property of men who were out of favour, to divert the products from it and even go so far as to deny them the income from their normal allocations of rice fields and households. As the *Eiga monogatari* says of Fujiwara no Korechika when, after his fall from grace, he had recovered his rank but not his function:

> Korechika had regained his allocation of households, but the provincial governors treated him with disdain and withheld his entitlements.[13]

For, at least up to the mid-11th century, rank and function remained one of the most valuable assets that a father could bequeath. They gave an entitlement to a stipend and down to the fifth rank to an allocation of rice fields. Being able to access this income was heavily dependent on the provincial administrations. Actual ownership of movable property – cloth and rice – was as important as having title deeds to properties. This is evident in the case of Fujiwara no Sukefusa. When his father-in-law died, his concern, like that of his two brothers-in-law, Norimune (?-?) and Norisue (?-?), was to find out what was in the storehouses of the deceased, those in the capital and those in the province of which he was governor. However they were thwarted, as Minamoto no Norisuke had left the keys to the wife he had taken after the death of the mother of his children. This woman, protected by the chancellor Yorimichi because she was no doubt related to his wife Takahime (995-1087), seems to have taken possession of the contents of the storehouses.

A very clear example of the total neglect both of the articles and spirit of the code is provided by Fujiwara no Sanesuke. A grandson of the chancellor Saneyori, he had been chosen by his grandfather as his heir, in preference to his father, uncle and two older brothers. He thus owned the patrimony of his family branch: the magnificent Ononomiya residence in the capital, estates (the precise number is unknown) and above all the pasture at Takada in the province of Chikuzen, an extensive region that supplied him with all sorts of products, including objects imported from the continent, for the estate officials he had appointed there carried on trade with Chinese merchants. At the beginning of 1020, aged over sixty, he took measures to deal with his succession. His only surviving child was a daughter, not yet married, whose mother was no doubt of fairly low birth and who had perhaps been in the service of the princess Kyōshi (?-998), his second wife. He had adopted as his son and heir his nephew Sukehira and had done everything that could have been expected to further his career; normally he should have left him the assets he had received as his grandfather's heir. He also had a son who was a monk, and whose mother had probably not been recognized even as a secondary wife. He seems to have been extremely fond of the daughter of his mature years. He had raised her as a princess. He bequeathed her all his immovable and movable property, as well as his valuable objects. He even decided that the documents, journals of his forebears, archives and books – all of which were of use only to a man – would be kept for his daughter's male children. His two sons, Sukehira and the monk, each received an estate and instructions not to raise any objections.[14] Sanesuke had long been seen as an enemy and critic of Michinaga and his family. However, when it came to finding a protector for his daughter, he chose a grandson of Michinaga, Kaneyori, the eldest son of Fujiwara no Yorimune, whom he thought would be capable of safeguarding his wishes.

In this world of the court, testamentary freedom was restricted by pressure from those ranking higher up the social scale and, especially in the case of the Fujiwara, by the intervention of the head of the family, who could always ensure that he was given either rare books or documents such as a copy of the journal of an emperor, or valuable objects – vases or musical instruments – belonging to a deceased person. Michinaga made sure that he was given the title deeds to the house of his mother-in-law, which she had wanted to bequeath to the children of her younger daughter, Rinshi's sister.[15] Similarly, the minister of the right Fujiwara no Akimitsu, who, it is true, was not considered very astute, found himself obliged to leave his Horikawa residence to his elder daughter Genshi, whereas he wished to leave it to the younger one Enshi and her children.[16] Genshi had been a consort of Ichijō Tennō, who had had Horikawa rebuilt after a fire (in fact, he had given orders to a provincial governor to bear the restoration costs), since this residence was where Genshi came when she left the palace. However, after the emperor's death, this imperial consort disobeyed her father and had an affair, which ended in marriage, with the son of the imperial prince Tamehira (952-1010), Minamoto no Yorisada. Michinaga had brokered a kind of uneasy truce between father and daughter. But Akimitsu wanted to deprive Genshi of any rights over the Horikawa residence. The empress Shōshi, Michinaga's daughter, supported Genshi's claims, using the argument of its reconstruction in the time of Ichijō Tennō.

The majority of families had the utmost difficulty in maintaining their social status. Which is why alliances, marriages and successions were at the heart of all family strategies, at least for those who did not take the decision to leave the capital for the harsher and less civilized environment of the provinces.

The stages of life

The great aristocrats and wealthy officials welcomed with equal joy the birth of boys and girls. The 3rd, 5th, 7th and 9th nights were celebrated by a banquet, both in the case of children of the nobility and imperial children. The guests who came to offer their congratulations differed according to the father's rank; a man of a higher rank than the father did not attend this type of rejoicing. The children of emperors were always born away from the palace, which must not be defiled by the birth blood. Michinaga took care to invite the most efficacious monks, exorcists and masters of the way of Yin and Yang for his daughters' confinements.[17] All families did likewise, with more or less ostentation according to their wealth and influence. The sons of emperors benefited from additional rituals; for example, over several days morning and night, the reading of a classic such as *The Classic of Filial Piety*, *The Book of Rites* or

Records of the Historian, by a scholar-official.[18] The children of the nobility were given into the care of wet-nurses, women serving in the household. The imperial princes had seven or eight. The wives of middle-ranking officials sought these positions, which allowed them, if their prince became emperor, to obtain favours for their husband and sons. A further invitation was issued for a banquet on the 50th and 100th day after the birth of the child, to whom his grandfather gave, at least symbolically, his first meal of rice and fish. Then, to mark the passage from babyhood to childhood, around two or three years of age there took place the "putting on of the trousers" (*hakamagi*), which was the occasion for another banquet (where of course the child did not appear).

Even in the highest society, the child was not absent from the lives of its parents. The historical narratives and journals often show the affection that men had for their sons and daughters. Sanjō Tennō, on a visit to Tsuchimikado to see for the first time his daughter Teishi aged around two months, had the baby brought inside his dais and entranced by her beauty caressed her for a long time, refusing to come out even though the entire court was waiting for him. Michinaga liked to take his grandsons with him. He relates in his journal how, when he had come to visit his daughter the empress Shōshi, the second little prince Atsuyoshi climbed for fun into his carriage and refused to get down again. The minister then gave in to his whim and left with him.[19] Children were taken to see and enjoy the processions of the Kamo and Iwashimizu festivals.

In his journal, the kind of document that, in principle, did not lend itself to the expression of personal feelings, Sanesuke tells of the last days of his first daughter, born in 985. The child had lost her mother very early. Over the next five years, she was often ill and her father tried everything possible to fortify her health, organizing recitations of *sūtras* and esoteric Buddhist rituals. But all to no avail and, in 990, after an illness lasting ten days or so, she died.[20] Yet Sanesuke had summoned the monks he believed to be the most efficacious, had made vows and had Buddhist statues carved, in a word, done his utmost to save her.

He writes soberly on the day of her death that he is devastated and is crying tears of blood. Fujiwara no Sukefusa, too, in his notes of 1039, relates in detail an illness of his daughter, the treatments followed, the visits of two physicians (as he did not want to rely on only one opinion) and his turmoil when told of a change for the worse.[21]

Boys' education began around five or six years of age. The initial step in learning to read was considered an important date for young princes. Their first reading lesson, purely symbolic, took place with great solemnity in the presence of the court and scholar-officials. A doctor of letters had the child repeat the first five characters of *The Classic of Filial Piety*. The session was followed by a meal, then the composition of Chinese poems, and ended with a concert and songs.

Basic instruction was given to all the children in a family. Elementary Chinese manuals were used, such as the *Mōgyū* (Ch. *Mengqiu*), "(Answers) to the unlettered who seek (explanations)", which, in a simplified and easy to memorize form, presented a series of edifying stories drawn from the Chinese classics and histories; or the *Senjimon* (Ch. *Qianziwen*), *The Thousand Characters*, divided into groups of five, dealing with various fields: astronomy, morality, food, plants, and so on; or again the *Ri Kyū hyakunijūei* (Ch. *Li Jiao baiershiyong*), *One Hundred and Twenty Poems of Ri Kyū*, a collection of poems in lines of five characters by Ri Kyū (644-713), twelve sections of ten poems each. In the late 10th century, primers that included knowledge specific to Japan began to be written. Minamoto no Tamenori (?-1011), a scholar-official who was in charge of the education of a son of Fujiwara no Tamemitsu, wrote for his pupil a short work called *Kuchizusami* (*Fun by Mouth*), in which, using lists intended to be recited much like nursery rhymes (*kuchizusami* means 'to hum', 'recite in a sing-song voice'), many kinds of information were assembled, in nineteen sections; some, like astronomy and the way of Yin and Yang, grouped together mainly Chinese terms, while others, such as palace buildings and functions, were purely Japanese. The section on books gave the list of the Chinese classics and the terms relating to Chinese prosody, but also the titles of the six official histories of Japan, the titles of the codes, collections of decrees and regulations, as well as the list of chapters in the administrative code – incomplete, with notable omissions, such as the chapters relating to households and cultivated lands. These two chapters are the ones that most especially concern the common people; the others deal mainly with officials. The same Tamenori wrote for Yorimichi, the eldest son of Michinaga, a similar work, *Sezoku genbun* (*Proverbs of Our Time*), a series of maxims, with commentary, indispensable for anyone living in society. Also deserving of mention is the dictionary *Wamyō ruijushō* (*Categorized Notes on Japanese Words*), the work of Minamoto no Shitagō (911-983), in which words, mostly concrete terms, are classified by categories: the entries and explanatory sentences are written in Chinese characters, but a Japanese translation is nearly always given. Evidence that these texts were used may be found in the journal of Fujiwara no Yukinari, *Gonki*. In 1011, he writes that one of his sons has just asked him for *Kuchizusami* and *Wamyō ruijushō*.[22] Some precocious children already knew the *Senjimon* by heart at the age of four, as told about a son of the doctor of letters Miyoshi no Kiyoyuki.[23] However Ōe no Masahira, descended from a line of scholars, says that he learned the *Mōgyū* at six years of age, when he rode hobby-horses at play. Two years later, he began writing Chinese poetry and no doubt reading the classics. His grandfather, the second counsellor Koretoki (888-963), lecturer to the emperor, seems to have taken an interest in his early studies and encouraged him, promising him a career as distinguished as his own. Up to the age of fourteen, Masahira studied at home, with such zeal, he says, that he denied himself walks and games.[24] He then attended lectures at the Office of Higher Learning and, in a year, passed an examination that allowed him to present for the competitive examination of the Department of Regulations Relating to Civil Officials. However he gives no information about his teachers at the Office. The sons of senior nobles and even of officials, all those not intending to pursue literary studies, did all their education at home or attended the house of a teacher, who was not necessarily a doctor of the classics or letters.

The education of Michinaga's youngest son, Nagaie, was entrusted to a member of the Ōe family, Kinyori (?-1040), who may well have been a student of letters in his youth, although it is not known for certain. At the age of twelve, Nagaie finished reading the first scroll of the *Records of the Historian*, which, together with the *Anthology* and the works of Haku Kyoi (Bo Juyi), was the main source of reading for the senior nobles. To mark the occasion, the doctor of letters Fujiwara no Hironari (977-1028) invited seven or eight scholars to compose poems.[25] Kinyori must have kept in contact with his pupil, for much later he transferred one of his properties to him. In fact, he hoped that Nagaie's protection would enable his descendants to retain rights over this property.[26]

Besides the classics and histories, some men, even from the very highest ranks of the aristocracy, had wider interests and read the *Rōshi* (Ch. *Laozi*) or the *Sōshi* (Ch. *Zhuangzi*), works of two thinkers classified as Taoist, or else took an interest in the way of Yin and Yang. Others did not neglect the law, as was the case, for example, with Fujiwara no Yukinari, who had the penal code, *ritsu*, explained to him.[27] However many did not go beyond a fairly basic level of education. Michinaga often complained that the young auditors were incapable of writing correctly, when this was asked of them during meetings of the council. He writes, in 1012, no doubt with a slight exaggeration:

> Many of the auditors cannot read or write, which is very painful to see when the council takes decisions.

Sanesuke was equally hard on the young second generals of the palace guard. An anecdote tells how Minamoto no Toshikata, a member of the Control Board no less, having to write a document in front of the council of senior nobles and not knowing how to write a character correctly, saved face by making an inkblot.[28]

As was to be expected, the scholar-officials took particular care with the education of their children. Fujiwara no Tametoki

(?-?), the father of Murasaki Shikibu, was teaching his son Nobunori (972-1011) to read the classics and histories. Recalling her childhood memories, Murasaki writes:

> When my brother was having his reading lesson, he would hesitate or have memory lapses in certain passages that I, curiously, understood. My father, who was very knowledgeable in Chinese literature, would say ruefully: "It's a great pity she's not a boy."[29]

For daughters were supposed to learn to read and write only the syllabary. In fact, quite a few had a good knowledge of the characters, but social conventions prevented them from displaying this too openly.

Girls and boys learned music, but girls practised the koto, which was played as a solo instrument. The image of the solitary woman plucking the strings of her instrument by moonlight before an overgrown garden forms part of the romantic imaginings of this period. Boys, while not disdaining the koto, played all the instruments of the orchestra, mainly the various kinds of flute, the mouth organ and small drums. They could be taken to display their proficiency at the court. A brother of Sanesuke, Takatō (949-1013), celebrated for his playing, gave flute lessons to the young Ichijō Tennō. Dance also formed part of a man's education. Fathers saw to it that their sons had good teachers and were very pleased when they were noticed at court celebrations or shrine festivals. Archery was also an opportunity to display skill and elegance, and any young aristocrat who had some ability practised it. Young women, for their part, were expected to know how to sew. For one of a wife's duties was to sew her husband's garments and see to the making of clothes for the members of the household as well as their re-sewing after washing. The author of the *Kagerō Diary* and wife of Kaneie, irritated by his infrequent visits and receiving from him packets of garments to prepare, returns them on several occasions without having sewn them herself or having had them sewn by women of her household.

Everyone, young men and young women alike, but in varying degrees, was required to learn the social conventions, good manners, the correct use of honorific terms and male or female vocabulary, and a host of details relating to dress: colours, patterns and way of wearing it. They had to be able to write a good hand and be capable of composing Japanese poetry. For this, it was necessary to be familiar with its conventions, and know many poems by heart in order to recognize the allusions contained in those of other people and be able to skilfully insert lines into one's own compositions.

Entry into adulthood took place between ten and twelve years of age for crown princes and the sons of very senior nobles, and between fourteen and sixteen years of age for the others. At this time, the young man adopted the hairstyle of an adult man, with his hair drawn up in a knot under the cap. He received his first rank and from then on could wear court dress. The ceremony, "putting on of the male cap" (*genpuku*), was held in public, at the residence of the father or that of one of his patrons, and one of the guests, preferably the most important, undertook the placing of the cap. A banquet and gifts were offered to the guests. Often, on this occasion, ministers adopted young men of their family, so as to assure them of their first rank. However these adoptions were more like sponsorship.[30] When the young man was the son of a senior noble, he then visited the palace to express his gratitude for the rank he had received. It was often not his first visit, as the young men of very high birth had previously received permission to come once to the palace, no doubt to familiarize themselves with the place and its ways.

For young women, a comparable celebration had been created, the "putting on of the train" (*mogi*), which preceded marriage or an appointment to the upper ranks of the female palace staff. The ceremony took place earlier or later, according to the plans of the family. Michinaga, for instance, held it for his two older daughters Shōshi and Kenshi when they were barely eleven years old, as he was anxious to marry them to the emperor and crown prince. Later, to the utter amazement of

Sanesuke, he appointed his youngest daughter Kishi, aged eleven, head of the palace women's services, even though she had not yet celebrated her coming-of-age.[31]

Marriage for men usually coincided with their first appointments. But the sons of very important personages began to conduct affairs with women in service at the palace, and, if they were capable of doing so, exchanged poems with them. The author of the *Eiga monogatari* says of Yorimune, a son of Michinaga and Minamoto no Meishi, that he was very charming and had amorous exploits with many women by whom he had children,[32] who of course do not appear among his descendants. Parents, whether senior nobles or officials, arranged marriages that they deemed to be the most advantageous for their family. Michinaga, whose position protected him from all financial worries, tried to obtain for his son and heir Yorimichi a daughter of the imperial prince Tomohira (964-1009). He apparently said at the time that a man's worth is measured by the rank of his wife. Matters were handled as if the marriage proposal came from the prince – normal practice since, strictly speaking, he was of a higher rank than the minister –, whereas it was Michinaga who had arranged everything, contrary to the secret wish of Tomohira. The senior nobles, who had no hope of placing their daughters as imperial consorts in the palace, tried to obtain Michinaga's sons as sons-in-law. Nagaie, the youngest, at the age of fifteen, was the object of their covetousness. The major counsellor Fujiwara no Yukinari sounded out Michinaga on the subject of a marriage with a daughter aged twelve, whom he had raised with the utmost care. Michinaga accepted, saying that it would be charming as a dolls' marriage. On the appointed day, Nagaie presented himself in the evening at Yukinari's residence and was welcomed with torches by the brothers of the young wife. In accordance with the custom, he left her next morning and sent her a poem:

> Why, this morning, did I wish to remain abed without ever getting up again and, once up, must I await the coming of evening to sleep?

Reading it, Yukinari realized that the poem was the work of Michinaga. The girl did not know how to respond appropriately, but her mother helped her and her father, a renowned calligrapher, imitating the writing of a young girl, wrote the poem:

> Sky of such pale blue, calm spring day; the evening, they say, is slow in coming.[33]

According to custom, the young man presented himself on three successive evenings at the residence of his father-in-law. On the third evening, a tray of glutinous rice cakes was offered to the newly-wed couple. A banquet made the marriage public.

Sometimes, it was after the birth of a child that a marriage was made official. Yorimune, mentioned earlier, had ceased his amorous exploits for a time to devote all his attention to the daughter of Fujiwara no Korechika. This man had died despairing at the thought of the unhappy fate that awaited the daughters of a man in disgrace. Clearly he did not wish them to marry a son of the man who had caused his downfall, any more than that they should enter the palace in the service of an empress who was the daughter of his enemy. For he himself had hoped to become the father of an empress. The *Eiga monogatari* relates that:

> The second general (Yorimune) was visiting the daughter of the late governor-general (Korechika). A pretty little girl was born. Lord Michinaga took her in his arms, saying that she was worthy of being a future empress. For the seventh-night celebration, congratulations poured in from all sides and not only did Lord Michinaga send his own, but he also took care of all the expenses.[34]

In this way, the marriage of Yorimune was henceforth recognized by his father.

Promotions and appointments marked the other stages in men's lives. Each time it was an opportunity for them to give a banquet to their equals and inferiors and to go and thank their superiors. The prohibition on displaying too much ostentation for these kinds of banquets was often renewed, but to no avail.

The provincial governors went to pay their respects to the important personages, their patrons, before leaving to take up their post. Michinaga and Sanesuke were pleased to offer their protégés refreshments and a session of poetic composition.

When men or women (at least empresses, princesses and mothers of empresses) reached the age of forty, fifty or sixty, they received wishes for a long life and festivities were organized by their families, according to a custom borrowed from China. In Japan, a Buddhist celebration brought the programme to a close. Many poems composed on these occasions have been preserved, one of the models being:

> Ten thousand years await you lord, object of our wishes, may we shelter a thousand years in your shade![35]

This text, rather banal at first sight, includes two word-plays: 'wait', *matsu*, has a homonym *matsu*, 'pine', symbol of longevity; the verbal auxiliary *tsuru*, which expresses finality, has a homonym *tsuru*, 'crane', symbol of good fortune. These word-plays allow the mental image of a crane on a pine tree to be introduced into the poem.

For his mother's fortieth birthday, Ichijō Tennō came to the Tsuchimikado residence, which Michinaga had decorated superbly for the occasion. Poems had been composed by the most skilful poets for the screens adorned with paintings. The garden and its hills were decked out in autumn colours and the boats carrying the musicians moved about on the lake. Michinaga's two eldest sons, Yorimichi and Yorimune, aged nine, each performed a dance.[36] When, in 1015, his daughter the empress Shōshi organized the celebration for Michinaga's fiftieth birthday, she assembled at least two hundred monks who, magnificently attired, went in procession around the lake, chanted invocations and recited *sūtras*. The minister's sons and daughters had all contributed to the expenses. The great personages had sent poems that were brushed on the screens by Fujiwara no Yukinari. During the banquet, the guests improvised and sang congratulatory poems. To Fujiwara no Kintō who said to him while proffering a cup:

Aging pine, to whom go all our wishes, as for a thousand years
we shall be able to shelter in its millennial shade,

Michinaga replied:

It has indeed aged, but as no-one knows this, they jest, saying
of the pine in the valley that it cannot feel the weight of years.[37]

In 1023, her children organized the celebration for the sixtieth birthday of Minamoto no Rinshi. There was the customary
Buddhist religious service, after which the banquet went on into
the night.

The moon soon rose, allowing them to see into the distance,
and the torches, set in the ground or carried by servants, lit up
the scene. The cups reflecting the moonlight circulated all the
while among the assembled lords; then the major counsellor
Kintō said: "Long life to her, let us make this acclamation
heard today, joining all our voices to that of the pines on the
hills."[38]

And all the participants in turn presented their poem.

Even the less well-to-do families organized this kind of
celebration. In 1004, Michinaga made sure that the sons of an
elderly deserving official had enough to recompense one of the
monks they had invited for their father's sixtieth birthday.[39]

The senior nobles often reached the age of sixty. Of the
twenty-one members of the council of senior nobles, in 1011, at
the time of Ichijō Tennō's death, three were over eighty, four
over seventy, nine over sixty and three over fifty. Only one died
prematurely aged forty-three. Thanks to the journals, we are
quite well informed about the most common illnesses: in
summer diarrhoea and malaria were rife; in winter colds and
coughs. In all seasons, men and women had boils and abscesses.
Diabetes and dropsy were also present. Women often died in
childbirth. From time to time, a smallpox epidemic struck the
court and the city, as in 995.

Physicians – certain branches of the Wake and Tanba
families provided most of them – belonged to the court
personnel, though not necessarily to the Office of Medicine.

They studied medicine from Chinese books. However, in the late 10th century, Tanba no Yasuyori (912-995) compiled a medical treatise, *Ishinpō* (*The Essence of Medicine*), covering all areas of physical and mental health, internal and external disorders, and treatments: this by means of quotations from Chinese works. Yet this treatise does not appear to have circulated widely. Physicians treated patients using herbs grown in gardens attached to the palace. But they also used imported remedies, notably drugs whose main ingredient was cinnabar, renowned in China as a life-prolonging medicine. Baths and compresses were also part of the therapeutic stock, as was the moxa. The journals do not mention acupuncture, which nevertheless appears in the medical treatises available in Japan at the time. Monks and their efficacious practices – prayers and exorcisms – were called just as often as physicians to patients' bedsides.

Death was surrounded by Buddhist rituals. For some it was an occasion to offer a final poem. Michinaga, in his journal, has preserved the one uttered by Ichijō Tennō on his death-bed:

> On this night, the emperor, whose suffering was extreme, raised himself to say to the empress, who was at the foot of his curtained bed: "In this transitory abode and bathed in tears, I leave you; I depart, I think, to shake off the dust of the world."[40]

Michinaga himself, when he was about to enter his last hours, sent his daughter the empress Shōshi a final poem:

> Songs like leaves are fated to end; in our world, nothing can hold back our bodies, which are like the autumn leaves. [41]

Then he awaited death in the Amida chapel, facing west, in the direction of Amida's paradise, holding between his hands ribbons that connected him to the nine aligned statues of Amida, ceaselessly reciting the *nenbutsu*.

As a house in which a death occurred was defiled and the defilement was transmitted to those inside, officials avoided waiting there for a dying person to draw their last breath. Thus

Michinaga left his mother-in-law's house when the end was nigh and Fujiwara no Sukefusa did likewise when his father-in-law was about to expire. He even took the precaution of having his clothes removed from the house of the deceased in order to be able to continue his service at the court.[42]

The body was then washed, placed in the coffin and taken outside the city, usually to the east, to the place where the dead were cremated. The smoke that rose and mingled with the clouds was used as a symbol for the precariousness of life. After Michinaga's cremation, a monk wrote:

> The smoke has vanished; the snow-covered plains of Toribe seem to us like the crane grove.[43]

The expression "crane grove" recalls the trees illuminated by whiteness under which the Buddha entered into Nirvana.

The code, copying the articles of the Chinese code, had established strict rules concerning the period of mourning. However, in the 11th century, the Japanese had greatly shortened this time. By and large they suited themselves when mourning relatives other than a father or mother, as officials were reluctant to be absent from the palace for too long.

Women in society

As already noted, with regard to marriages and successions, women were pawns in family strategies and were dependent on their father. But a certain amount of sexual freedom was accepted, more so for women belonging to the middle and lower levels of society than for the wives and daughters of the senior nobles. For men were obliged to exercise care in respect of these ladies so as not to be viewed unfavourably by their aristocratic families. The beauty, intelligence or adroitness of certain women of lowly birth enabled them to achieve unexpected success. Fujiwara no Sanesuke, after becoming minister of the right, treated as his principal wife the mother of the daughter whom he loved dearly, a woman he had probably known as someone in the service of his second wife Kyōshi, daughter of the imperial prince Tamehira.

All were expected to be beautiful. The criteria of beauty were whiteness of complexion, length of the hair, delicacy of features, slenderness of the figure and elegance of deportment. They were also expected to be educated in what was suitable for their sex. A good knowledge of the anthology compiled in the early 10th century, *Kokin wakashū* (*Collection of Ancient and Modern Poems*), was considered essential. In her *Makura no sōshi* (*Pillow Book*), Sei Shōnagon recounts in some detail how the empress Teishi set her ladies a kind of test, by giving them the first two lines of poems from this anthology and asking them to supply the remainder. The result was less than satisfactory and the empress reminded them of an imperial consort of Murakami Tennō and daughter of Fujiwara no Moromasa, Hōshi (?-967), who replied without error to the questions put to her by the emperor on the whole anthology. Her father, who by her education had laid the groundwork for this brilliant result, was so overjoyed by it that he had the monks in various temples recite *sūtras* in thanksgiving.[44]

Women of very high birth were destined for three kinds of future: entering the palace as an imperial consort, becoming the principal wife of a great nobleman, or becoming a nun. If their father was in disgrace, they fell back into the category of girls of the middle-ranking nobility, but their fate was considered even more unfortunate. Imperial princesses were especially difficult to marry off and the condition of nun suited them well. From among them and the daughters of imperial princes (namely sons of emperors) were chosen the Vestal-princesses in charge of worship at the Ise and Kamo shrines. Towards the end of a reign or when they were defiled by a bereavement, they left their functions and could marry.

Entry into the palace as an imperial consort or a lady of the bedchamber was relatively open in the 10th century: Daigo Tennō and Murakami Tennō each had a considerable number. The first had fourteen sons and twenty-three daughters by fourteen women, of whom only one, Onshi, a daughter of

Fujiwara no Mototsune, was elevated to the rank of empress. The second had nine sons and some twelve daughters by nine women, one of whom, Anshi, daughter of Fujiwara no Morosuke, became empress. The author of the *Eiga monogatari* praises Daigo Tennō because he treated all these women with kindness and saw to it that there was no jealousy.[45] However Anshi sometimes displayed a certain impatience at the all too obvious interest shown by the emperor Murakami in others than herself.[46] In addition to the two successive empresses, Teishi, daughter of the chancellor Fujiwara no Michitaka, and Shōshi, daughter of the minister of the left and head of the council, Michinaga, Ichijō Tennō had three imperial consorts: Genshi, Gishi (974-1053) and Sonshi (984-1022), daughters of the minister of the right, Fujiwara no Akimitsu, the third minister Fujiwara no Kinsue and the chancellor who died in 995, Fujiwara no Michikane. But none had a child. After the emperor's death, two of them married senior nobles, whose careers were undistinguished. When Goichijō Tennō came to the throne, the number of imperial consorts decreased markedly: for the three reigns of Michinaga's grandsons, only his grand-daughters were chosen.

An empress who was the mother of an emperor enjoyed a certain importance. It is said that Michinaga owed his attainment of the highest post at the court to the influence of his sister Senshi, the mother of the emperor (Ichijō). Later, when his daughter Shōshi was a widow and mother of the crown prince and future emperor (Gosuzaku), he seems to have often sought her advice. In 1040, prior to the appointment as head of the Chancellery of Fujiwara no Nobunaga (1022-1094), a son of Norimichi, hence a nephew of Shōshi, she was consulted, at least as a matter of form.[47] Even young empresses, through their female attendants, could also influence their father. Fujiwara no Sukefusa relates his conversation with a Control Board official:

> Towards evening, (Taira no) Sadachika came to chat: the lord chancellor had reprimanded him. This is why he remains shut away at home. The reprimand was not because of a mistake he

had made in the course of his duties, but concerned his wife. He left her a month or two ago and this woman, full of resentment, went and spoke ill of him to the empress (Genshi). It is because she went to the empress and slandered him that he left her. When the chancellor learned of the matter, he roundly criticized Sadachika. There are so many such stories that I have no time to tell them.[48]

Women who became the wife of a senior noble had a much more sheltered and peaceful life, unless, like those of Minamoto no Rinshi, their daughters entered the palace as imperial consorts and then empresses. Rinshi's presence at the palace with her daughters is often mentioned by Michinaga. However the wife of a major counsellor had no place here. She could not be seen in the entourage of an empress, as she would have demeaned her husband's rank. Rinshi, and later Takahime, the wife of the chancellor Yorimichi, had some influence over their husbands, who showed them an unwavering preference. The wife of the scholar-official Ōe no Masahira, Akazome Emon, author of a collection of poems and quite possibly of the *Eiga monogatari*, was a lady in Rinshi's service. The very successful career of her son no doubt benefited as much from this as from the reputation of her husband. Takahime had no children. Yorimichi was therefore obliged to contract other marriages, but the journal of Fujiwara no Sukefusa gives several examples of the weight Takahime's advice carried with the chancellor. She also intervened to protect a daughter of one of her uncles, although born to a secondary wife, from a woman who no doubt did not have the status of a wife and whose children do not appear in the Minamoto genealogy. This person was the second wife of Sukefusa's father-in-law, the stepmother of his wife. He complains of the protection she was given by the chancellor, when she became a widow, and which allowed her to gain control of most of the inheritance, to the detriment of the children.[49]

However the wives of major and second counsellors could seldom have the satisfaction of establishing themselves as protectors. They lived in relative luxury, surrounded by a household full of people and a large female staff: attendants and

wet-nurses of their children. In novels as in real life, these wet-
nurses had some influence over their young charges and could
facilitate their amorous intrigues. When Genshi, the former
imperial consort and daughter of Akimitsu, against her father's
wishes, began a relationship with a young auditor, Minamoto no
Yorisada, her wet-nurse helped her to get away from her
father's house.[50] The wives of senior nobles supervised their
daughters' education and, if they were capable of doing so,
exchanged letters with friends and relations. From time to time,
they could admire the processions of the shrine festivals from a
closed carriage. Visits and sojourns in temples in the countryside were a way of breaking the monotony of everyday life.
Some women, like the daughter of the major counsellor
Fujiwara no Kintō, had to put up with the rather dissolute
conduct of their husband. The author of the *Eiga monogatari*
says of Fujiwara no Norimichi:

> He was always having affairs; he went after the attendants of
> his sisters the empresses and even had relations with women in
> his household, which had alienated his wife and had drawn
> criticism from the ladies in service at his home.[51]

The daughters of officials who were not senior nobles had
the possibility of marrying a high nobleman if their grandfather
had been one, or if their father had made his fortune in provincial governorships. As in the case of the wife of Fujiwara no
Sukefusa, this assured them of no more than a modest level of
comfort. And their situation was hardly any different from that
of the wives of officials. Some lived very amicably with their
husband who, like Sukefusa, consulted them about everything
relating to family life and even kept them informed about their
work. If they married an official, they could remain at home or
seek to go into service. Some also had no hesitation in accompanying their husband to the provinces when he had been
appointed there, like the wife of the governor of the distant
province of Kōzuke, to whom, before her departure, the
empress Shōshi presented a fan, on which the minister Michinaga had written a poem to go with the picture of a hut:

If the dew wets your travel shelter with its grass pillow, may the wind blow only to dissipate it![52]

This situation, which may be called "middle-class", was that of the women about whom Sei Shōnagon says in her *Pillow Book*:

I was contemptuously imagining the thoughts of women with no future, who watch faithfully over the indifferent happiness of a home.[53]

However not all women were fortunate enough to be a man's only wife. They sometimes had to be satisfied with being a second wife, or even a concubine with a more precarious status, there being only a slight difference in some cases. The author of the *Kagerō nikki* rather had the status of a wife: Kaneie had spoken to her father before visiting her home. But, as we have seen, she was not the only one and what she found difficult to accept were not so much Kaneie's visits to Tokihime, the mother of his numerous children, as those he began making to a third person. She even had him followed in order to find out where this person lived and who she was. For many years, she waited for Kaneie's visits, consumed by jealousy and incapable of breaking things off, even if she refused to receive him on occasion and no doubt tired him out with her recriminations.

Relations between two wives sometimes took a most unpleasant turn. Ōnakatomi no Sukechika (954-1038), head priest of the Ise Shrine and a high-ranking official in the Ministry of Religious Affairs, had a wife known by the sobriquet of Kura. She had served at the court and was the wet-nurse of Norimichi, the younger brother of Yorimichi. So she was not in the first flush of youth in 1010 and Sukechika himself was fifty-six years old, when the house of the widow of Minamoto no Kanenari (?-1010) was extensively damaged by a band of thirty people made up of male and female servants of Norimichi. It was an attack provoked by the jealousy of the lady Kura against Kanenari's widow, whom Sukechika was visiting. Two years later, in 1012, there was a disturbance at Sukechika's home, where Kura was living. According to those who informed Michinaga, it was a case of revenge by the second wife.[54] The vocabulary of the time even had a specific term, *uwanari-uchi*, to describe the attack of the first wife against the second.

One way of escaping the monotony of life within the family and finding opportunities of being noticed, as well as in the longer term helping one's family, was to enter the palace women's services or become one of the empresses' attendants. The Naishidokoro was headed by two grand mistresses, a function which, in the 11th century, had become no more than a stepping-stone before entry into the palace as an imperial consort. The real work was handled by four assistants, often experienced women, and third-class officials. Their role was to convey certain orders from the emperor and to assist him in his daily life. They took part in the ceremonies, carrying the sword and the casket containing the jewel and transmitting the list of those present. They had places reserved for them at the ceremonies, a little to one side and not with the male officials. They were assisted by people of lower status who performed the practical tasks. They received ranks and stipends and were promoted in the same way as men. Moreover, wives of men of at least the fifth rank, while having no actual functions, were admitted to the palace as attendants of the empresses or imperial princesses: they accompanied them and lived at the palace when they were in residence there.

As Sei Shōnagon says, these women were sometimes considered frivolous, for they had the opportunity of meeting many men. However they had the advantage of mingling with the most élite company, at the centre of elegance, refinement and good taste. Even those who, confined within their family, seldom came to the palace any more, did at least know its conventions and could avoid being made to look foolish. Sei Shōnagon, on the one hand, who lived in the entourage of the empress Fujiwara no Teishi, and on the other Murasaki Shikibu, who was an attendant of the empress Fujiwara no Shōshi, give an almost identical picture of court life, but which their personalities colour in a different way.

The first sums up, in this scene, what she considers to be the height of happiness:

> How delightful it is to place carelessly in a vase a long branch of beautifully flowering cherry blossom. And even more delightful that guests dressed in a cerise costume or the noble brothers of the empress come to sit there and chat.[55]

A valuable object, a natural-looking floral arrangement, male guests elegantly attired in a white tunic lined with purple and pleasant conversation: these are what make her happy. Sei Shōnagon was proud of her presence of mind, and of her ability to immediately recognize allusions and dash off a poem. She smugly relates how Fujiwara no Narinobu, one of the most brilliant young aristocrats, having distanced himself from her, put her as it were to the test and sent her a line from a poem by the Chinese poet Bo Juyi, in which, exiled, he depicts the contrast between the lives of his friends still in service at the palace and his own solitary life in a thatched hut. Narinobu sent Sei Shōnagon the line about the glories of the court and she replied: "Who would go and visit a poor thatched hut?" She thus showed that she knew the poem and, out of sheer coquetry, rather gave Narinobu the impression that she was not particularly keen to renew their relationship. He eagerly did so, and let everyone know her response, which even became known to the emperor.[56]

Murasaki Shikibu, on the other hand, places more emphasis on the negative aspects of court life: the impossibility of isolating oneself – the screens and curtains made it difficult to avoid male indiscretions –, the chatter and gossip of the other ladies, the tiresome presence of young aristocrats, the enmities and jealousies, the jokes one had to put up with, the nicknames one could be given, the fear of mistakes and ridicule. However, called on several times by Michinaga to compose a poem on the spot, she complied and took care to preserve her work.

Men and women at the palace had many opportunities to embark on amorous affairs. The exchange of poems was an important part of this. The imperial anthologies and personal collections are full of poems that express passionate feelings or light banter. Certain women had a long career of love affairs and exchanged poems with many men. The lady known as Uma (?-?), who seems not to have contracted a regular marriage, was greatly loved for a time by a future senior noble, Fujiwara no Asateru (951-995). One of their first poetic exchanges may be given as an example of the playful tone of this type of correspondence. When Asateru was still only an adjutant of the gate guard and aged eighteen or nineteen, he sent her:

> I hear the voice of the nightingale, ah! how I long to see the branches in flower.

This was a first invitation to begin an exchange of letters. The nightingale is Uma, already known for her writing skill. Asateru apologizes for his beginner's awkwardness: he literally writes "I am not used to trampling branches in flower", with a word-play on the verb 'trample', *fumu*, which, in the suspensive form, *fumi*, is a homonym of the word 'letter'. The lady replied:

> What the nightingale sings softly, could you hear it too in the oak wood?[57]

The expression "oak wood", through a series of word-plays, is an allusion to the young man's function in the gate guard.

The women who served in the palace were in contact with the important personages. Murasaki Shikibu writes that when senior nobles had a message for the empress they usually entrusted this to an experienced lady, in whom they could confide and who could act as their informant. It certainly appears that she herself played this role for Sanesuke. She was perhaps the lady whom this major counsellor questioned in order to have news of the crown prince Atsunari, who was ill in 1013. Similarly, Fujiwara no Sukefusa received confidential information from Gosuzaku's wet-nurse about the emperor's state of mind.[58]

Provided they were clever and circumspect, the women serving in the palace could gain a good reputation and be in a position to help their families. Those who had been chosen as wet-nurses for the emperors or other important personages maintained relations with their charges that allowed them to request favours, such as appointments for their husband and sons.

Literature in the Japanese language has been made famous primarily by women belonging to the middle and lower levels of the aristocracy and having served at the palace. Of course, besides their works in *kanbun*, some men, the most distinguished being Fujiwara no Kintō, have left collections of Japanese poems and short treatises on art and poetry, but the women have given us the greatest masterpieces in the genres of narrative, essay or diary, the last of these often resembling memoirs. Several composed enough poems for them to be collected into anthologies. One may mention those of Uma, Akazome Emon, Sei Shōnagon, Murasaki Shikibu, Izumi Shikibu and Ise no Tayū (or Taifu), all of whom, in the early 11th century, belonged to the entourage of the empress Shōshi, which shows just how much care Michinaga had taken in selecting it.

The oldest was the third-class official Uma, of whose family little is known. She moved in various circles around empresses, as well as in that of the Vestal-princess Senshi (964-1035). Akazome Emon was the daughter of a lower-ranking officer in the gate guard; her real father may have been the poet Taira no Kanemori (?-990). She was the wife of the distinguished scholar Ōe no Masahira and was very familiar with the household of Michinaga and his wife Rinshi. Murasaki Shikibu, in her descriptions of people at the court, does not rank her among the very best talents, but credits her with dignity and restraint. On the other hand, Murasaki criticizes the way Sei Shōnagon parades her talents and knowledge. Sei Shōnagon was the daughter of Kiyohara no Motosuke (908-990), who was one of the officials appointed to select the poems for the imperial anthology *Gosen wakashū* (*Later Collection of Poetry*) compiled after 951. Izumi Shikibu (974?-1030?) was the daughter of Ōe no Masamune (?-?), an official in the household of a dowager empress. She was married to another official in the same household, who was appointed governor of Izumi, from where she took the name by which she is known. She caused something of a scandal by her successive affairs with two imperial princes, the sons of Reizei Tennō. After the death of the second, she entered the service of the empress Shōshi. It was here that Murasaki Shikibu came to know her. In the description she gives of her, Murasaki credits her with a genuine talent for epistolary exchanges and a lack of affectation in poetic improvisation.[59] As noted earlier, Murasaki Shikibu was the daughter of the scholar-official Fujiwara no Tametoki. She was married for only three years. After being widowed, she was called to serve in the entourage of the empress Shōshi. Tayū (fl. ca. 1007-1060) took her sobriquet from the functions exercised by her father Ōnakatomi no Sukechika at the Ise Shrine. Her grandfather Ōnakatomi no Yoshinobu (921-991) was a well-known poet. She too was placed in Shōshi's entourage. Up until her death, at a very advanced age, she graced the poetry contests organized at the court.

To these female authors of poetry collections must be added the name of the Vestal-princess of the Kamo Shrine, a daughter of Murakami Tennō, Senshi. For many years, she served the shrine, which obliged her to lead a more secluded and peaceful kind of life than that at the palace. With a natural gift for poetry, she took pleasure in gathering around her ladies capable of appreciating it and of composing poems.

Apart from Uma, Ise no Tayū and the Vestal-princess Senshi, these women have left other works, all containing poems, because they speak about their daily lives steeped in poetry. Sei Shōnagon's *Pillow Book* is a mixture of accounts of events that have taken place at the court, descriptions and various lists, such as depressing things, amusing things and others. The work called *Izumi Shikibu nikki* is a collection of the poems she exchanged with the princes Tametaka (977-1002) and Atsumichi (981-1007) by whom she was loved, linked by a few sentences noting the dates, her state of mind or the circumstances. In her diary, Murasaki Shikibu depicts the situation at the court at the time of the birth of the two sons of the empress

Shōshi, to which she adds the rather unkind descriptions of some of her companions.

A little earlier than *The Diary of Izumi Shikibu* is the work by the Mother of Michitsuna, *The Kagerō Diary*, which has a slightly different tone, for its author, confined at home, was obsessed with her grievances. A little later, *The Sarashina Diary* is the work of the daughter (name unknown, 1008-?) of a scholar-official, Sugawara no Takasue (973-?). It is more a collection of reminiscences than a diary. Its author served only briefly in the household of a very young princess. This text attests to the eagerness of women of this time for romantic tales. Such reading pleasurably filled their over-abundant leisure hours. Many titles of 10th-century narratives remain, but the works have been lost, except for three or four, including Murasaki Shikibu's masterpiece, *Genji monogatari.*

The first two parts are devoted to a prince named Hikaru, the Shining One, son of an emperor and a lady of the bedchamber, his favourite. They relate the vicissitudes of the life of this person, handsome and multi-talented, his first successes at the court, his doomed love for one of his father's wives, his numerous affairs with women, his disgrace, his self-imposed exile, his return to the court and his concern for the women he has loved. The last part relates the ill-starred loves of the son of his last wife, a child who, in actual fact, is not his. This long narrative, which extends over several decades and presents several hundred characters, has a somewhat melodramatic element: the hidden fault of the prince – his brief relationship with an imperial consort – making him, without anyone being aware of it, the real father of an emperor. The depiction of the hero and his attitude towards women seems somewhat ideal-ized, as does the reversal of fortune that allows him to resume his place at the court. Yet the contrasting and varied situations always appear plausible in their detail. This work quickly became a success. The empress Shōshi read it and the author of *The Sarashina Diary*, in her youth, dreamed only of being able to obtain a copy. Since then, it has never ceased to be read and commentated on; it has fostered the nostalgia for the Heian court, the refinement of which has been exaggerated by later generations. It has inspired illustrators and poets.

Akazome Emon, for her part, wrote the *Eiga monogatari*, which, divided into chapters with titles imitating those of the *Genji monogatari*, presents only the world of the court, beginning with Michinaga and his family. Akazome Emon was a witness to the events of her time and this is often apparent in her narrative, but she favours the sentimental and anecdotal aspects, although errors as to dates or the precise status of the people of whom she speaks are relatively few overall.

Only the collections of anecdotes, another production of the time, appear to escape the female dominance of literature. This is understandable for those belonging to the genre of edifying Buddhist tales, even if they often go beyond it. The two best known collections are *Sanbō ekotoba* (*Illustrated Tales of the Three Treasures*), the work of Minamoto no Tamenori, author of the primers for children mentioned earlier, written for the instruction of a princess, Sonshi (966?-985), who had become a nun; and *Konjaku monogatarishū*, with more than a thousand anecdotes about India, China and Japan. In its later books, there are many secular anecdotes, in which are clearly recognizable a large number of people known through the historical sources. The other category of collections of anecdotes deals with the relationships between men and women; each short tale, many very brief, is organized around one or more poems. The *Ise monogatari* (*Tales of Ise*), like the *Yamato monogatari* (*Tales of Yamato*), dates from the 10th century, but their authors (women, or more likely men) remain unknown.

As most modern readers have no interest in the literary works written exclusively by men in *kanbun*, much of the literature in the Japanese language – poetry, narratives and anecdotes – from the Heian period appears to have as its favourite subject the relations between men and women. On this point, Japan differs from China, its model. This fact accounts for the criticism sometimes levelled at the Heian period: that of being effeminate. However the novel is not the whole of reality. The senior nobles and officials did not spend all their time sighing at the moon and composing poems on the seasons. A good deal of their energy was taken up with securing positions or maintaining their rank, if not simply with survival. In order to achieve this, many were obliged to take roads that distanced them from the pomp of the court.

Notes

1. *Hossō shiyōshō*, a summary and reordering of the articles of the 8th-century penal code, compiled at the end of the Heian period.
2. *Shunki*, Chōryaku 3.10.7., 1039.
3. *Shōyūki*, Shōryaku 1.10.16. and 1.11.2., 990. Sanesuke sells the Nijō residence for five thousand bushels of rice.
4. *Midō kanpakuki*, Chōwa 5.7.21., 1016. Fire at Tsuchimikado; rebuilding begins from 5.8.7., and is completed the following summer. According to the *Eiga monogatari*, chap. 12, the provincial governors bore the costs and directed the work, and Minamoto no Yorimitsu (948-1021), a wealthy provincial governor, offered the furniture and interior furnishings.
5. *Gonki*, Chōtoku 4.10.29., 998.
6. *Heian ibun*, texts 409 and 410, Chōhō 3.6.26., 1001. According to the Taira genealogy, Korenaka had an adopted son, but he does not mention him in the dispositions he made in 1001.
7. *Shūgaishō* (*Collection of Fragments*), a small encyclopaedia dealing with the early court, compiled by a court noble in the 14th century, fasc. 2, "Aristocratic residences"; and *Eiga monogatari*, chap. 1.
8. *Shūgaishō*, fasc. 2, and *Eiga monogatari*, chap. 14.
9. *Eiga monogatari*, chap. 3.
10. *Eiga monogatari*, chap. 3. Masanobu could no longer hope to make his daughter an imperial consort, as the Fujiwara of the regents' branch were beginning to exercise very strict control over the group of imperial consorts and to no longer tolerate entry into it of any but their own daughters.
11. *Midō kanpakuki*, Kankō 1.11.8., 1004. The child left by a woman at Michinaga's residence was just over three months old. The following year, a lady in the service of the empress sent Michinaga a poem possibly referring to this child. She was requesting the minister's protection for the girl.

12. *Kugyō bunin* (*Appointments of Senior Nobles*). Fujiwara no Yasuchika (922?-996), the brother of Tokihime, was appointed an auditor in Eien 1., 987.

13. *Eiga monogatari*, chap. 8.

14. *Shōyūki*, Kannin 3.12.9., 1020. Sanesuke made these dispositions long before being able to marry off his daughter. He also made a gift to the Miidera.

15. *Shōyūki*, Chōwa 3.12.22., 1014, Michinaga is given a valuable vase from the estate of a brother of Sanesuke. *Midō kanpakuki*, Kankō 1.9. intercalary day 12. and 1.10.3., 1004, Kankō 7.10.3. and 7.10.27., 1010, Michinaga is given some books belonging to the estates of deceased officials; Chōwa 5.12.3. and 5.12.12., beginning of 1017, Michinaga has the title deeds to the residence of his mother-in-law brought to him.

16. *Eiga monogatari*, chap. 14. Akimitsu had married his younger daughter Enshi to the imperial prince Atsuakira, the eldest son of Sanjō Tennō, and for a time crown prince. She had borne him children and it was said that Akimitsu fondly entertained the idea that he would have his chance if all the imperial princes who were grandsons of Michinaga disappeared.

17. *Midō kanpakuki*, Kankō 5.9.11., 1008, and *Murasaki Shikibu nikki*; also *Eiga monogatari*, chap. 8. The residence resounded to the din of the exorcists and the cries of the women possessed by spirits.

18. *Murasaki Shikibu nikki* and *Gosan buruiki* (*Extracts Relating to Princely Births*), Kankō 5.9.11. to 16., 1008.

19. *Midō kanpakuki*, Chōwa 2.6.3., 1013.

20. *Shōyūki*, Kanna 1.4.28., 985, birth of Sanesuke's daughter, and Eiso 2.7.4. to 11., 989, her illness and death.

21. *Shunki*, Chōryaku 3.10., 1039. The treatment for an abscess consisted of compresses moistened with a mixture of gardenia and rhubarb juice and washes with lotus water. When the abscess burst, application of an amulet coated with fat and more washes with lotus water.

22. *Gonki*, Kankō 8.11.20., 1011.

23. *Fusō ryakki* (*Abbreviated Record of Japan*, Fusō being a poetical name for the country), Kōhō 1.11.21., 964, obituary of a son of Kiyoyuki.

24. *Gōrihōshū*, the works of Masahira, which include a long poem describing his formative years.

25. *Midō kanpakuki*, Kannin 2.2.16., 1018. Nagaie, already a second general of the palace guard, has not yet turned thirteen. Michinaga presents gifts to his son's teacher.
26. *Heian ibun*, text 4692, from Daiji 3.8., 1128, mentions the transfer to Nagaie of a pasture owned by Kinyori. However he retained some rights over it, which passed to his grand-daughter.
27. *Gonki*, Kankō 1.7.10., 1004.
28. *Midō kanpakuki*, Chōwa 1.12.16., beginning of 1013. On Toshikata, see *Kojidan*, anec. 133.
29. *Murasaki Shikibu nikki*. Murasaki was secretly explaining the Chinese poet Bo Juyi to the empress Shōshi.
30. *Midō kanpakuki*, Chōhō 1.8.2., 999, Michinaga accompanies the young Fujiwara no Tadatsune (?-1014) to the palace before the celebration of his coming-of-age; Kankō 8.8.23., 1011, Michinaga has adopted a son of his half-brother Michitsuna, in order to facilitate his first appointment; Kannin 2.12.6., beginning of 1019, Michinaga receives at his residence for the celebration of his coming-of-age a son of his nephew Takaie.
31. *Shōyūki*, Kannin 2.11.15., 1018. The same day, Michinaga had one of his grand-daughters, Fujiwara no Seishi, aged four, appointed to the post of intendant of the wardrobe.
32. *Eiga monogatari*, chap. 8.
33. *Eiga monogatari*, chap. 14.
34. *Eiga monogatari*, chap. 9.
35. *Kokin wakashū* (*Collection of Ancient and Modern Poems*), No. 356.
36. *Shōyūki*, Chōhō 3.10.9., 1001, and *Eiga monogatari*, chap. 7.
37. *Midō kanpakuki*, Chōwa 4.10.25., 1015, and *Senzai wakashū* (*Collection of Poems of a Thousand Years*), No. 959.
38. *Eiga monogatari*, chap. 20. Michinaga, who had taken religious vows four years earlier, attended the gathering and he too composed a poem for Rinshi.
39. *Midō kanpakuki* and *Gonki*, Kankō 1.9.25., 1004. The sons of Taira no Chikanobu (946-1017) organize the celebration for his sixtieth birthday.
40. *Midō kanpakuki*, Kankō 8.6.21., 1011.
41. *Eiga monogatari*, chap. 30. Michinaga died at the end of 1027.
42. *Midō kanpakuki*, Chōwa 5.7.26., 1016, death of Michinaga's mother-in-law; *Shunki*, Chōryaku 3.10.7., 1039, death of Sukefusa's father-in-law.

43. *Eiga monogatari*, chap. 30, and *Goshūi wakashū* (*Later Collection of Gleanings*), No. 544.
44. *Makura no sōshi*, 23. (NKBT edition)
45. *Eiga monogatari*, chap. 1.
46. *Eiga monogatari*, chap. 1, Anshi's jealousy towards her own sister, deeply loved by the emperor.
47. *Shunki*, Chōryaku 3.12.17., beginning of 1040.
48. *Shunki*, Chōryaku 2.11.28., 1038.
49. *Shunki*, Chōryaku 3.10.7. and 15., 1039. This is a very good example of the subtle influence of women in aristocratic society.
50. *Eiga monogatari*, chap. 11. Besides the help of her wet-nurse, Genshi benefited from the complicity of a monk who was this woman's lover.
51. *Eiga monogatari*, chap. 21.
52. *Midō kanpakuki*, Kankō 2.8.27., 1005, and *Shinsenzai wakashū* (*New Collection of Poems of a Thousand Years*), Nos 742 and 743.
53. *Makura no sōshi*, 24.
54. *Gonki*, Kankō 7.2.18., 1010, and *Midō kanpakuki*, Chōwa 1.2.25., 1012.
55. *Makura no sōshi*, 4.
56. *Makura no sōshi*, 82.
57. *Shinkokin wakashū* (*New Collection of Ancient and Modern Poems*), Nos 1045 and 1046.
58. *Shōyūki*, Chōwa 2.5.25., 1013. Learning from a woman, who is probably Murasaki Shikibu, that the young crown prince has still not fully recovered, Sanesuke suggests that his continuing illness is due to the delay in sending offerings to the shrines, ordered by Michinaga to enable monks to continue celebrations for the prince; *Shunki*, Chōryaku 2.10.3., 1038.
59. *Murasaki Shikibu nikki*.

CHAPTER 5

FAILURE AND ITS REMEDIES

Whereas in the 9th century it had still been possible for men born into families of local notables – mainly through their abilities in letters, law and mathematics – to enter the central administration and thereby enable some of their relatives to be registered in the capital, in the 10th century this opening became closed off. The world of the court could no longer renew and enrich itself by bringing in outsiders. On the contrary, it was burdened with individuals who could not find employment. Since the central administration was confining its activities more and more to the organization of the annual celebrations, had given up direct control of life in the provinces and was allowing the governors considerable freedom, the number of posts could not increase. Many officials and senior nobles, who practised polygamy, had a large number of children. The world of the court was thus producing a host of younger sons, individuals without a future; almost all their descendants were condemned to slide down the social scale.

Except for the regents of the illustrious Northern branch of the Fujiwara, a senior noble could seldom have more than one heir, whether or not he was the eldest by birth. The younger sons had to be satisfied with a more modest future. The genealogical tables make it possible to trace the gradual decline of many lines of descent, even if, from time to time, an exception appears to invalidate the general trend. For example, a son of Saga Tennō, Minamoto no Tōru, a minister renowned for the gardens of his residences, had five sons recorded in the Minamoto genealogical tables. The first reached the grade of major counsellor, but the best placed of his own four sons did not rise above that of a minor assistant in the Department of Palace Affairs. Tōru's second, fourth and fifth sons were only middle-ranking officials and their sons continued the downward slide. The third son was also a major counsellor. Yet his five sons did not rise above employment as provincial governors and many of his grandsons could not secure even a middle-level post. In three or four generations, Tōru's descendants fell into the group of minor employees and guards. The Fujiwara family also provides a host of similar examples. Fujiwara no Kane-michi, who became chancellor in 974, had seven sons by five different mothers. Four entered the group of senior nobles. The eldest, Akimitsu, even attained the rank of minister, but his three sons gave up all hope of a career. The second, Tokimitsu (948-1015), a second counsellor, could not bring any of his three sons to the grade of auditor. The third, Asateru, who was a major counsellor, had five sons, of whom only one was able to enter the council of senior nobles in the modest post of auditor. However the four sons of this auditor fell into the group of middle-ranking officials. The fourth of Kanemichi's sons to become a senior noble, Masamitsu (957-1014), was only an auditor; he had three sons who had to be satisfied with a middle- or low-level post.[1]

This downward movement, which affected more or less all lines of descent, produced a host of individuals in a precarious or difficult situation. Depending on the opportunities or their position in the hierarchy at the time, families and individuals had a choice between several possibilities: monopolizing a branch of knowledge, becoming the client or more modestly the servant of an important personage, joining the armed guard of a provincial governor, or seeking their fortune in the provinces. Otherwise, they had no alternative but to totally give up all ambition of a career in the administration, either by renouncing the world, or by taking up a life of crime.

Socially acceptable ways of arresting the decline

Some middle-ranking families gradually gained control of the posts reserved for the members of certain branches of learning. Thus, during the 11th century, the Abe and Kamo established themselves as specialists in astronomy and related sciences: the calendar, divination and the interpretation of omens. In 1000, the celebrated doctor of calendrical studies, Kamo no Mitsuyoshi (939-1015), was instructed to train a disciple, but he refused to pass on his knowledge to anyone other than his sons.[2] The law remained a little more open, but was gradually taken over by the Nakahara, as was mathematics by the Miyoshi, and medicine by the Tanba and certain of the Wake. The classics became the preserve of the Nakahara and Kiyohara. The most prestigious discipline, that of letters, which allowed its members to display their talents in the composition of Chinese poems and set texts in prose, was colonized by the Sugawara, Ōe and certain branches of the Fujiwara. The possession of a library, annotated books, oral traditions of interpretation and, in some cases, the tendency to keep secret a particular aspect of knowledge, enabled certain descendants to ensure for themselves positions that were reasonably secure, even if only mediocre. The specialists in astronomy and medicine, in addition to their official functions, gave private consultations for which they were handsomely rewarded.[3] As for the specialists in the classics or letters, they could earn a living by writing for important personages applications for posts or letters of resignation (since it was usual for ministers to periodically offer a formal resignation, which was never accepted) and giving lessons to their sons, as did Ōe no Masahira who wrote letters of resignation for Fujiwara no Michinaga, Minamoto no Tamenori who wrote small manuals for the sons of the minister Fujiwara no Tamemitsu and for those of Michinaga, and Ōe no Kinyori, the teacher of Michinaga's youngest son Nagaie.

According to the administrative code promulgated in the early 8th century, men of the first three ranks were entitled to a household consisting of two to five officials of very low rank, and between sixty and one hundred servants. It was intended that the latter would be recruited either among the sons of the lowest two ranks or the sons of commoners. However, over time, these rules had become a dead letter and, in the 10th century, the senior nobles, especially the ministers and major

counsellors, had larger numbers of staff who were recruited
even among men holding the fifth rank. The status of these new
"household intendants", *keishi*, was only semi-official, as they
were appointed by the household to which they were attached.
But the documents issued by that household, with its seal
affixed and bearing their name, had official validity. In 1015,
the household of a major counsellor, a close associate of the
minister Fujiwara no Michinaga and an excellent poet of
Japanese verse, Fujiwara no Kintō, had fourteen officials. After
a fire that destroyed Kintō's residence and in which the title
deeds to an estate and the certificate of tax exemption for these
men had been lost, they all signed a report, presented to Harima
province, to request the drawing up of new documents. The text
was signed by six men who, it may be surmised, were of the
fifth rank: two former provincial governors, two officials
between appointments and two officials from the household of
the senior grand empress Junshi (957-1017), the sister of Kintō
who managed her household. Next came eight other lesser
officials, below the fifth rank: three being regular members of
the household of a senior noble, and the others a minor
secretary of the Control Board or clerks of various agencies. In
total, of the fourteen individuals listed, only four had no other
functions.[4]

It goes without saying that the minister of the left and head
of the council, Fujiwara no Michinaga, had a household with
many more staff. In 1003, when he visited the Kamo Shrine,
twenty of his household intendants below the fifth rank escorted
him, which suggests that he had in addition well over a dozen
officials of the fifth rank.[5] Reading his journal, it is clear that
these men were responsible for many different tasks: secretarial
duties, supervising the work of construction or the fitting out of
a residence, preparing celebrations, various errands such as
carrying messages, sending offerings to religious establishments, providing escorts, raising horses, and loaning their house
if need be. Besides their actual employment, they sometimes
took on quite large expenses: Minamoto no Yorimitsu (948-
1021) offered the furniture for the Tsuchimikado residence in

1018, after its rebuilding.[6] But this loyal servant had already held four appointments as a provincial governor and was in his fifth term.

Michinaga's household also had a large number of minor officials divided between the various bureaux: administration, which was mainly concerned with financial management and controlled all the services, armed guards, general hands, and those in charge of the stables, the preparation of meals and the library. Fujiwara no Sanesuke, a very wealthy senior noble, maintained a construction bureau to which seven or eight carpenters were permanently attached.[7]

Those officials who joined the household of a senior noble as an intendant hoped it would give them protection for their career in the central administration and above all an appointment as a provincial governor. In this way they had the opportunity of making profits, some of which they returned to their patrons in the form of gifts or help with the collection of their revenues. Fujiwara no Korenori (963-1033) provides one of the best examples of a successful career due to the work he performed in the household of Michinaga, then in that of his son Yorimichi. He had no less than four important provincial governorships and, when he left the one in Inaba in 1005, his successor felt obliged to grant a discharge to a man who enjoyed such favour. Michinaga gives the following account of the matter:

> There was a discussion between the predecessor and successor of the governorship of Inaba province concerning the discharge. The successor stated that his predecessor, without a full hearing at the Ministry, had sent word that his discharge must be granted, that this conduct was very odd, and he wanted to know whether what his predecessor had stated was reasonable. This successor was questioned several times; he had nothing to say. Consequently, instructions were given to grant the discharge.[8]

Korenori later held the post of principal assistant at the Government Headquarters in Kyūshū, where, according to

Fujiwara no Sanesuke, he grew rich and was the object of complaints by Chinese merchants he had apparently robbed. When he returned to the capital, Sanesuke wrote in his journal:

> Korenori is due back in the capital the day after tomorrow. It is impossible to count the treasures he is bringing with him. He has plundered the nine provinces and the two islands, not to speak of Chinese products, and all that without the slightest sense of shame. Nowadays it is the rich who are called sages.[9]

Belonging to Michinaga's household presented opportunities for receiving a promotion: for example, when the emperor made a visit to his minister, ranks were bestowed on the sons and on members of the household. Another advantage was that a person would be treated leniently if he made a mistake, or at the time of submitting the accounts of a provincial administration. In 1017, after the resignation of Michinaga in favour of Yorimichi, Fujiwara no Sanesuke paints an eloquent little picture, when the council of senior nobles examined the management of Shinano province by Fujiwara no Kinnori (?-?):

> Yesterday the commandant of the military guard read the opinion relating to the discharge of the governor of Shinano: a most irritating document. Everyone present noticed it. There was a semblance of a decision, which resolved nothing. Kinnori is an intimate of the ex-regent. This is why the senior nobles turned a blind eye. There were some problematical points in the management of the rice reserves and the provision of horses. However the major counsellor Narinobu, who knew about them, remained tight-lipped. The decision by the senior nobles was terrible, an absolute farce.

Yet Sanesuke, too, protected his men when their requests were not submitted in the proper form: something he did for a governor of Ise, Minamoto no Kanesuke (960-1002), a man belonging to his household.[10]

Moreover, the senior nobles saw it as their duty to look after their household intendants, provide them with medical help in the event of illness, contribute to the cost of religious ceremonies in case of death, and protect their children. Examples of heredity among the officials attached to a household are by no means isolated. Even the menial servants found in these posts ways of making a living and protection when, as quite often happened, they had an altercation with the police. But it was acceptable to find a new and more influential patron. Similarly, it was possible to serve in an informal capacity in a household other than that to which one was attached. For, side by side with the household intendants, who benefited from a kind of official appointment, there existed another category of clients of important personages called "housemen", *kenin*, who attended their religious ceremonies, swelled the numbers in their escort and performed various services for them.[11]

When provincial governors were appointed, they formed their own entourage. From the late 10th century, in fact, officials of the capital invested with a minor provincial post no longer left to take it up. The governor himself recruited a band of men. On arrival in the province, he found locally recruited people – local notables – in the offices of the chief town and in those of the administrative subdivisions. He naturally needed to come to an arrangement with them. However he could not turn up alone in front of those he had been sent to govern. He therefore recruited between thirty and fifty men, most of them armed and able to defend him on the journey, as well as keep order. But some were also capable of doing office work. Governors who had frequent appointments could afford to retain quite a large number of these subordinates in their service. Those who, not so well protected, had no hope of obtaining another post for quite a long time disbanded their household as soon as they returned to the capital. It could also happen that their patron died; these men then went off to seek other employment. As Fujiwara no Sukefusa wrote on the death of his father-in-law:

> It appears that the servants of the deceased soon intend to go their separate ways. Some have even left already, which is quite understandable. They are like animals; they are going to look elsewhere for a way of making a living.[12]

Attributed to the doctor of letters Fujiwara no Akihira (989?-1066) is a text called *Shinsarugakuki* (*Notes on Some New Comic Entertainments*), in which he describes the family of a minor officer of the gate guard who have come to see a kind of variety show. He gives this man thirty sons and daughters, a fiction that allows him to list functions and occupations, as well as the vocabulary specific to each. The fourth son is one of these men in the service of a provincial governor:

He knows the roads of all the provinces. In a boat, he estimates the time a storm will last; on horseback, he is skilled at showing the way on the plains and in the mountains. He is quite skilful at archery. He is quite good at arithmetic and writing. Some may equal him, but there is no-one better at pointing out the protocol for taking up a post and for paying one's respects to the deities, hand-over procedures, matters relating to the discharge issued to one's predecessor and the verification of the official documents. Without seeking them, he finds himself entrusted with the tasks of general secretary of the provincial administration, tax collector, secretary, head of the militia bureau or those of the police, rice fields, public loans, tributes, constructions and repairs, or again manager of the stables, or the servants, or the table, or the household, or again in charge of the land register, the collection of taxes, the purchase of tribute products, the rice fields cultivated by the various bureaux and the imposition of special corvées. He is skilled at getting in the taxes without putting pressure on the people and preventing any losses to his patron, all the while making a profit himself.

The list of duties that could be given to the men whom the governors took with them produces a comical effect intended by the author. As first and foremost a civil official, Akihira stresses in particular the various administrative tasks that could be entrusted to these men recruited among the younger sons of minor officials. However other accounts place far more emphasis on their role as police and on their fighting capabilities, sometimes also on their brutality. One article in the petition presented by the inhabitants of Owari province, in 988, shows that the governor, amongst other violent acts, confiscated some of the district administrators' rice fields to give to his men.[13] A text issued by the court for use by provincial governors advised them to select honest and brave men for their entourage.[14] There were often complaints about their depredations in the provinces. Akihira ends the part concerning the fourth son by saying that his house is filled with all kinds of products. He has brought them back from the provinces in which he has served and sells them in the capital. All those who as a last resort took a position with a provincial governor did not succeed brilliantly and did not become rich. But, with an average of thirty to fifty men recruited by each provincial governor, the sixty-eight provinces could provide a livelihood for over two thousand five hundred individuals and their families.

Another way of making a living was to establish oneself in the provinces, which was quite easy for those who had been appointed administrators there. However, according to the code, the two categories of administrators – those who belonged to the staff of the central administration and those recruited in the provinces – were clearly distinguished. The former, who usually stayed only four years in a province, did not have the right to contract alliances, matrimonial or other, or to acquire land, or to clear land for rice fields. Since the 8th century, provincial administrators had sought to use their position and the prestige of the court to carve out landholdings for themselves or had formed alliances with local notables. From the 10th century, in the provinces of the North and East, and in those of Kyūshū and elsewhere, there were individuals descended from fairly well known families in the capital and permanently resident in these provinces. But, often, they also sought to maintain links with the capital, so as to have ranks and functions conferred on themselves.

A great-grandson of Kanmu Tennō (r. 781-806), Takamochi (?-?), when he was removed from the register of princes, received the family name of Taira in 889. He was invested with the function of assistant for a province in the Kantō region, that of Kazusa (of which the governor was an imperial prince who never exercised the functions). It is not known whether he returned, at least temporarily, to the capital, once his term of office was completed. But he must have acquired interests in the region for, of the eight sons attributed to him by the Taira genealogy, six are mentioned as having been invested with functions in the provinces of the North-East; another is said to have lived in a village of Musashi province, adjoining Kazusa. In fact, there were always governors sent by the court and responsible to it in the provinces where these sons of Takamochi were supposed to hold positions of authority. Their descendants, strong in their heritage and their ancient ties with the world of the court, thus often secured ranks and functions. Among the many descendants of Takamochi were a few rebels, like Masakado (903?-940) who, from 931, was engaged in a struggle with members of his family and later attacked some provincial government headquarters, or Tadatsune (967-1031) who, on a smaller scale, also sowed discord in the provinces of the East. Others managed to obtain the functions of policing and keeping order in the region. Yet even those who ended up becoming rebels had attempted to maintain their links with the capital: Masakado acknowledged himself as the servant of the regent Fujiwara no Tadahira, even though, in the last stage of his revolt, calling on his ancestor Kanmu Tennō, he had himself proclaimed emperor of the East. Although Tadatsune died a rebel, in the 12th century his descendants had police duties on an estate belonging to Toba Tennō (r. 1107-1123) and took the name of this estate. They founded the Chiba, a warrior family of the East.

While their deeds have perhaps been less often talked about and their origin is more modest, the Ōkura of Kyūshū may also be mentioned. In the mid-10th century, Haruzane (?-?), an officer of the gate guard, was assistant to the official tasked with pursuing and arresting Fujiwara no Sumitomo (?-941), who had robbed some public storehouses and had allied himself with pirates from the Inland Sea. Haruzane distinguished himself in the final battle, which took place, in 941, near the seat of the Government Headquarters in Kyūshū. He stayed on in

Kyūshū and his grandson Taneki (?-?), in the early 11th century, was known as an official of the Dazaifu. In 1007, he assassinated the governor of Ōsumi in the south of the island, with no action being taken by the police. Then, in 1019, when pirates attacked the north-west coast of Kyūshū, he apparently played an effective role in its defence and was appointed governor of the island of Iki.[15] Two warrior families of the following period, the Harada and Akitsuki, were descended from these Ōkura.

One could mention still other cases of officials from the capital who remained in a province where they had most of their interests, while attempting to maintain ties in the capital that could enable them to obtain a local function and a rank. These ties were possible if the officials helped to safeguard property belonging to members of the court aristocracy or if they obtained property for them: for example, by handing over lands owned by themselves to a minister and being granted in exchange rights of policing and administration.

Men named Fujiwara, Minamoto, or some other name found among the court aristocracy, appear in estate documents as owners of quite extensive landholdings; one is Fujiwara no Sanetō (?-?, not included in the genealogical tables) who, in the mid-11th century, owned more than forty hectares of cultivated lands in the province of Iga. But there is no evidence that all these Fujiwara and others actually belonged to a family of officials in the central administration. For civil status fraud was not unknown. Ōkura no Taneki, mentioned earlier, attempted in 1031 to pass his son off as a descendant of a prince in order for him to have a chance of reaching the fifth rank. The affair was discovered and the imperial prince, who was head of the Department of Regulations Relating to Civil Officials, was forced to resign.[16] Besides, a minor local notable could always find a destitute offspring and purchase his name. However, the existence of so many families who had put down roots in a province claiming to be descended from an official in the capital proves that it was a possibility.

Taking religious vows

One way, in theory quite austere, of escaping from the worries of the struggle for positions and the obligations of the life of officials was to take religious vows and become a Buddhist monk. But there were several kinds of monk. Many took religious vows – it was said in this case that they "entered the Way" – at the end of their career, as a kind of retirement and a preparation for death. This step could be taken with a greater or lesser degree of enthusiasm. Some of these late-comers to the monk's calling observed only a few basic rules: they stayed in their home, changed their dress, shaved their head and thus partly escaped from the rituals and obligations of society. The minister Fujiwara no Michinaga, following an illness, retired and took religious vows in 1019. However he moved into a magnificent temple, the Hōjōji, and remained the real head of his family, to the point where his son, the regent Yorimichi, did nothing without consulting him, slowing down an appointments session for example, because he had to send a messenger several times to consult his father.[17] Few men began a true new life. Yoshishige no Yasutane, a scholar-official who had always been very devout, took religious vows aged over fifty, when he could not expect much more from the court. He left his house and went to live for a time in the company of the celebrated monk Shōkū (?-1007) at the Enkyōji in Harima province. Taking religious vows instead of retirement was not an escape. It aroused no pity and was favourably viewed by society.

Far more significant are the cases where religious vows were taken at an earlier age (called "leaving home"), either voluntarily or imposed by the family in order to find employment for their excess sons. For a man facing a charge (true or false), taking religious vows was a convenient way of avoiding prosecution and a conviction. It also made it possible to save face after a failure or to get out of a difficult situation, especially for provincial governors who had problems submitting correct accounts when they left office. The number of men who resolved on this course appears to have increased quite markedly in the late 10th century. Even an emperor, Kazan, who ascended the throne aged sixteen, abdicated to become a monk at eighteen, when he realized that, without the support of his maternal family – his grandfather Fujiwara no Koremasa had died in 972 and his uncle Yoshichika was not sufficiently advanced in his career to carry any weight –, it was better to renounce the throne. Urged on, it seems, by Michi-kane, whose father Kaneie wished to place his own grandson (Ichijō) on the throne, he left the palace in secret to take shelter in a temple not far from the capital and there perform the first act needed to become a monk.[18] However, after a short time, he led anything but a monastic life and returned to live in the capital. He had children, who could have no legal existence since monks were in principle obliged to be celibate. He nevertheless succeeded in assuring them of a place in society by having them adopted by his own father Reizei.[19] It was said that Kazan also found the ceremonial surrounding the life of an emperor very tedious. Having taken religious vows, he could freely indulge his love of poetry, music and the fitting out of residences, and lead a comfortable existence.

His uncle Yoshichika, who at the age of twenty-nine was then a second counsellor, as well as the Control Board official Fujiwara no Koreshige (?-989) who, during the two years of this brief reign, apparently initiated measures for a return to more orderly administrative practices, both took religious vows when quite young. No doubt Yoshichika's motivation was that after having been highly influential for two years, he did not wish to return to an inferior position. The *Ōkagami* says of him:

> He was not very well educated, but he was extremely capable and thoroughly conversant with the workings of the court; in the time of Kazan Tennō, this lord and the controller Koreshige conducted government affairs in such a way that everything ran very smoothly. [...] The taking of religious vows by this second counsellor was on the advice of the controller Kore-shige who, as a far-sighted man, said to him: "Can you still be involved with the court, now (that you no longer have any family relationship with the emperor)? That would be too

distressing." He at once realized the truth of this remark and became a monk. It was not that he had wished to do so at the outset. People wondered how he would fare. But he, quite at peace with himself, lived without neglecting his duties.[20]

Not all men who had already attained the position of senior noble had that attitude when they suffered a setback. One may compare the conduct of Yoshichika with that of Fujiwara no Korechika and his younger brother Takaie, when their uncle (Michinaga) became the most important man at the court and they were sent into temporary exile. The first hoped that the accidents of princely births would deny Michinaga a grandson. The second resigned himself to being a second counsellor for the rest of his life and was content to seek economic compensations, by having himself appointed to the Government Headquarters in Kyūshū, which permitted him to arrange a suitable future for his children.

In spite of the respect that Yoshichika had gained by his secluded life in a temple of the Mountain and the protection he could therefore offer his sons by his recommendations, the eldest, Narifusa (982-?), on whom rested all the hopes of this branch of the Fujiwara, did not feel that he had the strength, abilities or courage shown by his cousin Fujiwara no Yukinari. In fact, Yukinari was also a grandson of the chancellor Koremasa, but his father Yoshitaka (954-974) had died very young, even before being appointed an auditor. However, he proved to be an effective and conscientious official at the Control Board and at the head of the Chancellery. His exceptional talent as a calligrapher also helped him to secure Michinaga's favour and he was thus able to attain the grade of major counsellor.

We are familiar through the journal of Yukinari, *Gonki*, with the circumstances that led to Narifusa, then aged twenty, taking religious vows, because he spoke of his wish to leave the court on several occasions and at some length to his cousin, who was eight years older. Yukinari tried in vain to persuade him to stay. At the end of 1000, the two cousins together attended the Buddhist celebration of the Litanies of the August Names of the

Buddhas, which took place at the court to end the year. They returned in the same carriage, talking about the difficulty of living in this uncertain world. The next day, Yukinari sent Narifusa a letter beginning with a poem:

"We think life in this world is oppressive. But we get up and go to bed and day follows night." In this transient world, all that we see and hear causes us sadness.

There, in essence, Yukinari was advising patient acceptance. Narifusa replied:

We know well the vanity of the things of this world; being so oppressed, everything moves us to tears.

The following day, Narifusa visited his father to tell him of his wish to renounce the world and become a monk. However Yoshichika put it to him that a monk's life was not easy, that it required constancy, that many understood the idea of Enlightenment, but lacked perseverance. He also told him that he was the main provider for his younger brothers and asked him to return to the court to serve the emperor.[21] It seems that even Michinaga, informed of this wish, attempted to restrain Narifusa, who was promoted to second general of the palace guard and chosen for the very prestigious mission of imperial messenger at the festival of the Iwashimizu Shrine in the 3rd month of 1001. But all efforts were futile and finally, in the 2nd month of 1002, Narifusa left his home and shaved his head. Shortly afterwards, his wife apparently sent him a pillow in the shape of a box, with a poem:

Am I alive, am I dead, I no longer know; in this box, my disembodied spirit.[22]

A year earlier, two other young aristocrats (and not of the lowest rank at the court) had also given up careers that could only be inferior to those of their fathers and grandfathers. One, Fujiwara no Shigeie (977-?), aged twenty-four or twenty-five, was the only son of the minister of the right Akimitsu and an imperial princess (a daughter of Murakami Tennō); the other, Minamoto no Narinobu (979-?), aged twenty-two or twenty-three, was the grandson of Murakami Tennō and of the minister of the left Minamoto no Masanobu. The *Great Mirror* says that the first was very gifted and had a good reputation. In her *Pillow Book*, Sei Shōnagon portrays the second as a ladies' man who, besides his wife, visits several women, herself included. One can obviously suspect these accounts of embellishing these portraits, if only because of the noble origins of the two men. Yet clearly they were two young officials with no obvious handicaps. In the spring of 1001, they went together to the Miidera, where they took religious vows. It is difficult, at such a remove from the events, to look into their hearts, but, of Shigeie, one can say that he may have been discouraged by the inability of his father, the minister of the right, to impose his opinions when faced with Michinaga. Yukinari, who went to visit them shortly after they had become monks, relates that, according to them, the dilapidated condition of the buildings of the Court of Abundance and Pleasures, where certain formal banquets were held, had given them an acute sense of the precariousness of all things. According to the same Yukinari, Narinobu, a man of little education but with a lively mind, was protected by Michinaga and had shown himself to be very diligent when the minister was ill for three months in the summer of 1000. He could thus have hoped for a reward. He apparently said to some old friends from the court who came to see him:

> How vain is glory. Even a man belonging to a line that must not die out, when faced with illness and danger, does not obtain the least advantage from it. [...] I began to understand the idea of Enlightenment when I saw the minister lying ill in bed. I am realizing it now with the protection of the buddhas.[23]

In 1012, Akinobu, the third son of Fujiwara no Michinaga and the second of his wife Minamoto no Meishi, aged eighteen and at the time director of the Office of Horses, went to Hieizan to become a monk. An ecclesiastical dignitary immediately sent a messenger to obtain the opinion of the minister, who did not oppose such a wish by this younger son, whereas he would not have tolerated it from his eldest son Yorimichi. Akinobu was no doubt disheartened, as his father had just refused to appoint him head of the Chancellery.[24] He could therefore have no great expectations regarding his future career. Michinaga, somewhat hypocritically, writes:

> He had nurtured this wish all by himself, but had not yet realized it. What a painful thought! This action can only be explained by the payment necessary for misdeeds (in a previous existence).[25]

The minister's words show that he does not consider the taking of religious vows at a young age by a man belonging to the nobility to be a good thing, since he attributes this to the cause often invoked when sudden misfortunes occurred: the misdeeds of a past life. Michinaga went up to Hieizan in the 5th month to attend the reception of the precepts and at this time had suitable gifts prepared for the religious dignitaries.[26] But he did not help his son to gain ecclesiastical ranks and functions.

When the taking of religious vows did not have family approval, it was possible to revoke it. In his journal, Fujiwara no Sukefusa mentions the case of the eldest son of the major controller and future major counsellor Fujiwara no Tsunesuke, a man in favour with the chancellor Yorimichi. This young man, Moroie (1027-1058), aged thirteen, had just celebrated his coming-of-age and a marriage had been arranged for him. However, without warning, he cut his hair, revealing his wish to become a monk. His family, in despair, appealed to the chancellor, who ordered that he be returned to the status of a layman.[27] Moroie was to die quite young, while occupying the post of second controller.

Thus, joining the Buddhist priesthood allowed aristocrats to save face after a failure. As for young men who were eligible to become senior nobles, but who had to struggle against quite fierce competition for a success which, in any case, was inferior to that of their forebears, provided they were devout and convinced of the possibility of obtaining Enlightenment, they found a refuge in the taking of religious vows, especially if they were unsure of their abilities and lacked influential support.

The late 10th century was not an auspicious time for those officials who had passed the competitive examinations in letters. For their chances of attaining the grades of auditor or second counsellor had disappeared. But the majority of them, like Yoshishige no Yasutane already mentioned, did not become monks until the end of their lives. Ōe no Sadamoto (962?-1034) is an exception. This member of one of the two important families of literati at the court, after a normal start to his career, took religious vows in 986, when he was governor of Mikawa province. Until then, he had had the posts he could reasonably have expected, with no disappointments. He did not complete his term in Mikawa and abruptly became a monk. An anecdote in *Tales of Times Now Past* attributes this sudden resolve to his sorrow at the death of a woman he loved.[28] One of the advantages of being a monk, especially important for a literatus, was that in the absence of official relations between China and Japan it made possible the voyage to China. In fact, only monks obtained permission from the court to leave. Ōe no Sadamoto, who became the monk Jakushō, requested this authorization in 1002, but he did not arrive in China until 1004. He was to remain there until his death in 1034. He had taken with him lists of questions on Buddhist doctrine to submit to Chinese monks. He sent back the replies and continued to correspond with members of the court. Can one attribute this taking of religious vows by a relatively young literatus to his wish to go to China?

Until the 10th century, the Buddhist priesthood was not normally recruited from the important families of the court. The genealogy of the descendants of Fujiwara no Fuyutsugu, founder of the regents' branch, does not include any monks before the mid-10th century. This does not appear to be due to an incomplete listing, as they subsequently become very numerous. When the contraction of the activities of the administration reduced the number of available posts, it became customary for families to get excess sons off their hands by sending them at a very young age to a temple. So by choice it was most often the sons of women of low birth who were destined for a religious life, but not always. Of the twelve sons of Fujiwara no Morosuke, there were three monks born to the imperial princesses Gashi and Kōshi; two had very successful ecclesiastical careers. The only one of Fujiwara no Yorimichi's sons to become a monk had the same mother as his heir Morozane (1042-1101). The latter had sixteen sons: eleven became monks and the majority religious dignitaries; one of them had the same mother as the son designated as heir. Lower down the social scale, Fujiwara no Sukefusa sent the eldest of his three sons to Hieizan: he refers to him in the years around 1038-1040 as "the little monk".

In her *Pillow Book*, Sei Shōnagon says of this custom:

It breaks one's heart to see promising children forced to become monks. The parents do this for the benefit it brings to the family. But this is to have no more feeling than a piece of wood. How sad! Monks eat poor, frugal meals and sleep little. Young monks may have a certain curiosity: they must stay away from the places where women are, but would they be able to refrain from having a look? Should they do so, they are gossiped about unmercifully.[29]

The benefit mentioned by Sei Shōnagon is that sons who are monks can perform the rites for the deceased of the family and their merits can be applied to their forebears. Monks were expected to lead an ascetic life, which was rather daunting for laymen. However they were not all holy men secluded in mountain temples. Many kept up very close links with the outside world. The most important families of the court, in the 11th century, were able to reserve the high ecclesiastical ranks for their offspring, provided they had done a certain amount of study in their youth and had undergone some training. After-wards, their lives could become quite comfortable, for the religious establishments, as a result of gifts, often made by the most important families, had significant revenues at their disposal. It would be unwise to generalize, but it is possible that the invasion of the high Buddhist priesthood by the aristocracy and its secular interests partly contributed to the disturbances that became more frequent in the temples from the 11th century.

Socially unacceptable ways: the descent into criminality

There were underground links between the aristocracy and a floating world of individuals who had descended into crime, some of good family. The capital harboured gangs of thieves and arsonists, no doubt recruited for the most part among the unemployed descendants of low-ranking officials. The Police Bureau was tasked with pursuing them. This agency had been established in the early 9th century. It recruited its staff of inspectors from the men of the gate guard, at most about ten officers and under-officers, assisted by armed followers: between ten and twenty for each inspector. It gradually extended its jurisdiction, which at first involved inquiries, tours of inspection and arrests. From the late 9th century, it conducted interrogations, using torture to obtain confessions, and handed down sentences. It also managed prisons. However, except for arrests of criminals caught in the act during a tour of inspection, the inspectors could detain a person only on the orders of the senior noble in charge of the Police Bureau. As regards minor officials and commoners, the procedures leading to a conviction were entirely dependent on the Bureau, which, until the early 11th century, always had jurists on its staff. When the matter concerned a man invested with a rank, especially one of the first five, interrogations and convictions were subject to approval by the council of senior nobles.

Cases of collusion between minor officials of the Police Bureau and thieves were quite common. In fact, freed prisoners often remained in the service of the Bureau, a situation that offered the advantage of allowing information to be gathered, but also the disadvantage of links between members of the Bureau and criminals. Moreover, the work of the police was continually hindered by the intervention of senior nobles who protected their servants. When these men were denounced or suspected of a crime, they took refuge in the home of their patron. The inspectors could not enter the residences of the important personages. On the other hand, they had no qualms about searching and robbing the houses of low-ranking officials who lacked adequate protection or those of commoners.

Even men of good birth and already embarked on careers as officials committed reprehensible acts. Thus, in 961, the son of an imperial prince was denounced as the head of a gang of thieves. When the police went to arrest him, his father said he was ill. His accomplices were the son of a supernumerary governor of Tosa and the son of an official in the Department of Palace Affairs.[30] One of the best-known cases is that of the grandsons of a major counsellor, Fujiwara no Motokata (888-953). His daughter Genshi (?-?) was a consort of Murakami Tennō and gave birth to an imperial prince;[31] his son Munetada (?-?), like many others of the same birth, could have a career only as a middle-ranking official, though still honourable. Munetada himself had three sons; his two eldest, captains in the military guard, began to be talked about in 985. For a reason that is not specified, they wounded two officials, one of whom was Ōe no Masahira, at that time just beginning his career and a minor assistant at the Board of Censors (Danjōdai). The facts having been established, the Police Bureau was ordered to arrest them. But the elder of the two brothers, Nariakira (?-?), escaped by boat and appears to have gone and joined a band of pirates. A month later, the inspectors dispatched in pursuit of these pirates received a reward. The *Nihon kiryaku* (*Abridged Annals of Japan*), which recounts the incident, does not specify that Nariakira was killed, but this is highly likely, as there is no further mention of him. The younger brother, Yasusuke (?-?), took refuge at his father's home. When the inspectors arrived, they learned that he had gone to the Hasedera. However the father undertook to hand over his son as soon as he returned. This first case must have been closed, for there seems to have been no penalty at that time. In 988, a theft occurred at the residence of the ex-governor of Echizen; one of Yasusuke's armed followers was caught at the home of an official of the Weaving Bureau and denounced his master as the perpetrator of the theft and the head of a gang of thieves. Moreover, he had shot arrows at an inspector of the Police Bureau. The order was given to arrest Yasusuke, who first hid at the residence of Fujiwara no Akimitsu, future minister of the right and at the time a second counsellor; he then attempted to escape, at least temporarily, by shaving his head and taking on the appearance of a monk. The police then arrested his father Munetada. Yasusuke surrendered or was captured: this point is not specified. However, once arrested, he immediately committed suicide. He was no doubt remembered as the head of a gang of thieves and his legend grew: no less than three collections of anecdotes devote one to him. The *Uji shūi monogatari* (*Supplement to the Tales of Uji*), from the early 13th century, relates that he lured to his house men who had cloth or arms to sell and killed them.[32] Numerous other cases could be mentioned, like that of a court physician's son who, posted on their route, held to ransom the pilgrims who travelled each month to the Kiyomizudera.[33]

Most of the thefts committed at the palace or at the residence of Fujiwara no Michinaga were with the connivance of the menial servants. They concerned the main source of wealth – silk fabrics and garments –, namely what served, together with rice, as a substitute for money, which had gone out of use at the time. The most important aristocrats also used gold dust. In 1017, some two thousand ounces of gold (nearly three kilogrammes) were stolen from one of Michinaga's storehouses. Six weeks later, the Police Bureau recovered most of the gold. The investigation established that the guilty parties were a servant of a senior noble and a retainer of an intendant in Michinaga's household, at the time a former and a future member of the Police Bureau. Moreover, the instigator was apparently a son of a former governor of Suruga province, a client of Michinaga. When he found out who was suspected, Michinaga revoked the order to question him that he had just issued.[34] This kind of leniency and such interventions in investigations impeded the work of the Police Bureau and greatly displeased its members. The Bureau in turn came into conflict with the men of the households that interfered in its work: it thus had a series of disputes with the household of the empress Shōshi.

However many of the misdeeds of middle- or low-ranking officials went unpunished. Nariakira and Yasusuke had a younger brother, Yasumasa (958-1036), whose career was more distinguished than that of his father Munetada. He was an intendant in Michinaga's household and so enjoyed his protection. He therefore had provincial governorships throughout his life. Quite a skilful poet and married for a time to Izumi Shikibu, he also had a reputation for courage and skill in military exercises. He had built up a formidable entourage in competition with that of another official, also protected by Michinaga and appointed several times to provincial governorships, Minamoto no Yorichika (ca. 970-after 1050? probably the son of his sister, or at least a half-sister). Michinaga writes in 1017:

> The intendant of the Police Bureau came and said: "During the imperial visit to Iwashimizu, towards four in the afternoon, a certain Kiyohara no Munenobu was in a small house situated at the corner of Rokkaku and Tomi streets. This man belonged to Yasumasa's retinue. Seven or eight men on horseback and some ten on foot surrounded the house and murdered Munenobu. Inspectors from the Police Bureau were sent to the scene. Here is their report." I looked at it and saw that the son of Hata no Ujimoto was implicated in the affair. When I asked the whereabouts of Ujimoto, I learned that he belongs to Yorichika's retinue. So I had them continue the investigation and it appears that Yorichika is responsible for the murder of Munenobu. It is said everywhere that Yorichika is a very clever killer and has often been involved in similar incidents. This present one, they say, is apparently in retaliation for the murder of a certain Tameyori of Yamato province.[35]

In principle, the penal code punished the instigator of a murder more harshly than the man who had done the deed.[36] Murder was punishable by death, but the death penalty had not been applied since the early 9th century. Moreover, through a loss of rank and function, as well as the payment of a fine, it could be commuted to exile for officials. It is probable that, in the present case, there was not even a judgement: it seems that Yorichika was merely deprived for a time of the post of governor of Awaji that he held when these events took place. However he did not lose the favour of Michinaga. In fact, the following year, when his son was sitting for the competitive examination in letters and the jury had rejected his poem, he complained to the minister, who gave him a sympathetic hearing.[37]

Men like Yasumasa, Yorichika and his brother Yorinobu (968-1048), as well as other middle-ranking officials often employed in the provincial governments, had no hesitation in ordering killings and taking the law into their own hands. In the eyes of the law, had it been strictly applied, they were guilty of murder. But they were seldom pursued, except when they attacked the interests of religious establishments. They usually got out of their predicament with a temporary period of exile.

The under-officers of the palace guard, or those of the gate guard, and among these most especially those who were assigned as members of the escort of a minister or a senior noble, were also very unruly and their masters gave them a great deal of latitude, particularly if they were good archers, good horsemen or good dancers and brought honour to them. Quarrels over gambling, or for other reasons, were frequent between under-officers and guards. Yet they all united behind one of their number who had a dispute with a civil official. In 1015, a guard having refused to escort a member of the Chancellery right to his destination, this man threw water in his face. Next day, not only the two sections of the palace guard, but also those of the gate guard and military guard gathered to support their colleague's complaint.[38] In 1018, the men of Fujiwara no Michinaga's escort behaved badly towards the scholar-official Fujiwara no Hironari, who was principal assistant in the Department of Regulations Relating to Civil Officials. However their master merely saw to it that they were stood down for two months. One of the men implicated in the affair of 1018, a sergeant, committed another quite serious indiscretion three years later:

> Yesterday, the chancellor was leaving the palace, escorted by some senior nobles, including the intendant of the Police Bureau. One of the guards in his escort, Kintada, north of the inner palace library, shot several arrows at the ex-assistant of Sagami province, Munemitsu, whose cap fell off. The chancellor ordered the intendant to put Kintada in the prison of the right section. The intendant dispatched some low-ranking officers of the Police Bureau to apprehend Kintada, who returned to the palace. Munemitsu in tears went to tell the minister who has taken religious vows (Michinaga), who became very angry. He several times criticized his son's stupid order and the fact that the intendant had not immediately had Kintada imprisoned by the overseer who was in his retinue. Kintada's house is in the west, near the right section prison. The minister who has taken religious vows ordered that he be transferred to the left section prison. Kintada is the biggest scoundrel in the realm.

This sergeant probably did not remain long in prison, for he continued his career.[39] While not a daily occurrence, incidents of this kind (not always serious) were by no means uncommon. They go some way towards correcting the portrayal of aristocratic life given by female literature and by poetry.

Generally speaking, the great nobles did not like violence and they refrained from spilling blood, a source of defilement that disqualified them from service in the palace. However, their servants were quick to take up their quarrels or to fight on their own account with servants of rival households. If a man was killed, the Police Bureau would take action. But the investigation often came to nothing. In fact, using all kinds of excuses, the senior nobles did their best to protect their servants. So it was that Fujiwara no Sanesuke, who was critical in other cases when prosecutions were not sufficiently rigorous, in 1005 requested and obtained the return of one of his men who had taken part in a brawl and had been imprisoned. The reason he gave in his letter to the intendant of the Police Bureau was that he was in an ill-omened year. Which simply meant that he did not want to be responsible for a punishment, as if being lenient somehow brought good fortune.[40] Again in 1018, Sanesuke decided that he was in an unlucky year, and had returned to him a murderer who was the son of servants in his household and had been raised there.[41] The court, which had borrowed from China the custom of proclaiming an amnesty on the occasion of an enthronement or the naming of a crown prince, prompted by the belief that the higher powers would reward its leniency, extended this practice to other cases, far more numerous: illnesses of the emperor, empress or chancellor, natural disasters and misfortunes. The very frequent granting of amnesties contributed to an increase in the number of repeat offences.

There was sometimes quite a fine line between service in the household of a senior noble and the descent into petty or serious criminality. It remains difficult to determine the true extent of the latter. Fujiwara no Sanesuke, always critical, on several occasions laments the increased incidence of fires and thefts. However not all the homes of former provincial governors (who supposedly had full granaries) were burgled. Not all governors were attacked and murdered while travelling between their provincial headquarters and the capital, even if one or other of them was occasionally waylaid. Many had no hesitation in leaving with their wife and sometimes a daughter, one being the author of *The Sarashina Diary*, who spent part of her childhood in the distant province of Kazusa. The senior nobles and officials often moved about at night in the capital, as celebrations could go on until very late. Thieves sometimes waited in the shadows for men without an escort. But this type of incident did not happen every night. Debauchery, drunkenness and gambling were quite common among the menial servants and led to altercations, which were not always serious. Yet, all things considered, insecurity was probably no greater in the 11th century than in the 9th. However, the difficulty of finding employment and the experience of a permanent decline in the fortunes of certain families fostered a sense of the impermanence of all things and of irreparable decay. There remained one solution: trust in the protection of the deities and buddhas.

Notes

1. *Sonpi bunmyaku* (*Noble and Base Lineages*): genealogies of the Fujiwara of the Northern branch and those of the Minamoto descended from Saga Tennō.
2. *Gonki*, Chōhō 2.7.9., 1000. The limited number of books made it much easier to transmit one's knowledge only to a select few.
3. *Shunki*, Chōryaku 3.10.5., 1039. The physician Wake no Sukenari (987-1056) received thirteen pieces of silk and five pounds of floss silk for a moxa treatment, which was far more than the yearly allocations assigned by the administrative code to men of the fifth rank.
4. *Chōya gunsai*, chap. 7, Chōwa 4.10.15., 1015.
5. *Gonki*, Chōhō 5.4.21., 1003. The most important personage of the court sometimes visited the Kamo Shrine shortly after the festival. The size of the escort showed the minister's prestige.
6. *Shōyūki*, Kannin 2.6.20., 1018. Yorimitsu offered partitions, chests, shelves, small chests of drawers, musical instruments, swords, silver objects, toiletries, pillows, screens, curtains and fabrics.
7. *Shōyūki*, Manju 1.12.13., 1024, and *Ōkagami*, section relating to Fujiwara no Saneyori.
8. *Midō kanpakuki*, Kankō 2.12.29., beginning of 1006. Korenori, on his return to the capital, must have trumpeted his merits. In fact, in the 4th month, his successor had requested a tax exemption for the province, but the council had refused to grant it, arguing that it was common knowledge that Korenori had restored the fortunes of the province.
9. *Shōyūki*, Chōgen 2.7.11., 1029. The previous year, Chōgen 1.10.10., Sanesuke had mentioned the increase in the number of complaints by Chinese merchants.
10. *Shōyūki*, Kannin 1.9.1., 1017. Protection given by Sanesuke to Kanesuke, who did not submit a request correctly in Jian 1.12.9., beginning of 1022.

11. *Shōyūki*, Manju 2.11.11., 1025. Sanesuke, speaking of one Fujiwara no Kanenari (?-?), who had been governor of Tōtōmi, says that he is an intendant of his household, *keishi*, and at the same time a houseman, *kenin*, of the third minister Fujiwara no Norimichi.

12. *Shunki*, Chōryaku 3.10.13., 1039. Some anecdotes in the *Konjaku monogatarishū* present former provincial governors, between appointments in the capital, living with a greatly reduced number of servants.

13. *Owari no kuni gebumi*, text 339 of the *Heian ibun*, article 29.

14. *Chōya gunsai*, chap. 22, an undated text titled "Duties of Provincial Administrators".

15. *Nihon kiryaku*, Kankō 4.7.1., 1007 and Chōgen 4.3.14., 1031, concerning the murder of the governor of Ōsumi by Taneki; *Shōyūki*, Kannin 3.7.13., 1019, his appointment as governor of Iki.

16. *Nihon kiryaku* and *Shōyūki*, Chōgen 4.3.14., 1031. Passing oneself off as a descendant of an imperial prince made it possible to solicit a promotion to the fifth rank.

17. *Shōyūki*, Kannin 1.11.16., 1017. A session held before Michinaga took religious vows, while he had still only resigned his office, but it provides the model for what happened subsequently, up until Michinaga's death; Sanesuke calls it a farce.

18. *Ōkagami*, section relating to Kazan Tennō.

19. *Midō kanpakuki*, Kankō 1.4.25. and 1.5.2., 1004. Kazan had two sons, probably born the same year to two women who shared the unusual distinction of being mother and daughter. Kazan seems to have greatly flattered Michinaga in order to have his sons registered as those of his own father, the cloistered Reizei Tennō, thereby enabling them to be made imperial princes.

20. *Ōkagami*, section relating to Fujiwara no Koremasa.

21. *Gonki*, Chōhō 2.12.18.19. and 20., beginning of 1001.

22. *Shūi wakashū* (*Collection of Gleanings*), No. 1209.

23. *Gonki*, Chōhō 3.2.4., 1001.

24. *Gonki*, Kankō 8.12.19., 1011.

25. *Midō kanpakuki*, Chōwa 1.1.16. and 17., 1012.

26. *Midō kanpakuki*, Chōwa 1.5.23., 1012.

27. *Shunki*, Chōryaku 3.12. intercalary month 10., beginning of 1041. As this happened to the family of his colleague and rival Tsunesuke, Sukefusa relates it somewhat ironically and speaks of

the condolence visits they received, as though there had been a death.

28. *Konjaku monogatarishū*, chap. 19, anec. 2.
29. *Makura no sōshi*, 4.
30. *Fusō ryakki*, Tentoku 5.5.10. or Ōwa 1.5.10., 961.
31. The imperial prince born to Genshi (or Sukehime), Hirohira shinnō (948-969), was older than those born to Fujiwara no Anshi, daughter of Morosuke. When Anshi's first son, the future Reizei Tennō, was born, Motokata, realizing that his grandson would never become emperor, died a very angry man. From childhood, Reizei showed signs of mental disturbance that were attributed to the vengeance of the angry spirit of Motokata.
32. *Shōyūki*, Kanna 1.3.27., 985, the violent conduct of Nariakira and Yasusuke having become known, the order was given to pursue them "in accordance with the law". Their father's house was searched. Eien 2.5. intercalary day 9., 988, Yasusuke was denounced as the perpetrator of a robbery with violence and for having attacked an inspector of the Police Bureau. Eien 2.6.14. and 18., 988, he attempted to escape and committed suicide. *Nihon kiryaku*, Eien 2.6.13., 988, Yasusuke was said to be at the home of the second counsellor Akimitsu. *Uji shūi monogatari*, anec. 125.
33. *Midō kanpakuki*, Chōwa 2.2.18., 1013. This physician was able to continue his career in spite of his son's misdeeds.
34. *Midō kanpakuki*, Kannin 1.5.27., 1017, theft of the gold; 1.7.10.11. and 12., the gold reappeared. Michinaga had not revoked in time the order not to question the first suspect, so he was arrested, but at once released. However a lot of evidence had been produced against him.
35. *Midō kanpakuki*, Kannin 1.3.11., 1017.
36. *Hossō shiyōshō*, article 21.
37. *Shōyūki*, Kannin 2.10.29., 1018. According to Fujiwara no Sanesuke, Michinaga, informed by Yorichika, asked to review the examination papers. Akimitsu, minister of the left, replied that as the results had been made public, the papers could not be reviewed. Furious, Michinaga apparently insulted Akimitsu and had the papers brought to him.
38. *Shōyūki*, Chōwa 4.7.4. and 5., 1015. Michinaga reprimanded the member of the Chancellery but refused to accept the complaint.

39. *Midō kanpakuki*, Kannin 2.2.26., 1018, misconduct by the men of the escort. *Shōyūki*, Kannin 2.4.21., those guilty are pardoned. Jian 1.7.19., 1021, another incident. Manju 1.9.19., 1024, the person responsible is still employed.
40. *Shōyūki*, Kankō 2.2.16. and 18., 1005.
41. *Shōyūki*, Kannin 2.10.2.5. and 6., 1018.

CHAPTER 6

PRESCRIPTIONS FOR SUCCESS
AND SALVATION

As we saw in Chapter 2, the organization of religious rituals was an important part of the work of the court officials. Moreover, the court outlaid a significant proportion of its revenues rewarding monks and priests and having the material elements of worship prepared, as well as the offerings. Celebrations, prayers and offerings were regarded as matters of State. The presence in the code and the regulations of articles concerning the worship of the national deities and others relating to Buddhism clearly shows the court's desire to control the various forms of worship and thereby reserve for itself the privilege of using the power of rituals and benefiting from their efficacy, so as to fulfil its mission of maintaining order and prosperity. Over time, it seems that the officials of the central administration – the men in touch with the realities of life in the provinces were able to take practical measures – considered that when misfortunes or difficulties occurred, their main duty was to organize religious celebrations. It is very interesting to note the reaction of the court, in 1004, when insufficient rain fell during the summer and fears were held for the harvest. There is no trace of a directive recommending, for example, that the rice reserves be checked. On the contrary, from the 6th day of the 7th month until the 16th day of the 8th month, a series of measures was ordered: prayers by the emperor in person, recitation of the *Benevolent Kings Sūtra* in the Great Hall of State, recitation of the same *sūtra* by the monks of the seven great temples of Nara, sending of offerings to the shrines of Nihu and Kibune, as well as to seven shrines chosen by divination, prayers by the principal assistant of the Ministry of Religious Affairs, rituals for rain at the Murōji temple and celebration of the Five Dragons (Goryūsai) in the Shinsen-en.[1] All the resources of Shintō,

Buddhism and the way of Yin and Yang were brought into play, together with a change of era name. Again in 1019, when the coast of Kyūshū was attacked by pirates, the court, once informed, ordered celebrations at the temples and shrines, but took no military measures, leaving the initiative to its representatives on the spot and to the local notables. It did no more than recommend that the assailants be driven off and that those who had given good service be later rewarded.[2]

Onto the old stock of the worship of the national deities, which took the name of Shintō, "way of the gods", were grafted Buddhism (from the 6th century) and the body of doctrines of the way of Yin and Yang (from the 7th century). There were points of similarity and contamination between these three belief systems and a kind of syncretism began to appear from the 9th century. In the daily lives of the aristocrats, the three doctrines coexisted without difficulty. In his advice to his descendants, Fujiwara no Morosuke, combining the way of Yin and Yang, Buddhism and Shintō, writes:

> When you get up, utter seven times the name of your birth star, then take a mirror and look at your face. Next, take an almanac to determine whether the day is favourable or unfavourable. Then take a toothpick, turn towards the west and wash your hands. Then recite the names of the buddhas and those of the great shrines.[3]

However the awareness of a distinction between Shintō and Buddhism never disappeared. Without any overall comparison of their respective merits actually having been undertaken or Shintō having been declared superior, one can nevertheless detect a kind of wish to set it apart. Thus, monks were not permitted to enter the palace during festivals of the deities and Buddhist celebrations for the palace or at the palace could not be held at the same time as a Shintō ritual, this last-mentioned always taking priority. The Vestal-princesses of Ise and Kamo had to respect certain taboos and not use words from the Buddhist vocabulary, which was considered unclean. For example, they said "coloured papers" for *sūtra* and "long hair" for monk.

Shintō

With the organization of the codal system came a clear desire to place the worship of the country's deities at the highest level, in the face of Buddhist beliefs from the continent, even if, from the early 7th century, these were protected by the court, which set great store by their efficacy. The deities were those of communities throughout the country or the ancestral deities of the great clans, foremost among them those of the imperial family, worshipped at Ise. The court was anxious to extend its control over the greatest possible number, thereby contributing to the extension of its influence and showing its superiority over the great clans and all the communities. Already, in the 8th century, the central administration was registering shrines in every province. However it seems that the list was drawn up in the early 9th century; the final form appears in the *Engishiki* (*Regulations of the Engi Era*) of the early 10th century. This list includes the names of three thousand one hundred and thirty-two shrines, of which seven hundred and thirty-seven were to be given regular offerings by the court, with the others receiving them from the provincial governors.

The central administration – the Ministry of Religious Affairs – not only kept the list of shrines, but also classified them according to their importance. The court adopted the practice of conferring ranks on deities, just as on officials, and there are many examples of promotions. This involved the gift of rice fields, as well as households, whose taxes and labour were used for the upkeep of the buildings. The central administration also registered, appointed and conferred ranks on the priests. The provincial governors were responsible for ensuring that shrines were kept in good repair and for the correct performance of the rituals, the main purpose of which was to ward off misfortunes and bring good fortune.

In the distant past, men and especially women in the service of shrines or even common people could be possessed by a deity and transmit its oracles. From the 8th century, the court was very wary and suspicious of these practices. It sought to contain them by organizing a body of divination specialists inside the Ministry of Religious Affairs and expelling from the capital individuals who claimed to be mediums. As for sudden oracles occurring in the provinces, the court refused to accept them without a prior and rigorous investigation by the local authorities, who took the responsibility of sending a report and risked a reprimand if the court later rejected it.[4]

Priests and officials had above all to take care to maintain absolute purity around shrines, meaning that anything polluting – blood and corpses – must not be found there and that anyone in mourning or in an unclean state must not approach them. Slaughtering and butchering animals close to a shrine was strictly forbidden. When an ill-starred event occurred, divination was used to determine its cause. Often the response was that one or other deity or the deity of a certain direction was angry. Inspectors from the Police Bureau were then sent to make inquiries near the shrine in question to ascertain whether or not there had been a defilement and who was responsible for it. Respect for the purity of everything concerning the shrines was taken to such lengths that Fujiwara no Sukehira, who, in accordance with the custom, was to provide trousers for the dancers at the Kamo festival, was excused from this obligation because he had accidentally contracted a defilement.[5]

The rituals consisted of prayers and offerings of rice, saké, cloth and, for the most important shrines, musical instruments and valuable metal objects, such as weapons. All the shrines on the list received offerings for the celebration of the Prayers for the Year, in the 2nd month, at the start of the agricultural year, in order to obtain favourable weather and good harvests. A slightly smaller number received offerings in the 6th and 12th months, on the occasion of the Monthly Celebration. According to the *Engishiki*, the priests of the shrines that received offerings from the court had to come to the capital to collect their deities' share, even if they lived in a distant province. They attended a ceremony at the Ministry of Religious Affairs, in the presence of senior nobles and officials of the Control Board and the Ministry. After the proclamation of the Prayers came the distribution of offerings. However, if one is to believe Miyoshi no Kiyoyuki, most priests, even from nearby provinces, no longer bothered to turn up and those who did wasted no time in reselling the offerings.[6]

The central administration therefore gave up its desire for direct control of a large number of shrines throughout the country, and from the 10th century restricted itself to exercising this control for a limited number of large establishments, all located in the provinces closest to the capital. There were still only sixteen shrines receiving offerings from the court in 966; they increased to nineteen in 991 and to twenty-one before the end of the century. The number was set at twenty-two in 1039 and did not change after that. However, on the occasion of an enthronement, messengers were still sent – one for each of the seven circuits and one for the central provinces – to announce this to all the deities of the country and take offerings to them.[7]

The most important was the Great Shrine at Ise, which housed the ancestral deity of the dynasty in the "inner" shrine and a food-protecting deity in the "outer" shrine. It was entitled to very special treatment. No-one but an imperial messenger could go and have prayers offered up: even the crown prince did not have the right to send a messenger without permission from the emperor. A priest who had said prayers for a disgraced minister in 969 was punished.[8] The court sent a messenger for the Prayers for the Year, on the occasion of the celebrations of the 6th and 12th months, and in the 9th month for the First Fruits Festival at Ise. Moreover, every twenty years, the inner and outer shrines were rebuilt and the "sacred objects" they housed were moved to the new building. At this time, an imperial messenger brought special offerings for the deities' treasure. There were many priests at the shrine, belonging to two local families, the Watarai and Arakida. In addition, the court appointed a head priest, a member of the Ōnakatomi family, who was usually also a senior official in the Ministry of Religious Affairs. He went several times a year to Ise where he was the eyes of the court. An imperial princess (daughter of an emperor) or a princess (grand-daughter of an emperor) was sent there at the beginning of each reign to serve the deities. The presence of a female member of their family at Ise was considered by the emperors to be very important. When Gosuzaku Tennō heard the report of Sukefusa who had just returned after accompanying the Vestal-princess to Ise:

> His Majesty was moved to tears by it and I too was in tears. The emperor said to me: "The departure of the Vestal-princess for Ise is an event of the greatest importance for the imperial family. From what I have been told, earlier journeys have never been entirely without incident. However, this time, there have been no complaints from the people and the conduct of the men of her retinue has been beyond reproach. Everything has gone just as I had hoped. [...] This sending of the Vestal to Ise is the most important event in my life."[9]

The court gradually allowed this shrine full management of most districts of the province of Ise. From the 11th century, there were frequent disputes between the priests, the head priest, the provincial governor and the director of the Office of the Vestal-Princess of Ise (Saigūryō). In 1031, an oracle transmitted by the Vestal during a storm in rather dramatic circumstances demanded the punishment and removal of the director, who had organized a kind of popular worship of the Ise deities. The court took a very dim view of this matter, which it regarded as a sacrilege and a crime of high treason.[10] Then, in the years 1038 and 1039, on two occasions, the chancellor Yorimichi attempted to impose a head priest who was not acceptable to the priests, thus starting a further series of oracles.[11] The priests did not have the right to bring their grievances to the capital and had to send these through the head priest. But being in dispute with him, large numbers of them arrived in the capital several times during the 11th century.

The emperors were very concerned about what happened at Ise. In 1040, on a windy day, the collapse of the outer shrine terrified the emperor, who realized that his family deities were displeased and were no longer protecting the country.[12] Goichijō and Gosuzaku appear to have been especially devoted to the Ise deities. They also had a superstitious respect for the sacred mirror of the palace, regarded as a "sacred object" of the Ise deity. When this object melted in 1040 in a palace fire, feverish efforts were made to find in the ashes small fragments of molten metal, which were treated with the utmost care.[13] The presence of the sacred mirror and the other two regalia, objects conceded by the founding deity at the same time as the mandate to rule, showed the legitimacy of the imperial line and the protection of its ancestors. Hence any accident that befell them was considered to be a serious warning and set in train divinations, consultations, prayers by the emperor at the palace (the emperors of the ancient period never went to Ise) and by the head priest at Ise, as well as the sending of special offerings.

In second place behind Ise on the list of the principal shrines were the lower and upper Kamo shrines. They pre-dated the establishment of the court at Heiankyō. Located north-east of the palace, they were taken over as shrines of the imperial family, which assigned a Vestal-princess to them from 810. The two annual Kamo festivals, especially that of the 4th month, were among the great events of the year. It began at the palace where the emperor, after having purified himself, paid his respects to the offerings, provided refreshments for the members of the procession and watched the programme of music and dances prepared for the deities. Then the procession of messengers of the emperor, crown prince, palace guard and women's services, enhanced by some ten horses, magnificently caparisoned, left the palace. It returned at night and a dance performance recalling an episode from a legend about the deities was given by the light of a brazier. The procession was one of the spectacles most enjoyed by the senior nobles and officials, as well as by the common people. The head of the Fujiwara family was also in the habit of visiting the shrine shortly before the festival.

The third most important shrine was that of Iwashimizu, south of Heiankyō. It was founded in 859 to house, among other deities of the Usa Shrine in north-east Kyūshū, the god Hachiman, who was believed to be the emperor Ōjin, regarded as an ancestor of the emperor and identified with a bodhisattva. His festival, which took place in the 3rd month, occasioned the same ceremonial as for Kamo. This shrine also had a Buddhist temple, whose intendant was often a member of one of the priestly families attached to Usa and Iwashimizu. Here in the 8th month was celebrated the Freeing of Living Creatures (Hōjōe), which involved releasing birds and fish, because:

> Do the swarming little animals not fear death? Do insects not like their bodies? This is why, by giving them life, we ensure for ourselves the happiness of a long life; by depriving them of it, we risk cutting short our future.[14]

At Iwashimizu, as at Usa, relations between the shrine and the temple were not always smooth, as there was competition for a share of the revenues from the large landholdings offered by the court.

Kasuga at Nara was the shrine of the Fujiwara, the maternal family of the emperors. Its two annual festivals were therefore celebrated in the same way as those of Kamo and Iwashimizu. The Kasuga deities had also been installed on the outskirts of Heiankyō, in the Ōharano Shrine, which was accorded special honour by the Fujiwara empresses.

Hirano was the shrine of the maternal family of Kanmu Tennō, the founder of Heiankyō. As such, it was included in the list of the most important shrines. Like Kamo, Iwashimizu, Kasuga and Ōharano, the Hirano Shrine could be honoured with an imperial visit.

Worshipped at the Sumiyoshi Shrine, in the province of Settsu, by the sea, was the consort of Ōjin Tennō, the empress Jingū, who is credited with conquests in Korea, together with deities protecting the country and navigation. The site was famous and was a place of pilgrimage (and tourism) for retired empresses and emperors, as well as for senior nobles.

Nihu and Kibune, which were on the list of twenty-two shrines, received as offerings black horses in the event of drought or white horses in the event of too much rain. Thus hardly a year went by that the court, besides the regular offerings, did not have occasion to send horses there.

Among the last shrines to be included in the list of twenty-two were those of Kitano and Yasaka. The first was founded in 959 and dedicated to the spirit of the renowned literatus Sugawara no Michizane, who died in exile in 903. The Fujiwara, responsible for Michizane's downfall, supported its foundation, as they feared the angry spirit of their victim.[15] As for the second, its origin is rather obscure. From the late 9th century, a deity who warded off epidemics was worshipped in this place. A Buddhist temple was attached to it. From 970, a ritual was performed in the middle of the 6th month to appease the evil spirits responsible for epidemics. This celebration soon became very popular and attracted all kinds of side-shows.[16]

Just as a new list of the shrines receiving regular offerings from the court was drawn up, so in each province a kind of reclassification was carried out. When they took up their duties, governors began by paying their respects to the deities of the shrine at the top of the list.

Relations between provincial governors and shrines were sometimes difficult. Disputes concerned the situation of the men belonging to the shrines: they took advantage of exemptions that the provincial administrators refused to recognize, as they feared a reduction in the number of those liable for taxes. Or else they centred on the management of the shrines' property, over which the governors claimed to have a right of inspection. So it was that in the early 11th century, the Usa Shrine presented to the court a petition in nine articles against the governor-general of Kyūshū, Taira no Korenaka. The grievances concerned the civil authorities' claiming the right to interfere in the administration of the shrine's property and impose their own men, their discourteous behaviour towards the priests and even the theft of objects from the treasure-house. Although he had arguments in his favour, Korenaka was dismissed – a fate suffered by many governors-general of Kyūshū for precisely the same reasons.[17]

Already in the Nara period, when Buddhism enjoyed great favour at the court, temples had been built near important shrines, as it were to help the deities to benefit from the teaching of the buddhas. In the early 9th century, the monk Kūkai provided a formula that made possible a kind of synthesis between the deities and the buddhas and bodhisattvas. The latter two were the original entities and the former were one of their manifestations. Thus the god Hachiman at Usa was considered to be an avatar of Amida and the goddess Amaterasu that of the original Buddha Dainichi. This compromise worked satisfactorily for the most part, and when disputes erupted between the shrines and their adjoining temples they involved the sharing of revenues and the management of property and not discussions relating to doctrinal matters.

In the Fujiwara period, the major festivals of the principal shrines were lavishly celebrated and the court was anxious to avoid any oversight that, in its eyes, could have had serious consequences. The senior nobles sought for their sons the role of imperial messenger. The fine bearing and elegant costume of the young man were thus clear for all to see and he was usually promoted as a reward. The heads of the Fujiwara clan visited their family shrine (Kasuga) from time to time with much pomp and ceremony. However apart from the cases of the emperors Goichijō and Gosuzaku, who seem to have been deeply devoted to and fearful of their ancestral deity, one finds very few expressions of fervent religious sentiment for the deities in the journals of the aristocrats. On the other hand, they were emotional and moved to tears when they attended Buddhist celebrations or sermons.

Buddhism

Buddhism appears to have been more in evidence in the daily lives of the senior nobles than Shintō, if only because of their familiarity with monks, which increased with the custom of sending some of their sons to temples. The Buddhism of the 10th and 11th centuries offers a number of different aspects. In the seven great temples of Nara, which owned substantial libraries, the tradition of study, notably of the doctrines of the Hossō sect, was maintained. The monks of the most powerful sects of the time, Tendai and Shingon, continued to produce commentaries. The court gave them the opportunity to face each other in quite frequent disputations, as the important personages seem to have taken far more interest in these than in the disputations on the classics that took place only once a year.

The principal Tendai establishments occupied Hieizan, the Mountain, and its environs. They housed very large numbers of monks: some devoted themselves most especially to study, others practised seated or ambulatory meditation, or gained a reputation for efficacy in the celebration of esoteric rituals, or followed simpler devotional practices. Tendai possessed an exoteric and an esoteric teaching. In the 11th century, it developed an early form of Amidism: faith in the promise of Amida Buddha to welcome into the Pure Land of the west all those who placed their trust in him. It was in the early 11th century that the monk Genshin (942-1017)[18] wrote *Ōjōyōshū* (*Compendium of Essentials for Rebirth in the Pure Land*). Another type was the administrator-monk, skilled at managing the wealth of his temple. Below these, a host of converts with an indeterminate monastic status wielded cudgels and bows. The Tendai abbot-general Ryōgen (912-985), the great reformer of the sect in his day, is credited with the organization of the first monastic troops. Since the late 9th century, the Tendai sect had been split into two branches, the Mountain on the one hand, and the Onjōji on the other, which clashed fiercely from the 11th century.[19] The Shingon sect was founded on esoteric doctrines. Its main centre, Mount Kōya, was located in the southern mountains of Yamato province. But it owned an important temple in the capital, the Tōji. This sect also split into two branches in the 10th century.

Originally, the central administration restricted the numbers taking religious vows (called "leaving home") and gave permission only to those who had passed examinations. Monks, in fact, paid no taxes and it was necessary to prevent tax evasion.

There were few ordination platforms (places for "receiving the precepts"): in the central areas the one at the Tōdaiji in Nara and the one at Hieizan for the Tendai monks. To control Buddhist affairs, in the 8th century the court had created an ecclesiastical hierarchy consisting of monastic rectors and prefects and masters of discipline, numbering only five at first. But in the 11th century, all this had become largely a formality. Permits to take religious vows were still issued at the time of important celebrations to honour the high-ranking monks, who gave them to their disciples. Monks who pursued serious studies and took part in disputations also received permits and, after reception of the precepts, a certificate. However, many men became monks of their own accord. Furthermore, the number of ecclesiastical dignitaries increased to such an extent – in the 12th century there were around a hundred masters of discipline – that the titles of monastic rector or monastic prefect became mainly honorary.

Emperors, senior nobles and even lesser officials vied with each other to found temples, adorn them with statues and endow them. The most important became registered temples and received official recognition. They were very numerous in the immediate vicinity of Heiankyō. Each establishment managed its own affairs and had a hierarchy at its head; the court appointed the superiors or intendants of these registered temples. The choice of the Tendai abbot-general gave rise to intrigues and disturbances.

The aristocracy tended to increase the number of Buddhist ceremonies. The emperor, who was subject to interdictions because of Shintō celebrations – mainly in the 2nd, 4th and 11th months as well as at the beginning of the 6th and 12th months –, confined himself to the celebration of the *Golden Light Sūtra* at the start of the year, the Litanies of the August Names of the Buddhas at the end of the year, the two celebrations of spring and autumn, and offerings for the celebration of the *Sūtra for Souls in Suspense* (*Urabongyō*) for the dead in the 7th month. Whenever it was possible and necessitated by difficulties, he ordered readings of the *Lotus Sūtra* or the *Benevolent Kings*

Sūtra, reputed to be beneficial for the protection of the country. But Fujiwara no Michinaga organized many more celebrations. He inaugurated at his residence an entire month (usually the 5th) devoted to readings of the *Lotus Sūtra*. Each year he had the same *sūtra* celebrated over four days for his father Kaneie; he did the same for his sister Senshi. He organized celebrations in spring and autumn, as was done at the palace. These ceremonies were an opportunity for him to gauge his authority and prestige by the number of participants and the offerings of food and alms they made to the monks. Readings and sermons were enhanced by processions, songs and dances. A meal was offered to the participants; sometimes a session of poetic composition was organized. The beautiful garments of the monks, who wore sumptuous kinds of stoles, combined with music and incense to delight sight, hearing, smell and taste.

The aristocracy increased the number of orders for religious statues, both for the temples it built and for its private chapels. The preference of the time was for wooden statues, assembled according to a technique (*yosegi-zukuri*) thought to be specific to Japan, which involved joining five or many more blocks set lengthwise or crosswise. The master sculptor active in the early 11th century, Kōshō, with a workshop of nearly a hundred artisans, worked for the Hōjōji, founded by Michinaga, who commissioned some two hundred statues from him.[20] Kōshō's successor, Jōchō (?-1057), worked at the Byōdōin. Religious painting also saw major developments, in accordance with established iconographical models. However, paintings representing the descent of Amida show very naturalistic landscapes in the background.

At the least sign of danger, Michinaga summoned monks to his residence. When he and members of his family were ill, he consulted a physician, but he also had recourse to monks who celebrated rituals of esoteric Buddhism. These rites were not ordered only to obtain health or prosperity or rain. They could also have a more sinister use: that of harming an enemy. Since they had been deemed efficacious and therefore dangerous if left in the hands of unqualified people, the court had attempted to restrict their use to purposes relating to the happiness of the emperor and thus of the country.[21] But in the 11th century, the emperor no longer had exclusive rights to them and the prohibition on subjects ordering their use was no longer respected. The Fujiwara regents had them celebrated for their own prosperity: Michinaga and his son Yorimichi could take the view that that their successes were useful for the good of the State. However many officials no longer had any hesitation in requesting rituals from monks for their own benefit.

The devoutness of lay people led them to increase the number of invitations to monks for recitations of *sūtras* as well as for those of invocations to Amida. For monks, this practice was a means of concentration, whereas for laymen it seems rather to have been the expression of a faith in the promise of this Buddha and the most effective way of moving him. In 1021, two years after taking religious vows, Fujiwara no Michinaga organized a recitation of seven hundred thousand invocations in five days. Later, at the end of the 11th century, one million would be exceeded.

Pilgrimages would increase significantly in the 12th century. However, already in the 11th century, the aristocracy visited temples close to the capital: the Kiyomizudera, the Miidera or Onjōji, not far from Lake Biwa, the Ishiyamadera of Ōtsu south of Lake Biwa, the establishments of Hieizan, the Hasedera in Yamato and the great temples of Nara; when the head of the Fujiwara went to the Kasuga Shrine, he also visited the family temple, Kōfukuji. These temples were sometimes used as resting places in the heat of summer, enabling devotion and pleasure to be reconciled. People would also spend the night there in the hope of receiving a communication in the form of a dream.

In the early 9th century, the founder of Tendai in Japan, the monk Saichō (767-822), had developed the idea, known in China since the 6th century, of a continuous decline in the knowledge and understanding of the doctrines preached by the Buddha. Entry into the period called "the end of the Law" (*mappō*) was predicted for 1052. This climate of a sense of powerlessness to be able to achieve Enlightenment by oneself led to the development of Amidism, which promised Amida's help. Many Amida chapels were set up in temples, as at the famous Byōdōin, founded by Fujiwara no Yorimichi in his villa at Uji, the very same year as entry into the final period. Another method frequently used to overcome this terrible destiny of the Law was the copying of *sūtras*, practised assiduously by the emperors and important personages. Fujiwara no Michinaga was one of the first, if not the first, to bury *sūtras*, a method of conservation that became very widely practised. Archaeologists have recovered from the sacred mountain of Kinpusen, where he made a pilgrimage in 1007, the *sūtras* he had buried there.[22] The casket bears an inscription in which he mentions all the buddhas and bodhisattvas from whom he hopes for aid: Shaka the past Buddha, Kannon the present Buddha and Miroku the future Buddha.

Protected, constantly called on for assistance by the court and enriched by it, the monks of the most important temples began early in the 11th century to assert their independence from the provincial governors, who were attempting to curb their greed. The first slightly serious case was instigated by the Kōfukuji, in dispute with the Yamato governor Minamoto no Yorichika, a client of Michinaga. In 1006, following skirmishes in the province and damage caused to rice fields, for which some monks had been punished, a threatening band arrived in the capital to lay siege to Michinaga's residence and set up camp at the palace gates. Michinaga had sufficient authority to get them to leave and after eight days agreed to receive a delegation of ecclesiastical dignitaries. They presented a document in four articles requesting the lifting of sanctions and the dismissal of the governor and one of his subordinates – demands deemed outrageous and improper by the minister. He threatened to deprive the dignitaries of their office and make sure they were no longer invited to palace celebrations. Order was restored.[23] Thirty years later, his son, the chancellor Yorimichi, was less successful in dealing with the monks of the Mountain. When it became necessary to appoint a new Tendai abbot-general in 1038, he wished to name an eminent monk, his protégé, who belonged to the rival Onjōji sect. Just when it was feared there would be problems, Fujiwara no Sukefusa writes:

> In the morning, the monk Kyōshō came to chat. He warned me that disturbances were about to erupt on the Mountain. They have learned that the emperor is going to appoint as abbot-general the grand monastic rector Myōson, and there is talk of rebellion.[24]

Shortly before this, the emperor, who was troubled, had secretly sought the advice of Fujiwara no Sanesuke, whose reply (conveyed to the emperor by Sukefusa) was as follows:

> I have nothing to suggest. If it were known that the emperor has consulted me, it would be most inconvenient. All I can say is that it is of the utmost importance for the imperial family that everything should go smoothly. The chancellor is leaning heavily towards Myōson, as he undoubtedly considers him to be the best candidate. He is not wrong. However, in the period of the "end of the Law", that may lead to the destruction of the Mountain form of Buddhism. It is extremely worrying that the whole of the Mountain might be sacrificed for one monk. It is also very serious for the imperial family.[25]

Several hundred monks arrived in the capital. Some ecclesiastical dignitaries signed a petition, which was presented to the court. Others intentionally abstained, either out of loyalty to the chancellor, or so as to be able to be chosen as a mediator. The chancellor was obliged to back down. But shortly afterwards, to show his displeasure and on the pretext that the abbot-general had not yet been appointed, he delayed the awarding of certificates to monks of the Mountain who had recently taken religious vows, causing Fujiwara no Sukehira to say:

> At the present time, the precepts are not being conferred in Tendai and, for this reason, many novices from all parts of the country are returning home in tears. [...] The monks of the Mountain are returning to their temples, empty-handed. This conduct is contrary to previous rules and is a source of grave

offences for future generations. Encouraging even one man to become a monk procures countless merits. Preventing even one man from taking religious vows is a very grave offence indeed.[26]

The disputes between Buddhist establishments became more acrimonious in the 12th century. The court, which was in the middle, had great difficulty in having its wishes respected, but it retained the privilege of conferring ecclesiastical honours.

The way of Yin and Yang

This developed significantly from the second third of the 9th century, after the reign of Saga Tennō, who had some reservations about this body of doctrines based on a cosmology and a knowledge of the interaction of the five elements and the succession of the two principles, Yin (female and darkness) and Yang (male and brightness). The study of these factors made it possible to determine auspicious and inauspicious days, either for everyone, or for a category of individuals based on date of birth, defined by the system of the ten stems (the five duplicated elements) and the twelve branches (the twelve animals). The combination of the two produced a cycle of sixty days, as well as others of sixty months and sixty years. Certain combinations were reputed to have a special influence. Thus, in the years Junior of Metal and Cock – years of changes –, it was advisable to adopt a new era name. The observation of the movements of real or even imaginary planets made it possible to determine directions – auspicious or inauspicious, open or closed – and dangerous days during which it was necessary to shut oneself up at home and see no-one from outside, that is, observe an interdiction. Therefore, if the emperor had to send a line of caparisoned horses to parade around a shrine on a day when he was obliged to observe an interdiction, the horses had to be kept at the palace overnight. Naturally the officials who attended personally on the emperor were required to shut themselves up in the palace with him at such times. Movements from one place to another and building work, called "violation of the earth", could be forbidden at certain times and in certain directions. Besides the foreseeable interdictions, there were accidental ones: the result of an omen, or coming upon a corpse, human or animal (which caused a defilement and necessitated the observance of an interdiction to get rid of it), or meeting an individual in mourning or who had contracted a defilement.

A whole casuistry, originally Chinese, but greatly expanded and complicated in Japan by the members of the way of Yin and Yang, was the object of reflections and of almost daily consultations. Many senior nobles were very familiar with it. Thus someone who sat down in the same place as a man in mourning contracted a defilement, but not if he remained standing. Which is why Fujiwara no Sukefusa, after the death of his father-in-law, when he went to speak with his wife, remained standing.[27] Defilements contracted were calculated as being of the first, second or third degree, of decreasing seriousness and demanding the observance of a shorter and shorter period of interdiction. Likewise, the seriousness differed according to whether the corpse found in a place was intact or not. Elements from the remotest Japanese antiquity and others brought by the way of Yin and Yang, hence of Chinese origin, were combined in the idea that the Japanese had formed of defilement, its effects and the means of cleansing oneself of it. Yet, rightly or wrongly, they were convinced that this abhorrence of defilement was unique to them. Fujiwara no Sanesuke writes in 1027:

> Yorimichi said that in India there is no fear of contracting a defilement. My reply was that the fear of defilement is Japanese and that in China no-one fears it.[28]

The lesser officials seem to have observed fewer interdictions than the senior nobles, as their absences would have been too frequent. However an important minister like Fujiwara no Michinaga observed a prohibition on about seventy days a year.

All kinds of expedients were possible to get around interdictions when they were simply too inconvenient. If a direction was closed, it was usual to make a detour in order to proceed in an open direction. Or else when construction was required during a prohibited period, the work was begun. In early 1040, it was necessary to erect a pavilion at the palace in the days devoted to the Earth element, a time when "violation of the earth" was not permitted. It was decided to erect the platform the evening before the prohibited period and place a temporary roof over it.[29]

In the early 11th century, there were two very well known masters of the way of Yin and Yang: Kamo no Mitsuyoshi, a calendrical specialist, and Abe no Seimei (921-1005), who was adept in rituals designed to ward off evil influences. Some slightly later anecdotes attribute magical powers to him.[30] These men passed on their knowledge to their descendants.

The members of the way of Yin and Yang had various tasks, as much in the service of the State as in that of the senior nobles in a private capacity. They drew up the calendar each year, determined the auspicious and inauspicious days, fixed the dates and the hours for ceremonies and travel, and interpreted omens. They celebrated the star of the birth year of those who requested this of them. They performed divinations by means of the short lines forming the hexagrams in the fundamental work, *The Book of Changes* (J. *Ekikyō*; Ch. *Yijing*). In general, when the court requested a divination, regular or exceptional, it simultaneously enlisted the services of officials from the Ministry of Religious Affairs, using the interpretation of the small cracks on a tortoise shell, and officials of the Office of Divination, thereby enabling these two groups to check each others' results. The masters also provided opinions on the seriousness of defilements contracted by a person or place. They performed purification rites near rivers. They took part in the rituals of entry into a new house in order to expel the evil forces, as well as in rituals of departure. They performed offices for rain in a Five Dragons ritual. They also had certain responsibilities in celebrations intended to prevent epidemics.

The very ancient belief in spirits had become associated with the three religious and cosmological systems: Shintō, Buddhism and the way of Yin and Yang. These spirits were either those of malevolent and demonic beings (or things according to the euphemism used in referring to them), or those of the dead, especially men who had died a violent death, and therefore angry and seeking vengeance. The fear of this latter category developed markedly from the second half of the 9th century. Which is why a temporary measure – the suspension of the application of the death penalty – adopted in the early 9th century, no doubt to imitate the emperor Xuan Zong (r. 712-756) of the Tang, remained in force up to the end of the 12th century. In fact, it was above all the aristocracy of the capital that was susceptible to the fear of posthumous vengeance, as it showed in the worship offered at the Kitano Shrine to the spirit of the disgraced minister Sugawara no Michizane. Provincial governors, like Fujiwara no Yasumasa or Minamoto no Yori-nobu mentioned in the previous chapter, were not as fearful. However, the members of the Police Bureau, who had no qualms about shooting arrows at people and quite possibly killing them, apparently began in the early 11th century the practice of offering a reading of the *Lotus Sūtra* each year, in order to receive pardon for their violent conduct and protect themselves from the vengeance of their victims.[31]

In the late 9th century, the court began to hold ceremonies at the beginning of summer, in the Shinsen-en south of the palace and in temples around the capital, to propitiate evil spirits and appease the spirits of the dead, in order to prevent them from causing harm by spreading epidemics. To the same end, rituals were celebrated on the roads leading to the capital to protect it against evil influences.[32] The former were mainly entrusted to monks, but were celebrated in temples associated with shrines, like the Kanjin-in or Kitano. The latter were offered in some cases by Shintō priests, and in others by masters of the way of Yin and Yang. Japan thus provided a model of peaceful co-existence of doctrines and beliefs.

Fear of evil spirits, abhorrence of defilements, observation of the movements of stars and planets, fear of divine retribution, terror when faced with incantations and rituals intended to cause harm: all these things would suggest that the aristocrats lived in fear and dread. Some qualification is needed, however. There were always means of warding off evil influences, avoiding interdictions, regaining lost purity, and obtaining the help of the deities and buddhas: Amida in particular was seen at the time as the best recourse. Miroku, the future Buddha, and Yakushi, the healing Buddha, were called upon whenever necessary. A host of powerful tutelary deities offered their support.

However, with the death of Fujiwara no Michinaga in 1027, some aristocrats were assailed by a pessimism fuelled by the increase in the number of incidents bringing the religious establishments into conflict with each other and with the local authorities, and by the disturbances that spread in the North from the middle of the century. The court had to give the power to suppress them to warrior-officials, who thereby gained increasing independence and looked after their own interests, without ceasing to revere it. At the same time, its sources of revenue were changing, without actually declining, but the new system, based on estates holding tax exemptions, was more complex and more difficult to manage because of the large number of agents required and the ambitions of each person. When informed of the events that had taken place at the Ise Shrine – oracles and the collapse of buildings –, the emperor wondered whether the realm was not doomed and whether the deities were not abandoning it. Those members of the aristocracy who were unable to keep up their status – a category typified by the author of the *Shunki*, Fujiwara no Sukefusa – were haunted by the thought of the inescapable nature of decay, exacerbated by the Buddhist belief of entry into the final period of the Law. But these bursts of pessimism were counterbalanced by the persistence of the idea according to which the loss of divine protection and decline were the result of a bad government, thus liable to punishment, and by the consoling promises of Amidism.

Notes

1. *Ruijū fusenshō* (*Systematically Classified Collection of Imperial Orders and Ministerial Decrees*), chap. 3, Kankō 1.7.6. and 9., 1004; *Midō kanpakuki*, Kankō 1.7.10.14. and 20., 1.8.1.5.6.9.11. and 16., 1004; *Nihon kiryaku*, Kankō 1.8.4., 1004.
2. *Nihon kiryaku*, Kannin 3.4.17.21. and 3.5.26., 1019; and *Shōyūki*, Kannin 3.4. and 5. It should be noted that, two and a half centuries later, at the time of the Mongol invasions, the court referred back to the measures taken in 1019 for ordering religious celebrations.
3. *Kujō-dono yuikai* (*Instructions Left by the Lord of Kujō*).
4. *Ruijū sandai kyaku* (*Systematically Classified Decrees of Three Eras*), decrees of Hōki 11.12.14., 780, and Daidō 2.9.26., 807, prohibition of the activities of mediums; Kōnin 3.9.26., 812, provincial governors forbidden to transmit oracles pronounced by common people; *Nihon kiryaku*, Chōgen 5.8.20., 1032, opinion of jurists on the offence of the governor of Izumo, who transmitted an oracle rejected by the court.
5. *Shunki*, Chōryaku 2.11.27., 1038.
6. *Iken jūnikajō*, article 1.
7. *Midō kanpakuki*, Chōwa 5.2.26. and 5.3.8., 1013.
8. *Daijingū shozōjiki* (*Record of Various Matters Pertaining to the [Ise] Great Shrines*), a text written by Ise priests, and reworked in the late 12th century; Anna 2.4.26., 969, a shrine dignitary loses his post for having offered prayers for Minamoto no Takaakira.
9. *Shunki*, Chōryaku 2.10.4., 1038.
10. *Daijingū shozōjiki*, Chōgen 4.4.17. and 19.; and *Shōyūki*, Chōgen 4.7.3., 1031.
11. *Daijingū shozōjiki*, Chōryaku 3.4.1., 1039, oracle against the head priest who had had a dispute with the priests the previous year, and 3.8.7., dismissal of a second head priest because he did not belong to the Ōnakatomi line from which these dignitaries were always chosen.
12. *Daijingū shozōjiki*, Chōkyū 1.7.27., 1040, collapse of one of the Ise shrines; *Shunki*, Chōkyū 1.8. and 9., discussions at the court on the significance of the event and the emperor's fears.
13. *Shunki*, Chōkyū 1.9.9., 1040, palace fire and search for the remains of the sacred mirror. *Midō kanpakuki*, Kankō 2.11.15.,

1005, palace fire; 2.12.9., what was recovered of the mirror gave off an auspicious glow.

14. *Ruijū sandai kyaku*, Gangyō 6.6.3., 882.

15. *Shōyūki*, Kanna 1.9.8., 985, Eiso 1.3.19., 989, Shōryaku 4.6.26., 990. Oracles in the entourage of the retired emperor and the Fujiwara empresses request posthumous promotions for Michizane, reflecting Fujiwara fears of possible posthumous vengeance.

16. The establishment called Kanjin-in consisted of a temple and a shrine. In 935, the temple was given official recognition; in 939, the shrine received offerings from the court.

17. *Iwashimizu monjo* (*Documents of the Iwashimizu Shrine*), text of Chōhō 5.8.19., 1003, submission of a petition from the Usa Shrine to the court. *Midō kanpakuki*, Kankō 1.3.24., 1004, several hundred men from the shrine came to voice their complaints at the palace gate.

18. He declined honours in order to devote himself to meditation and the writing of his celebrated work, *Ōjōyōshū*; in Japan, the first exposition intended for everyone of the Amidist doctrine. In 1039, *Shunki*, Chōryaku 3.10.8., during the mourning period after the death of the empress Genshi, the courtiers read this text.

19. The differences relate to details of the esoteric doctrines and rituals, those of the Mountain deriving from Ennin, who travelled in China from 838 to 847, and those of the Onjōji from Enchin (814-891), who was in China from 853 to 858.

20. No trace remains of the works ordered by Michinaga for the Jōmyōji in 1005 and for the Hōjōji after he took religious vows, except a statue of Fudōmyōō preserved in Kyōto at the Dōshuin temple.

21. *Ruijū sandai kyaku*, decree of Shōtai 4. (Engi 1.) 2.14., 901. It reiterates the prohibition, already formulated in the late 8th century, on having rituals celebrated for private individuals. These celebrations were to be reserved for the emperor and the country.

22. *Midō kanpakuki*, Kankō 4.8.11., 1007.

23. *Midō kanpakuki*, Kankō 3.7.15., 1006.

24. *Shunki*, Chōryaku 2.10.16., 1038.

25. *Shunki*, Chōryaku 2.10.12., 1038.

26. *Shunki*, Chōryaku 2.12.7., 1039.

27. *Shunki*, Chōryaku 3.10.11., 1039.

28. *Shōyūki*, Manju 4.8.25., 1027.

29. *Shunki*, Chōryaku 3.12.18., beginning of 1040.
30. *Konjaku monogatarishū*, chap. 19, anec. 24, he performs a ritual that prevents the death of a monk. *Uji shūi monogatari*, anec. 26, he causes the temporary disappearance of the servants of a monk who wanted to put his powers to the test.
31. *Kokon chomonjū* (*Collection of Ancient and Modern Traditions*), anec. 69.
32. On the question of spirits and celebrations for appeasing them, see B. Frank, Annuaire de l'École pratique des hautes études, IVe section, 1970-1971.

CONCLUSION

In the early 11th century, the group of those who, according to a saying of the time, lived protected by nine gates, in other words the court, began to shroud its activities under a veil of secrecy that reinforced the sacred respect inspired by its role of intermediary with the deities and buddhas, as well as that of guardian of the civilization and the traditions. The leading members of the court tended to focus mainly on their ritual duties and on ceremonial. From the former, they expected an efficacy that would bring peace and prosperity to the country; from the latter, that it should make visible the order of the world and society. They performed their task with care, but knew how to find the strategies necessary to ensure that it was not too onerous.

At the same time, the court continued to keep a tight rein on the provincial governors, who had not yet shortened – or all but discontinued, as happened in the 12th century – their sojourns in their provincial seats of government and acknowledged themselves as clients of the members of the council of senior nobles. In this way, the court could receive without any real difficulty a major share of the available wealth of the country: what it needed to live and meet the costs incurred in the building of palaces, residences and temples and the organization of the annual cycle of celebrations. These governors provided the timber, corvée labour, cloth and rice used as means of payment, together with all the necessary provisions and furnishings.

Thus, in the early 11th century, at the time when Fujiwara no Michinaga dominated the court, there was a fairly brief period of stability and relative peace. The provinces experienced only the usual small-scale disturbances, but no major clashes. In the capital, a few thieves and arsonists operated freely, but there were no serious plots or problems caused by the religious establishments. The prestige, good fortune and astuteness of Michinaga stifled all opposition. A well-governed and refined society had ample opportunity to foster a splendid flowering of literature and the arts. Women occupied quite an important place in this society, though one that later generations have undoubtedly over-estimated, because the only part of the literary productions of the time that is still widely read is due in large measure to them.

The most obvious and best-known legacy of this period is the literature. About a hundred years after the first texts written in the syllabary, a work as dense, complex and refined as the *Genji monogatari* was able to appear, not in isolation, but as part of a powerful current of diverse productions: romantic tales, short tales, poetry and essays. These works in Japanese are the only ones that are still appreciated. However the poems in Chinese and the writings in *kanbun*, in a word the productions reserved exclusively for men, enjoyed a higher status at the time, as serious works carrying a moral and political meaning. Yet only the romantic literature that served as a diversion and the poetry continue to be read and appreciated. They determined certain aspects of taste in matters of style: a partiality for ellipsis, abridgement and allusion, as well as the search for amusing word-plays and for sentences with a double meaning. They inspired a large part of the medieval theatre, the *nō*. At least three contemporary novelists, including Tanizaki Junichirō, have produced versions of the *Genji monogatari* in the modern language. This novel continues to be read and imitated in our own day. It has been translated into almost all European languages and even in this form has elicited great admiration.

The mid-Heian period saw important developments in architecture. A large number of palaces, aristocratic residences and temples were built. But many had only a short existence because of fires, and hardly any survived beyond medieval times. There remain only some plans, descriptions and a few examples: incomplete like the Byōdōin or rustic like the Jōruriji. However, these at least make it possible to understand their structure and to imagine their grandeur and beauty. The civil architecture of the Heian period is really only found in the imperial palace in Kyōto, located in the same place since the 14th century, noticeably farther to the east than the palace of the early 11th century, and reduced to the inner palace alone. The reconstructions of 1789 and 1856 are considered to be quite faithful reproductions of the main buildings of the old inner palace, as they benefited from the scholarly investigations conducted in the Edo period. In the medieval and modern periods, the symmetry that characterizes the architecture of the Fujiwara era was abandoned. But the notion of the gallery surrounding the central part of a pavilion and largely open to the garden during the day persisted. The bare nature of the interior décors remained a permanent feature of the aristocratic residences, always compensated for by the refinement, at once restrained and opulent, of the few objects, notably lacquerware.

This high point of early Japanese civilization did not leave traces only in literature, the arts and, more generally, the customs. In this area may be mentioned, for example, table etiquette and the exchange of saké cups. The concern with protocol – respect for the social order – is another legacy of this time, inherited by later periods up to our own day. The programme of a modern-day ceremony is very similar to those established by the court officials: it is just as painstakingly drawn up. Also dating from this time are principles of administrative organization that have never entirely disappeared and that were studied and imitated in the Edo period and even at the beginning of Meiji. Throughout the medieval period (13th-16th centuries), writing retained its importance: all procedures, notably judicial, had to be written down. The ideal that early Japan had not been able to achieve – total control of the people and lands through the establishment of population registers and land surveys – was to be realized on a large scale in the Edo period. Already in the Middle Ages, the daimyō had attempted to do this. The practice of taking decisions through committees and of asking the opinion of the most junior people before going up to the most senior ones also comes from the early period, as does that of conducting an official procedure in parallel with unofficial discussions.

The progression towards formalism begun in the late 10th century continued, to the point where, in the late 11th century, officials in the bureaux of the capital fabricated in large quantities tax registers purporting to come from the provinces, registers inspected by these same bureaux: an ingenious way of presenting documents that conformed to the rules. However this sclerosis of the agencies of the court, which gradually went to sleep in a ritual role where it was irreplaceable, is perhaps one of the factors (no doubt not the only one) that helped to ensure its survival during the disturbances of the Middle Ages. Since the Edo period took over and applied more rigorously the administrative rules already established in the Heian period, the founding role of the latter in this area is often forgotten. On the other hand, the aesthetic principles elaborated at the apogee of the Heian period have remained alive and have always been acknowledged as a great achievement.

APPENDIX 1

Writing in Heian Japan

The Heian period, and in particular the so-called Fujiwara era, has left an enormous number of documents. From the foundation, in the early 8th century, of the system described by historians as that of the "code-governed State", writing has played a very important role in Japanese life. The administration relied heavily on it, but only in the 9th century did it abandon the use – on the whole not very practical – of wooden tablets, as the supply of paper must by then have become sufficient. This dominant place of the written word in early Japanese society was not self-evident, given the extreme complexity of reading and writing. Japan, in fact, borrowed the Chinese characters, even though its language does not belong to the same family as Chinese. Thanks to continuing efforts over several centuries by anonymous people, many of whom were no doubt monks, and largely completed by the early 10th century, a syllabary was able to be perfected; it was formed using abbreviated or truncated characters for their sound, thereby making it possible to write spoken Japanese. It served to write down poetry and gave an impetus to the flowering of a literature of tales, personal accounts and essays written by women, who were not permitted by social convention to use Chinese characters.

The officials, for their part, used Chinese, the language of government, to write regulations and decrees, official histories, manuals and poetry. It was often a very degraded form of Chinese. But whether it was poetry, the Chinese classics and histories (their main intellectual nourishment), or texts composed in Japan, they read them "in the Japanese manner", in other words they engaged in mental gymnastics that involved modifying the word order by moving the verb to the end of a sentence, and inserting the case particles and flexional endings unknown in Chinese. Moreover, some characters were read in their "Japanese reading", hence translated. Others, for which there were no corresponding Japanese readings, were read in what is called Sino-Japanese, the pronunciation differing markedly from that of Tang-period Chinese. To further complicate matters, early in the 9th century, the court failed in its attempt at reform of the Sino-Japanese sounds, meaning that at least two series, introduced at different dates, were used at the same time. Words of Sino-Japanese appearance were quite common in the language of the officials, but not all were Chinese words, as the Japanese had created new compounds for their own use.

Thus, for the century from about 967 (after which date the Fujiwara regents and chancellors succeeded one another without interruption) until 1067 (date of the accession of Gosanjō Tennō, marking the start of the waning of Fujiwara influence), we have a wealth of documents. These comprise regulations (the earliest ones not yet abolished and the new ones issued periodically), imperial edicts, ministerial decrees and orders relating to various subjects, appointments, diplomas of rank, addresses to the throne, requests for posts, resignations, reports and official proceedings of the Police Bureau: texts collected together for use by the administration. Of all this output, there remain the codes, penal and administrative, *Yōrō ritsuryō*, compiled in the early 8th century, but still not forgotten in the 11th century. The *Regulations of the Engi Era* (*Engishiki*), from the early 10th century, were still partially applied. The two major collections of decrees are *Ruijū sandai kyaku* (*Systematically Classified Decrees of Three Eras*) and *Ruijū fusenshō* (*Systematically Classified Collection of Imperial Orders and Ministerial Decrees*). Many texts of different dates and scope were collected into manuals for use by officials; the two most important are the *Compendium of Administration* (*Seiji yōryaku*), by a jurist of the early 11th century, Yoshimune no Tadasuke (?-?), and *Writings of the Court and Provinces* (*Chōya gunsai*), by Miyoshi no Tameyasu (1049-1139), a collection of models of administrative documents.

The compilation of the official histories prepared by a committee of officials and presented to the throne was interrupted at the very beginning of the 10th century. However, some officials, basing their work primarily on official registers, kept alive the tradition of annals in *kanbun*, the Chinese written by Japanese. Also, a copious output of protocol manuals, which provide detailed information about procedures and ceremonies and give lists of dated examples, took over where the output of annals left off. In the category of histories on the model of the previous official histories, the *Abridged Annals of Japan* (*Nihon kiryaku*) ends at 1036. It can be supplemented by the *Abbreviated Record of Japan* (*Fusō ryakki*), also in *kanbun*, compiled in the early 12th century, and by *Notes One Hundred Times Polished* (*Hyakurenshō*) from the second half of the 13th century. One particular episode, the insurrection of Taira no Masakado from 935 to 940, became the subject of an account in *kanbun*, *Shōmonki* or *Masakadoki*. The three main protocol manuals are *Notes of the Western Residence* (*Saikyūki*), from the late 10th century, *Notes of the Northern Hills* (*Hokuzanshō*), from the early 11th century, and *Order of Procedures and Celebrations According to the Ōe Family* (*Gōke shidai*), from the late 11th century; all three are the work of senior nobles: Minamoto no Takaakira, Fujiwara no Kintō and Ōe no Masafusa. We also have collections of archival documents: deeds of sale, wills, petitions, arbitration judgements and texts relating to estate administration, these being mainly of monastic origin. A modern compiler, Takeuchi Rizō, reclassified chronologically in a major collection, *Heian ibun*, a large part of the surviving documents, most of them produced by local administrations or religious establishments, the texts issued by the court being in a minority.

Anthologies compiled by officials recorded Chinese poems, examination papers, prefaces composed on the occasion of sessions of poetic composition at the court, and wishes expressed at Buddhist celebrations: a whole literature influenced by the official ideology. For prose, most of the output is found in the *Literary Essence of Our Country* (*Honchō monzui*) by

Fujiwara no Akihira, and for poetry in the *Collection of Japan* (*Fusōshū*) by Ki no Tadana (957-999) and *Outstanding Poems from Our Country* (*Honchō reisō*) by Takashina no Moriyoshi (?-1014?), as well as in Ōe no Masahira's *Anthology of the Ministry of Ceremonial's Official Ōe* (*Gōrihōshū*).

Lastly, and these documents are by no means the least interesting, are the surviving notes kept on a daily basis by some senior nobles, notes not intended to be made public and therefore presumed to be reasonably accurate, as they were expected to enable heirs, thus provided with good precedents, to correctly perform their functions at the court. In principle, they were intended only as an unvarnished record of the procedures and celebrations attended by their authors and it was not considered advisable to mention feelings and personal judgements. One can, however, to a greater or lesser degree depending on the individual, get an idea of the passions that stirred them. The journals preserved include, for the end of the 10th and the first third of the 11th century, those of Fujiwara no Michinaga, *Midō kanpakuki*, Fujiwara no Sanesuke, *Shōyūki*, Fujiwara no Yukinari, *Gonki*, Minamoto no Tsuneyori (976-1039), *Sakeiki*, and, for the mid-11th century, that of Fujiwara no Sukefusa, *Shunki*. To these may be added *Instructions Left by the Lord of Kujō* (*Kujō-dono yuikai*), a small treatise of moral advice written by Fujiwara no Morosuke for his descendants, and collections of anecdotes in *kanbun*, such as *The Ōe Conversations* (*Gōdanshō*), anecdotes heard directly from the second counsellor and literatus Ōe no Masafusa and full of reminiscences of the previous hundred years, and *Remarks on Past Matters* (*Kojidan*), attributed to Minamoto no Akikane (1160-1215), from the early 13th century. One of the first treatises on the study of words, by the scholar-official Fujiwara no Akihira and written in Sino-Japanese, *Notes on Some New Comic Entertainments* (*Shinsarugakuki*), lists and describes the activities of a large group of inhabitants of the capital in the mid-11th century.

Next to these works by men in a more or less "Japanized" form of *kanbun*, the literature by women casts a very different light on the society of the early 11th century. This mainly consists of personal diaries, often akin to reminiscences: *The Kagerō Diary* (*Kagerō nikki*), *The Diary of Murasaki Shikibu* (*Murasaki Shikibu nikki*), *The Diary of Izumi Shikibu* (*Izumi Shikibu nikki*), this last-mentioned filled with poems, and *The Sarashina Diary* (*Sarashina nikki*); essays, such as *The Pillow Book* (*Makura no sōshi*) by Sei Shōnagon; romantic tales, the most famous being *The Tale of Genji* (*Genji monogatari*) by Murasaki Shikibu; and historical narratives, such as *A Tale of Flowering Fortunes* (*Eiga monogatari*) by Akazome Emon.

Some men wrote works in Japanese prose, but without putting their name to them: these include a history, *The Great Mirror* (*Ōkagami*), a series of biographies of emperors and Fujiwara ministers, ending with the greatest, Michinaga; a tale of the fighting that disturbed the north of the country from 1051 to 1062, the *Account of the Uprising in Mutsu* (*Mutsu waki*); and also collections of anecdotes. Those from the late 11th and early 12th century have preserved a somewhat distorted re-collection of many of the men who lived during the heyday of the Heian court, but one often corroborated by authentic documents. This is especially true of *Tales of Times Now Past* (*Konjaku monogatarishū*), the final chapters of which are a mine of information on the society of the early 11th century. Of a later date, as it comes from the early 13th century, the *Supplement to the Tales of Uji* (*Uji shūi monogatari*) presents men who lived in the 10th and 11th centuries. A particular type of collection is the one that brings together very short tales containing one or more poems; the best known are *Tales of Ise* (*Ise monogatari*) and *Tales of Yamato* (*Yamato monogatari*), both from the mid-10th century.

The Fujiwara period has left us an abundance of poems, many of which are concerned above all with worldly matters and provide us with information about the society that produced them. They are found in numerous anthologies, some compiled at imperial command, or in personal collections. From the late 10th and early 11th century are those of the ladies Izumi Shikibu, Murasaki Shikibu, Sei Shōnagon and Akazome Emon, and that of the major counsellor Fujiwara no Kintō. In each of these collections, nearly half the poems are not by the person whose name it bears, for poetic composition, a social activity, enters into a dialogue.

APPENDIX 2

Learning and Artistic Pursuits

The journals of members of the aristocracy, the senior nobles and their sons, often give the impression that they live in a closed society, animated it is true by competing tensions and ambitions, but considerably removed from their subordinates. However Heian-period society, especially at its apogee, did not consist solely of Fujiwara, Minamoto, Taira, Sugawara and Ōe. The still functioning parts of the administration employed men from many other families, some of whom had developed a specialization: in government offices, learning or the arts. The households of the important personages were full of retainers and through these men they had contact with a cross-section of society, even at times its criminal element, despite claiming to distance themselves from violence of any kind. With a view to correcting the common perception of a court society centred almost exclusively on the senior nobles, we shall discuss here some members of the various branches of learning and their functions, as well as a number of artists.

Most areas of study were controlled by the Office of Higher Learning. Normally, in order to gain access to the different disciplines – the classics, law and mathematics –, it was necessary to pass an entrance examination from which the sons of men of the fifth rank were exempt. Classes seem to have consisted of explicated readings of the works prescribed for each discipline. Students needed to have a very good memory, especially as there were probably insufficient books during the Nara period and the first century of the Heian period. The regulations – it is not known how they were applied in the 10th century – prescribed periodic examinations consisting of questions on the meaning of the passages read in class. Each discipline had doctors, sometimes assistants, and students, the numbers being set down in the regulations. The best students were called graduates. But it is unclear whether the law was still applied, even as early as the 10th century. In fact, one has the impression that teachers were free to select and instruct disciples who were often family members and that, if they came across very talented individuals from outside, they gave them their name. Graduates were selected not by a competitive examination, but based on the recommendation of the doctors. Heredity was already in evidence from the early 10th century. This did not entirely rule out the possibility for men belonging to provincial families or those holding very minor posts to study, become known to a teacher, progress in a discipline and on the threshold of old age obtain a position.

The curriculum for the classics consisted of *The Analects of Confucius*, *The Classic of Filial Piety* (two compulsory works for students in all fields), *The Book of Odes*, *The Book of Documents*, *The Book of Changes*, *The Spring and Autumn Annals* and *The Book of Rites*. These were explicated by a doctor, two assistants and readers, originally supported by two doctors specializing in the reading of Chinese sounds and two doctors of writing. But it seems that in the 10th century the latter were no longer appointed. By that time, the documents mention only the doctor, sometimes an assistant, readers and the four graduates (the best students originally receiving a kind of scholarship), mostly relatives of the teachers. As Nakahara no Munetoki (946?-?) remarked in 995: of itself the study of the classics did not lead to any useful outcome for the students.[1] This discipline could, at best, and then not every year, put forward two or three students for a very minor post. By contrast, readers and graduates, as well as the doctor, had employment opportunities that enabled advancement, however slow. The court sometimes requested advice from the doctor on a point relating to ceremonial. In principle, each year on the day after the Confucian celebration in the 8th month, the court was supposed to invite into its presence the principal members of this discipline for a lecture and an interrogation of students followed by the distribution of gifts, but certainly did not hold this spectacle every year. However in 1007, Fujiwara no Michinaga, wishing to set himself up as a patron of learning, invited the staff members and students of the classics, law and mathematics to a public session of disputations, in fact an interrogation of three students, preceded by a lecture given by the doctor of the classics, Kiyohara no Hirozumi (934-1009). Michinaga notes that the reader Yoshizumi, the brother of Hirozumi and responsible for asking questions, has a distracted air and that the participants wonder whether he is deranged or intoxicated.[2] Clearly this man, who at nearly sixty years of age was only a reader, was not accustomed to being in the presence of senior nobles, who had little regard for these teachers. The career paths of specialists in the classics were far from being rapid and easy, as is shown by that of the first Kiyohara, Hirozumi, who founded a line of doctors. He was made a reader in 983 at almost fifty, then a minor secretary in the Ministry of State Affairs in 986, principal secretary in 988 and the same year promoted to the fifth rank. In 1004 he became a doctor of the classics, after an appointment as governor of Ōsumi. Nakahara no Munetoki became a doctor in 991, while principal secretary in the Ministry; in 1008 he took part in the readings of passages from the classics in the presence of the new-born imperial prince Atsunari;[3] he was then governor of Ise. During the 11th century, his descendants retained the posts of doctor and members of the ministerial secretariat, posts that continued to have a certain importance. In fact, these officials, thanks to their bureau register that preserved precedents, were frequently consulted by the members of the council and played an important role in the preparation of council meetings and celebrations. Specialists in the classics could also be employed in the Control Board secretariat as principal and minor secretaries, who participated in the activities of the controllers, reading and classifying documents. But their numbers never compared with those for the literati. Thus, in the 10th century, the ministerial secretariat had only four or five doctors, readers or graduates of the classics compared with more than thirty students or graduates of letters, and of course even among the latter there were no Fujiwara, Minamoto or Taira.[4] The decline of this discipline from the 10th century is shown by the fourth article presented by Miyoshi no Kiyoyuki in 914 aimed at correcting errors that had crept into the administration. It seems that the provincial authorities no longer provided enough rations to feed the students who were dying of hunger and cold. Kiyoyuki adds that the Office of Higher Learning has become a refuge for failures and that families are reluctant to send their sons there.[5]

The study of law is not mentioned in the code, but was organized in the first half of the 8th century with two doctors and twenty students, two of whom were graduates. As it was concerned with punishments, it had a poor reputation. Moreover it did not deal with the major principles of government, the first being that the emperor acts more by morality and example[6] than by laws, notably penal, and regulations, often subject to change, and about which the prevailing political morality said that the fewer there were the better the country was governed. No curriculum was prescribed for the legal specialists, whose field was naturally the explanation and commentary of the codes, decrees and regulations of the country. It may reasonably be supposed that they also consulted the Chinese legislation. Thus, among the families specializing in the law, one finds no Fujiwara, Minamoto, Taira, Sugawara or Ōe, but families thought to be descended from immigrants of the very early period. In the 10th and 11th centuries, the doctors were unable to put forward a student each year for a very minor post, generally in the gate guard, Police Bureau or Department of Justice. But those appointed, often aged over thirty, could remain in the same post for more than twenty years, as happened with a man who in 1001 was made a fourth-class official in the gate guard and was still at the same grade in 1025. There were even fewer jurists in the ministerial secretariat than specialists in the classics: three between 991 and 1015. The doctors were called upon for advice – notably on the subject of misdeeds by officials –, as were the principal judicial advisors, a function often given to doctors or graduates. As with the other disciplines, heredity tended to become the norm from the 10th century. The best known doctor of the late 10th century was the fifth generation of a family of jurists: his grandfather Koremune no Kinkata (?-?) had been active during the reign of Murakami Tennō. Tadasuke (?-?) changed his family name to Yoshimune in 999. He was a graduate, then doctor and held posts as a judicial advisor and member of the gate guard. He did not consider his career to be a rewarding one; he wrote that after he graduated he had dream in which a deity told him he would have a career in the Police Bureau, a rather shameful function since it required chaining people up. He also wrote: "As the court has no respect for the law and despises the judicial officials, those who pass the law examinations are usually not wise and many of them are vulgar."[7] Yet he ended his career at the fourth rank and between 1006 and 1008 was governor of Kawachi. He was also reputed to have had a very good knowledge of Chinese literature. He is the author of the important *Seiji yōryaku* and several smaller works. He has remained famous, because in 999 he invited a group of literati to his residence for a lecture on the law. On this occasion, the guests composed poems in Chinese: the literatus Ōe no Mochitoki wrote a poem in praise of the law with its "deep meaning": "those who obey it live in peace, those who go against its principles lay themselves open to dangers".[8] Yoshimune no Tadamasa (?-1015), possibly the brother of Tadasuke, was also a doctor of law. They had a descendant in the person of Michinari (?-1052?), considered the best jurist of the 11th century. But the Yoshimune did not monopolize the posts of doctor; in the 10th and 11th centuries one also finds Mimana no Tadatoki (?-?), Ono no Fumiyoshi (?-?) and Kuni no Masashige (?-?). Fujiwara no Michinaga employed in his household, as guardian of his treasure, a jurist named Kannabi no Yasusuke (?-?), who in 1020 became a doctor.[9] In the 11th century and beyond, there were doctors from the Nakahara and Sakanoue families, notably Sakanoue no Akikane (1079-1147) and his grandson Akimoto (1138-1210) who are credited with recasting the legislation and compiling the *Hossō shiyōshō*. However the unrest of the late 11th century gave a more important role to the law, more of whose members could be put forward for appointments.

The study of mathematics was based on Chinese books and dealt with the four operations, linear measures, distances, areas, weights, and the extraction of square and cube roots. There were two doctors who taught twenty students, and two graduates who after seven years of study sat a final examination. As elsewhere, posts tended to become hereditary from the 10th century and it was sometimes difficult to appoint examiners who were not fathers of the candidates. This discipline was dominated by members of immigrant families who had come to Japan before the 8th century and were employed in managing the storehouses. Among them one finds Hata, Nishiki, Kusakabe, Nibu and Miyoshi. The doctors and graduates could find work in the offices of Accounts, Public Resources and Grains, where they kept the books. From the 10th century, five generations of Otsuki succeeded one another as doctors. The fourth was Tadaomi (933?-1009) who in 960 was a fourth-class official in the Accounts Office, director in 990 and principal secretary of the Control Board. His son Tomochika (963?-1024) also had a career as a Control Board secretary and doctor of mathematics. Just as the best men in the classics and law could compete on more or less equal terms with those specializing in letters, as evidenced by the jurist Yoshimune no Tadasuke, in the late 11th century a doctor of mathematics, namely Miyoshi no Tameyasu (1049-1139), also excelled in letters. He illustrates the case of a son of a local notable from Etchū province who came to study in the capital with the doctor of mathematics (who probably had only a few students). His teacher Miyoshi no Tamenaga considered him so talented that he gave him his name and promoted his career, actually begun when he was already fifty years old. Ten years later, Tameyasu became a doctor of mathematics. It seems that Tamenaga was descended from Miyoshi no Kiyoyuki; had he inherited an interest in letters? Be that as it may, though Tameyasu never passed a literary examination, he became known for a number of works, including *Chōya gunsai*, which has various kinds of texts in *kanbun* – poems and models of administrative documents. Also extant by him are fragments of a small encyclopaedia as well as a primer of rhymes for the composition of Chinese verse and a few poems in Chinese. He demonstrated his faith in Amidism by writing *Gleanings of Stories about Rebirth in the Pure Land* (*Shūi ōjōden*).[10] His career path shows that the boundaries between specializations were not rigid, especially after the virtual disappearance of examinations in the classics, law and mathematics and the emergence of a style of teaching no longer intended primarily to fill government posts, but where a few disciples grouped themselves around a master.

What was officially known as the study of history, but whose members were called doctor, graduate and student of letters, took on its final form during the first third of the 9th century and was the pinnacle of the system of learning. The curriculum was based mainly on the *Anthology*, *Records of the Historian*, *History of the Former Han Dynasty* and *History of the Later Han Dynasty*. The twenty students were recruited by a competitive examination organized not by the Office of Higher Learning but by the Department of Regulations Relating to Civil Officials. The test consisted of the composition of a poem in Chinese. The doctors then conferred together and selected as graduates the two whom they considered to be the best. After a period of seven years, in principle, but that could be shorter or longer, each graduate sat a final examination consisting of two compositions on set topics. These examinations were held up to the 12th century. Throughout the 10th century, men belonging to families of lower- and middle-ranking officials with names such as Ōkura, Ki, Ono, Hata, Tomo, Otsuki and more than forty others, could pass the competitive examination as a student of letters. But the level of graduate was very soon almost monopolized by the Sugawara and Ōe, to which were added some Fujiwara and Taira. The literati produced by this discipline never ceased to extol it. Ōe no Masahira writes: "Letters, centre of the universe, seed of all virtues, source of the hundred joys, gateway to all things. The ruler who uses them becomes an enlightened ruler, he who cherishes them has a saintly reign." Former students of letters had the possibility of a career in the secretariats of the Ministry of State Affairs and Control Board, as well as in the Department of Regulations Relating to Civil Officials and at the head of government offices. The court turned to them for the drafting of various kinds of texts: edicts, regulations, consultations, petitions to deities, vows to the buddhas, and the senior nobles had them write their applications for posts or their resignations. Many of their works are found in anthologies such as the *Honchō monzui* by Fujiwara no Akihira, and its sequel *Honchō zoku monzui*, possibly by the doctor of letters Fujiwara no Suetsuna (?-?). The commissions that compiled the *Decrees of the Engi Era* (*Engi kyaku*) and *Engishiki* were largely made up of literati, some of them doctors or future doctors. The scholar-officials were chosen as lecturers to the emperor and crown prince, they taught the sons of senior nobles and some owed their relatively successful careers to the links forged during these activities as tutors, beginning with the grandfather of Sugawara no Michizane, Kiyotomo (Kiyokimi), lecturer to the emperors Saga and Ninmyō, who participated in the compilation of the three anthologies of Chinese verse prepared in Japan before 827. The scholar-officials steadfastly maintained the tradition of poetic composition in Chinese and have left quite a few anthologies.

The 9th century saw the establishment of the family tradition of the Sugawara with Koreyoshi (812-880) and the Ōe with Otondo (811-877), who each founded a line of doctors. In the late 9th century and during the 10th century, some literati were sufficiently famous to be able to enter the group of senior nobles. The best known success story is that of Sugawara no Michizane, the eminent poet, who even attained the post of minister and so offended the Fujiwara that they caused his downfall, but his father Koreyoshi, an auditor, had paved the way. Michizane's fall from grace meant that his descendants could only retain the post of doctor, with the exception of his great-grandson Sukemasa (925-1009) who became an auditor late in life. The destiny of the Ōe was similar; three of them were able to gain entry into the council of senior nobles in the 10th century after Otondo: Koretoki, a second counsellor, Asatsuna (886-957), an auditor, and Tadamitsu (934-987), also an auditor. When the apogee of the Heian period came to an end in the late 11th century, Ōe no Masafusa, thanks no doubt to his talents but also to the links forged as a teacher with the emperors Gosanjō, Shirakawa (1053-1129, r. 1072-1086) and Horikawa (1079-1107, r. 1086-1107), was able to become an auditor in 1088 then a second counsellor in 1094. In the 10th century, there were still a few senior nobles belonging to families who would later cease to be represented in this select group. They gained entry because they excelled in letters: Ki no Haseo, a graduate and lecturer to Daigo Tennō, reached the rank of second counsellor. Haseo was able to advance his son Yoshiteru (869-939), who became an auditor in 934. Miyoshi no Kiyoyuki had a difficult career: his final examination compositions submitted in 881 were rejected, but the decision was overturned in 883; he became a doctor in 900 and an auditor in 917. There is also Tachibana no Hiromi (837-890), a graduate then a doctor of letters and tutor to the crown prince, who became an auditor in 884; and again in the 10th century among the senior nobles several Tachibana, Taira or Minamoto who had studied literature. However their appointment appears to be due not to the talents they had acquired, but to other reasons such as their birth or for the second counsellor Taira no Korenaka his close links with Fujiwara no Kaneie. Most literati among the senior nobles were Fujiwara. The Southern branch distinguished itself in the person of Sugane (856-908), a doctor and tutor to the future Daigo Tennō, in whom he instilled a high idea of his duties with the aid of explanations from the Chinese classics and histories. He was a second counsellor at his death. His son Motokata was also tutor to the crown prince but did not rise above the grade of auditor; many of his descendants continued to cultivate letters but with middle- or lower-level posts in the administration. Some men of the Ceremonial branch passed the literary examination and a few even became doctors, but only Okinori (844-917) was promoted to auditor in

911. Various lines of descent from the Northern branch had quite a number of senior nobles who had passed the literary examination. The following may be mentioned: Kunimoto (874-932), the son of a minister, a student of letters in 893, an auditor in 921 and a second counsellor in 932; Moriyoshi (896-974), the grandson of a second counsellor, a student of letters in 924 and appointed an auditor in 972 at the end of a mediocre career; Tadasuke (944-1013), the grandson of a minister, a graduate of letters in 968, an auditor in 996 and a second counsellor in 1013. No descendant of these three men entered the council. Only the descendants of Fujiwara no Arikuni (good at Chinese verse and a client of Michinaga) were able to remain for a time in the group of senior nobles, albeit at a low rank. Arikuni, none of whose forebears for the previous hundred years had become an auditor, was appointed to this post in 1001; his son Hironari, a doctor of letters, also reached the grade of auditor, while another son Sukenari (988-1070) only became a non-participating auditor in the council. Sukenari's son Sanemasa (1019-1093), a graduate in 1037, was tutor to the future Gosanjō Tennō and was appointed an auditor in 1080. This line of descent from Arikuni continued to provide senior nobles in the 12th century.

If one looks at the works produced by the literati, there are no political or philosophical commentaries inspired by the Chinese classics and histories, which at most supplied them with a fairly small number of quotations. Poems, on the other hand, abound, being considered the embodiment of the highest values of the society. Besides the three major personal collections, that of Ki no Haseo, *Collected Works* (*Kike shū*), and those of Sugawara no Michizane, *Sugawara Family Literary Drafts* (*Kanke bunsō*) and *Sugawara Family Later Collection* (*Kanke kōshū*), there is the *Gōrihōshū* of Ōe no Masahira. Anthologies by other literati have been lost. However, Chinese poems by scholar-officials are found in various collections, notably the *Fusōshū*, compiled by Ki no Tadana and bringing together the best poems written between 827 and 998, and the *Honchō reisō* with poems selected by the scholar-official

Takashina no Moriyoshi. Some lesser works have also survived. Other anthologies contain poems but especially prose texts, models of those required of the literati, the earliest being the *Collection for Ruling the Country (Keikokushū)* of 827. The two main ones are *Honchō monzui* compiled by Fujiwara no Akihira (descended from the Ceremonial branch of the Fujiwara), containing a few poems but mostly prose texts written between 810 and 1037; and its sequel *Honchō zoku monzui*, attributed to Fujiwara no Suetsuna and containing texts composed between 1018 and 1140.

In the 10th century, besides their important participation in the compilation of various collections of decrees and regulations, scholar-officials composed several texts dealing with the administration of the country and its reform: *Opinions on Twelve Matters (Iken jūnikajō)* by Miyoshi no Kiyoyuki (914), *Opinions on Three Matters (Fūji sankajō)* by Sugawara no Fumitoki (957), and the earlier *Regulations of the Chancellery (Kurōdōshiki)*, compiled mainly by Tachibana no Hiromi. In the early 12th century, Ōe no Masafusa produced *Gōke shidai*. By way of learned works, the doctor Fujiwara no Sukeyo (847-897) compiled the *Catalogue of Extant Texts in Japan (Nihonkoku genzaisho mokuroku)*. Miyoshi no Kiyoyuki is also the author of a small volume dealing with the way of Yin and Yang, *Opinion on [Preventing] Great Changes (Kakumei kanmon)*. Minamoto no Shitagō, despite having become an authority on Chinese language and literature while a very young man, lacked patronage and so could only become a student of letters at the age of forty-three. However, he distinguished himself in the composition of both Chinese and Japanese verse and is the author of the *Wamyō ruijushō*, a dictionary organized by topics and giving the definitions of the Chinese terms followed by their Japanese translation noted by means of characters used for their phonetic value. Shitagō may also have written *Basics of Composition (Sakumon daitai)*. It is to another scholar-official of the 12th century, Tachibana no Tadakane (?-?), that we owe the dictionary *Iroha jiruishō* (that is, classified according to the *iroha* sounds).

Literati were also the authors of biographies: Sugawara no Aritsune (?-?), grandson of Michizane, wrote the first account of this unfortunate minister who was deified and worshipped at the Kitano Shrine, *The Kitano Heavenly Deity* (*Kitano tenjin goden*). Nobutsune (born Kamo) took the name of Sugawara because he had studied both letters and calendrical science; he wrote the second account of Michizane, *Kanke godenki*. Miyoshi no Kiyoyuki is the author of biographies of an exemplary provincial governor, *Fujiwara no Yasunori den*, and the Tendai monk Enchin, *Chishō daishi den*. Fujiwara no Atsumitsu (1063-1144), a son of Akihira, wrote *A Record of the Life and Teaching of Kōbō Daishi* (*Kōbō daishi gyōkeki*), an account of the founder of the Shingon sect in Japan. Ōe no Masafusa wrote *Lives of the Japanese Immortals* (*Honchō shinsen den*) and *Stories of Rebirth in the Pure Land from Our Country, Continued* (*Zoku honchō ōjōden*).

From the late 11th century, literati produced works in a slightly different style. Fujiwara no Akihira wrote a manual of (private) correspondence (*Meikō ōrai*) and a kind of handbook of terms, *Shinsarugakuki*, a portrait gallery of minor officials and artisans of the capital treated in a humorous way. Ōe no Masafusa also produced short prose texts: *An Account of Puppeteers* (*Kairaishiki*), *An Account of Prostitutes* (*Yūjoki*) and *An Account of Country Music in the Capital* (*Rakuyō dengakuki*). Both Akihira and Masafusa broke new ground by showing an interest, with no moralizing purpose, in the life of the people of the capital.

From the 10th century, learned men tended to go beyond the limits of their official field of study; literati such as Ōe no Masafusa took an interest in Taoist writings that were not included in the curricula, certain exponents of the highly specialized disciplines of law and mathematics dabbled in literature, and many educated men acquired some knowledge of the way of Yin and Yang, be it astronomy, astrology, the calendar, geomancy or the arts of divination. Distinguished men of letters, such as Minamoto no Shitagō and many others, also excelled in the composition of Japanese poetry. But for the most part, Chinese prose literature in the Heian period produced only practical works for the administration – laws and regulations, models of the various documents required –, biographies of eminent individuals and dictionaries, but no philosophical works.

The highly specialized studies of medicine and the science of Yin and Yang were controlled not by the Office of Higher Learning, but by the Office of Medicine and the Office of Divination respectively. From the 10th century, physicians belonged mostly and by reason of heredity to the Wake and Tanba families, and the officials of the Onmyōryō to the Kamo (mainly specialists in calendrical science) and Abe families.

Artists occupied a rather unusual position. Even if they held ranks and functions in the administration, their activity depended on commissions from the court, senior nobles and temples and they were paid according to their talent. The Department of Court Affairs originally had a Painting Bureau (Gakōshi); it was abolished in 808 and its members transferred to the Office of Skilled Artisans (Naishōryō). But in fact, from the 9th century, décors and paintings were normally produced in the Skilled Artisans Workshop (Tsukumodokoro), probably created in the mid-9th century, and the Painting Workshop, which existed at the end of that century. It was in this setting that the artists worked. Painters with the name of Kose distinguished themselves from the late 9th century up to the 11th century. Several were directors of the Palace Women's Bureau, but this function was purely formal and gave them a rank. In fact, they were artist-painters who provided the court and senior nobles with movable partitions painted in both the Chinese style with Chinese subjects (landscapes and famous men) and the Japanese style (landscapes, human and animal figures). Besides partitions, they decorated sliding screens, notably those taken by the daughters of senior nobles when they entered the palace as imperial consorts. They could also decorate fans, or provide the design for an emperor's garment or for a garden. The first Kose, Kanaoka, worked for the court and Fujiwara no Mototsune; his son Kintada was active during the reign of Murakami

Tennō, and his grandson Hirotaka painted during the reign of Ichijō Tennō for Michinaga as well as Fujiwara no Yukinari. It may be said that they lived by their art.

Sculpture made important advances, with senior nobles, led by Michinaga and his son Yorimichi, commissioning a great many works for their foundations when the period known as the end of the Law approached and the worship of Amida developed. The two most famous sculptors, Kōshō and Jōchō, took a monastic name and received a nominal function in the Buddhist establishment. Kōshō's origins are unclear; a later document, *Sonpi bunmyaku*, says he was the son of Minamoto no Yasuyuki (?-?), a provincial governor, descended from Kōkō Tennō. Kōshō was probably active between 991, when he may have belonged to a workshop of the Tōji temple, and 1020 when he is mentioned for the last time. He was already known in 998, as Yukinari gave him an imperial order conferring on him the function of provincial instructor of Tosa that included control of the temples of that province, a function he could not of course take up, Tosa being in the southern part of Shikoku. He worked for Michinaga, carving a statue of Yakushi in 1005 and three life-size statues of Michinaga for which he received twenty-four ounces of gold (about 333 grams) in 1013. In 1020, he carved a statue of Yakushi for the Sekidera in Ōmi. He began work on some of the statues for the Hōjōji,[11] already assisted by his son Jōchō. Kōshō is credited with perfecting the carving of statues made up of several pieces of wood, in a so-called Japanese style, flexible, smooth and elegant, and with the production of more than a hundred statues, since he had some tens of assistant sculptors to help him. None of this output has survived.

Jōchō, Kōshō's successor, was working with him from 1020 on the nine Amida statues for the Muryōjūin. He certainly played a major role in filling the chapels of the Hōjōji with statues, notably that of Dainichi nyorai (more than six metres high) in the main chapel; for this he was given in 1022 the title of Bridge of the Law (*Hokkyō*), the first person outside the ecclesiastical hierarchy to receive a rank. In 1026, in order to prepare for the safe delivery of Fujiwara no Ishi, third daughter of Michinaga, Jōchō was commissioned to execute twenty-seven life-size statues of Ishi, for which he received a thousand bushels of rice, wood of varying quality, some 223 grams of gold dust and a hundred and thirty iron hoe blades. The work was completed in a month with the help of a hundred and fifty-eight men, including twenty-eight sculptors. Jōchō was given three pieces of silk and a little over a hectare of cultivated land; the assistant sculptors each received one piece of silk and a smaller area of land. Jōchō worked for the emperors Goichijō and Gosuzaku. After a fire at the Kōfukuji, he replaced the Buddhist statues, which earned him a promotion to Eye of the Law (*Hōgen*). He worked finally in 1053 at the Byōdōin, built for Yorimichi, where the statue of Amida nyorai attributed to him can still be seen. He may even have carved statues for the chapels of wealthy officials who had grown rich from provincial governorships, such as Fujiwara no Kunitsune (986-1067) for whom Jōchō carved a statue of Amida. This Amida may have pre-dated the one in the Byōdōin and served as its model. It is Jōchō's principal surviving work. He may also have carved on occasion secular objects such as the heads of dragons and birds that decorated the boats filled with musicians moving around on the lakes of aristocratic residences during banquets.[12] The careers of Kōshō and Jōchō, like those of Kanaoka and Hirotaka, perfectly illustrate the position occupied by artists in 11th-century society: at the head of quite large workshops, they were relatively independent of the court administrative offices. In his *Shinsarugakuki*, Fujiwara no Akihira gives no other function to the painter and the carver of Buddhist images than the practice of their art.

Music and dance continued to be controlled by the Office of Music, in charge of the instructors responsible for teaching the instruments of the orchestra and dance movements. But the performers in the court celebrations were professional musicians and dancers, often members of the palace guard. However, unlike painting and sculpture, music was practised, sometimes extremely well, by many officials and senior nobles who, after childhood, no longer appeared in public on official occasions.

Certain people who moved in the court's orbit may also be thought of as artists. These were often younger sons who had only been able to obtain a very low rank with no real function and earned a modest living thanks to a special talent. Akihira gives the examples of the calligrapher and the poet. Until the early 11th century, calligraphers classed as outstanding were important officials and even an emperor. The author of the *Shinsarugakuki* does not think it necessary to give a rank or function to the skilled calligrapher he presents, and emphasizes the very high price paid for his works. There were also men who made a living from their ability to compose verse. (The various kinds of Japanese poetry were constantly practised by the members of the court.) These men were useful in social exchanges, banquets and poetic contests. The person depicted by Akihira is modelled on a 9th-century member of the Fujiwara family who had neither rank nor function but was a good poet. He lives by composing poems that he can give to officials lacking inspiration and by invitations to banquets: in short, like a kind of parasite.

Still drawing on the *Shinsarugakuki*, it is possible to add to these artists men on the fringes of the court, individuals who have left a reputation recorded in small encyclopaedias of the time as having excelled at *sumō* or *go*. The *sumō* bouts held at the court in the emperor's presence were very popular and the victors, it seems, were handsomely rewarded. As for the skilled *go* players, their games verged on the illegal in the sense that betting was prohibited.[13]

Notes

1. *Ruijū fusenshō*, Book 9, Chōtoku 1.8.19., 995.
2. *Midō kanpakuki*, Kankō 4.5.30., 1007.
3. *Midō kanpakuki*, Kankō 5.9.12., 1008.
4. See *Geki bunin* (*Chronology of Appointments of Ministerial Secretaries*).

5. See *Iken jūnikajō*, article 4.

6. See *Honchō monzui*, Book 8, preface to the *Kōnin kyaku* (*Decrees of the Kōnin Era*); *Ruijū sandai kyaku*, Book 17, Jōwa 1.12.5.

7. *Seiji yōryaku*, Book 61, account of the dream and overall judgement on jurists. Tadasuke was in fact an inspector in the Police Bureau. From 984, *Shōyūki*, Eikan 2.11.17., he was a doctor of law and an assistant in the Discharge Investigation Bureau (Kageyushi). The last mention of him is in the *Midō kanpakuki*, Kankō 4.5.30., 1007.

8. *Nihon kiryaku*, Chōhō 1.6.2., 999 and *Honchō reisō*, 101.

9. Later, as a doctor of law and a member of the gate guard and Police Bureau his career took him as far as the fourth rank and the governorship of Shinano in 1024.

10. For details concerning him, see Kawaguchi Hisao, *Heianchō Nihon kanbungakushi no kenkyū*. His biography is found in the work dating from 1151, *Honchō shinshū ōjōden* (*New Biographies of Japanese Reborn in Paradise*) by Fujiwara no Munetomo (?-?).

11. *Gonki*, Chōtoku 4.12., 998/999, he is appointed to Tosa; *Zoku Kojidan*, Shōryaku 2.3., 991, statue of Shaka in the Kawara no in; *Midō kanpakuki*, Kankō 5.8.2., 1008 and Chōwa 2.3.6., 1013, he delivers statues to Michinaga; *Chūgaishō*, Kannin 4.2., 1020, installation in the Muryōjūin of nine statues of Amida; Kōchō had his son carve the faces.

12. *Sakeiki*, Jian 2.7.16., 1022, Jōchō is elevated to *Hokkyō*; Manju 3.8.8., 1026, he receives the materials for the commission of twenty-seven statues, 3.10.10., he is paid; *Shunki*, Chōkyū 1.5.2., 1040, Gosuzaku Tennō commissions a statue from him; Chōkyū 2.2.24., 1040, a commission for dragon and bird heads for the boats that will sail on the lake; *Shoreishō* (*Notes on the Earliest Precedents*) Eishō 2.3.3., 1047, Jōchō is elevated to *Hōgen* for his work at the Kōfukuji after the fire of the previous year; *Shunki*, Tengi 2.5.3., 1054, Sukefusa goes to see the statue of Amida in the chapel of Fujiwara no Kunitsune, which Minamoto no Morotoki (*Chōshūki*, Chōshō 3.6.12., 1134) states is by Jōchō and the model for the one in the Byōdōin.

13. See, in the *Shinsarugakuki*, the painter (sixth son), the carver of Buddhist images (seventh son), the musician (ninth son), the calligrapher (eldest son), the poet Tsuneyuki (lover of the

eleventh daughter), the wrestler Tanji no Sujio (husband of the sixth daughter) and the *go* player Sukeharu (husband of the eldest daughter).

APPENDIX 3

Status and Role of Provincial Governors at the Apogee of the Heian Period

The code gives only a very general idea of the role of the provincial administrators, foremost among them the governors. These men were appointed by the central administration for four years. They were expected to oversee Shintō worship, keep the population registers, be a father figure to the people, encourage agriculture and silkworm breeding, right wrongs, attend to the police and complaints, keep the household and rice-field registers, raise taxes and corvée labour, maintain the irrigation system and public buildings, as well as the pasture lands, and keep the province in a state of readiness to defend itself by means of militias, weapons and signal fires; in short, exercise control over every aspect of the peoples' lives. All of which implied, even if the provinces were not heavily populated, in addition to the governor, his (two to six) trusted officials from the four classes and clerks who had accompanied him from the capital, a relatively large number of locally recruited staff: district administrators and minor officials.

It was during the 8th and 9th centuries that this programme was developed and that the very general indications given in the code were completed and spelled out in detail by means of regulations and decrees. Almost four hundred decrees – issued over two centuries – are extant, which implies a greater number, whereas after the first third of the 10th century and up to the late 11th century, there are only a few dozen and these often deal with a minor point. This abundance of decrees, often repetitive or contradictory, does not suggest an efficiently functioning local administration. In the early 10th century, the *Engishiki* and *Engi Period Regulations on Transferring Office* (*Engi kōtaishiki*) perfected this legislation. Budgets calculated in rice were established for each province. Part of the provincial public resources, also calculated in rice and made up of the accumulated land tax was loaned out at interest. This interest was used for the various expenses incurred: administering the province or deliveries to the capital. Payments in kind, an important part of the tax system, were also carefully specified and in principle calculated for each taxpayer. The *Engi kōtaishiki* was quite detailed and dealt with the drawing up of the annual population registers, the upkeep of the public buildings, religious establishments and the irrigation system, the management of the public resources, mainly rice, as well as deliveries in full and within the allotted time of goods to be sent to the capital. These documents, which could number several dozen, had to be verified and above all accepted by the supervisory bodies in the capital. In principle, no administrator, whatever his rank, could be re-employed if he did not leave everything in perfect order. With two to six (sometimes three to seven) administrators in a province, the problem soon arose as to how responsibilities should be shared and a distinction was made between responsibility and liability; that is, in the very frequent case of tax arrears not delivered to the capital, liability was shared and all the current administrators had to reimburse the shortfall by advance deductions from their stipends, but penal sanctions were imposed on the official chiefly responsible. For the offices in the capital, this was a good way of establishing mutual oversight. Moralizing speeches on the role of father figures and educators made to the administrators appointed by the capital, still quite common in the 8th century, were becoming less frequent. As time went on, so the two main concerns of the court, namely taxation – it had to maintain the capital and its body of officials – and the control it could exercise over the local administrations became the most important considerations. Only then did it become apparent that the immense effort of codification and the constraining and detailed regulations built up over two centuries were an unwieldy, onerous and very impracticable solution. Paradoxically, it was when the legislation was completed that it began to be more or less circumvented, rather than abolished, and that whole sections simply fell into disuse. The solution was to hold only one person, the *zuryō*,[1] accountable and allow him a good deal of initiative.

We shall look first at the actual work of the provincial governors, next at how they were chosen, then at their relations with those they governed, and finally at the procedures used to supervise their work in the late 10th and early 11th century, when the *Genji monogatari* was written.

Functions of the zuryō

From the 10th century, the tax system, which according to the code was based on a precise knowledge of the population – assumed not to decrease or move elsewhere –, was in total disarray. Although governors were obliged to keep exact registers of those they governed, since the imposts, payments in kind and corvées were levied mainly on individuals, the few known examples of fragments of 10th-century civil status registers clearly show that they are incorrect: some contain more than 80% of women and a very large number of old people; in others the proportion is slightly lower, but the number of non-taxpayers among the men is significant or unknown.[2] This suggests that payments in kind could not be levied according to the criteria stipulated in the laws and that redistributions of personal plots granted for life were becoming impossible. The public resources of the province were increasingly used to make up deficits and therefore tended to decrease. But the management of the province depended on the interest from the rice loaned to the holders of these plots. It is known, moreover, that in the 10th century the periodic allo-cation of such plots ceased, even though, in his *Iken jūnikajō*, Miyoshi no Kiyoyuki recommended that new allocations be made, but only to bona fide households. The earlier plots now belonged to those who could work them, in the same way as cleared rice fields were registered in the name of the clearer. It is also known that the obligatory loan of public rice could only be imposed on those able to repay the debt with interest. In the

10th century, it was no longer necessary to make actual loans with all the handling this involved. It was sufficient to require the holders of rice fields to pay interest according to the area under cultivation, which in effect meant transferring the main part of the tax system to the land. This measure reduced the burden of managing the provincial storehouses. Moreover, in order to obtain the rice needed to pay the stipends of the central administration officials, a certain number of so-called excess rice fields were declared administration rice fields and assigned to each department and office. In some provinces, excess or public rice fields were managed either directly by the officials who had them cultivated by paid labourers, or indirectly by being leased out for a year (with the lease renewable). The rents derived from these fields were often used to purchase payments in kind and some decrees even stipulated this.[3] Gradually, during the 10th century, the meaning of "public rice field" changed and the important distinction was no longer between rice fields granted for life or held in perpetuity and those that remained under the control of the administration, but between exempt rice fields (belonging to the religious establishments and to senior nobles by virtue of their rank), and the public rice fields subject to taxation. What complicated matters was that the old names persisted, the old registers could still be consulted and the supervisory bodies in the capital – the offices of Accounts and Public Resources and the Discharge Investigation Bureau (Kageyushi) – continued, at any cost and not very successfully, to apply provisions that had largely become obsolete.

In short, the *zuryō* basically needed reliable land surveys together with registers containing the names of the holders of rice fields subject to taxation. They had to levy enough rice to set aside reserves, either permanent or intended for use in the near future, even if these were far less than prescribed in the regulations. Up to the mid-11th century, the most prudent governors officially requested the central administration to verify the new figures. If pressed for details, the majority simply said that the quantities had already been markedly reduced during their predecessors' time in office. By means of this rice, they were responsible for maintaining public property: the irrigation system, buildings, storehouses and especially shrines and temples. The responsibility for irrigation was soon left to the users and the number of public storehouses gradually decreased with the reduction in the public rice resources, but in the 10th and 11th centuries governors often had problems with the temples they were obliged to keep in good repair. These governors also had to send rice to the capital and contribute to the stipends of the central administration officials, according to the amount required from their province. In addition, they had to levy the products in kind or, quite often, purchase them and have them delivered to the capital, according to need and the requests they received, in more or less the same quantities as set out in the regulations and on dates that were not always precisely fixed.

In the early 10th century, Miyoshi no Kiyoyuki wrote a biography, or rather a hagiography, of Fujiwara no Yasunori (825-895), presented as the paragon of virtuous administrators. Kiyoyuki, who may have known Yasunori and claims to have based his account on documents and oral testimony, emphasizes above all his integrity and the kindly way he treated his subordinates and the people of the provinces he governed. He presents him as an adept of government by example, as one who demonstrates his prestige and power but as far as possible does not resort to arms. However this text, full of Chinese expressions and allusions, in fact tells us very little about the practical aspects of Yasunori's administration.[4]

By contrast, in the late 10th century, the petition by the district administrators and principal inhabitants of Owari against their governor, Fujiwara no Motonaga, *Owari no kuni gebumi*, is very explicit regarding the questionable actions of the governor and especially his management of the tax system. The authors of this petition may have been encouraged to formulate it because, in the previous year (987), one of the last important texts dealing with the duties of governors issued by the central administration had been promulgated in thirteen articles.[5] Unlike this and other similar documents, earlier and later, the thirty-one articles of the Owari petition have been preserved. Motonaga probably went too far in exploiting the province, but perhaps not all that much further than others who were astute enough not to allow a petition to reach the capital. For their part, the complainants may also have exaggerated the cruelty and malpractices of the governor. However, this text can provide some useful elements for describing the administration of the *zuryō*.

Already in the 10th century, relations between governors and those they governed were not always good: cases of attacks against their person are not unknown and nine have been identified (no doubt not the only ones) without counting the troubles stirred up by Taira no Masakado and Fujiwara no Sumitomo. The petition, a legal means, was not unknown either, since Miyoshi no Kiyoyuki included in his reform proposals that of not accepting petitions from subordinates against their superiors.[6] Normally, any complaint had to follow the hierarchical path and go through the governor. If the one from Owari reached the court, it was probably because, among the district administrators or local notables, were men who, looking after the interests of a patron – a senior noble or an official in the capital – could find protectors there. Informal links existed between officials of all ranks in the capital and the provinces where already younger sons had gone to seek their fortune. It is likely that these relations were more numerous than can be seen in a novel such as the *Genji monogatari*, whose author clearly seeks to put a vast distance between the inhabitants of the highest heaven and other mortals.

Motonaga was accused of using various means to exact more rice (now the principal tax) than was justified. Without going into details, it may be said that he levied taxes shown in the models for provincial budgets – assistance to the needy, upkeep of religious establishments, repair of dykes and canals, stipends of minor officials and expenses for official posts – even though some no longer existed, and kept the others for himself. He was also accused of levying the interest on forced loans, loans that existed only in name, but with real interest calculated in proportion to the areas cultivated, and levying it on the volume of loans shown in the *Engishiki*, whereas the quantity was routinely reduced by about half. He also made a profit on the payments in kind, notably pieces of silk and various products. In fact, it had become customary to estimate the price in rice. All that was needed was to arbitrarily fix the value of these products, extract the required amount of rice from the peasants and purchase them at a lower price. He was accused of sending large quantities of rice and silk to his residence in the capital. It must not be forgotten, however, that administrators often stocked in their private warehouses goods that they later delivered to the court.

In his administration, Motonaga made little use of local officials appointed according to the normal criteria, but primarily used individuals chosen by himself – members of his family or allied to it –, and especially a band of men recruited by him, the *rōdō*. From their first appearance in the documents, shortly before the mid-10th century, they were called upon to bear arms, provide policing in the province and protect the governor: "men-at-arms" is normally a suitable translation. However the word is also used to describe men employed by their patron for administrative tasks, such as conducting the land survey and levying taxes. (In this latter case, their being armed was quite useful.) Motonaga had with him his son and even some officials between appointments from the capital, including one man of the fifth rank who did not normally have the right to leave the central region without authorization. Younger sons of middle-ranking officials had no means of making a living other than to find employment as *rōdō* with governors. These were the men used by Motonaga to conduct the land survey. The inhabitants claimed that they recorded larger areas of rice fields than actually existed in order to levy more taxes, and that they dragged out the work so as to live off the locals. They also perpetrated acts of violence in order to collect the taxes.

Normally, when a governor arrived in a province, he found district administrators and household retainers who were very familiar with all the business of the previous administrations. It is known that local administrations were organized in several respects like the central administration, with what may very loosely be termed bureaux. In fact their number and specialization depended on the province. However at least four were found almost everywhere: the land bureau, which kept the registers of rice fields with the names of their owners, plans and results of actual inspections; the bureau of taxation returns; the bureau of official documents and archives, and the bureau of general affairs. A governor was more or less obliged to use his own men, the *rōdō*, as well as locals.[7]

Three points should be noted in connection with the *zuryō*, besides the fact that they actually went to the province assigned to them, even if, in the case of a province not too far distant from the capital, they often did not reside there continuously. The first point is that they enjoyed a certain amount of freedom in the way they levied taxes, a freedom they owed in part and paradoxically to an over-abundance of legislation, which had never been repealed and was sometimes disjointed. But, on the other hand, this same legislation required them to keep reasonably accurate accounts, at least on the face of it, and so led them to produce large numbers of false registers. This enabled a sizeable group of clerks and other copyists about whom little is known to flourish both in the provinces and in the capital. The fact remains that if the governor supplied the needs of the court, which were not arbitrarily fixed but also did not conform to those found in the regulations of the early 10th century, then he fulfilled his function. Until the first third of the 11th century, it seems that he was well able to hold his own against the aristocratic households, who were looking to extend their landholdings and gain tax exemptions for them, and that he was more or less in a position to preserve the contributory capacity of his province. The second point is that, to a greater or lesser degree, the *zuryō* and their men engaged in trade – payments in kind were very often purchased – and controlled the circulation of goods, to an extent that is difficult to evaluate precisely but that was undoubtedly significant. To illustrate this point, we might make mention of the *rōdō* who appears in the *Shinsarugakuki*.[8] This man goes into service with successive governors and accumulates in his residence in the capital various goods that people come to buy from him. His patron probably shares in the profits. The third point is that the *zuryō* had of necessity to make profits in addition to their regular stipend, if only because they essentially paid the wages of most employees in the local administrations. However the example of Motonaga shows that, in order to avoid problems, they also had to rely on the locally recruited district administrators and employees. It therefore required tact and diplomacy to get the best out of both categories of subordinates, keep them on mutually good terms and take care to satisfy both groups. It must also be remembered that many *zuryō* were not continually employed during their careers and had to survive as best they could when in between appointments, a period that could last for several decades.

Selecting the zuryō

In the early Heian period, careers alternated between postings in the capital and the provinces, and those of the most fortunate or deserving men could end with entry into the group of senior nobles. In the 11th century, this possibility had all but ceased to exist and the trend towards specialization in the provincial administration gradually increased. When a senior noble obtained a post as *zuryō* for one of his sons, he essentially mapped out his career in advance; at best it could see him reach the fourth rank and the governorship of large provinces.[9] Posts as *zuryō* were highly sought after. The literary texts provide ample evidence of the feverish activity in the capital when appointments were about to be announced. We see in the *Makura no sōshi* the picture of the residence of a hopeful candidate, besieged by visitors who are already celebrating, while servants are dispatched to the palace gates to find out what is happening and convey the news without delay. When the sound of the processions of senior nobles leaving the palace signals the end of the appointments session, when the servants are late returning and it is announced that the host remains an ex-governor, the residence empties and the old retainers calculate the number of posts that may become vacant in the coming year.[10]

In theory, any official who had reached the fifth rank and a sufficient number of years of service could submit an application prior to a regular appointments session or when a post became vacant. But it was preferable to do this under the auspices of the bureau or department in which one had served, or after already having proved oneself as a *zuryō*, or after having shown exceptional merit. Being put forward by a retired emperor or an empress could carry weight in certain cases. The following four criteria were therefore taken into account in determining an appointment: the support of a branch of the central administration, the services already rendered in a provincial governorship, the recommendation of a member of the imperial family and proof of exceptional service. This is evident from the list given by Fujiwara no Sukefusa of the *zuryō* appointed early in 1040. He had been involved in classifying the applications and was thus very familiar with the situation of each candidate.[11]

Among the factors taken into account when selecting *zuryō*, the procedure involving the support of a retired empress or emperor should be considered separately. In fact, these personages were officially entitled to present only a third-class official for a provincial post, but examples exist regarding the appointment of a *zuryō*. Thus, in 992, after becoming a nun, the mother of Ichijō Tennō had one of her household intendants appointed to Sanuki. When Atsuakira gave up the rank of crown prince in 1017, Michinaga granted his request to retain the right of recommending a *zuryō*. There is even an instance of such an appointment being made after the death of the retired emperor Enyū.[12] But it appears that this right was unable to be exercised each year and these appointments are fairly rare.

Certain regulations, while not spelled out in any officially promulgated text, allowed some organs of the central administration to put forward, in turn, one of their members for a post as *zuryō*. This custom is already mentioned in 977. But soon afterwards the only applications considered in appointments sessions were those transmitted to members of the council.[13] In all cases, these applications concerned men who had reached the fifth rank.

The principal ministerial secretaries or those of the Control Board had often put in twenty or more years of service, at first in minor posts that carried few responsibilities. After promotion to the fifth rank, they could obtain governorships, usually of small or distant provinces, such as Izu, Tosa, Higo or Chikugo. For example, the jurist Ono no Fumiyoshi, who worked in the ministerial secretariat from 1007 until 1022, before being appointed to Tosa; or Sugano no Atsuyori (?-?), a mathematician, who after eighteen years of service was posted to Chikugo.[14] The known examples show that a third-class official of the Shikibushō obtained an appointment as *zuryō* each year, whereas neither the Minbushō nor the gate guard was similarly rewarded. It was better to transfer to the Shikibushō and take one's turn, which each man tried to protect.[15] Once they had been promoted to the fifth rank, third-class officials from these two departments could also transfer to another branch of the central administration, but the post of *zuryō* was more sought after. When one considers specific cases, it is difficult to know whether the posting was awarded immediately after a promotion or whether the candidate had to remain for some little time between appointments.

Former provincial governors were quite often preferred because of their experience, notably at supplementary sessions held as and when necessary. These men were required to have submitted full accounts from their previous administration and have a duly certified final discharge in order to re-apply. This is why the appointments sessions in the 1st month were preceded by meetings of the senior nobles who granted (or not) the final document.[16]

The expression "exceptional services" is a euphemism; it simply means 'buying a position'. Another expression was "having performed a (meritorious) deed", which for an official consisted of using his private resources to fund the construction costs of public buildings or religious establishments, the upkeep of which was the court's responsibility. For minor posts, venality was the norm, since the emperors, imperial princes, empresses and senior nobles had available to them a right of recommendation for provincial offices carrying no responsibility, but a social rank. They sold that right according to a well known scale of charges. However, for the office of *zuryō*, the language used was more attenuated and the practices more covert and varied. One particular merit was to bear the costs associated with building works for the court or else those for celebrations. This enabled a man to be appointed without his having previously governed a province and with little seniority. Sometimes a wealthy and highly placed father helped out, as seems to be the case for Akimasa, a son of the minister Minamoto no Shigenobu. Akimasa was appointed governor of Echizen as a reward for having funded the construction of the building housing the Shikibushō. In 1027, a director of the Library Office was appointed after having arranged for the carving of objects of worship and thirteen thousand images. On rare occasions, a father, even a senior noble, resigned in return for a post as *zuryō* for one of his sons. The direct purchase of such offices, paid for in rice and cloth, was never acknowledged. Clients who owed their appointment to their patron nonetheless provided him with financial services and, once appointed, gave him handsome gifts, especially in their first year: cloth, products from their province, rice, horses and oxen. To give a few of the most striking examples: the governor of Sanuki, in 1004, sent twelve hundred bushels of rice to Michinaga and the minister came out to see the arrival of the procession of a hundred and sixty ox-drawn carts. In 1013, the man appointed governor of Shinano the previous year presented Michinaga with ten horses. The governor appointed to Mutsu in 1010 had at least twenty-nine horses sent to Michinaga during his term of office, twenty in the year after his arrival in the province. A rather curious case is that of a Chinjufu general who, in 1014, before a large crowd of curious onlookers, paraded a line of twenty horses, some fully caparisoned, as well as men carrying quivers, feathers, gold dust, silk fabrics, floss silk and linen cloth, all in large quantities and presented to Michinaga. It was payment for his decree of appointment, causing Sanesuke to bemoan the fact that this was a time when offices could be bought.[17]

A closer look at what occurred prior to an appointments session shows that the candidates had very often informed ministers and senior nobles of their aspirations, either by having a confidant of the important personage speak to him on their behalf, or by having paid a personal visit to his residence. On several occasions, Sanesuke mentions the visits he receives from applicants. Candidates not only sought to present solid documentation, but also endeavoured to obtain a written re-commendation. If they satisfied all the necessary criteria, even if success was not assured because of the large number of eligible candidates, they had nothing to lose by submitting an application and joining the field. Fujiwara no Sukefusa, as head of the Chancellery, found himself at the centre of preparations for appointments sessions, the main one lasting three days. Each day, he received the dossiers to be discussed. These had already been seen by the ministerial secretariat, which could withhold a dossier, not due to the content but to the form. Sukefusa classified the applications, adding to each a brief summary of the contents. The posts of minor officials seldom required any discussion. On the other hand, the applications for the posts of *zuryō* or of important officials in the capital had already been seen by the chancellor. These were examined on the last day. The senior nobles reached agreement and their decisions were sent to the emperor. He could sometimes exercise a choice, but he normally received the same number of proposals as there were posts to be filled. Generally speaking, Fujiwara no Michinaga could be certain of having his preferred candidates accepted, but the other senior nobles occasionally had a say:

notably, when one of them wished to appoint a son or close relative, he added to the application a request addressed to the emperor.[18] The journals of Michinaga, Sanesuke and Sukefusa quite often give an insight into the discussions concerning the selection of *zuryō*.

In 1006, when a vacancy occurred, a single post was to be filled. Of the thirty applications, Michinaga thought that only four should be presented to the emperor: three from former governors and one from a man who could claim services. In the council discussion, only the former governors (all eligible) were considered, two of whom had been waiting a long time for a new post. The third minister Fujiwara no Kinsue rejected one candidate and substituted another. When the emperor was informed of this first selection, he expressed surprise at not seeing the names of the same individuals who had been presented to him as possible candidates on previous occasions. The discussion resumed and the senior nobles finally included in the four names put forward that of a previously unsuccessful candidate and the one proposed by Kinsue, who then objected that the man he supported said he was not a candidate. Contrary to appearances, this was not a complete farce. However it ended with Michinaga going alone to the emperor, presenting him with four names and returning with the appointment of the only candidate not mentioned during the discussion and who was clearly the one he had supported from the outset, even though he seems to have remained silent during the deliberations. Another minor appointments session, in 1014, recounted by Sanesuke, also shows something of what went on behind the scenes. Two posts needed to be filled and there were many applicants. The deliberations of the senior nobles were presided over by Michinaga and Kinsue. They narrowed the field down to seven, including one for exceptional services; Michinaga immediately had it excluded. The governorship of Echigo held by Fujiwara no Tametoki, who had resigned, was given to Fujiwara no Nobutsune (?-?), his nephew, and Sanesuke suspected that Tametoki had negotiated the outcome before resigning: surely not an isolated case.[19]

Often, though not always, the choices had been discussed informally before council meetings and Michinaga's opinion was known unofficially. The candidate appointed in 1006, referred to above, was a client of Michinaga, and most if not all appointees were either officials in the household of a minister or senior noble, or a client. The most successful careers were those of officials in Michinaga's household, none more so than Fujiwara no Korenori. He reached the fifth rank in 985, aged twenty-two, after a brief period in the Treasury; he began a career as a *zuryō* in 1001 and received successive appointments to Inaba, Kai and Ōmi. Michinaga transferred him from his household to that of the future Goichijō Tennō. He was promoted to the upper fourth rank in 1013. As a further sign of his patron's trust, he was made assistant director of the household of the future Gosuzaku Tennō. Around 1020, he was appointed governor of Harima and, to cap off his career, in 1023 he became a non-participating auditor and was sent to Kyūshū as principal assistant at the Dazaifu, just after the governor had died. As a new governor was not appointed until 1029, Korenori had total charge of the administration of Kyūshū from 1023 until his return to the capital in 1029, weighed down, according to Sanesuke, with the rich spoils of his depredations.[20]

If one considers the distribution of *zuryō* according to their family origin, the Fujiwara, as would be expected, provided just under half; Minamoto, Taira, Tachibana, Takashina, Ōe and Sugawara between them did not reach the number of Fujiwara. There was also a small group of "others" (Abe, Nakahara, Kiyohara, etc.), drawn from the secretariats. The majority of *zuryō* had only one posting; those with more than three were a tiny minority. One of the most successful men of the early 11th century was Minamoto no Yorinobu who had six provincial governorships. The *zuryō* considered capable of maintaining order, namely Taira and Minamoto, were often sent to the East and the North, as well as to Kyūshū. But the senior nobles distrusted them: in 1019, Sanesuke had Yorinobu's posting changed from Tōtōmi to Iwami. Up to that time this governor had been posted only to the East.[21]

Following the announcement, the successful appointees went to offer their thanks. After the usual compliments, the *zuryō* had to obtain their decree of appointment, with the imperial seal affixed. In order to receive this document, they were required to present a discharge issued by the administrative organ in which they had previously served. But the new appointees nearly always asked to be exempted from obtaining this. In fact, a document from 1044 is accompanied by a legal opinion stating that the holders of offices in the central administration where no financial responsibilities were involved did not need one.[22] For former *zuryō*, the final discharge received at the time of their previous rendering of accounts was sufficient. However, typical of the workings of the early administration, the requirement to present a discharge was not abolished and ways had to be found of gaining an exemption.

Having received their appointment, the *zuryō* made preparations for their journey. They went to take leave of their protectors – ministers and senior nobles – who might present them with a horse or garments. For certain *keishi* valued by their patron, a small reception was organized that included the composition of poems, a reminder of the customs of Chinese officials. Wives and children could accompany the governor; wives, especially if they served in the palace, were also presented with gifts by ministers and empresses.[23] On the departure of one of these women, Michinaga adds that she shows a manly determination. But this was probably more because she was leaving the court for the provinces than because the journey was particularly fraught with danger.

Arrival in the province and relations with the inhabitants

The duties, mainly ceremonial, of *zuryō* on arrival in their province are set out in a document containing forty-two articles, undated but written before 1132. Some of the information given corresponds to what was already occurring in the 11th century. These duties can be grouped under three headings. The first concerns the journey and arrival in the province, the selection of auspicious days for leaving the capital, the crossing of the provincial border, the move into the residence and the start of work. The convoy numbered several dozen members; it was therefore necessary to plan the overnight stops ahead and to ensure that the men-at-arms conducted themselves well. The visit to the principal shrine of the province and the greeting of the local administration employees, who came to introduce themselves and brought the new governor the seal and keys to the provincial storehouses, completed the installation process. The second heading relates to the hand-over of authority, assuming the outgoing governor had waited for his successor to arrive. The new governor had to look at the archives and inspect the storehouses to ascertain whether their contents corresponded to what was recorded in the registers, and generally examine the management of his predecessor so as not to be held responsible for arrears and deficiencies left by him. The third heading deals with the conduct of a good governor: he had to know the abilities of his subordinates, keep his distance from everyone, be economical, carefully choose his right-hand man who replaced him during any absence, not use *rōdō* of the fifth rank, have on his staff some good calligraphers, an efficacious monk and one or two skilled soldiers, even though a good governor should not normally need to use force. Unlike the ministerial decrees of the 8th and 9th centuries, this advice is of a very general nature and gives no concrete details about the way the provinces were governed.[24]

In fact, a good *zuryō* was one who could respond to circumstances, maintain order, and satisfy the court by his deliveries and ultimately by satisfactory reports and registers. He also had to avoid disputes with the inhabitants or, as could happen, with neighbouring provinces. In the period under consideration, a few governors were assassinated or were themselves assassins, sometimes for personal reasons. On the other hand, disputes between governors and well-connected local notables as well as between governors and religious establishments, while not very frequent, did occur. An interesting example concerns Nagato province, since it shows that the local notables, who held minor posts, could very well be known to the senior nobles and were certainly not without support in any conflict with governors. In 1008, the governor returned to the capital to complain about a local notable who had besieged him in his residence and wounded three of his *rōdō*. The man was summoned to the capital for questioning and the affair went no further, as he was pardoned: according to Sanesuke, through the intervention of Takashina no Naritō (965-1010), a valued client of Michinaga. Early in 1018, Naritō's son Naritoshi (?-?), the governor of Nagato, was dismissed following a complaint by the son of the local notable of 1008. Sanesuke expresses surprise that the dismissal was announced without a detailed examination of the matter and with no legal opinion at all, and he adds that the local notable presented oxen to Michinaga each year.[25]

The position of the governor of Yamato, where the Kōfukuji had large estates, was a difficult one. But in Michinaga's time the governor was not sacrificed to the monks. This was not so later in the 11th century. The case of Minamoto no Yorichika shows how much more serious it was for a governor to cross swords with a religious establishment than with an ordinary individual. In 1017, after being found guilty of killing a man, he lost his post as governor of Awaji. All the senior nobles knew that he had instigated the murder. The penal code punished incitement to murder, but he was not prosecuted and continued his career. In early 1050, while governor of Yamato, he vigorously repulsed an attack by the Kōfukuji that left several monks dead. Less than a month later, he was banished. This incident clearly shows how difficult it was to keep the great temples of Yamato in check during the time of Fujiwara no Yorimichi. In Kyūshū, relations between the provincial governors and the Dazaifu administration were not always harmonious. Moreover, the presence of large religious establishments – Usa and Kanzeonji – often caused problems for the governor-general and his assistant.[26] The administration wished to control the management of the households granted to this shrine and temple, whereas these sought to transform them purely and simply into tax-exempt estates.

As happened to Motonaga, governors risked having a complaint brought against them by the local administrators and notables. From 987 to 1041, a possibly incomplete count shows that eleven complaints reached the capital and have come down to us in some form, as well as at least fifteen "good letters", expressing satisfaction by local inhabitants. This type of document did not guarantee that the governor exercised wisdom and fairness; only that he was able to instil these qualities in some of those he governed. There was even an incident in 1014 where the governor of Kaga, who was the subject of a petition in thirty-two articles drawn up by certain district administrators and presented in the capital, arrived shortly afterwards escorted by other district administrators (or possibly those he had reinstated in the meantime) attesting to the integrity of his conduct.[27] Similarly, in 1019, some inhabitants of Tanba, two months after coming to the capital to complain about their governor, brought a "good letter" to the palace gate. In over sixty years in a country with more than sixty provinces, there were relatively few complaints. It may be noted that they concern mainly provinces close to the capital, those where the senior nobles quite possibly had most of their interests and thus knew certain local notables; in the eastern and northern provinces, disputes often seem to have been settled locally. This is evident from a note written by Fujiwara no Sanesuke early in 1024. He learned that the residence of the governor of Tanba, who it appears the population of the province accused of cruelty, had been burned down by a group of horsemen, and concluded that the capital was adopting the manners of the East. The same Sanesuke informs us that complaints by the people, although not legal, were tolerated as a matter of custom. In 1028, nights in the capital were disturbed by the angry shouts of inhabitants of Tajima province around the chancellor's residence, causing Sanesuke who was surprised at this behaviour to say that it was a long-established precedent for the people to present their petition by day at the palace gate. In fact, there had been no written complaint because the whole affair had been stirred up by a client of Sanesuke. This man had property in

Tajima, hence his dispute with the governor.[28] Of the eleven known petitions, only four led to the governor's dismissal, but with no further penalty.[29] For the others, either the governor kept his post[30] or the result is unknown.[31] It is clear that a dispute with a powerful religious establishment was far more dangerous for a *zuryō* than a complaint from those he governed: in the latter case, at worst he left his post a little sooner. Moreover, many of these incidents seem to have involved local disputes in which the governor was rather out of his depth. All things considered, a complaint from the inhabitants was perhaps not too serious for a *zuryō* and rarely spelled the end of his career.

Leaving office and submitting accounts

At the end of a period ranging from two to five years, a governor had to think about leaving office and preparing to submit his accounts. However some men requested a renewal or an extension, no doubt so as to be in a better position when the time arrived. The correct procedure for obtaining this favour was defined in principle, but in fact was often circumvented, and the author of the *Hokuzanshō* admits to some indecision, as the precedents are contradictory.[32] For a renewal, one normally had to be on an appointments list (implying an investigation of the previous management), but this was not necessary for an extension. Still according to the *Hokuzanshō*, in order to obtain an extension, one needed to have satisfied the tax obligations of the province, or restored the fortunes of a ruined province, or else had a fire in the provincial government headquarters near the end of one's term. In early 1006, the governor of Harima requested a renewal; some senior nobles considered that it could not be granted unless the previous management had been scrutinized, but this man made an interesting proposal at a time when the palace was in need of rebuilding: he undertook to rebuild two pavilions. The senior nobles added another for good measure and granted his renewal. In 1026, the governor of Ōmi made such a request; as he had funded the reconstruction of a bridge, the procedure was simplified and a ministerial decree was issued authorizing him to serve a new term. Twenty years earlier (in 1004), the governor of Tanba had been reappointed by an imperial order. In fact, in all the known examples from the early 11th century, the requester had either provided buildings for the court or promised to do so.[33] It is extremely difficult to verify the number of years spent by the *zuryō* in their provinces; one has the impression that some asked for an extension before completing their term.

It seems that these requests for quite lengthy extensions of two to four years were partly intended to give the departing governor more time to prepare his accounts. According to the earlier regulations, a governor could not return to the capital until the arrival of his successor, a full investigation into the state of the province and the signing of a discharge (*geyujō*) by both men. Before this document could be drawn up, the public and religious buildings had to be in reasonably good condition, the permanent rice reserves complete, the receipts showing that all tax liabilities had been met available for inspection and the registers proving this verified and approved. Since this ideal situation was never achieved, given that the outgoing governor could not finalize everything in a hundred and twenty days and could not remain in the province, the two men simply noted what the predecessor remained responsible for and signed a document stating the reason for the non-delivery of a discharge (*fuyogeyujō*). Sometimes, notably in the 11th century in an urgent situation, the successor provided a kind of *pro forma* discharge, enabling his predecessor to depart before the investigation into the state of the province. This was done later, in the capital, based on written evidence. Generally speaking, an outgoing *zuryō* was prepared to accept such a document allowing him to return to Heiankyō.[34] Men called back to the capital returned with only a *pro forma* discharge: for example, in 1014, Sanjō Tennō was ill and the governor of Ōsumi, who was a physician, was hastily summoned to the court. He arrived with this document, which Sanesuke had personally requested from the successor so that the physician could enter the palace and provide treatment for the emperor. In the early 11th century, it was considered important to respect the established norms and, also in 1014, Michinaga wished the first reading lesson of his grandson Atsunari to be given by Fujiwara no Hironari who was recalled from Iyo, but the successor did not provide a *pro forma* discharge. Hironari was in the capital but, while directing his anger towards the successor, Michinaga refrained from employing him at the palace because his situation was not in order. Yet a few years later, when Yori-michi was chancellor, Sanesuke several times had occasion to be critical of the immediate employment of men who had returned without the benefit of a *pro forma* discharge. An ex-governor of Mino became assistant director of the crown prince's household without this document, an ex-governor of Dewa received a post in the palace Library Office and another in the chancellor's household, prompting Sanesuke to say that this was not in accordance with court precedent.[35] In principle, a *pro forma* discharge was required to hold a position in the central administration, whereas a final discharge was necessary to apply for a new post as a *zuryō*.

On leaving office, a governor could in principle determine with his successor what he remained responsible for, such as damage to be repaired or arrears to make good, so as to avoid any disputed claims, something that was not always possible. If the hand-over formalities had posed problems due to a mis-understanding or simply because the predecessor had died, become a monk or returned too soon to Heiankyō, the new governor would then ask for an inspector[36] to be sent to draw up a register of the hand-over.

Having returned to the capital with a *fuyogeyujō*, the ex-governor began negotiations with the supervisory bodies: the Accounts and Public Resources offices. He needed to be able to produce the receipts for three types of register: those proving that the public buildings – the provincial government head-quarters and storehouses, as well as the listed provincial temples and shrines – were in good repair; those proving that all tax liabilities – what was owed to the court and also to the beneficiaries of conceded households – had been met; and lastly those for the provincial rice reserves. Which is appreciably less than is listed in the *Regulations on Transferring Office*. It was necessary to be able to present the decrees authorizing tax remissions, or the decrease in the public resources, or the authorization not to go further back than the final year of office of the outgoing governor, and so not be held responsible for decades of arrears. After inspection, the examining offices and the Kageyushi produced a kind of synthesis. But the senior nobles did not pronounce judgement based solely on this. In fact, they had available to them the complete dossier: receipts, legal opinions and documentary evidence, including extracts of precedents relating to the management of predecessors.[37]

It was incumbent upon the governor to assemble his own dossier and to prove that he had satisfied all his obligations. He then presented a request for a final discharge. The dossier was first handed to the emperor who immediately had it sent on to the Control Board. This body did an initial check and at this stage could withhold an incomplete dossier. Thus in 1003, the major controller Fujiwara no Yukinari removed that of Ōnaka-tomi no Sukechika, as a supporting document was missing. He later regretted his action, because his zeal did not please Michinaga who protected Sukechika. The senior nobles met to decide on the dossiers presented to them and there seems to have been a recorder for each one. This procedure probably began in the early 10th century. The *Gōke shidai* describes these sessions, generally presided over by a major counsellor. Members of the Control Board were present, primarily as readers, and the proceedings were taken down by an auditor. The main points considered for each dossier were the management of the province's rice (in the permanent reserves; steamed and dried), payment of the consolidated part of taxes and the condition of the provincial shrines and temples. In the *Chōya gunsai* is a document from 1072 setting out the request by a governor for a final discharge, but it may be no more than a model. It contains the following headings: receipts for a series of registers presented over four years, receipts for annual deliveries of the consolidated part of taxes, certificates proving that a certain quantity of rice has been set aside each year and new rice fields created, proof that shrines and temples have been repaired and lastly the notification of various building works for the palace without drawing on public resources, thus no doubt funded by the governor himself. The requester states that he found the province in a bad way and restored its fortunes. Under the first heading are listed a large number of registers: population, payments in kind, envoy to the imperial assembly, charitable granaries, rice from the public resources, public loans of rice, land tax and land tax on conceded households; at that date, many could only be dummy registers, since, for example, the charitable granaries had long ceased to exist. It is known from the *Chōya gunsai* that at least by the 12th century there were copyists in the Accounts and Public Resources offices whose task it was to fabricate large numbers of provincial registers.[38] Although not mentioned in the article of the *Gōke shidai* relating to the sessions involving decisions on the management practices of governors, it appears that having funded building works for the court counted heavily in one's favour.

During the sessions at which management practices were scrutinized, one or more cases (often three to five) could be dealt with. In spite of careful preparation, a dossier might be withheld and the requester be unable to receive his final discharge until the next year. Even under ideal conditions, it took about a year for a favourable decision to be handed down. But there are examples of far longer periods. A governor of Ise who resigned in 1006 obtained his final discharge only in 1013; and decisions made three, four and even five years after a governor left office are not unknown. The patronage of a minister sometimes enabled a final discharge to be obtained from the council despite an incomplete dossier. In 1017, the Kageyushi expressed an unfavourable opinion regarding a client of Michinaga; the senior nobles in session exchanged looks but all remained silent, and the administration of this ex-governor of Shinano was declared to be beyond reproach. But Michinaga could not do everything: in 1014, one of his protégés, the ex-governor of Bingo, submitted an incomplete dossier; the council of senior nobles agreed to overlook it, but Sanesuke opposed the decision. When informed of the incident, Michinaga backed down and blamed the Control Board for not having done its work properly. In his journal, Sanesuke refuted this argument for, he says, Michinaga who held the post of official document examiner had also seen the dossier. The matter was resolved a few months later.[39]

Resignation did not exempt a governor from the obligation to submit his accounts, whereas if he died in office the court could usually do no more than demand from his successor any arrears that might be outstanding from his administration. It seems that a governor who had been dismissed could quite easily get around the problem of the non-delivery of products expected by the court. Minamoto no Yorichika was dismissed in 1017; at the end of that year, Sanesuke, who managed the affairs of the Vestal-princess of Kamo, demanded the silk he had not delivered and was surprised at his response, namely that the court had not ordered him to pay in 1017. It is not known how the matter ended, but it certainly appears that Yorichika did not repay this debt. He was still able to obtain his final discharge in 1019.[40]

The case of governors who became monks while in office is more complicated. This step could be taken more or less by accident, during an illness. Which is what happened in 1015 to Minamoto no Kunitaka, who had not paid what his province owed in silk to the Vestal-princess of Kamo. Sanesuke urged him to pay up but Kunitaka tried to find a way out. The problem posed by a man becoming a monk was two-fold: firstly, he no longer had any social obligations and could no longer use his own name and the seal of his province; secondly, and increasingly so after the first third of the 11th century, everyone knew that many *zuryō* posts had been handed out following a personal pledge by the candidate to fund works for the court from his private resources (often acquired while exploiting the province on behalf of the court). In these circumstances, the wife and children shared responsibility and it seemed only right to expect them to pay, in view of the mix in the governors' warehouses of private and public goods, the latter needed in part to meet the requirements of the court. In 1025, Sanesuke began a discussion with Michinaga, mediated by Yorimichi, on the subject of three governors who had become monks without having finalized payment of what they owed. An initial order had been issued requiring the descendants to pay. When consulted, Michinaga preferred to have the obligation fall on the wife, arguing that she knew better than the children where the goods of the governor turned monk were located; these could only be movables such as rice, cloth and oil, distributed between several warehouses and therefore easy to conceal. Sanesuke reluctantly accepted this new formulation.

Cases of governors who died while in office also began to pose similar questions to those raised by governors who became monks. But it seems that, widow or children, the obligation to make good any arrears was most often decided in an arbitrary way. Fujiwara no Sukefusa had first-hand experience of this in 1039 when his father-in-law died. The widow circulated the rumour that the sons had robbed one of their father's warehouses, with the result that Yorimichi ordered the arrears to be paid by them. This incident gave Sukefusa the opportunity to mention the cases of two governors turned monks and continuing to enjoy their possessions without either themselves or their families being required to make any restitution.[41] The problems encountered by Sukefusa show that governors could easily hide their wealth by depositing it in the warehouses of subordinates, such as men-at-arms.

Conclusion

In the heyday of the Fujiwara regents and chancellors, the resident governors, who were often clients of senior nobles, played a very important role, since they were responsible for maintaining order in the country, as well as for financing the material needs and the religious and social activities of the court. They are often mentioned in the journals of ministers and other senior nobles, and some were the sons of ministers. The most highly placed men of the time, headed by Michinaga and Sanesuke, were the grandsons of governors and had spent their earliest years in the residence of their grandfather. They continued to seek for their sons unions with the daughters of *zuryō*. Sanesuke personally negotiated such marriages for his adopted son Sukehira and grandson Sukefusa. However, with Yorimichi's generation, the sons of ministers and major counsellors preferred to take a wife from the households of imperial princes and senior nobles, thus effectively sanctioning the social isolation of the innermost circle of the court. But the lack of a son and heir born to the principal wife led some men to assure their posterity by a secondary wife, a good example being Morozane (adopted by Takahime, wife of Yorimichi), in fact the grandson of a *zuryō* by his mother and who succeeded his father as chancellor.

The most important part of the actual administrative work done by the senior nobles was undoubtedly to carefully select the governors, that is, to examine the candidatures and dossiers relating to the submission of accounts during the appointments sessions. They were well aware, in fact, that the entire life of the court – the rebuilding and repair of palaces and temples and the organization of celebrations – depended on the governors' ability to administer the provinces. Up to the mid-11th century – while their role as tax collectors was not made too difficult by the expansion of estates and they did not come into too much conflict with local individuals or institutions like the religious establishments, who had direct links with the court –, the post of *zuryō* remained an enviable one. For many men it provided various satisfactions: the joys of command, a greater freedom in daily life, the pleasures of an active life, new and different landscapes, and in Kyūshū meetings with foreigners and the diversion of hunting. Despite the dangers in the provinces of Kyūshū, which were quite restive and exposed to threats from the sea, even senior nobles requested the post of governor-general, and Fujiwara no Takaie distinguished himself fighting off attacks from pirates. No doubt the greatest benefit of provincial posts was that they enabled those who were sufficiently astute to realize handsome profits. In spite of their feigned indifference, the least affluent senior nobles cast envious eyes at this wealth. The beauty of the residence that Fujiwara no Kunitsune had built for himself in the capital aroused melancholy thoughts in Sukefusa when he visited it in 1054: "A wealthy man can indulge his every whim; whenever one contemplates such things one is saddened at not being able to realize one's wishes." It is true that not all governors succeeded so well or were as rich as Kunitsune.[42]

Despite the major importance of the resident governors in Heian society and their fundamental role in the administration of the country and in the very existence of the court, they do not occupy a significant place in the fictional world of Murasaki Shikibu – daughter, sister, cousin and wife of *zuryō*. They make brief appearances, whether as the owner of a residence where Genji goes to effect a change of direction and incidentally take an interest in the ladies of the household (*Hahakigi*), or as a monk like the ex-governor of Harima, motivated by an almost irrational ambition for his daughter (*Akashi*), or again as anonymous figures who carry out work on the residence of the novel's chief protagonist. The only man portrayed in some detail, the governor of Hitachi and husband of the mother of Ukifune, is one of the most comical characters: a vulgar and pretentious upstart. Despite his not-so-humble birth, life among people considered as rather simple-minded and the need to employ ruthless men-at-arms have cut him off from the life of the court and left him in complete ignorance of its customs and refinement.[43]

Yet Murasaki Shikibu could not have been unaware that certain officials of the *zuryō* class were better educated, more informed about the affairs of the country, better poets and more refined in their tastes than most senior nobles, or that their daughters had sharper minds and a better knowledge of literature than those of senior nobles, and were equally familiar with the social conventions. It goes without saying that a work of fiction is not written with the aim of describing in precise detail the society in which it is set and that a measure of idealization of aristocratic society, and especially the main protagonists, could not but appeal to readers and especially female ones. I would venture another hypothesis. It is known that, after the organization of the codal system, the order and peace of the country were believed to be dependent on the preservation of the social hierarchy, but up to the 10th century promotions and changes in status based on merit were still possible to some extent. It was in Murasaki Shikibu's time that offices gradually became hereditary: could it be that her novel, which is somewhat condescending and even disdainful towards anyone not belonging to the innermost circle of the court, reflects the fact that the aristocratic society of the early 11th century was hardening its attitude and closing ranks? Can one go so far as to say that the novel could be a veiled criticism of this society?

Notes

1. The term appears in the *Ruijū sandai kyaku*, Daidō 4.2.2., 809; see also *Shoku Nihon kōki*, Kashō 1.12.12., 849, *Shōyūki*, Tengen 5.2.25., 982 and *Midō kanpakuki*.
2. See *Heian ibun*, text 188 (Engi 2, 902: Awa, Shikoku) and text 199 (Engi 8, 908: Suō). Miyoshi no Kiyoyuki (*Iken jūnikajō*) mentions a district in Bitchū where the number supposedly decreased from nineteen hundred (late 8th century) to seventy (late 9th century).
3. See *Seiji yōryaku*, decrees of Enchō 3.12.14., 925 and Tengyō 5.12.29., beginning of 943.
4. This biography was probably written in 907.
5. See *Nihon kiryaku*, Eien 1.3.4: only three survive intact and seven others in an abridged form. For *Owari no kuni gehumi*, see *Heian ibun*, text 339; also pp. 29, 158.
6. *Iken jūnikajō*, article 8.
7. The first occurrence seems to be in the *Tosa nikki*, Jōhei 4.12.26., beginning of 935, but their role as guards is not mentioned. However, in the *Shōmonki*, Jōhei 7, 937, it is clear that this group has been a fighting force from the outset.

8. Namely, the fourth son of the gate guard official.
9. In the early 11th century, the only known case is Taira no Chikanobu who governed Awa (977), Ōmi (985) and Echizen (991) and in 1010 became principal assistant at the Dazaifu. But his rise to non-participating auditor in 1001 was mainly due to building works done for the court and his promotion to auditor in 1015 was two years before his death.
10. Section 25 (NKBT edition), "Depressing Things". The thwarted hopes of Sugawara no Takasue, father of the author of the *Sarashina nikki*, may also be mentioned.
11. For details, see *Shunki*, Chōkyū 1.1.25., 1040.
12. For these instances see *Shōyūki*, Shōryaku 3.1.20., 992 and *Midō kanpakuki*, Kannin 1.8.6., 1017. Another example is Fujiwara no Takasuke (985-1069/74) who immediately after being promoted to the fifth rank became a *zuryō* on the recommendation of the retired emperor Sanjō in 1017 (Kannin 1.1.24.); see *Kugyō bunin*, Kōhei 2.
13. *Honchō monzui*, Book 6, application by Taira no Kanemori, Tengen 2.7.22., 977. See also *Shōyūki*, Kankō 8.2.1., 1011, Chōwa 2.1.24., 1013 and Jian 1.1.24., 1021. It is possible that only the ministerial secretariat and the Shikibushō had an application accepted each year, *Shōyūki*, Eiso 1.1.28., 989.
14. The former is mentioned frequently in the *Shōyūki* up to 1021, but does not reappear until Chōgen 2.3.2., 1028; the career of the latter official lasted from 983 until at least 1040.
15. *Shōyūki*, Manju 4.1.27., 1027, a dispute between two men over the order of their applications.
16. This document set out the merits or otherwise of a governor's administration.
17. *Shōyūki*, Eiso 1.2.1., 989 (Akimasa and another man); Manju 4.12.19., beginning of 1028 (Library Office official); Chōwa 1.8.17., 1012 (a father resigns his post in favour of his son). *Midō kanpakuki*, Kankō 1.3.4., 1004 (rice comes from Sanuki); Chōwa 2.4.19., 1013 (horses arrive from Shinano); Kankō 7.8.23., 1010 (Fujiwara no Nariie (?-?) leaves for Mutsu) and Chōwa 4.7.15., 1015 (number of horses presented by him to Michinaga). From early 958, Sugawara no Fumitoki urged the prohibition of venality. *Shōyūki*, Chōwa 3.2.7., 991 (Chinjufu general).
18. See *Shōyūki*, notably Eiso 1.2.1., 989.

19. *Midō kanpakuki*, Kankō 3.10.2., 1006 (selection of a client of Michinaga); *Shōyūki*, Chōwa 3.6.17., 1014 (appointment of Nobutsune).

20. Korenori's success and the protection of Michinaga caused a great deal of rancour. See his biographical notice in the *Kugyō bunin*; also p. 156 for Sanesuke's comments.

21. *Shōyūki*, Kannin 3.1.22. and 24.

22. The text is found in the *Chōya gunsai*, Book 22, Chōkyū 5.2.28., 1044.

23. See for example *Midō kanpakuki*, Kannin 3.2.18., 1019 (Minamoto no Yorimitsu leaves for Iyo); Kankō 6.9.2., 1009 (a female official departs with her husband for Izumo).

24. *Chōya gunsai*, Book 22.

25. *Shōyūki*, Kankō 5.7.26., 1008 and Kannin 2.12.7., beginning of 1019.

26. Two governors-general were recalled following disputes: Taira no Korenaka (despite being highly favoured by Michinaga) with the Usa Shrine, *Midō kanpakuki*, Kankō 1.3.24., 1004 and *Nihon kiryaku*, Kankō 1.12.28., 1005; the second (who even lost his rank as second counsellor) was Fujiwara no Sanenari (975-1044) with the Anrakuji, *Hyakurenshō*, Chōryaku 2.2.19., 1038.

27. In this case, there seems to have been no "good letter", only oral evidence.

28. *Shōyūki*, Chōgen 1.7.24., 1028.

29. See for example *Gonki*, Kankō 4.7.23. and 4.10.29., 1007; *Midō kanpakuki*, Kankō 5.2.27., 1008.

30. See for example *Gonki*, Chōhō 3.12.2., 1001; *Midō kanpakuki*, Chōwa 1.9.22., 1012 and Chōwa 2.12.9., beginning of 1014; *Shōyūki*, Kannin 3.6.20., 1019; *Shunki*, Chōkyū 1.6.3., 1040.

31. See for example *Midō kanpakuki*, Chōwa 5.8.25., 1016; *Shunki*, Chōkyū 1.12.23. and 2.2.1., 1041.

32. See *Heian ibun*, text 142, Jōgan 6.1.13., 864; also *Hokuzanshō*, Book 10.

33. See for example *Midō kanpakuki*, Kankō 2.12.21., beginning of 1006; *Sakeiki*, Manju 3.2.29., 1026.

34. The term *geyujō* seems to have been used in China after it came into use in Japan.

35. *Shōyūki*, Chōwa 3.2.26. and 3.11.28., 1014; Jian 1.1.8., 1021; Manju 4.5.15., 1027.

36. See *Ruijū sandai kyaku*, decree of Tenchō 2.5.10., 825.

37. Two copies of the *fuyogeyujō* were required: one being for the Shukeiryō and Shuzeiryō, and the other for the Kageyushi.
38. See *Gōke shidai*, Book 4; *Chōya gunsai*, Book 28, Enkyū 4.1., 1072 and Book 27, texts of Eikyū 6.2.15., 1118 and Tenei 1.12.17., beginning of 1111.
39. See *Shōyūki*, Chōwa 2.1.22., 1013; Kannin 1.9.1., 1017; Chōwa 3.1.23.24. and 3.10.15., 1014.
40. See *Midō kanpakuki,* Kannin 1.3.15., 1017; *Shōyūki*, Kannin 1.12.26. and 3.1.23., 1019; also pp. 173, 174, 195, 250.
41. *Shunki*, Chōryaku 3.10.15., 1039; also pp. 120 and 137.
42. *Shunki*, Tengi 2.5.3., 1054, Sukefusa and his father Sukehira decide to absent themselves from a meeting of the council in order to visit this fine residence. Kunitsune had already been appointed to several provincial governorships.
43. See his portrayal in *Azumaya*. The journals of Michinaga and Sanesuke are rather critical of men such as Minamoto no Yorinobu and his brother Yorichika, used to the turbulent life of the East and having little respect for human life: unlike their brother Yorimitsu who had quite close ties with some senior nobles, including Fujiwara no Michitsuna. Many *zuryō* appear in the *Shōyūki*; they provided the only sources of information available to a minister such as Sanesuke about the countryside and its administration.

Note: The original French text of Appendix 3 was published in Terada Sumie, ed., *Cipango*: *Autour du* Genji monogatari, Paris: Publications Langues O', 2008, pp. 292-332.

BIBLIOGRAPHY

Brief details of all primary sources referred to in the text may be found in the *Dictionnaire des sources du Japon classique/Dictionary of Sources of Classical Japan*, Paris: Collège de France, Institut des Hautes Études Japonaises, 2006.

Principal primary sources

Chiteiki, Nihon koten bungaku taikei, vol. 69.
Eiga monogatari, Nihon koten bungaku taikei, vols 75, 76.
Engishiki, Shintei zōho kokushi taikei, vol. 26.
Genji monogatari, Nihon koten bungaku taikei, vols 14-18.
Gōke shidai, Shintei zōho kojitsu sōsho, vol. 2.
Gonki, Zōho shiryō taisei, vols 4, 5; Shiryō sanshū, 3 vols (991-1010).
Gōrihōshū, Gunsho ruijū, vol. 9, fasc. 132.
Heian ibun, ed. Takeuchi Rizō, 15 vols & 2 index vols. Revised edition. Tokyo: Tōkyōdō shuppan, 1980.
Honchō monzui, Shin Nihon koten bungaku taikei, vol. 27.
Iken jūnikajō, Nihon shisō taikei, vol. 8.
Kagerō nikki, Nihon koten bungaku taikei, vol. 20.
Kokin wakashū, Nihon koten bungaku taikei, vol. 8.
Konjaku monogatarishū, Nihon koten bungaku taikei, vols 22-26.
Makura no sōshi, Nihon koten bungaku taikei, vol. 19.
Midō kanpakuki, Dai Nihon kokiroku, 3 vols.
Murasaki Shikibu nikki, Nihon koten bungaku taikei, vol. 19.
Ōkagami, Nihon koten bungaku taikei, vol. 21.
Ononomiya nenjūgyōji, Gunsho ruijū, vol. 6, fasc. 84.
Owari no kuni (gunji hyakushōra) gebumi, Nihon shisō taikei, vol. 8.
Ruijū sandai kyaku, Shintei zōho kokushi taikei, vol. 25.
Saikyūki [*Saigūki, Seikyūki*], Shintei zōho kojitsu sōsho, vols 6, 7.
Shinsarugakuki, Nihon shisō taikei, vol. 8.
Shōyūki, Zōho shiryō taisei, vols 1-3; Dai Nihon kokiroku, 10 vols & index.
Shunki, Zōho shiryō taisei, vol. 7.
Sonpi bunmyaku, Shintei zōho kokushi taikei, vols 58-60 & index.
Yōrō ritsuryō, Nihon shisō taikei, vol. 3.

Secondary sources

Acta Asiatica 99 (August 2010): Studies on the *Ritsuryō* System of Ancient Japan: In Comparison with the T'ang. (Special issue)

Adolphson, Mikael, *et al.*, eds, *Heian Japan, Centers and Peripheries*, Honolulu: University of Hawai'i Press, 2007.

Batten, Bruce L., *Gateway to Japan: Hakata in War and Peace, 500-1300*, Honolulu: University of Hawai'i Press, 2006.

Beaujard, André, trans., *Sei Shōnagon: Notes de chevet*, Paris: Gallimard, 1966.

Bock, Felicia Gressitt, trans., *Engi-shiki: Procedures of the Engi Era*, *Monumenta Nipponica* Monographs, Tokyo: Sophia University, 1970 (Books I-V) and 1972 (Books VI-X).

Borgen, Robert, *Sugawara no Michizane and the Early Heian Court*, Cambridge (Mass.) and London: Harvard University Press, 1986.

Bowring, Richard, trans., *The Diary of Lady Murasaki*, London: Penguin Classics, 1996. [Revised edition of *Murasaki Shikibu: Her Diary and Poetic Memoirs*, Princeton, N.J.: Princeton University Press, 1982]

——, *The Religious Traditions of Japan 500-1600*, Cambridge: Cambridge University Press, 2005.

Ceugniet, Atsuko, *L'Office des études supérieures au Japon du VIIIe au XIIe siècle et les dissertations de fin d'études*, Genève: Droz, 2000.

Dictionnaire des sources du Japon classique/Dictionary of Sources of Classical Japan, ed. Joan Piggott, Ivo Smits, Ineke Van Put, Michel Vieillard-Baron and Charlotte von Verschuer, Paris: Collège de France, Institut des Hautes Études Japonaises, 2006.

Dictionnaire historique du Japon, 20 vols. Tokyo: Maison Franco-Japonaise/Librairie Kinokuniya, 1963-1995. [Reprinted in 2 vols, Maisonneuve et Larose, Paris, 2002]

Dykstra, Yoshiko Kurata, trans., *Miraculous Tales of the Lotus Sutra from Ancient Japan: The* Dainihonkoku Hokekyōkenki *of Priest Chingen*, Osaka: Kansai University of Foreign Studies, 1983.

Farris, William Wayne, *Heavenly Warriors: The Evolution of Japan's Military, 500-1300*, Cambridge, Mass.: Harvard University Press, 1992.

——, *Japan to 1600: A Social and Economic History*, Honolulu: University of Hawai'i Press, 2009.

Faury, Julien, "Les banquets poétiques au Japon à l'époque Heian" (794-1192), *Journal Asiatique* 299.2 (2011): 651-676.

Fiévé, Nicolas, *L'architecture et la ville du Japon ancien*, Paris: Maisonneuve et Larose, 1996.

——, ed., *Atlas historique de Kyōto*, Barcelona: Unesco/Les Éditions de l'Amateur, 2008.

Fischer, Peter, *Studien zur Entwicklungsgeschichte des Mappō-Gedankens und zum "Mappō-tōmyō-ki"*, Wiesbaden: Harrassowitz, 1975.

Frank, Bernard, *Kata-imi et kata-tagae: Étude sur les interdits de direction à l'époque Heian*, Tokyo: Maison Franco-Japonaise, 1958. [Revised edition, Paris: Collège de France, Institut des Hautes Études Japonaises, 1998]

——, trans., *Histoires qui sont maintenant du passé (Konjaku monogatari shū)*, Paris: Gallimard, 1968. [Revised edition, 1987]

——, *Le panthéon bouddhique au Japon*, Paris: Réunion des musées nationaux, 1991.

——, *Amour, colère, couleur: Essais sur le bouddhisme au Japon*, Paris: Collège de France, Institut des Hautes Études Japonaises, 2000.

——, trans., *La mère du révérend Jōjin: Un malheur absolu*, ed. Francine Hérail and Jacqueline Pigeot, Paris: Gallimard, 2003.

——, *Démons et jardins: Aspects de la civilisation du Japon ancien*, Paris: Collège de France, Institut des Hautes Études Japonaises, 2011.

Friday, Karl F., *Hired Swords: The Rise of Private Warrior Power in Early Japan*, Stanford, California: Stanford University Press, 1992.

——, *The First Samurai: The Life and Legend of the Warrior Rebel, Taira Masakado*, Hoboken, N.J.: John Wilby & Sons, 2008.

Fujishima Ryauon, *Le bouddhisme japonais: Doctrines et histoire des douze grandes sectes bouddhiques du Japon*, Paris: Maisonneuve et Ch. Leclerc, 1889. Re-edited as *Les douze sectes bouddhiques du Japon*, afterword by B. Frank, Paris: Éditions Trismégiste, 1983.

Girard, Frédéric, *Traité sur l'acte de foi dans le Grand Véhicule*, Tokyo: Keiō University Press, 2004. (trans. of *Daijō kishinron*)

Grapard, Allan Georges, *La vérité finale des trois enseignements*, Paris: Poiesis, 1985. (trans. of *Sangō shiiki* by the monk Kūkai)

——, "Aspects économiques du rituel pendant l'époque Heian", *Cipango* 6 (1997): 111-150.

Hakeda Yoshito S., *Kūkai: Major Works Translated, With an Account of His Life and a Study of His Thought*, New York: Columbia University Press, 1972.

Hempel, Rose, *Japan zur Heian-Zeit: Kunst und Kultur*, Stuttgart: W. Kohlhammer, 1983. [French trans. by Madeleine Mattys-Solvel, *L'âge d'or du Japon: L'époque Heian 794-1192*, Fribourg: Office du Livre, 1983; English trans. by Katherine Watson, *The Heian Civilization of Japan*, Oxford: Phaidon Press Ltd., 1983]

Hérail, Francine, "Un lettré à la cour de l'empereur Ichijō, Ōe no Masahira (953-1012)", in *Mélanges offerts à M. Charles Haguenauer*, Paris: L'Asiathèque, 1980, pp. 369-387.

——, *Histoire du Japon des origines à la fin de l'époque Meiji: Matériaux pour l'étude de la langue et de la civilisation japonaises*, Paris: Publications Orientalistes de France, 1986.

——, trans., *Notes journalières de Fujiwara no Michinaga, ministre à la cour de Hei.an (995-1018). Traduction du Midō kanpakuki*, 3 vols. Genève-Paris: Droz, 1987, 1988, 1991.

——, trans., *Poèmes de Fujiwara no Michinaga, ministre à la cour de Hei.an (995-1018)*, Genève-Paris: Droz, 1993.

——, "Une succession difficile au XIᵉ siècle", in *Mélanges offerts à M. le Professeur Sieffert, Cipango* (Special issue): Paris: Publications Langues O', 1994, pp. 383-396.

——, "Lire et écrire dans le Japon ancien", in Viviane Alleton, ed., *Paroles à dire, paroles à écrire*, Paris: EHESS, 1997, pp. 253-74.

——, trans., *Notes journalières de Fujiwara no Sukefusa. Traduction du Shunki*, 2 vols. Genève-Paris: Droz, 2001, 2004.

——, "La cour de Heian à travers le *Shunki* de Fujiwara no Sukefusa", *Ebisu* 27 (Autumn-Winter 2001): 45-68.

——, "Quelques caractères des célébrations à la cour du Japon au XIᵉ siècle", *Cahiers Kubaba* IV-2, "Rites et Célébrations", Paris: L'Harmattan, 2002, pp. 39-58.

——, trans., *Gouverneurs de province et guerriers dans les Histoires qui sont maintenant du passé*, Paris: Collège de France, Institut des Hautes Études Japonaises, 2004.

——, *La cour et l'administration du Japon à l'époque de Heian*, Genève: Droz, 2006. [Revised edition of *Fonctions et fonctionnaires japonais au début du XIᵉ siècle*, 2 vols. Paris: Publications Orientalistes de France, 1977]

——, "Dans la législation japonaise des VIIIᵉ et IXᵉ siècles", *Ebisu* 38 (Autumn-Winter 2007): 105-130.

——, trans., *Recueil de décrets de trois ères méthodiquement classés, Ruijū sandai kyaku*, 2 vols. Genève-Paris: Droz, 2008, 2011.

——, "L'Époque ancienne" (Chapters 5-10), in *L'Histoire du Japon des origines à nos jours*, Paris: Hermann, 2009. [Reprint with additions of *Histoire du Japon*, Horvath, 1990]

——, trans., *Notes sur de nouveaux divertissements comiques, Shin-sarugakuki*, Paris: Les Belles Lettres, 2013.

Hurst, G. Cameron, "Michinaga's Maladies: A Medical Report on Fujiwara no Michinaga", *Monumenta Nipponica* 34.1 (Spring 1979): 101-112.

Itasaka Gen *et al.*, eds, *Kōdansha Encyclopedia of Japan*, 9 vols. Tokyo: Kodansha, 1983.

Joüon des Longrais, Frédéric, *L'Est et l'Ouest: Institutions du Japon et de l'Occident comparées*, Tokyo: Maison Franco-Japonaise, 1958.

——, trans., *Tashi, le roman de celle qui épousa deux empereurs*, 2 vols. Tokyo: Maison Franco-Japonaise, 1965, 1969.

Kakimura Shigematsu, ed., *Honchō monzui chūshaku*, 2 vols. Reprint of 1922 edition. Tokyo: Fuzanbō, 1968.

Kokushi daijiten, 14 vols & 3 index vols. Tokyo: Yoshikawa kōbunkan, 1979-1997.

Konishi Jin'ichi, *A History of Japanese Literature*, vol. 1, *The Archaic and Ancient Ages*, trans. Aileen Gatten and Nicholas Teele, ed. Earl Miner, Princeton, N.J.: Princeton University Press, 1984.

Lurie, David B., *Realms of Literacy: Early Japan and the History of Writing*, Cambridge, Mass.: Harvard University Press, 2011.

Macé, Mieko, "La médecine dans la civilisation de l'époque Heian", in Gérard Siary and Hervé Benhamou, eds, *Médecine et société au Japon*, Paris: L'Harmattan, 1994, pp. 57-83.

McCullough, Helen Craig, trans., "A Tale of Mutsu", *Harvard Journal of Asiatic Studies* 25 (1964-1965): 178-211.

——, trans., *The Great Mirror: Fujiwara Michinaga (966-1027) and His Times*, Princeton, N.J.: Princeton University Press, 1980.

——, ed., *Classical Japanese Prose: An Anthology*, Stanford, California: Stanford University Press, 1990.

McCullough, William H. and Helen Craig, trans., *A Tale of Flowering Fortunes: Annals of Japanese Aristocratic Life in the Heian Period*, 2 vols. Stanford, California: Stanford University Press, 1980.

McKinney, Meredith, trans., *Sei Shōnagon: The Pillow Book*, London: Penguin Classics, 2006.

Mills, Douglas E., A Collection of Tales from Uji: A Study and Translation of *Uji shūi monogatari*, Cambridge: Cambridge University Press, 1970.

Miner, Earl, *et al.*, eds, *The Princeton Companion to Classical*

Japanese Literature, Princeton, N.J.: Princeton University Press, 1985.

Morris, Ivan, *The World of the Shining Prince: Court Life in Ancient Japan*, New York: Alfred A. Knopf, 1964. [French trans. by Madeleine Charvet, *La vie de cour dans l'ancien Japon au temps du prince Genji*, Paris: Gallimard, 1969]

——, trans., *As I Crossed a Bridge of Dreams: Recollections of a Woman in Eleventh-Century Japan*, New York: Dial Press, 1971.

Mostow, Joshua S., "Mother Tongue and Father Script: The Relationship of Sei Shōnagon and Murasaki Shikibu to Their Fathers and Chinese Letters", in Rebecca L. Copeland and Esperanza Ramirez-Christensen, eds, *The Father-Daughter Plot: Japanese Literary Women and the Law of the Father*, Honolulu: University of Hawai'i Press, 2001, pp. 115-142.

——, trans., *At the House of Gathered Leaves: Shorter Biographical and Autobiographical Narratives from Japanese Court Literature*, Honolulu: University of Hawai'i Press, 2004.

—— and Royall Tyler, trans., *The Ise Stories: Ise Monogatari*, Honolulu: University of Hawai'i Press, 2010.

Nagahara Keiji *et al.*, eds, *Nihonshi jiten*, Tokyo: Iwanami shoten, 1999.

Pigeot, Jacqueline, *Femmes galantes, femmes artistes dans le Japon ancien – XIe-XIIIe siècle*, Paris: Gallimard, 2003.

——, trans., *Mémoires d'une Éphémère (954-974) par la mère de Fujiwara no Michitsuna*, Paris: Collège de France, Institut des Hautes Études Japonaises, 2006.

——, *Michiyuki-bun: Poétique de l'itinéraire dans la littérature du Japon ancien*, Paris: Collège de France, Institut des Hautes Études Japonaises, 2009. [Revised edition of *Michiyuki-bun*, Paris: Maisonneuve et Larose, 1982]

Piggott, Joan R., ed., *Capital and Countryside in Japan, 300-1180: Japanese Historians Interpreted in English*, New York: Cornell University Press, 2006.

—— and Sanae Yoshida, eds, *Teishinkōki: The Year 939 in the Journal of Regent Fujiwara no Tadahira*, New York: Cornell University Press, 2008.

Rabinovitch, Judith N., trans., *Shōmonki: The Story of Masakado's Rebellion*, *Monumenta Nipponica* Monograph, Tokyo: Sophia University, 1986.

Renondeau, Gaston, trans., *Contes d'Ise*, Paris: Gallimard, 1969.

——, trans., *Anthologie de la poésie japonaise classique*, Paris: Gallimard, 1971.

Robert, Jean-Noël, *Les doctrines de l'école japonaise Tendai au début du IXe siècle: Gishin et le Hokke-shū gi shū*, Paris: Maisonneuve et Larose, 1990.

——, trans., *Le Sūtra du Lotus*, Paris: Fayard, 1997.

Rohlich, Thomas H., trans., *A Tale of Eleventh-Century Japan: Hamamatsu Chūnagon Monogatari*, Princeton, N.J.: Princeton University Press, 1983.

Rotermund, Hartmut O., ed., *Religions, croyances et traditions populaires du Japon*, Paris: Maisonneuve et Larose, 2000.

Sakamoto Tarō, *Rikkokushi*, Tokyo: Yoshikawa kōbunkan, 1970. [English trans. by John S. Brownlee, *The Six National Histories of Japan*, Vancouver and Tokyo: UBC Press and University of Tokyo Press, 1991]

Seidensticker, Edward G., trans., *The Gossamer Years: The Diary of a Noblewoman of Heian Japan*, Tokyo: Charles E. Tuttle Co., 1964.

Shimizu, Christine, *L'art japonais*, Paris: Flammarion, 1997.

Shirane Haruo, ed., *Traditional Japanese Literature: An Anthology, Beginnings to 1600*, New York: Columbia University Press, 2007.

Sieffert, René, trans., *Journal de Murasaki Shikibu*, Paris: Publications Orientalistes de France, 1978.

——, trans., *Journal de Sarashina*, Paris: Publications Orientalistes de France, 1978.

——, trans., *Contes de Yamato suivis du Dit de Heichū*, Paris: Publications Orientalistes de France, 1979.

——, trans., *Murasaki Shikibu: Poèmes*, Paris: Publications Orientalistes de France, 1986.

——, trans., *Supplément aux contes d'Uji*, Paris: Publications Orientalistes de France, 1986.

——, trans., *Le Dit du Genji*, 2 vols. Paris: Publications Orientalistes de France, 1988.

——, trans., *Izumi Shikibu: Journal et Poèmes*, Paris: Publications Orientalistes de France, 1989.

Shively, Donald H. and William H. McCullough, eds, *Heian Japan*, vol. 2 of *The Cambridge History of Japan*, Cambridge [England] and New York: Cambridge University Press, 1999.

Sorensen, Joseph T., "The Politics of Screen Poetry: Michinaga, Sanesuke, and the Court Entrance of Shōshi", *The Journal of Japanese Studies* 38.1 (Winter 2012): 85-107.

Tanabe, Willa J., *Paintings of the Lotus Sutra*, New York and Tokyo: Weatherhill, 1988.

Terada Sumie, ed., *Cipango* (Special issue): *Autour du* Genji monogatari, Paris: Publications Langues O', 2008.

Torao Toshiya, ed., *Engishiki*, 2 vols. Tokyo: Shūeisha, 2000, 2007.

Tsunoda Bun'ei *et al.*, eds, *Heian jidaishi jiten*, 3 vols. Tokyo: Kadokawa shoten, 1994.

Tyler, Royall, trans., *The Tale of Genji*, 2 vols. New York: Viking Press, 2001.

Verschuer, Charlotte von, *Les relations officielles du Japon avec la Chine aux VIIIe et IXe siècles*, Genève-Paris: Droz, 1985.

——, *Le commerce extérieur du Japon des origines au XVIe siècle*, Paris: Maisonneuve et Larose, 1988. [English trans. by Kristen Lee Hunter, *Across the Perilous Sea*, Cornell East Asia Series No. 133, 2006]

——, *Le riz dans la culture de Heian, mythe et réalité*, Paris: Collège de France, Institut des Hautes Études Japonaises, 2003. [English revised edition, Ch. von Verschuer with W. Cobcroft, *Agriculture and the Food Supply in Premodern Japan*. Forthcoming 2014]

——, "Le coffret de toilette (*tebako*) de la fille de Fujiwara no Chikataka", in *Les Rameaux noués: Hommages offerts à Jacqueline Pigeot*, ed. Cécile Sakai, Daniel Struve, Terada Sumie and Michel Vieillard-Baron, Paris: Collège de France, Institut des Hautes Études Japonaises, 2013, pp. 153-176.

Watson, Burton, trans., *Japanese Literature in Chinese*, vol. 1: *Poetry and Prose in Chinese by Japanese Writers of the Early Period*, New York and London: Columbia University Press, 1975.

INDEX

– Entries marked * are referred to only in a note to the text or an appendix.
– Page numbers in italics refer to the Notes.
– Additional explanatory material is taken from *Histoire du Japon* (POF, 1986), *Notes journalières de Fujiwara no Sukefusa* (Droz, 2001 & 2004), *La cour et l'administration du Japon à l'époque de Heian* (Droz, 2006), all by Francine Hérail, and *Nihonshi jiten* (Iwanami, 1999).

Administration, religion, rituals...

akō jiken 阿衡事件 political incident (887) *35*
Amidism 191, 195, 201, 221

Benkan 弁官 Control Board 8, 27, 28, 30, 42, 47, 126, 136, 154, 163, 164, 184, 217, 220, 222, 243, 255, 257
Buddhism 22, 37, 41, 44, 46, 56, 58, 69, 79, 85, 98, 123, 131-133, 146, 162, 164, 167-170, 181-183, 188-197, 199, 201, 209, 211

Chinese classics 9, 12, *34*, 39, 40, 42, 44, 45, 51, 59, 83, 124-127, 133, 153, 191, 199, 209, 216, 217, 223, 224
Chinjufu 鎮守府 military government of the North 245
Chinkonsai 鎮魂祭 Pacification of Souls ritual 55
Chōwa 長和 era (1012-1016) 43
Chōyō no sechie 重陽節会 Triple Yang banquet 49
Chūgūshiki 中宮職 Service of the Empress 9
chūnagon 中納言 second counsellor 7, 14, 21, 22, 27, 110, 112, 116, 118, 125, 137, 152, 163, 164, 168, 172, 223, 224, *263*
Classics (*myōgyōdō* 明経道) 12, 51, 126, 153, 191, 215, 217, 218, 220, 221

Daigakuryō 大学寮 Office of Higher Learning 9, 33, 44, 51, 86, 125, 215, 218, 221, 227
Daijōsai 大嘗祭 Great Thanksgiving 38, 85, 86
dainagon 大納言 major counsellor 7, 22, 27, 33, 45, 81, 111, 113, 129, 132, 137, 138, 142, 151-154, 156, 164, 167, 171, 214, 255, 259
Daizenshiki 大膳職 Service of the Table 9
dajōdaijin 太政大臣 prime minister 7, 83, 111, 115, 116

Dajōkan 太政官 Ministry of State Affairs 7, *34*, 42, 51, 217, 222

Danjōdai 弾正台 Board of Censors 171

Dazaifu 太宰府 Government Headquarters in Kyūshū 75, 112, 117, 155, 160, 161, 164, 247, 250, *262*

Edo jidai 江戸時代 Edo period (1603-1867) 2, 3, 207, 208

Edokoro 絵所 Painting Workshop 96, 227

Emonfu 衛門府 gate guard 14, 97, 142, 143, 158, 160, 170, 174, 218, 219, 243, *261*

Enchishi 園池司 Bureau of Gardens and Lakes 9

Engi 延喜 era (901-923) 5

fuyogeyujō 不与解由状 document in lieu of a discharge 253, 254, *264*

Gagakuryō 雅楽寮 Office of Music 48, 60, 61, 229

Gakōshi 画甲司 Painting Bureau 227

genpuku 元服 putting on of the male cap 128

geyujō 解由状 official discharge document 243, 248, 253-257, *263*

Gion *no matsuri* 祇園祭 festival 80

go 碁 Japanese chequers 230

Goryūsai 五龍祭 Five Dragons celebration 181, 199

Gosaie 御斎会 Buddhist celebration in the 1st month 41, 56

gunji 郡司 district administrator 29, 233, 237-239, 241, 251

Gyōbushō 刑部省 Department of Justice 8, 14, 219

hakamagi 袴着 putting on of the trousers 123

Han 漢 dynasty 97

Hiden-in 悲田院 Hospital of Compassion 15

hisangi 比参議 non-participating auditor 115, 224, 247, *262*

Hōgen 法眼 Eye of the Law (ecclesiastical title) 229

Hōjōe 放生会 Freeing of Living Creatures 188

Hokkyō 法橋 Bridge of the Law (ecclesiastical title) 228

Hossōshū 法相宗 Buddhist sect 191

Hyōbushō 兵部省 Department of Military Affairs 8, 30

Hyōefu 兵衛府 military guard 21, 86, 156, 171, 174

Iba hajime 射場始 Inauguration of the Archery Ground 57

Jian 治安 era (1021-1023) 43

Jibushō 治部省 Department of Noble Affairs 8

Jingikan 神祇官 Ministry of Religious Affairs 6, 37, 41, 53-55, 139, 181, 183-185, 199

Kageyushi 勘解由使 Discharge Investigation Bureau *231*, 236, 255, 256, *264*

Kaji no tsukasa 梶司 Blacksmiths Bureau 9

kanbun 漢文 Sino-Japanese 6, 143, 146, 206, 210-212, 221

Kanbutsue 潅仏会 Aspersions of the Buddha 41, 57

Kannamesai 神嘗祭 First Fruits Festival (Ise Shrine) 56, 185

Kannin 寛仁 era (1017-1020) 43

kanpaku 関白 chancellor 2, 18, 19, 21-24, 27, 28, 32, 88, 92, 99, 120, 136, 137, 152, 164, 167, 175, 176, 186, 195, 196, 210, 245, 251, 254, 258, 259

Kebiishichō 検非偉使庁 Police Bureau 13, 14, 28, 29, 77, 78, 100, 170-173, 175, 176, 184, 200, 210, 218, 219

keishi 家司 household intendant 154-157, 242, 247

kenin 家人 houseman, client 31, 157

Kinensai 折年祭 Prayers for the Year 53, 56, 184, 185

kojōhai 小朝拝 Minor Reverence 47

Konoefu 近衛府 palace guard 13, 25, 28, 39, 53, 57, 61, 62, 70, 86, 91, 126, 165, 174, 187, 229

Kōshin 庚申 Senior of Metal and Monkey day 65

Kunaishō 宮内省 Department of Palace Affairs 8, 151, 171

Kuraryō 内蔵寮 Office of Palace Storehouses 8, 9, 86

Kurōdodokoro 蔵人所 Chancellery 13, 14, 21, 25, 28, 44, 47, 91, 92, 100, 101, 111, 136, 164, 167, 174, 245

Kyotōshi 筥陶司 Utensils Bureau 9

Law (*myōhōdō* 明法道) 9, 12, 126, 151, 153, 170, 215, 217-221, 226

Letters (*kidendō* 紀伝道) 12, 13, 19, *34*, 39, 41-45, 51, 59, 60, 63, 124-126, 151, 153, 158, 168, 174, 218, 220-226

mappō 末法 final period of the Law 194-196, 201, 228

Mathematics (*sandō* 算道) 9, 151, 215, 217, 220, 221, 226

Medicine 9, 133, *148*, 153, 227

Medieval period 82, 206-208

Meiji jidai 明治時代 Meiji period (1868-1912) 207

Meryō 馬寮 Office of Horses 31, 166

mikado 御門 palace gate 77

Minbushō 民部省 Department of Population 8, 243

mogi 裳着 putting on of the train 128

Mokuryō 木寮 Constructions Office 9, 28

naidaijin 内大臣 third minister 7, 22, 27, 82, 136, 246

Naikyōbō 内教坊 Female Dancers Room 61

nairan 内覧 document examination function 18, 19, 21, 22, 87, 257

Naishidokoro 内侍所 Bureau of Palace Women's Services 129, 140

Naishōryō 内匠寮 Office of Skilled Artisans 227

Naizenshi 内膳司 Bureau of the Imperial Table 88

Nakatsukasashō 中務省 Department of Court Affairs 8, 30, 227

Nara jidai 奈良時代 Nara period (710-784) 85, 190, 215

nenbutsu 念仏 prayer to Amida Buddha 133

nō 能 classical Japanese theatre 206

Nuidonoryō 縫殿寮 Sewing Office 86

Obutsumyōe 御仏名会 Litanies of the August Names of the Buddhas 41, 56, 164, 165, 192

ōchō jidai 王朝時代 "age of the court" 1

Ōiryō 大炊寮 Grains Office 9, 77, 83, 220

Ōkurashō 大蔵省 Department of the Treasury 8, 86, 247

Onmyōryō 陰陽寮 Office of Divination 9, 42, 199, 227

Oribe no tsukasa 織部司 Weaving Bureau 9, 99, 101, 172

Regalia (mirror, sword and jewel) *35*, 86, 89, 103, 140, 187

ritsu 律 penal code 5, 109, 110, 125, 126, 173, 210, 250

ritsuryō kokka 律令国家 "code-governed State" 1, 6, 11, 14, 209

rōdō/rōtō 郎頭; 郎等 armed follower of a provincial governor 30, 157, 239-241, 249, 250, 258, 260

ryō 令 administrative code 5, 6, 99, 101, 109, 110, 113, 120, 125, 134, 153, 159, *177*, 210, 233, 235

sadaiben 左大弁 major controller of the left 8, 27, 167, 255

sadaijin 左大臣 minister of the left 7, 38, 118, 136, 154, 166, *179*

saibara 催馬楽 stable-boy songs 61

saigū 斎宮 Ise Vestal-princess 85, 115, 135, 182, 186

Saigūryō 斎宮寮 Office of the Ise Vestal-princess 186

sai-in 斎院 Kamo Vestal-princess 52, 80, 135, 144, 145, 182, 187, 257

sangi 参議 auditor 7, 14, 22, 111, 115, 117, 126, 138, 152, 164, 168, 222-224, 255, *262*

Sekiten 釈奠 ceremony in honour of Confucius 51, 216

sesshō 摂政 regent 2, 18, 19, 21, 24, 84, 87, 88, 96, 97, 115, 118, 151, 156, 160, 162, 168, 210, 258

Shikibushō 式部省 Department of Regulations Relating to Civil Officials 8, 16, 30, 33, 125, 161, 174, 221, 222, 243, 244, *262*

Shingonshū 真言宗 Buddhist sect 44, 79, 191, 226

Shinjōsai 新嘗祭 First Fruits Festival 49, 54, 55, 61, 85, 88, 100, 185

Shintō 神道 national religion 37, 40, 41, 44, 46, 52, 57, 58, 79, 80, 181-185, 190, 192, 199, 200, 233

Shoryōryō 諸陵寮 Office of Imperial Tombs 9

Shukeiryō 主計寮 Accounts Office 8, 9, 31, 220, 236, 254, 256, *264*

Shurishiki 修理職 Repair Service 28

Shusuishi 主水司 Water Bureau 9

Shuzeiryō 主税寮 Office of Public Resources 8, 9, 31, 220, 236, 254, 256, *264*

sumō 相撲 Japanese wrestling 57, 230

Taoism 6, 42, 46, 58, 226

Tang 唐 dynasty 5, 83, 85, 200, 210

tatami 畳 103

Tendaishū 天台宗 Buddhist sect 24, 45, 191, 192, 194-196, 226

Tenyakuryō 典薬寮 Office of Medicine 9, 79, 132, 227

tone 刀禰 municipal officer 78

Tonomoryō 主殿寮 Palace Office 62

Toyo no akari no sechie 豊明節会 "Intoxication" banquet 55

Tsukinamisai 月次祭 Monthly Celebration 53, 56, 184

Tsukumodokoro 作物所 Skilled Artisans Workshop 227

udaiben 右大弁 major controller of the right 8

udaijin 右大臣 minister of the right 7, 16, 27, 110, 114, 121, 134, 136, 165, 166, 172

Uneme no tsukasa 采女司 Palace Women's Bureau 88, 97, 227

uta-awase 歌合 contest of Japanese poems 70, 230
uwanari-uchi 後妻打 attack by the first wife against the second 140

Yakuin 施薬院 Hospice 15
yamato-e 大和絵 Japanese-style painting 96, 97, 227
Yin/Yang (principle) 陰陽 42, 197
Yin and Yang, way of (*onmyōdō* 陰陽道) 42, 43, 46, 58, 85, 122, 124, 126, 197-200, 225-227
Yōrō 養老 era (717-723) 5, 15
yosegi-zukuri 寄木造 joined-wood technique 193, 228

Zōshushi 造酒司 Saké Bureau 9
zuryō 受領 resident provincial governor 12, 29-31, 33, *36*, 45, 50, 53, 55, 80, 81, 83, 110-112, 114-116, 119, 120, 122, 131, 138, 144, *147*, 151, 152, 154-162, 168, 171-174, 176, *178*, 183, 186, 189, 195, 200, *202*, 205, 217, 219, 226, 228, 229, Appendix 3 *passim*
Zushoryō 図書寮 Library Office 8, 31, 244, 254

People, families, buddhas and deities

Abe-shi 阿倍氏 specialists in divination, astronomy 152, 227, 247
Abe no Seimei (921-1005) 阿倍晴明 master of Yin and Yang 199
Akazome Emon (960?-1041?) 赤染衛門 wife of Ōe no Masahira; mother of Takachika; author of *Eiga monogatari* 20, 104, 137, 143, 146, 213
akitsu kami 現神 emperor; visible deity 5
Akitsuki-shi 秋月氏 warrior family 161
*Akutagawa Ryūnosuke (1892-1927) 芥川竜之介 author *105*
Amanouzume no mikoto 天鈿女命 Shintō deity 40
Amaterasu Ōmikami 天照大御神 sun goddess 6, 40, 53, 56, 89, 190
Amida butsu 阿弥陀仏 Amida Buddha 133, 190, 191, 193-195, 201, 228, 229
Arakida-shi 荒木田氏 priests attached to the Ise Shrine 185
Ariakira shinnō (910-961) 有明親王 son of Daigo Tennō 113
Atsuakira shinnō; Koichijōin (994-1051) 敦明親王; 小一条院 eldest son of Sanjō Tennō and F. no Seishi; grandson of F. no Naritoki 24, 118, *148*, 242

Atsumichi shinnō (981-1007) 敦道親王 son of Reizei Tennō and F. no Chōshi; brother of Sanjō Tennō and Tametaka shinnō; half-brother of Kazan Tennō; grandson of Kaneie; lover of Izumi Shikibu 144

Atsunari shinnō 敦成親王 *see* Goichijō Tennō

Atsuyasu shinnō (999-1018) 敦康親王 son of Ichijō Tennō and F. no Teishi; half-brother of emperors Goichijō and Gosuzaku; nephew of Korechika and Takaie; father of Genshi (adopted daughter of F. no Yorimichi) 22, 68, 69

Atsuyoshi shinnō 敦良親王 *see* Gosuzaku Tennō

Azukabe Tsunenori (?-?) 飛鳥部常則 painter 97

Bo Juyi (J. Haku Kyoi 772-846) 白居易 Chinese poet 67, *73*, *106*, 126, 141, *149*

Black Warrior (J. Genbu 玄武) 84

Buddha 41, 57, 134, 194

Chiba-shi 千葉氏 warrior family, active in eastern Japan 160

Chikuzen 筑前 court lady 103

Chinese merchants 75, 121, 156

Chōshin (1014-1072) 長信 seventh son of Michinaga; Shingon monk 118

Daigo Tennō (885-930, r. 897-930) 醍醐天皇 son of Uda Tennō; father of emperors Suzaku and Murakami, Kōshi naishinnō and M. no Takaakira; grandfather of M. no Meishi 16, 18, 19, 23, 38, 113, 115, 118, 135, 223

Dainichi nyorai 大日如来 Great Sun Buddha 190, 228

Enchin (814-891) 円珍 Tendai monk *203*, 226

Ennin (794-864) 円仁 Tendai monk 45, *203*

Enyū Tennō (959-991, r. 969-984) 円融天皇 son of Murakami Tennō and F. no Anshi; brother of Reizei Tennō; grandson of Morosuke; father of Ichijō Tennō; grandfather of emperors Goichijō and Gosuzaku 19, 21, 65, 87, 115-117, 242

*Fudōmyōō 不動明王 Buddhist deity *203*

Fujiwara-shi 藤原氏 dominant political family of the mid-Heian period 2, 7, 14-18, 20-22, 52, 80, 82, 87, 110, 112, 113, 118, 119, 121, *147*, 151-153, 161, 164, 187-190, 194, 207, 209, 210, 213, 215, 218, 221-225, 230, 247, 258

Fujiwara no Akihira (989?-1066) 藤原明衡 literatus; compiler of *Honchō monzui*; author of *Shinsarugakuki* 158, 159, 212, 222, 225, 226, 229, 230

Fujiwara no Akimitsu (944-1021) 藤原顕光 eldest son of Kanemichi; brother of Tokimitsu, Asateru and Masamitsu; cousin of Michinaga; father of Shigeie and Genshi; minister of the right, later minister of the left 27, 82, 113, 121, 122, 136, 138, *148*, 152, 165, 172

Fujiwara no Akinobu (994-1027) 藤原顕信 second son of Michinaga and Meishi; brother of Yorimune, Nagaie, Kanshi and Sonshi; became a monk 118, 166, 167

Fujiwara no Anshi/Yasuko (927-964) 藤原安子 eldest daughter of Morosuke; sister of Koremasa, Kanemichi, Kaneie and Tōshi; principal consort of Murakami Tennō; mother of emperors Reizei and Enyū and Tamehira shinnō 19, 115, 116, 136, 179

Fujiwara no Arikuni (943-1011) 藤原有国 father of Hironari and Sukenari; literatus; auditor 59, 224

Fujiwara no Asateru (951-995) 藤原朝光 third son of Kanemichi; lover of Muma; major counsellor 142, 152

Fujiwara no Atsumitsu (1063-1144) 藤原敦光 son of Akihira; literatus 226

Fujiwara no Atsutada (906-943) 藤原教忠 third son of Tokihira; grandson of Mototsune; cousin of Morosuke; second counsellor 112, 115

Fujiwara no Bokushi/Mutsuko? (?-1016) 藤原穆子 wife of M. no Masanobu; mother of Rinshi and Tokinaka 118, 121, 134

Fujiwara no Chōshi/Yukiko (?-982) 藤原超子 elder daughter of Kaneie and Tokihime; sister of Michitaka, Michikane, Michinaga and Senshi; consort of Reizei Tennō; mother of Sanjō Tennō and princes Tametaka and Atsumichi 19, 21, 116

Fujiwara no Enshi/Nobuko? (?-?) 藤原延子 younger daughter of Akimitsu; sister of Genshi; wife of Atsuakira shinnō 122

Fujiwara no Fuhito (659-720) 藤原不比等 second son of Nakatomi no Kamatari; father of Muchimaro, Fusasaki and Kōmyōshi; grand-father of Shōmu Tennō 15-17

Fujiwara no Fusasaki (681-737) 藤原房前 second son of Fuhito; founder of the Northern branch 15

Fujiwara no Fuyutsugu (775-826) 藤原冬継 son of Nakamaro; father of Nagara and Yoshifusa; grandfather of Montoku Tennō 16, 17, 168

Fujiwara no Genshi/Motoko (?-?) 藤原元子 elder daughter of Akimitsu; sister of Enshi; consort of Ichijō Tennō, later wife of M. no Yorisada 89, 122, 136, 138

Fujiwara no Genshi/Motoko (1016-1039) 藤原元子 daughter of Atsuyasu shinnō and F. no Teishi; adopted daughter of Yorimichi and Takahime nyoō; consort of Gosuzaku Tennō 137, *203*

Fujiwara no Genshi/Sukehime (?-?) 藤原元子; 祐姫 daughter of Motokata; sister of Munetada; consort of Murakami Tennō; mother of Hirohira shinnō 171

Fujiwara no Gishi/Yoshiko (974-1053) 藤原義子 daughter of Kinsue; consort of Ichijō Tennō 136

Fujiwara no Gyōshi/Toshiko? (?-?) 藤原曉子 elder daughter of Nakahira; sister of Meishi; wife of Ariakira shinnō 112, 113

Fujiwara no Hironari (977-1028) 藤原広業 son of Arikuni; literatus; auditor 126, 174, 224, 254

*Fujiwara no Hirotsugu (?-740) 藤原広嗣 son of Umakai (694-737) 藤原宇合; grandson of Fuhito; led a revolt in Kyūshū *35*

Fujiwara no Hōshi (?-967) 藤原芳子 daughter of Moromasa; consort of Murakami Tennō 135

Fujiwara no Ishi/Takeko (999-1036) 藤原威子 third daughter of Michinaga and Rinshi; sister of Yorimichi, Norimichi, Shōshi, Kenshi and Kishi; principal consort of Goichijō Tennō 23, 69, 118, 229

Fujiwara no Junshi/Nobuko (957-1017) 藤原遵子 daughter of Yoritada; sister of Kintō; consort of Enyū Tennō 154

Fujiwara no Kaneie (929-990) 藤原兼家 third son of Morosuke and Moriko; brother of Koremasa, Kanemichi, Anshi and Tōshi; father of Michitaka, Michikane, Michitsuna, Michinaga, Chōshi, Senshi and Suishi; grandfather of emperors Ichijō and Sanjō; prime minister; regent 19, 21, 70, 79, 82, 114, 116-118, 127, 139, 163, 193, 223

Fujiwara no Kanemichi (925-977) 藤原兼通 second son of Morosuke and Moriko; brother of Michitaka, Kaneie, Anshi and Tōshi; uncle of Michinaga; father of Akimitsu; prime minister; chancellor 27, 113, 114, 152

*Fujiwara no Kanenari (?-?) 藤原兼成 household intendant of Sanesuke; provincial governor *178*

Fujiwara no Kaneyori (1014-1063) 藤原兼頼 eldest son of Yorimune; grandson of Michinaga; second counsellor 62, 121

Fujiwara no Kanshi/Hiroko (998?-1025) 藤原寛子 elder daughter of Michinaga and Meishi; sister of Yorimune; principal consort of Atsuakira shinnō 118

Fujiwara no Kenshi/Yoshiko/Kazuko (994-1027) 藤原妍子 second daughter of Michinaga and Rinshi; sister of Yorimichi, Norimichi, Shōshi, Ishi and Kishi; principal consort of Sanjō Tennō; mother of Teishi naishinnō 23, 32, *107*

Fujiwara no Kinnori (?-?) 藤原公則 provincial governor 156

Fujiwara no Kinsue (957-1029) 藤原公季 son of Morosuke and Kōshi naishinnō; uncle of Michinaga; prime minister 27, 82, 116, 136, 246

Fujiwara no Kintō (966-1041) 藤原公任 son of Yoritada (924-989) 藤原頼忠; brother of Junshi; grandson of Saneyori; major counsellor; celebrated poet; author of *Hokuzanshō* 26, 27, *35*, 39, 65, 131, 132, 138, 143, 154, 211, 214

Fujiwara no Kishi/Yoshiko (1007-1025) 藤原嬉子 fourth daughter of Michinaga and Rinshi; sister of Yorimichi, Norimichi, Shōshi, Kenshi and Ishi; consort of the future Gosuzaku Tennō; mother of the future Goreizei Tennō 23, 118, 129

Fujiwara no Kōmyōshi (701-760) 藤原光明子 daughter of Fuhito; grand-daughter of Nakatomi no Kamatari; consort of Shōmu Tennō; founder of Hiden-in and Yakuin 15

Fujiwara no Korechika (974-1010) 藤原伊周 second son of Michitaka; brother of Takaie; nephew of Michinaga; uncle of Atsuyasu shinnō; third minister 22, 63, 64, 68, *108*, 120, 130, 164

Fujiwara no Koremasa/Koretada (924-972) 藤原伊尹 eldest son of Morosuke and Moriko; brother of Kanemichi, Kaneie, Anshi and Tōshi; father of Yoshitaka and Yoshichika; grandfather of Kazan Tennō and F. no Yukinari; prime minister; regent 21, *107*, 111, 114, 115, 163, 164

Fujiwara no Korenori (963-1033) 藤原惟憲 household intendant of Michinaga; wealthy provincial governor; non-participating auditor 155, 156, 247

Fujiwara no Koreshige (?-989) 藤原惟茂 close advisor of Kazan Tennō; controller 163

Fujiwara no Kunimoto (874-932) 藤原邦基 grandson of Fuyutsugu; second counsellor; auditor 224

Fujiwara no Kunitsune (986-1067) 藤原邦恒 wealthy provincial governor 229, *231*, 260

Fujiwara no Kyūshi/Miyako (?-754) 藤原宮子 daughter of Fuhito; mother of Shōmu Tennō 15

Fujiwara no Masamitsu (957-1014) 藤原正光 youngest son of Kanemichi; auditor 152

Fujiwara no Meishi/Akiko (?-?) 藤原明子 younger daughter of Nakahira; sister of Gyōshi; wife of F. no Atsutada 112

Fujiwara no Michikane (961-995) 藤原道兼 second son of Kaneie and Tokihime; brother of Michitaka, Michinaga, Chōshi and Senshi; regent; chancellor 21, 22, 114, 116, 117, 136, 163

Fujiwara no Michimasa (991-1054) 藤原道雅 son of Korechika; grandson of Michitaka; non-participating auditor 102

Fujiwara no Michinaga (966-1027) 藤原道長 fourth son of Kaneie (m: Tokihime); brother of Michitaka, Michikane, Chōshi and Senshi; half-brother of Michitsuna; father of Yorimichi, Norimichi, Shōshi, Kenshi, Ishi and Kishi (m: Rinshi); father of Yorimune, Akinobu, [Yoshinobu (996-1065) 能信], Nagaie, Kanshi and Sonshi (m: Meishi); grandfather of emperors Goichijō, Gosuzaku and Goreizei; uncle of Korechika and Takaie; minister of the left; regent; founder of Hōjōji; author of *Midō kanpakuki* 20-28, 32, 39, 60-70, 79, 80, 82, 87, 93-95, 97, 99, 101, 104, 111, 113, 114, 116-119, 121-123, 125, 126, 128-134, 136-138, 140, 141, 143, 146-150, 153-156, 162, 164-167, 172-175, 193-195, 198, 201, 205, 206, 212, 213, 217, 219, 224, 228, 229, 242, 244-248, 250, 253-259

Fujiwara no Michitaka (953-995) 藤原道隆 eldest son of Kaneie and Tokihime; brother of Michikane, Michinaga, Chōshi and Senshi; father of Teishi; regent; chancellor 21, 22, 70, 116, 136

Fujiwara no Michitsuna (955-1020) 藤原道綱 third son of Kaneie; grandson of Tomoyasu; half-brother of Michitaka, Michikane and Michinaga; major counsellor 116, 117, *149*, *264*

Fujiwara no Michitsuna no haha (936?-995?) 藤原道綱の母 daughter of Tomoyasu; mother of Michitsuna; secondary wife of Kaneie; author of *Kagerō nikki* 116, 117, 127, 139, 145

Fujiwara no Moriko/Shigeko (?-?) 藤原盛子 daughter of Tsunekuni; wife of Morosuke; mother of Koremasa, Kanemichi, Kaneie, Anshi and Tōshi 114-116

Fujiwara no Moriyoshi (896-974) 藤原守義 literatus; auditor 224

Fujiwara no Moroie (1027-1058) 藤原師家 son of Tsunesuke; second controller of the right 167

Fujiwara no Moromasa (920-969) 藤原師尹 fifth son of Tadahira; brother of Saneyori and Morosuke; father of Hōshi naishinnō; minister of the left 23, 38, 135

Fujiwara no Morosuke (908-960) 藤原師輔 second son of Tadahira; brother of Saneyori; grandson of Mototsune; nephew of Tokihira and Onshi; father of Koremasa, Kanemichi, Kaneie, Anshi and Tōshi (m: Moriko), Tamemitsu (m: Gashi naishinnō) and Kinsue (m: Kōshi naishinnō); grandfather of emperors Reizei and Enyū; minister of the right 19, 23, 38, 39, 114-116, 136, 169, 182, 212

Fujiwara no Morozane (1042-1101) 藤原師実 son and heir of Yorimichi; grandson of Michinaga; prime minister; chancellor 169, 259

Fujiwara no Motokata (888-953) 藤原元方 son of Sugane; father of Munetada and Genshi; major counsellor; auditor 171, *179*, 223

Fujiwara no Motonaga (?-?) 藤原元命 provincial governor 29, 237-239, 241, 251

Fujiwara no Mototsune (836-891) 藤原基経 nephew and adopted son of Yoshifusa; father of Tokihira, Nakahira, Tadahira and Onshi; uncle of Yōzei Tennō; grandfather of emperors Suzaku and Murakami, F. no Saneyori and Morosuke; prime minister; chancellor 18, 19, 112, 136, 227

Fujiwara no Muchimaro (680-737) 藤原武智麿 eldest son of Fuhito; father of Nakamaro 15

Fujiwara no Munemitsu (930-969) 藤原致光 provincial official 175

Fujiwara no Munetada (?-?) 藤原致忠 son of Motokata; brother of Genshi (Sukehime); father of Nariakira, Yasusuke and Yasumasa; prefect (of the capital) 171-173

Fujiwara no Munetada (1062-1141) 藤原宗忠 grandson of Yorimune; minister of the right; author of *Chūyūki* 81

*Fujiwara no Munetomo (?-?) 藤原宗友 literatus *231*

Fujiwara no Nagaie (1005-1064) 藤原長家 youngest son of Michinaga and Meishi; brother of Yorimune and Akinobu; half-brother of Yorimichi and Norimichi; third minister 113, 126, 129, 153

Fujiwara no Nagara (802-856) 藤原長良 father of Mototsune; brother of Yoshifusa; grandfather of Yōzei Tennō; second counsellor 112

Fujiwara no Nakahira (875-945) 藤原仲平 son of Mototsune; brother of Tokihira and Tadahira; minister of the left 112, 113

*Fujiwara no Nakamaro (706-764) 藤原仲麿 son of Muchimaro; grandson of Fuhito; father of Fuyutsugu *35*

Fujiwara no Nakamasa (?-?) 藤原中尹 father of Yasuchika and Tokihime; provincial governor 116

Fujiwara no Nariakira (?-?) 藤原斉明 son of Munetada; grandson of Motokata; brother of Yasusuke and Yasumasa; brigand 171, 173

Fujiwara no Narifusa (982-?) 藤原成房 nephew of Yorichika; cousin of Yukinari; became a monk 164, 165

*Fujiwara no Nariie (?-?) 藤原済家 provincial governor *262*

Fujiwara no Narinobu/Tadanobu (967-1035) 藤原斉信 son of Tamemitsu; major counsellor; poet 26, 27, 141, 156

Fujiwara no Naritoki (941-995) 藤原済時 father of Seishi (Yoshiko); grandfather of Atsuakira shinnō; major counsellor 32

Fujiwara no Nobunaga (1022-1094) 藤原信長 eldest son of Norimichi; grandson of Michinaga; prime minister 136

Fujiwara no Nobunori (972-1011) 藤原惟規 son of Tametoki; brother of Murasaki Shikibu 127

Fujiwara no Nobutsune (?-?) 藤原信経 nephew of Tametoki; provincial governor 246

Fujiwara no Norimichi (996-1075) 藤原教通 younger son of Michinaga and Rinshi; brother of Yorimichi, Shōshi, Kenshi, Ishi and Kishi; son-in-law of Kintō; prime minister; chancellor 39, 101, 136, 138, 139, *178*

Fujiwara no Okinori (844-917) 藤原興範 literatus; auditor 224

Fujiwara no Onshi/Yasuko (885-954) 藤原穏子 daughter of Mototsune; sister of Tokihira and Tadahira; aunt of Morosuke; consort of Daigo Tennō; mother of emperors Suzaku and Murakami 116, 135

Fujiwara no Sanemasa (1019-1093) 藤原実正 son of Sukenari; literatus; major controller; auditor 224

*Fujiwara no Sanenari (975-1044) 藤原実成 second counsellor; provincial governor *263*

Fujiwara no Sanesuke (957-1046) 藤原実資 grandson and adopted son of Saneyori; brother of Takatō; uncle and adoptive father of Sukehira; grandfather of Sukefusa; minister of the right; author of *Shōyūki* 27, 28, 31, 32, *35*, 38, 45, 69, 111, 113, 120, 121, 123, 124, 127, 129, 131, 134, 142, 155, 156, 175, 176, 196, 198, 212, 245-247, 250, 251, 253, 254, 257-259, *264*

Fujiwara no Sanetō (?-?) 藤原誠任 provincial landowner 161

Fujiwara no Saneyori (900-970) 藤原実頼 elder son of Tadahira; brother of Morosuke; grandfather and adoptive father of Sanesuke;

grandfather of Kintō and Takatō; prime minister; chancellor 19, 27, 39, *71*, 120, *177*

Fujiwara no Seishi/Nariko (1014-1068) 藤原生子 daughter of Norimichi; grand-daughter of Michinaga; consort of Gosuzaku Tennō 92, *149*

Fujiwara no Seishi/Yoshiko (971-1025) 藤原成子 daughter of Naritoki; grand-daughter of Moromasa; consort of Sanjō Tennō; mother of Atsuakira shinnō 32

Fujiwara no Senshi/Akiko (961-1001) 藤原詮子 younger daughter of Kaneie and Tokihime; sister of Michinaga and Chōshi; consort of Enyū Tennō; mother of Ichijō Tennō 19, 21, 22, 83, 93, 112, 116-118, 136, 193, 242

Fujiwara no Shigeie (977-?) 藤原重家 only son of Akimitsu and a daughter of Murakami Tennō (Seishi/Moriko naishinnō (?-998) 盛子内親王 or Kishi/Noriko naishinnō (949-986) 規子内親王); became a monk 165, 166

Fujiwara no Shōshi/Akiko (988-1074) 藤原彰子 eldest daughter of Michinaga and Rinshi; sister of Yorimichi, Norimichi, Kenshi, Ishi and Kishi; principal consort of Ichijō Tennō; mother of emperors Goichijō and Gosuzaku 22, 23, 97, 104, 118, 122, 123, 128, 130, 132, 133, 136, 138, 140, 143-145, *149*, 173

Fujiwara no Sonshi/Takako (984-1022) 藤原尊子 daughter of Michikane; consort of Ichijō Tennō 136

Fujiwara no Sonshi/Ryūshi/Takako (?-?) 藤原尊子; 隆子 younger daughter of Michinaga and Meishi; wife of M. no Morofusa (1008-1077) 源師房 118

Fujiwara no Suetsuna (?-?) 藤原季綱 literatus; ?compiler of *Honchō zoku monzui* 222, 225

Fujiwara no Sugane (856-908) 藤原菅根 descendant of Muchimaro; father of Motokata; literatus; second counsellor; auditor 223

Fujiwara no Suishi/Yasuko (974?-1004) 藤原綏子 youngest daughter of Kaneie; consort of the future Sanjō Tennō 117

Fujiwara no Sukefusa (1007-1057) 藤原資房 elder son of Sukehira; son-in-law of M. no Norisuke; brother-in-law of Norimune and Norisue; head of the Chancellery; auditor; author of *Shunki* 25, 28, 29, 31, 32, *35*, 56, 91, 92, 100, 110, 111, 120, 124, 134, 136-138, 142, 157, 167, 169, 186, 196, 198, 201, 212, *231*, 242, 245, 246, 258-260

Fujiwara no Sukehira (986-1067) 藤原資平 nephew and adopted son of Sanesuke; father of Sukefusa; head of the Chancellery; major counsellor 27, 28, 110, 121, 184, 196, 259

Fujiwara no Sukenaka (1021-1087) 藤原資仲 younger son of Sukehira; brother of Sukefusa; governor-general of Kyūshū; second counsellor 56

Fujiwara no Sukenari (988-1070) 藤原資仲 son of Arikuni; brother of Hironari; father of Sanemasa; literatus; non-participating auditor 224

Fujiwara no Sukeyo (847-897) 藤原佐世 literatus 225

Fujiwara no Sumitomo (?-941) 藤原純友 provincial official; became a rebel leader 160, 238

Fujiwara no Tadahira (880-949) 藤原忠平 youngest son of Mototsune; brother of Nakahira and Tokihira; uncle of emperors Suzaku and Murakami; document examiner; prime minister; chancellor; regent 19, 21, 38, 114, 160

Fujiwara no Tadakimi (?-968) 藤原忠君 son of Morosuke and Moriko; brother of Koremasa, Kanemichi, Kaneie, Anshi and Tōshi 115

*Fujiwara no Tadasuke (944-1013) 藤原忠輔 literatus; second counsellor; auditor 224

*Fujiwara no Tadatsune (?-1014) 藤原忠経 son of Michiyori (971-995) 藤原道頼; grandson of Michitaka *149*

Fujiwara no Takaie (979-1044) 藤原隆家 youngest son of Michitaka; brother of Korechika; nephew of Michinaga; second counsellor 22, *149*, 164, 259

Fujiwara no Takasuke (985-1069/74) 藤原隆佐 provincial governor; non-participating auditor *262*

Fujiwara no Takatō (949-1013) 藤原高遠 grandson of Saneyori; brother of Sanesuke; non-participating auditor; good musician 127

Fujiwara no Tamemitsu (942-992) 藤原為光 son of Morosuke and Gashi naishinnō; half-brother of Kaneie and Kinsue; prime minister 83, 111, 115, 116, 124, 153

Fujiwara no Tametoki (?-ca. 1016) 藤原為時 father of Murasaki Shikibu and Nobunori; uncle of Nobutsune; literatus; provincial governor 126, 144, 246

Fujiwara no Teishi/Sadako (976-1001) 藤原定子 daughter of Michitaka; niece of Michinaga; cousin of Shōshi; consort of Ichijō Tennō; mother of Atsuyasu shinnō 22, 23, 135, 136, 140

Fujiwara no Tōkazu (?-?) 藤原遠量 half-brother of Kaneie 117

Fujiwara no Tokihime (?-980) 藤原時姫 daughter of Nakamasa; sister of Yasuchika; principal wife of Kaneie; mother of Michitaka, Michikane, Michinaga, Chōshi and Senshi 21, 116, 117, 119, 139

Fujiwara no Tokihira (871-909) 藤原時平 eldest son of Mototsune; brother of Nakahira and Tadahira; father of Atsutada; minister of the left; document examiner 19

Fujiwara no Tokimitsu (948-1015) 藤原時光 son of Kanemichi; second counsellor 152

Fujiwara no Tomoyasu (?-977) 藤原倫寧 father of the mother of Michitsuna; provincial governor 116, 117

Fujiwara no Tōnori (?-989) 藤原遠度 son of Morosuke; half-brother of Koremasa, Kanemichi, Kaneie, Tamemitsu and Kinsue; non-participating auditor 115

Fujiwara no Tōshi/Nobuko (?-975) 藤原登子 younger daughter of Morosuke; sister of Koremasa, Kanemichi, Kaneie and Anshi; consort of Murakami Tennō 115

Fujiwara no Tsunekuni (?-?) 藤原経邦 father of Moriko; grandfather of Kaneie; provincial governor 114

Fujiwara no Tsunesuke (1006-1081) 藤原経輔 son of Takaie; grandson of Michitaka; nephew of Korechika; father of Moroie; rival of Sukefusa; major controller of the left; major counsellor 29, 167

*Fujiwara no Yasuchika (922?-996) 藤原安親 son of Nakamasa; brother of Tokihime; head of the Chancellery; provincial governor; auditor *148*

Fujiwara no Yasumasa (958-1036) 藤原保昌 son of Munetada; younger brother of Nariakira and Yasusuke; grandson of Motokata; provincial governor; poet 173, 174, 200

Fujiwara no Yasunori (825-895) 藤原保則 prov. governor *34*, 237

Fujiwara no Yasusuke (?-?) 藤原保輔 son of Munetada; brother of Nariakira and Yasumasa; grandson of Motokata; brigand and assassin 171-173

Fujiwara no Yorimichi (992-1074) 藤原頼通 eldest son of Michinaga and Rinshi; brother of Norimichi and imperial consorts Shōshi, Kenshi, Ishi and Kishi; father of Morozane; regent; chancellor 23-25, 27-29, 58, 60, 62, 64, 65, 70, 82, 97, 118, 120, 125, 129, 131, 137, 139, 155, 156, 162, 167, 169, 186, 194, 195, 198, 228, 229, 250, 254, 258, 259

Fujiwara no Yorimune (993-1065) 藤原頼宗 eldest son of Michinaga and Meishi; brother of Akinobu, [Yoshinobu], Nagaie, Kanshi and Sonshi; half-brother of Yorimichi; father of Kaneyori; minister of the right 29, 113, 121, 129-131

Fujiwara no Yoritada (924-989) 藤原頼忠 eldest son of Saneyori; brother of Sanesuke; father of Kintō and Junshi; prime minister; chancellor 19

Fujiwara no Yoshichika (957-1008) 藤原義懐 son of Koremasa; brother of Yoshitaka; uncle of Kazan Tennō and F. no Yukinari 21, 163-165

Fujiwara no Yoshifusa (804-872) 藤原良房 son of Fuyutsugu; grandfather of Seiwa Tennō; brother of Nagara; adoptive father of his nephew Mototsune; prime minister; regent 17, 18, 112

Fujiwara no Yoshitaka (954-974) 藤原義孝 son of Koremasa; brother of Yoshichika; father of Yukinari *107*, 164

Fujiwara no Yukinari (972-1027) 藤原行成 son of Yoshitaka; grand-son of Koremasa; cousin of Narifusa; father of Yukitsune; major controller of the left; major counsellor; celebrated calligrapher; author of *Gonki* 27, 105, 125, 126, 129-131, 164-166, 212, 228, 255

Fujiwara no Yukitsune (1012-1050) 藤原行経 son of Yukinari; head of the Chancellery; auditor; rival of Sukefusa 25

Gashi/Masako naishinnō (909-954) 雅子内親王 daughter of Daigo Tennō; Vestal-princess of Ise Shrine; wife of Morosuke; mother of Tamemitsu 115, 169

Genmei Tennō (661-721, r. 707-715) 元明天皇 daughter of Tenji Tennō; mother of emperors Monmu and Genshō; grandmother of Shōmu Tennō 17

Genshin (942-1017) 源信 Tendai monk 191

Genshō Tennō (680-748, r. 715-724) 元正天皇 daughter of Genmei Tennō; younger sister of Monmu Tennō; grand-daughter of Tenji Tennō; aunt of Shōmu Tennō 18

Goichijō Tennō (1008-1036, r. 1017-1036) 後一条天皇 elder son of Ichijō Tennō and F. no Shōshi; brother of Gosuzaku Tennō; grandson of Michinaga 23, 24, 64, 68, 87, 104, 118, 136, 142, 186, 190, 217, 229, 247, 254

Goreizei Tennō (1025-1068, r. 1045-1068) 後冷泉天皇 son of Gosuzaku Tennō and F. no Kishi; brother of Gosanjō Tennō; grandson of Michinaga 23, 87

Gosanjō Tennō (1034-1073, r. 1068-1072) 後三条天皇 son of Gosuzaku Tennō and Teishi naishinnō; brother of Goreizei Tennō; grandson of Sanjō Tennō 210, 223, 224

Gosuzaku Tennō (1009-1045, r. 1036-1045) 後朱雀天皇 younger son of Ichijō Tennō and F. no Shōshi; brother of Goichijō Tennō; grandson of Michinaga 23-25, 28, 58, 64, 68, 87, 92, 118, 123, 142, 186, 190, 229, 247

Hachiman 八幡 bodhisattva 187, 190

Harada-shi 原田氏 warrior family 161

Hata-shi 秦氏 specialists in mathematics 220, 221

Hata no Ujimoto (?-?) 秦氏元 armed follower (along with his son) of M. no Yorichika 173

Higashi Sanjōin 東三条院 *see* Fujiwara no Senshi

Hikaru Genji 光源氏 "hero" of *Genji monogatari* 89, 145, 260

Hirohira shinnō (948-969) 廣平親王 son of Murakami Tennō and F. no Genshi; half-brother of emperors Reizei and Enyū *179*

Horikawa Tennō (1079-1107, r. 1086-1107) 堀河天皇 second son of Shirakawa Tennō 223

Hoshi/Yasuko naishinnō (949-987) 保子内親王 daughter of Murakami Tennō; briefly visited by Kaneie; became a nun 117

Ichijō Tennō (980-1011, r. 986-1011) 一条天皇 son of Enyū Tennō and F. no Senshi; grandson of Kaneie; nephew of Michinaga; father of Atsuyasu shinnō and emperors Goichijō and Gosuzaku 21, 22, 50, 64, 83, 87, 89, 93, 104, 105, 112, 117, 118, 122, 127, 131-133, 136, 163, 228

Ise no Tayū (var. Taifu, ?-after 1060) 伊勢大輔 poet 143, 144

Izumi Shikibu (974?-1030?) 和泉式部 poet 143, 144, 173, 213

Jakushō 寂照 *see* Ōe no Sadamoto

Jingū Kōgō (?-?) 神功皇后 empress; mother of Ōjin Tennō 52, 188

Jōchō (?-1057) 定朝 son of Kōchō; wood carver 193, 228, 229

Junna Tennō (786-840, r. 823-833) 淳和天皇 son of Kanmu Tennō; brother of Saga Tennō 13

Kamo-shi 賀茂氏 specialists in divination, astronomy 152, 226, 227

Kamo no Mitsuyoshi (939-1015) 賀茂光栄 master of Yin and Yang 153, 199

Kanmu Tennō (737-806, r. 781-806) 桓武天皇 father of emperors Saga and Junna 16, 159, 160, 188

Kannabi no Yasusuke (?-?) 甘南備保資 jurist; provincial governor 219

Kannon 観音 present Buddha 195

Kazan Tennō (968-1008, r. 984-986) 花山天皇 son of Reizei Tennō and F. no Kaishi (945-975) 藤原懐子; half-brother of Sanjō Tennō and princes Tametaka and Atsumichi; grandson of Koremasa; nephew of Yoshichika; became a monk 21, 22, 70, 78, 80, 95, 163

Ki-shi 紀氏 specialists in letters 221

Ki no Haseo (845-912) 紀長谷雄 literatus; second counsellor 59, 223, 224

Ki no Tadana (957-999) 紀斉名 poet; compiler of *Fusōshū* 212, 224

Ki no Yoshiteru (869-939) 紀淑光 son of Haseo; auditor 223

Kintada, Shimotsuke no (?-?) 下毛野公忠 household intendant of Michinaga and Yorimichi 175

kita no kata 北方 principal wife 114

Kiyohara-shi 清原氏 specialists in the classics 153, 217, 247

Kiyohara no Hirozumi (934-1009) 清原広澄 literatus 217

Kiyohara no Motosuke (908-990) 清原元輔 father of Sei Shōnagon; literatus; provincial governor 143

Kiyohara no Munenobu (?-1017) 清原致信 armed follower of F. no Yasumasa 173

Kiyohara no Yoshizumi (?-?) 清原善澄 brother of Hirozumi; literatus 217

kokka 国家 emperor; state 85

Kōkō Tennō (830-887, r. 884-887) 光孝天皇 son of Ninmyō Tennō; brother of Montoku Tennō; uncle of Seiwa Tennō; father of Uda Tennō 18, 228

Koremune no Kinkata (?-?)惟宗公方 grandfather of Yoshimune no Tadasuke; jurist 219

Kose-shi 巨勢氏 family of painters 227

Kose no Hirotaka (?-?) 巨勢弘高 grandson of Kanaoka; painter 97, 101, 105, 227, 229

Kose no Kanaoka (?-?) 巨勢金岡 painter 96, 97, 227, 229

Kose no Kintada (?-?) 巨勢公忠 son of Kanaoka; painter 97, 227

Kōshi/Yasuko naishinnō (920-957) 康子内親王 daughter of Daigo Tennō and F. no Onshi; sister of Murakami Tennō; cousin and wife of Morosuke; mother of Kinsue 115, 116, 169

Kōshō (var. Kōjō, fl. 990-1020) 康尚 son of M. no Yasuyuki?; father of Jōshō; wood carver 193, 228, 229

Kūkai (774-835) 空海 Shingon monk 44, 79, 190

Kuni no Masashige (?-?) 国雅重 jurist 219

Kura no myōbu 蔵の命婦 wife of Ōnakatomi no Sukechika 139, 140

Kusakabe-shi 日下部氏 specialists in mathematics 220

Kyōshi nyoō (?-998) 恭子女王 daughter of Tamehira shinnō; wife of Sanesuke 121, 135

Kyōshō (?-?) 慶昭 Tendai monk 196

Li Jiao (J. Ri Kyū 644-713) 李嶠 Chinese poet 124

Louis XIV (1638-1715; r. 1643-1715) king of France 1, *3*

Masami ō (799-863) 正躬王 grandson of Kanmu Tennō; auditor 12

Midō kanpaku 御堂関白 *see* Fujiwara no Michinaga

Mimana no Tadatoki (?-?) 美麻那直節 jurist 219

Minamoto-shi 源氏 descendants of emperors, but excluded from the imperial family 16, 22, 38, 113, 137, 151, 161, 215, 218, 223, 247

Minamoto no Akikane (1160-1215) 源顕兼 ?compiler of *Kojidan* 212

Minamoto no Akimasa (?-?) 源明理 son of Shigenobu; brother of Michikata; provincial governor 244

Minamoto no Kanenari (?-1010) 源兼業 provincial governor; supported by Kazan Tennō 139

Minamoto no Kanesuke (960-1002) 源兼資 household intendant of F. no Sanesuke; provincial governor 156

Minamoto no Koremasa (929-980) 源惟正 undistinguished career; auditor 111

Minamoto no Kunitaka (?-1023) 源国挙 provincial governor 257

Minamoto no Masanobu (920-993) 源雅信 grandson of Uda Tennō; father of Rinshi and Tokinaka; grandfather of Norisuke; minister of the left 20, 23, 118, 166

Minamoto no Masasuke (?-?) 源雅亮 author of *Masasuke shōzokushō* 98

Minamoto no Meishi/Akiko (965?-1049) 源明子 daughter of Takaakira; sister of Toshikata; grand-daughter of Daigo Tennō; secondary wife of Michinaga; mother of Yorimune, Akinobu, [Yoshinobu], Nagaie, Kanshi and Sonshi 23, 117, 118, 129, 166

Minamoto no Michikata (969-1044) 源道方 son of Shigenobu; brother of Akimasa; second counsellor 27, 28

*Minamoto no Morotoki (1088-1136) 源師時 literatus; author of *Chōshūki 231*

Minamoto no Moroyori (1068-1139) 源師頼 great-grandson of Tomohira shinnō; major counsellor 113

Minamoto no Narinobu (979-?) 源成信 grandson of Murakami Tennō and M. no Masanobu; protected by Michinaga; became a monk 166

Minamoto no Norimune (?-?) 源経宗 son of Norisuke; brother of Norisue; grandson of Tokinaka; brother-in-law of F. no Sukefusa; provincial governor; good musician 120

Minamoto no Norisue (?-?) 源経季 son of Norisuke; brother of Norimune; grandson of Tokinaka; brother-in-law of F. no Sukefusa; minor official; accomplished musician 120

Minamoto no Norisuke (979-1039) 源経相 son of Tokinaka; grandson of Masanobu; father-in-law of F. no Sukefusa; provincial governor 31, 111, 120, 134, 137, 157, 198, 258

Minamoto no Rinshi/Tomoko (964-1053) 源倫子 daughter of Masanobu and Bokushi; sister of Tokinaka; principal wife of Michinaga; mother of Yorimichi, Norimichi, Shōshi, Kenshi, Ishi and Kishi 20, 22, 23, 62, 93, 104, 111, 117, 118, 121, 132, 137, 143

Minamoto no Shigenobu (922-995) 源重信 father of Michikata and Akimasa; minister of the left 244

Minamoto no Shitagō (911-983) 源順 literatus; compiler of *Wamyō ruijushō* 125, 225, 226

Minamoto no Takaakira (914-982) 源高明 son of Daigo Tennō; father of Toshikata and Meishi; minister of the left 23, 38, 39, 82, 118, *202*, 211

Minamoto no Tamenori (?-1011) 源為憲 tutor of F. no Tamemitsu and Yorimichi; compiler of *Kuchizusami*, *Sezoku genbun* and *Sanbō ekotoba* 124, 125, 146, 153

Minamoto no Tokinaka (941-1001) 源時中 son of Masanobu and Bokushi; father of Norisuke; major counsellor 111

Minamoto no Tōru (822-895) 源融 son of Saga Tennō; minister of the left 94, 151, 152

Minamoto no Toshikata (960-1027) 源俊賢 son of Takaakira; brother of Meishi; major counsellor 27, 126

Minamoto no Tsuneyori (976-1039) 源経頼 grandson of Masanobu; auditor; author of *Sakeiki* 212

Minamoto no Yasuyuki (?-?) 源康行 descendant of Kōkō Tennō; perhaps the father of Kōshō 228

Minamoto no Yorichika (970?-after 1050) 源頼親 son of Mitsunaka (912-997) 源満仲; brother of Yorimitsu and Yorinobu; client of Michinaga; provincial governor 173, 174, 195, 250, 257, *264*

Minamoto no Yorimitsu (948-1021) 源頼光 son of Mitsunaka; brother of Yorichika and Yorinobu; client of Michinaga; wealthy provincial governor *147*, 154, 155, *264*

Minamoto no Yorinobu (968-1048) 源頼信 son of Mitsunaka; brother of Yorichika and Yorimitsu; provincial governor 174, 200, 247, *264*

Minamoto no Yorisada (977-1020) 源頼定 son of Tamehira shinnō; grandson of Murakami Tennō; auditor 117, 122, 138

Miroku 弥勒 future Buddha 195, 201

Miyoshi-shi 三善氏 specialists in mathematics 153, 220

Miyoshi no Kiyoyuki (847-918) 三善清行 literatus; auditor; author of *Iken jūnikajō 34*, 45, 59, 125, 185, 218, 220, 223, 225, 226, 235, 237, 238, *261*

Miyoshi no Tamenaga (?-?) 三善為長 mathematician; literatus 220

Miyoshi no Tameyasu (1049-1139) 三善為康 compiler of *Chōya gunsai* 210, 221

Mongols *202*

Monmu Tennō (683-707, r. 697-707) 文武天皇 son of Genmei Tennō and Kusakabe no miko (662-689) 草壁皇子; brother of Genshō Tennō; grandson of emperors Tenji and Tenmu; father of Shōmu Tennō 15, 17

Montoku Tennō (827-858, r. 850-858) 文徳天皇 son of Ninmyō Tennō and F. no Junshi (?-?) 藤原順子; brother of Kōkō Tennō; grandson of Fuyutsugu; father of Seiwa Tennō; grandfather of Yōzei Tennō 17

Muma no myōbu (?-?) 馬の命婦 court lady 102, 142-144

Murakami Tennō (926-967, r. 946-967) 村上天皇 son of Daigo Tennō and F. no Onshi; brother of Suzaku Tennō; grandson of Mototsune; father of Hirohira shinnō and emperors Reizei and Enyū 19, 37, 115, 117, 135, 136, 144, 166, 171, 219, 227

Murasaki Shikibu (973?-1014?) 紫式部 daughter of F. no Tametoki; author of *Genji monogatari* 102, 127, 140-145, 213, 260, 261

Myōson (971-1063) 明尊 ecclesiastical dignitary 196

Nagaya ō (684-729) 長屋王 grandson of Tenmu Tennō (631?-686, r. 672-686) 天武天皇 15

Nakahara-shi 中原氏 specialists in the classics, law 153, 219, 247

Nakahara no Munetoki (946?-?) 中原致時 literatus; provincial governor 216, 217

Nakatomi-shi 中臣氏 family attached to the national religion 15

Nakatomi no Kamatari (614-669) 中臣鎌足 father of Fuhito; close advisor of Tenji Tennō 14, 15, 17

Nibu-shi 丹生氏 specialists in mathematics 220

Ninmyō Tennō (810-850, r. 833-850) 仁明天皇 son of Saga Tennō; father of Montoku Tennō 16, 222

Nishiki-shi 錦氏 specialists in mathematics 220

Ō no Masakata (?-1045) 多政方 celebrated dancer 62, 63

Ōe-shi 大江氏 specialists in letters 13, 126, 153, 215, 218, 221, 222, 247

Ōe no Asatsuna (886-957) 大江朝綱 grandson of Otondo; literatus; auditor 223

Ōe no Kinyori (?-1040) 大江公資 nephew of Mochitoki; tutor of F. no Nagaie; provincial governor 126, 153

Ōe no Koretoki (888-963) 大江維時 grandson of Otondo; grandfather of Masahira; second counsellor 125, 223

Ōe no Masafusa (1041-1111) 大江匡房 son of Narihira (?-?) 大江成衡; grandson of Takachika; literatus; second counsellor; auditor; author of *Gōke shidai* 39, 211, 212, 223, 225, 226

Ōe no Masahira (952-1012) 大江匡衡 father of Takachika; literatus; provincial governor 44, 59, 60, 63, 66, 94, 95, 125, 137, 143, 153, 171, 212, 221, 224

Ōe no Masamune (?-?) 大江雅致 brother? of Masahira; father of Izumi Shikibu 143

Ōe no Mochitoki (955-1010) 大江以言 uncle of Kinyori; literatus *73*, 219

Ōe no Otondo (811-877) 大江音人 literatus 222, 223

Ōe no Sadamoto (962?-1034) 大江定基 became a Tendai monk (Jakushō); spent thirty years in China 168

Ōe no Tadamitsu (934-987) 大江斉光 son of Koretoki; auditor 223

Ōe no Takachika (978?-1046) 大江挙周 son of Masahira and Akazome Emon; grandfather of Masafusa; literatus; provincial governor 44

Ōjin Tennō (?-?) 応神天皇 son of Jingū Kōgō 52, 187, 188

Ōkura-shi 大蔵氏 warrior family, active in Kyūshū 160, 161, 221

Ōkura no Haruzane (?-?) 大蔵春実 grandfather of Taneki 160

Ōkura no Taneki (?-?) 大蔵種材 grandson of Haruzane 161

Ōnakatomi-shi 大中臣氏 Jingikan officials closely associated with the Ise Shrine 185, *202*

Ōnakatomi no Sukechika (954-1038) 大中臣輔親 Jingikan official; priest of the Ise Shrine; father of Ise no Tayū; poet 139, 144, 255

Ōnakatomi no Yoshinobu (921-991) 大中臣能宣 Jingikan official; grandfather of Ise no Tayū; poet 144

Ono-shi 小野氏 minor officials 221

Ono no Fumiyoshi (?-?) 小野文義 jurist; provincial governor 219, 243

Otsuki-shi 小槻氏 specialists in mathematics 220, 221

Otsuki no Tadaomi (933?-1009) 小槻忠臣 mathematician 220

Otsuki no Tomochika (963?-1020/24) 小槻奉親 son of Tadaomi; mathematician; provincial governor 220

Reizei Tennō (950-1011, r. 967-969) 冷泉天皇 son of Murakami Tennō and F. no Anshi; brother of Enyū Tennō; grandson of Morosuke; father of emperors Kazan and Sanjō 19, 21, 115, 116, 144, 163, *179*

Ryōgen (912-985) 良源 Tendai monk 191

Saeki no Kinyuki (?-?) 佐伯公行 provincial governor 83, 112

Saga Tennō (786-842, r. 809-823) 嵯峨天皇 son of Kanmu Tennō; brother of Junna Tennō; father of M. no Tōru 12, 13, 16, *34*, 151, 197, 222

Saichō (767-822) 最澄 Tendai monk 194

Sakanoue-shi 坂上氏 specialists in law 219

Sakanoue no Akikane (1079-1147) 坂上明兼 jurist; joint compiler of *Hossō shiyōshō* 219

Sakanoue no Akimoto (1138-1210) 坂上明基 grandson of Akikane; jurist 219

Sakyō 左京 court lady 103

Sanjō Tennō (976-1017, r. 1011-1016) 三条天皇 son of Reizei Tennō and F. no Chōshi; half-brother of Kazan Tennō; brother of princes Tametaka and Atsumichi; grandson of Kaneie; father of Teishi naishinnō 21, 23, 24, 32, 62, 64, 87, 99, 117, 118, 123, 253, *262*

Sanuki no Naganao (783-862) 讃岐永直 jurist 12

Sei Shōnagon (966?-1017?) 清少納言 daughter of Kiyohara no Motosuke; author of *Makura no sōshi* 80, 135, 139-141, 143, 144, 166, 169, 213

Seiwa Tennō (850-880, r. 858-876) 清和天皇 son of Montoku Tennō; nephew of Kōkō Tennō; grandson of F. no Yoshifusa; father of Yōzei Tennō 17, 18

Senshi naishinnō (964-1035) 選子内親王 daughter of Murakami Tennō; long-serving Vestal-princess of Kamo Shrine (975-1031); celebrated poet 143, 144

Shaka 釈迦 past Buddha 195, *231*

Shirakawa Tennō (1053-1129, r. 1072-1086) 白河天皇 son of Gosanjō Tennō 223

Shōkū (?-1007) 性空 Tendai monk 162

Shōmu Tennō (701-756, r. 724-749) 聖武天皇 son of Monmu Tennō and F. no Kyūshi; grandson of Genmei Tennō and Fuhito; nephew of Genshō Tennō 15, 17

Sonshi naishinnō (966?-985) 尊子内親王 daughter of Reizei Tennō; became a nun 146

Sugano no Atsuyori (?-?) 菅野教頼 mathematician; provincial governor 243

Sugawara-shi 菅原氏 specialists in letters 13, 153, 215, 218, 221, 222, 226, 247

Sugawara no Aritsune (?-?) 菅原在躬 grandson of Michizane; literatus 226

Sugawara no Fumitoki (899-981) 菅原文時 grandson of Michizane; literatus 59, 225, *262*

Sugawara no Kiyotomo/Kiyokimi (770-842) 菅原清公 literatus; joint compiler of *Kikokushū* 44, 222

Sugawara no Koreyoshi (812-880) 菅原是善 father of Michizane; literatus; auditor 222

Sugawara no Michizane (845-903) 菅原道真 literatus; celebrated poet; compiler of *Kanke bunsō* and *Kanke kōshū*; minister of the right 16, 17, 19, 63, 80, 189, 200, 222, 224, 226

Sugawara no Nobutsune (?-?) 菅原陳経 literatus 226

Sugawara no Sukemasa (925-1009) 菅原輔正 great-grandson of Michizane; literatus; auditor 222

Sugawara no Takasue (973-?) 菅原孝標 literatus; provincial governor 145, *262*

Sugawara no Takasue no musume (1008-?) 菅原孝標女 author of *Sarashina nikki* 145, 176, *262*

Susanoo no mikoto 須佐之男命 brother of Amaterasu 40

Suzaku Tennō (923-952, r. 930-946) 朱雀天皇 son of Daigo Tennō and F. no Onshi; brother of Murakami Tennō; grandson of Mototsune 19

Tachibana-shi 橘氏 specialists in letters 17, 223, 247

Tachibana no Hayanari (?-842) 橘逸勢 celebrated calligrapher 17

Tachibana no Hiromi (837-890) 橘広相 literatus; auditor 223, 225

Tachibana no Tadakane (?-?) 橘忠兼 literatus; compiler of *Iroha jiruishō* 225

Taira-shi 平氏 descendants of emperors, but excluded from the imperial family 16, *147*, 159, 160, 215, 218, 221, 223, 247

*Taira no Chikanobu (946-1017) 平親信 provincial governor; auditor *149, 262*

Taira no Kanemori (?-990) 平兼盛 ?father of Akazome Emon 143, *262*

Taira no Korenaka (944-1005) 平惟仲 Dazaifu official; second counsellor; auditor 112, 189, 223, *263*

Taira no Masakado (?-940) 平将門 descendant of Kanmu Tennō; rebel leader 160, 211, 238

Taira no Sadachika (995-1063) 平定親 literatus; major controller of the right; provincial governor; non-participating auditor 136, 137

Taira no Tadatsune (967-1031) 平忠常 provincial official in eastern Japan; became a rebel leader 160

Taira no Takamochi (?-?) 平高望 great-grandson of Kanmu Tennō; provincial official 159, 160

Takahime nyoō (995-1087) 隆姫女王 daughter of Tomohira shinnō; principal wife of Yorimichi 120, 137, 259

Takashina-shi 高階氏 specialists in letters 247

Takashina no Moriyoshi (?-1014?) 高階積善 third controller of the left; compiler of *Honchō reisō* 212, 225

Takashina no Naritō (965-1010) 高階業遠 provincial governor 250

Takashina no Naritoshi (?-?) 高階業敏 son of Naritō; provincial governor 250

Takeuchi Rizō (1907-1997) 竹内理三 scholar; complier of *Heian ibun* 35, 211

Tamehira shinnō (952-1010) 為平親王 son of Murakami Tennō and F. no Anshi; father of Kyōshi nyoō and M. no Yorisada 122, 135

Tametaka shinnō (977-1002) 為尊親王 son of Reizei Tennō and F. no Chōshi; brother of Sanjō Tennō and Atsumichi shinnō; half-brother of Kazan Tennō; grandson of Kaneie; lover of Izumi Shikibu 144

?Tameyori (?-?) 為頼 173

Tanba-shi 丹波氏 specialists in medicine 132, 153, 227

Tanba no Yasuyori (912-995) 丹波康頼 court physician; compiler of *Ishinpō* 133

Tanizaki Junichirō (1886-1965) 谷崎潤一郎 author 206

*Tao Yuanming (J. Tō Enmei 365-427) 陶淵明 Chinese poet *73*

Teishi naishinnō (1013-1094) 禎子内親王 daughter of Sanjō Tennō and F. no Kenshi; grand-daughter of Michinaga; mother of Gosanjō Tennō 62, 99, 123

Tenji Tennō (626-671, r. 668-671) 天智天皇 son of Jomei Tennō 舒明天皇 (?-641, r. 629-641) 14

tennō 天皇 celestial ruler; Pole Star 6, 88

tenshi 天子 son of Heaven 6

Toba Tennō (1103-1156, r. 1107-1123) 鳥羽天皇 son of Horikawa Tennō (1079-1107, r. 1086-1107) 堀河天皇 160

Tomo-shi 伴氏 minor officials (guards etc.) 17, 221

Tomohira shinnō (964-1009) 具平親王 son of Murakami Tennō; father of Takahime nyoō; calligrapher and poet 129

tsuma 妻 wife 114

Uda Tennō (867-931, r. 887-897) 宇多天皇 son of Kōkō Tennō; father of Daigo Tennō; grandfather of M. no Masanobu 16, 18, 23, 79, 117

Ukifune 浮船 female character in *Genji monogatari* 260

Uma *see* Muma

Wake-shi 和気氏 specialists in medicine 132, 153, 227

*Wake no Sukenari (987-1056) 和気相成 court physician *177*

Watarai-shi 渡会氏 priests attached to the Ise Shrine 185

Xuan Zong (685-762, r. 712-756) 玄宗 Chinese emperor 200

Yakushi 薬師 healing Buddha 201, 228

Yoshimune-shi 令宗氏 specialists in law 219

Yoshimune no Michinari (?-?) 令宗道成 son of Tadasuke or Tadamasa; jurist 219

Yoshimune [Koremune] no Tadamasa (?-1015) 令宗[惟宗]允正 brother? of Tadasuke; jurist 219

Yoshimune [Koremune] no Tadasuke (?-?) 令宗[惟宗]允亮 jurist; provincial governor; compiler of *Seiji yōryaku* 210, 219, 220

Yoshishige no Yasutane (?-1002) 慶滋保胤 son of Kamo no Tadayuki (?-?) 加茂忠行; author of *Chiteiki*; became a monk 82, 83, 94, 162, 168

Yōzei Tennō (868-949, r. 876-884) 陽成天皇 son of Seiwa Tennō; grandson of Montoku Tennō and F. no Nagara; nephew of Mototsune 18

Place names

Ankamon 安嘉門 Gate of Peace and Happiness 83

*Anrakuji 安楽時 temple *263*

Atsuta jinja 熱田神宮 shrine 44

*Awa 阿波国 province (Shikoku) *262*

Awaji 淡路国 province 174, 250

Bingo 備後国 province 257

*Bitchū 備中国 province *261*

Biwadono 枇杷殿 aristocratic residence 82, 112, 113

Biwako 琵琶湖 lake 76, 194

Burakuden 豊楽殿 Pavilion of Abundance and Pleasures 86
Burakuin 豊楽院 Court of Abundance and Pleasures 86, 90, 166
Butokuden 武徳殿 Pavilion of Military Virtue 86
Byōdōin 平等院 temple 193, 195, 206, 229

Chikugo 筑後国 province 243
Chikuzen 筑前国 province 120
China 中国 5-7, 11-13, 17, 41, 43-46, 51, 58-60, 63, 67, 68, 75, 84, 104, 109, 131, 133, 146, 168, 176, 194, 198, *203, 263*
Chūka-in/Chūwa-in 中和院 Court of Central Harmony 53, 54, 88

Daigokuden 大極殿 Great Hall of State 47, 56, 85, 87, 181
Dantenmon 談天門 Gate of Heavenly Will 84
Dewa 出羽国 province 254
*Dōshūin 同聚院 temple *203*

Echigo 越後国 province 246
Echizen 越前国 province 171, 244, *262*
Enkyōji 円教寺 temple 162
Etchū 越中国 province 220

France 1
Fujitsubo 藤壷 Wisteria Arbour 89
Fujiwarakyō 藤原京 ancient capital 15, 75
Fukuoka 福岡 75

Gekkamon 月華門 Gate of the Moon's Radiance 88
Giyōden 宜陽殿 Pavilion of the Beneficent Yang Principle 88

Harima 播磨国 province 154, 162, 247, 252, 260
Hasedera 長谷寺 temple 171, 194
Hasshōin/Chōdōin) 八省院/朝堂院 Court of the Eight Departments 47, 84-87, 90
Heiankyō 平安京 Kyōto 2, 16, 43, 52, 75, 76, 80, 81, 83, 97, 187, 188, 192, 253, 254
Heijōkyō 平城京 Nara 75
Hieizan 比叡山 holy mountain; headquarters of the Tendai sect in Japan 23, 79, 164, 166, 167, 169, 191, 192, 194-196
Higashi Kyōgoku ōji 東京極大路 avenue 77, 82

Higashi Sanjōdono 東三条殿 aristocratic residence *73*, 82, 94, 112, 117

Higo 肥後国 province 243

Hirano jinja 平野神社 shrine 80, 188

Hitachi 常陸国 province 115, 116, 260

Hōjōji 法成時 temple 79, 162, 193, 228

Hōkōin 法興院 temple 79

Horikawa-in 堀河院 aristocratic residence 113, 121, 122

Ichijō-in 一条院 aristocratic residence 83, 93, 111, 112

Iga 伊賀国 province 161

Ikanmon 偉鑒門 Gate of Excellent Vigilance 84

Iki 壱岐島 island province 161

Inaba 因幡国 province 155, 247

Inari taisha 稲荷大社 shrine 80

India 146, 189

Inland Sea (J. Setonaikai 瀬戸内海) 76, 160

Ise 伊瀬国 province 156, 186, 217, 256

Ise daijingū 伊勢大神宮 Ise Great Shrine 23, 24, 56, 80, 85, 115, 135, 139, 144, 182, 183, 185-187, 201

Ishiyamadera 石山寺 temple 194

Iwashimizu Hachimangū 石清水八幡宮 shrine 52, 80, 100, 101, 123, 165, 173, 187, 188

Iyo 伊予国 province 254, *263*

Iyo 渭陽河 river (China) 66

Iwami 石見国 province 247

Izu 伊豆国 province 243

Izumi 和泉国 province 144

*Izumo 出雲国 province *202*, *263*

Jijūden 仁寿殿 Pavilion of Benevolence and Good Fortune 89

*Jōmyōji 浄妙寺 temple *203*

Jōneiden 常寧殿 Pavilion of Constant Tranquillity 55

Jōruriji 浄瑠璃寺 temple 206

Jōtōmon-in 上東門院 *see* Tsuchimikadodono

Kaga 加賀国 province 251

Kai 甲斐国 province 247

Kamogawa 鴨川 river 76, 79

Kamo jinja 賀茂神社 shrine 45, 52, 79, 100, 101, *107*, 123, 135, 144, 154, 182, 184, 187, 188

Kan-in 閑院 aristocratic residence 82

Kanjin-in 感神院 *see* Yasaka jinja

Kantō 関東 eastern region 159

Kanzeonji 観世音寺 temple 250

Kasuga taisha 春日大社 shrine 52, 80, 188, 190, 194

Katsura 桂川 river 76

Kawachi 河内国 province 219

*Kawara no in 河原院 aristocratic residence *107, 231*

Kaya no in 高陽院 aristocratic residence 82

Kazusa 上総国 province 159, 160, 176

Kibune jinja 貴布禰; 貴船神社 shrine 181, 188

Kinpusen 金峰山 mountain 195

Kiritsubo 桐壷 Paulownia Arbour 89

Kitano jinja 北野神社 shrine 80, 189, 200, 226

Kiyomizudera 清水寺 temple 79, 80, 172, 194

Koadono 小安殿 small palace pavilion 85

Kōfukuji 興福寺 temple 194, 195, 229, 250

Konmei (Ch. Kunming) 昆明池 lake 97

Konoemikado 近衛御門 Palace Guard Gate 77, 83

Korea 75, 78, 188

Kōyasan 高野山 holy mountain 191

Kōzuke 上野国 province 138

Kujōdono 九条殿 aristocratic residence 116

Kuzu 国栖 locality 48

Kyōgokudono 京極殿 *see* Tsuchimikadodono

Kyōto 京都 52, 75, 76, *203*, 207

Kyūshū 九州 75, 80, 112, 117, 155, 156, 159-161, 164, 182, 187, 189, 247, 250, 259

Matsunō jinja 松尾神社 shrine 80

Miidera *see* Onjōji

Mikawa 三河国 province 31, 111, 168

Mino 美濃国 province 254
Murōji 室生寺 temple 181
Muryōjūin 無量寿院 temple 228
Musashi 武蔵国 province 114-116, 160
Mutsu 陸奥国 province 116, 117, 244

Naden/Nanden 南殿 Southern Pavilion 47, 49-51, 56, 58, 88, 89, 93, 97, 103, *107*
Nagato 長門国 province 249, 250
Nakamikado 中御門 Middle Gate 77, 83
Naniwa 難波 port of Ōsaka 76
Nara 奈良 15, 43, 52, 75, 76, 83, 181, 188, 191, 192, 194
Nashitsubo 梨壷 Pear Arbour 89
Nihu jinja 丹生神社 shrine 181, 188
*Nijō-in 二条院 aristocratic residence *147*
Nikkamon 日華門 Gate of the Sun's Radiance 88
Ninnaji 仁和寺 temple 79
Nishi Kyōgoku ōji 西京極大路 avenue 77
Nishinomiyadono 西宮殿 aristocratic residence 38, 82

Ōharano jinja 大原野神社 shrine 80, 188
Ōigawa 大堰川 river 65
Ōimikado 大炊御門 Grains Office Gate 77, 83
Ōmi 大見国 province 112, 228, 247, 252, *262*
Ōmiya ōji 大宮大路 avenue 82
Oni no ma 鬼間 Demon Room 97
Onjōji 園城寺 temple *148*, 166, 191, 194, 196
Ononomiyadono 小野宮殿 aristocratic residence 113, 120
Ōsaka 大阪 76
Ōsumi 大隅国 province 161, 217, 253
Ōtenmon 応天門 Gate of Heavenly Obedience 84
Ōtsu 大津 194
Owari 尾張国 province 29, 158, 237, 238

Parhae (J. Bokkai 渤海) country 78

Rashōmon 羅城門 Enclosure Gate 76, 78, 79, *105*

Saga 嵯峨野 plain 97

Sagami 相模国 province 175

Saiji 西寺 temple 79

Sanuki 讃岐国 province 242, 244

Seiryōden 清涼殿 Pavilion of Purity and Freshness 37, 47, 50, 52, 55, 56, 88, 89, 91-93, 97, 103

Sekidera 釈寺 temple 228

Settsu 摂津国 province 116, 188

Shikoku 四国 228

Shinano 信濃国 province 156, *231*, 244, 256

Shingon-in 真言院 chapel 86

Shinkaden 神嘉殿 Pavilion of Divine Happiness 53, 54, 88

Shinsen-en 神泉苑 Garden of the Sacred Spring 87, 181, 200

Shishinden 紫宸殿 Pavilion of the Pole Star 88, 90, 91

Shōkeimon 昭慶門 Gate of Light and Good Fortune 85

Shōmeimon 承明門 Gate of Received Light 88

Sumiyoshi taisha 住吉大社 shrine 188

*Suō 周防国 province *261*

Suruga 駿河国 province 172

Suzakumon 朱雀門 Red Bird Gate 84-86

Suzaku ōji 朱雀大路 Red Bird Avenue 76, 77, 86

Taikenmon 待賢門 Gate of the Reception of Wisdom 83

Tajima 但馬国 province 251, 252

Takada *no maki* 高田牧 pasture 120

Takakuradono 高倉殿 aristocratic residence 82

Takaodera 高雄寺 temple 79

Takatsukasadono 鷹司殿 aristocratic residence 82

Tanba 丹波国 province 251, 253

Tenjō no ma 殿上間 Courtiers' Hall 47, 50, 89, 91, 101

Tōdaiji 東台寺 temple 192

Tōji 東寺 temple 79, 191, 228

Toribe 鳥辺野 cremation site east of Heiankyō 134

Tosa 土佐国 province 171, 228, 243

Tōtōmi 遠江国 province *178*, 247

Tsuchimikado 土御門 Extra Mud-brick Gate 77, 84

Tsuchimikadodono 土御門殿 aristocratic residence *74*, 82, 92, 93, 95, *108*, 111, 118, 123, 131, 193, 195

Uji 宇治 195
Ujigawa 宇治川 river 65, 76, 97
Umenomiya jinja 梅宮神社 shrine 80
Unmeiden 温明殿 Pavilion of Warmth and Brightness 89
Usa Hachimangū 宇佐八幡宮 shrine 80, 187-190, 250, *263*

Yamato 大和国 province 11, 173, 191, 194, 195, 250
Yasaka jinja 八坂神社 shrine 80, 189, 200
Yodogawa 淀川 river 76

Works cited

Chishō daishi den 智証大師伝 *Biography of Chishō Daishi* 226
Chiteiki 池亭記 *Notes from the Pavilion by the Pond* 82, 94
*Chōshūki 長秋記 journal of Minamoto no Morotoki *231*
Chōya gunsai 朝野郡裁 *Writings of the Court and Provinces* 71, 210, 220, 255, 256
*Chūgaishō 中外抄 *Stories from Inside and Outside the Capital 231*
Chūyūki 中右記 journal of Fujiwara no Munetada 81

Daihannyakyō 大般若経 *Large Sūtra on Perfect Wisdom* 56
*Daijingū shozōjiki 大神宮諸雑事記 *Record of Various Matters Pertaining to the [Ise] Great Shrines 202*
Dairishiki 内裏式 *Inner Palace Regulations* 37

Eiga monogatari 栄華物語 *A Tale of Flowering Fortunes* 20, 62, 89, 104, 117, 118, 120, 129, 130, 136-138, 146, *147-150*, 213
Ekikyō (Ch. *Yijing*) 易経 *The Book of Changes* 199, 216
Engi kōtaishiki 延喜交替式 *Engi Period Regulations on Transferring Office* 233, 234, 255
Engi kyaku 延喜格 *Decrees of the Engi Era* 222
Engishiki 延喜式 *Regulations of the Engi Era* 5, *106*, 183, 184, 210, 222, 233, 239

Fūji sankajō 封事三箇条 *Opinions on Three Matters* 255
Fujiwara no Yasunori den 藤原保則伝 *Biography of Fujiwara no Yasunori 34*, 226, 237

Fusō ryakki 扶桑略記 *Abbreviated Record of Japan 148*, 211
Fusōshū 扶桑集 *Collection of Japan* 212, 224

*Geki bunin 外記補任 *Chronology of Appointments of Ministerial Secretaries 230*
Genji monogatari 源氏物語 *The Tale of Genji* 89, 102, 145, 146, 206, 213, 235, 238, 260, 261
Girai (Ch. *Yili*) 儀礼 *The Book of Etiquette and Ceremonial* 40
Gōdanshō 江談抄 *The Ōe Conversations* 212
Gokanjo (Ch. *Hou Hanshu*) 後漢書 *History of the Later Han Dynasty* 12, 221
Gōke shidai 江家次第 *Order of Procedures and Celebrations According to the Ōe Family* 39, 211, 225, 255, 256
Gonki 権記 journal of Fujiwara no Yukinari 125, 164, 212, Notes *passim*
Gōrihōshū 江吏部集 *Anthology of the Ministry of Ceremonial's Official Ōe* 63, *72*, *148*, 212, 224
*Gosan buruiki 御産部類記 *Extracts Relating to Princely Births 148*
Gosen wakashū 後選和歌集 *Later Collection of Poetry 143*
Goshūi wakashū 後拾遺和歌集 *Later Collection of Gleanings* 70, *150*
*Gyokuyō wakashū 玉葉和歌集 *Collection of Jewelled Leaves 106*

Heian ibun 平安遺文 archival documents *35*, *106*, *147*, *149*, 211, *261*
Hokekyō 法華経 *Lotus Sūtra* 69, 95, 192, 200
Hokuzanshō 北山抄 *Notes of the Northern Hills* 39, 211, 252
Honchō monzui 本朝文粋 *Literary Essence of Our Country* 34, 71-73, 211, 222, 225
Honchō reisō 本朝麗藻 *Outstanding Poems from Our Country 73*, *106*, 212, 224
Honchō shinsen den 本朝神仙伝 *Lives of the Japanese Immortals* 226
*Honchō shinshū ōjōden 本朝新修往生伝 *New Biographies of Japanese Reborn in Paradise 231*
Honchō zoku monzui 本朝続文粋 *Literary Essence of Our Country, Continued* 222, 225
Hossō shiyōshō 法曹至要抄 *Compendium of Laws* 109, 219

Iyakurenshō 百練抄 *Notes One Hundred Times Polished* 211, *263*

Iken jūnikajō 意見十二箇条 *Opinions on Twelve Matters* 45, 59, 218, 225, 235, 238, *261*

Iroha jiruishō 色葉字類抄 dictionary 225

Ise monogatari 伊勢物語 *Tales of Ise* 146, 213

Ishinpō 医心方 *The Essence of Medicine* 133

*Iwashimizu monjo 石清水文書 *Documents of the Iwashimizu Shrine* 203

Izumi Shikibu nikki 和泉式部日記 *The Diary of Izumi Shikibu* 213

*Jiga (Ch. *Erya*) 爾雅 Chinese dictionary *34*

Kagerō nikki 蜻蛉日記 *The Kagerō Diary* 116, 127, 139, 145, 213

Kairaishiki 傀儡子記 *An Account of Puppeteers* 226

Kakumei kanmon 革命勘文 *Opinion on [Preventing] Great Changes* 225

Kanke bunsō 菅家文草 *Sugawara Family Literary Drafts* 224

Kanke godenki 菅家御伝記 *Biography of Sugawara* 226

Kanke kōshū 菅家後集 *Sugawara Family Later Collection* 224

Keikokushū 経国集 *Collection for Ruling the Country* 225

Kike shū 紀家集 *Collected Works of Ki no Haseo* 59, 224

*Kintō shū 公任集 *Kintō's Collection of Poems 35*

Kitano tenjin goden 北野天神御伝 *Biography of the Kitano Heavenly Deity* 226

Kōbō daishi gyōkeki 弘法大師行化記 *A Record of the Life and Teaching of Kōbō Daishi* 226

Kojidan 古事談 *Remarks on Past Matters* 73, 212

*Kojiki 古事記 *Record of Ancient Matters 34*

Kokin wakashū 古今和歌集 *Collection of Ancient and Modern Poems* 135, *149*

*Kokon chomonjū 古今著聞集 *Collection of Ancient and Modern Traditions* 204

Kōkyō (Ch. *Xiaojing*) 孝経 *The Classic of Filial Piety 34*, 122, 124, 216

*Kōnin kyaku 弘仁格 *Decrees of the Kōnin Era* 231

Konjaku monogatarishū 今昔物語集 *Tales of Times Now Past* 55, 70, 76, 146, 168, *178*, 213

Konkōmyōkyō 金光明経 *Golden Light Sūtra* 56, 192

Kuchizusami 口遊 *Fun by Mouth* 124, 125

*Kugyō bunin 公卿補任 *Appointments of Senior Nobles* 148, 262, 263

Kujō-dono yuikai 九条殿遺戒 *Instructions left by the Lord of Kujō* 182, 212

*Kujō nenjūgyōji 九条年中行事 *Annual Cycle of Procedures and Celebrations According to the Lord of Kujō* 71

Kurōdōshiki 蔵人式 *Regulations of the Chancellery* 225

Makura no sōshi 枕草子 *The Pillow Book* 135, 139, 144, 166, 169, 213, 241

Masasuke shōzokushō 満佐須計装束抄 *Masasuke's Treatise on Costume and Décor* 98

Meikō ōrai 明衡往来 *Akihira's Models of Correspondence* 226

Midō kanpakuki 御堂関白記 journal of Fujiwara no Michinaga 101, 119, 123, 133, 154, 155, 167, 173, 212, Notes *passim*

Mōgyū (Ch. *Mengqiu*) 蒙求 *Youth Inquires* 124, 125

Monzen (Ch. *Wenxuan*) 文選 *Anthology* 12, 59, 126, 221

Murasaki Shikibu nikki 紫式部日記 *The Diary of Murasaki Shikibu* 102, 103, 213

Mutsu waki 陸奥話記 *Account of the Uprising in Mutsu* 213

Nihon kiryaku 日本紀略 *Abridged Annals of Japan* 106, 171, *178*, *202*, 211

Nihonkoku genzaisho mokuroku 日本国現在書目録 *Catalogue of Extant Texts in Japan* 225

Nihon sandai jitsuroku 日本三代実録 *Veritable Record of Three Reigns of Japan* 12, *34*, *71*

*Nihon shoki 日本書紀 *Chronicle of Japan* 34

Ninnōkyō 仁王経 *Benevolent Kings Sūtra* 41, 181, 194

Ōjōyōshū 往生要集 *Compendium of Essentials for Rebirth in the Pure Land* 191

Ōkagami 大鏡 *The Great Mirror* 20, 102, 163, 166, 213

*Ononomiya nenjūgyōji 小野宮年中行事 *Annual Cycle of Procedures and Celebrations According to the Lord of Ono* 71

Owari no kuni gebumi 尾張国解文 petition 29, 158, 237, 238

Raiki (Ch. *Liji*) 礼記 *The Book of Rites* 40, 58, 68, 122, 216

Rakuyō dengakuki 洛陽田楽記 *An Account of Country Music in the Capital* 226

Rikkokushi 六国史 *Six Official Histories* 11, 12, *34*, 125, 211

Ri Kyū hyakunijūei (Ch. *Li Jiao baiershiyong*) 李嶠百二十詠 *One Hundred and Twenty Poems of Li Jiao* 124

Rongo (Ch. *Lunyu*) 論語 *The Analects of Confucius 34*, 216

Rōshi (Ch. *Laozi*) 老子 Taoist classic 126

Ruijū fusenshō 類聚府宣抄 *Systematically Classified Collection of Imperial Orders and Ministerial Decrees* 202, 210, *230*

Ruijū sandai kyaku 類聚三代格 *Systematically Classified Decrees of Three Eras* 202, 203, 210, *261, 263*

Ruijū zatsuyōshō 類聚雑要抄 *Classified Notes on Various Important Customs* 98

Saikyūki 西宮記 *Notes of the Western Residence* 38, 39, 211

Sakeiki 左経記 journal of Minamoto no Tsuneyori 212, *231*

Sakumon daitai 作文大体 *Basics of Composition* 225

Sanbō ekotoba 三宝絵詞 *Illustrated Tales of the Three Treasures* 146

Sarashina nikki 更級日記 *The Sarashina Diary* 145, 176, 213, *262*

Seiji yōryaku 政事要略 *Compendium of Administration* 210, 219, *231, 261*

Sei Shōnagon shū 清少納言集 *Collected Poems of Sei Shōnagon* 105

Senjimon (Ch. *Qianziwen*) 千字文 *The Thousand Characters* 124, 125

Senzai wakashū 千載和歌集 *Collection of Poems of a Thousand Years 149*

Sezoku genbun 世俗諺文 *Proverbs of Our Time* 125

Shiki (Ch. *Shiji*) 史記 *Records of the Historian* 12, 123, 126, 221

Shikyō (Ch. *Shijing*) 詩経 *The Book of Odes 34, 72*, 216

Shingishiki 新義式 *New Ritual Procedures* 37

Shinkokin wakashū 新古今和歌集 *New Collection of Ancient and Modern Poems 150*

Shinsarugakuki 新猿楽記 *Notes on Some New Comic Entertainments* 158, 212, 226, 229, 230, 241

Shinsenzai wakashū 新千載和歌集 *New Collection of Poems of a Thousand Years 150*

Shinshō kyakuchoku fushō 新抄格勅符抄 *New Selection of Decrees and Edicts 105*

Shoku Nihon kōki 続日本後紀 *Later Annals of Japan, Continued 34, 261*

Shokyō (Ch. *Shujing*) 書経 *The Book of Documents 34, 216*

Shōmonki (*Masakadoki*) 将門記 *The Story of Masakado's Rebellion 211, 261*

Shoreishō 初令抄 *Notes on the Earliest Precedents 231*

Shōyūki 小右記 journal of Fujiwara no Sanesuke 27, 32, 45, 123, 156, 212, Notes *passim*

Shūgaishō 拾芥抄 *Collection of Fragments 147*

Shūi ōjōden 拾遺往生伝 *Gleanings of Stories about Rebirth in the Pure Land 221*

Shūi wakashū 拾遺和歌集 *Collection of Gleanings 178*

Shunjū sashiden (Ch. *Chunqiu Zuoshizhuan*) 春秋佐氏伝 *Commentary of Tso on the Spring and Autumn Annals* (*Annals of the Duchy of Lu*) 44, 216

Shunki 春記 journal of Fujiwara no Sukefusa 25, 28, 31, 56, 91, 92, 100, 111, 124, 136, 137, 157, 167, 169, 186, 196, 201, 212, Notes *passim*

Shūrai (Ch. *Zhouli*) 周礼 *The Zhou Rituals 34*

Shuzeishiki 主税式 *Regulations of the Office of Public Resources 106*

Sonpi bunmyaku 尊卑文脈 *Noble and Base Lineages 177, 228*

Sōshi (Ch. *Zhuangzi*) 荘子 Taoist classic 126

Tōkagenki (Ch. *Taohua yuanji*) 桃花源記 *Peach Blossom Spring 67*

Tosa nikki 土佐日記 *The Tosa Diary 261*

Uji shūi monogatari 宇治拾遺物語 *Supplement to the Tales of Uji 172, 204, 213*

Urabongyō 盂蘭盆経 *Sūtra for Souls in Suspense 192*

Wamyō ruijushō 和名類聚抄 *Categorized Notes on Japanese Words* (dictionary) 125, 225

Yamato monogatari 大和物語 *Tales of Yamato 146, 213*

Yōrō ritsuryō 養老律令 *Yōrō code* 5, 210
Yūjoki 遊女記 *An Account of Prostitutes* 226

Zenkanjo (Ch. *Qian Hanshu*) 前漢書 *History of the Former Han Dynasty* 12, 68, 221
Zoku honchō ōjōden 続本朝往生伝 *Stories of Rebirth in the Pure Land from Our Country, Continued* 226
*Zoku Kojidan 続古事談 *Remarks on Past Matters, Continued 231*

ILLUSTRATIONS

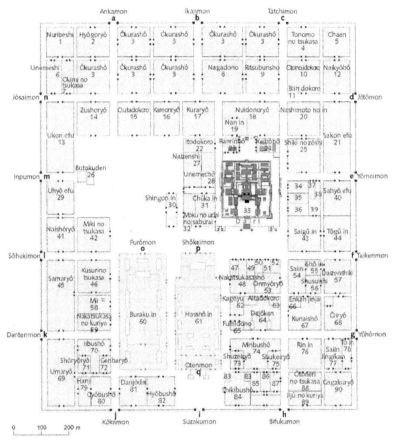

Le plan du palais impérial

© Nicolas Fiévé, *Atlas historique de Kyôto*, UNESCO/Ed. de l'Amateur, 2008

Map 1: The imperial palace (*daidairi*).

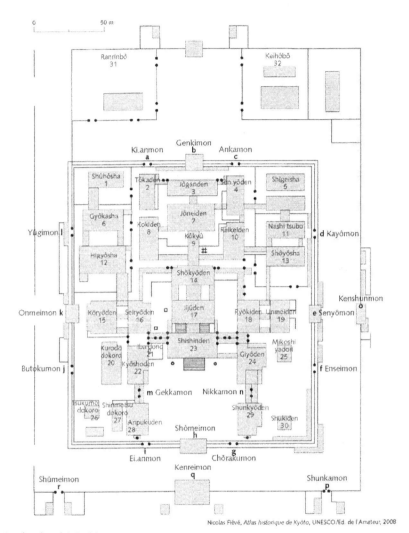

Le plan du palais intérieur

Nicolas Fiévé, *Atlas historique de Kyôto*, UNESCO/Ed. de l'Amateur, 2008

Map 2: The inner (residential) palace (*dairi*).

Printed in Great Britain
by Amazon